315

Interest Group Politics in America

INTEREST GROUP POLITICS IN AMERICA

Edited with an Introduction

ROBERT H. SALISBURY
WASHINGTON UNIVERSITY

Harper & Row, Publishers
New York, Evanston, and London

For Susan, Bob, and Matt

Contents

Interest Group Politics in America

Introduction

A decade or more ago a prime issue of discussion, disputation, and even research in political science was that to which we give the identifying label of "interest groups." From a number of different perspectives the phenomena of groups: their internal life and their lobbies, their cohesion and influence, their access and their goals, and the degree to which they constituted the fundamental building blocks of the discipline were all important issues.

Perhaps the latter—the essentiality of group focus to the construction of a usable analytic framework—was the most often and widely debated point. From Arthur Bentley on, some political scientists argued that the most appropriate conceptual unit for the study of politics was the group. A good many others argued that this was a wrong or foolish or inadequate view, and much of the group literature came to concentrate on this dispute: whether and to what extent a "group approach" to politics was fruitful. An important part of this argument, in turn, was one growing out of research interests in cross-national comparative politics. It was argued by a number of scholars that the phenomena of interest group activity simply did not have the relevance in political systems outside the United States that seemed so obvious to observers of the American scene. Ironically, a large portion of the recent studies of interest groups have been made in other systems especially in Western Europe. But the methodological criticism of group analysis—that it is culture bound and not generic—has remained powerful.

The group approach to politics, however, is only one dimen-

1

sion of both scholarly and popular attention to interest groups or, to use the more pejorative but perhaps more familiar term, pressure groups. Another line of concern, of far more importance in provoking popular notice of groups, begins with the lobby. From this perspective interest groups are interesting because they lobby, they pressure the government for special favors. They often engage in practices which are both corrupt and corrupting and hence have often aroused the wrath and reformist zeal of the political moralist. Even when they are technically honest, the special interest for which the pressure group works may cloud the vision of public servants and make it harder than ever to achieve the general or public interest. Thus lobbies have been regarded as at least undesirable and often close to criminal and accordingly crusading reformers, journalists, politicians, and sometimes academics have sought to expose pressure groups in order to destroy them. And hence a good deal of literature.

Not much less normative though manifesting a very different reading of the pressure group scene is a view of American politics which begins with James Madison in the *Federalist Papers* and continues through to such scholars as John Kenneth Galbraith and David B. Truman. This perspective has the following components. The United States is a large and diverse nation with many different kinds of people holding many different values. The pursuit of these diverse values often occurs through the medium of interest groups which contend against one another for the influence and power to gain their values. The competition among so many groups moderates the claims and counterclaims by forcing compromise and bargaining. It disciplines the groups thereby and they adjust and adapt to one another. If any sector of society is aggrieved, it may organize and seek redress through the bargaining among groups. Freedom for each group is thus maximized, goals are moderated, and social consensus is promoted. This benign view of the American system rests firmly on the assumption that interest groups play the major role in achieving both expression and accommodation of the "different senti-ments and views" of the people.

These very different perspectives on the role of interest groups in American politics have shared one important feature, they have stimulated research and writing. Muckrakers like Lin-coln Steffens exposed lobbyists as the heart of the "Shame of Cities," and new exposés still issue forth quite independent of the standing which group analysis may have in political science. The Madisonian optimism about groups, indeed about the whole po-litical system, is less in vogue now than it was for a time, but there remain many who argue that the route to social justice for the deprived is through pressure group organization and action.

It should be apparent that however one may resolve the is-sue of the role interest groups play in the political system, this is a different question from the one which Bentley raised and which has consumed so much attention from political scientists, namely, should the whole discipline adopt a group orientation. Yet even "the role of groups in the system" is an ambitious item on any research agenda. It might well be argued that since the early 1950s political scientists have been so preoccupied with one or another of these large questions that they have rather neg-lected some smaller ones: What are the various kinds of groups we see around us like? Who belongs and why? What do they do and to whom and with what effect?

It is these questions which are reflected in the construction of this volume. Whatever one decides about "the system" or "political science" and how best to study them, it is plain that many thousands of organized interest groups are engaged every day in politically relevant activity. Labor unions, business groups, and farm organizations—all with rather straightforward economic foundations—were once the almost exclusive objects of our attention. But no student of interest groups in the 1960s can miss the tremendous role of civil rights organizations and of the myriad of ideologically militant groups of the political left and of the right. The burgeoning academic interest in education as a policy issue cannot evade the role of education groups in that issue. Nor can the question of crime in the streets be understood without reference to the interests of police and prosecutors as well as black power militants. If the academic analysis of interest groups has lain relatively dormant for the past decade or so, the emergence of student groups with newly articulated interests fervently expressed within academic institutions compels any sensitive observer to think again about group phenomena.

This volume, then, is a collection of readings about interest groups in the United States. The essays all deal with group activity and ways of thinking about groups rather than with ways of conceptualizing politics or political systems more generally. The essays were chosen with two criteria principally in mind. I have sought to cover a wide range of groups and to select readings which would convey a substantial body of relevant information about those groups. Many of the essays themselves range over many groups and are thus hard to classify but there are at least ten quite different *kinds* of interest groups discussed in this volume, and the careful reader should come away knowing a good deal about who wants what and how they go about getting it.

Second, each reading illustrates especially one or another of the general questions I suggested earlier were important to an understanding of groups in American politics. The readings treat organizational form, leadership, membership, and goals; they examine national, state, and local levels of government; they cover legislative, executive, and judicial branches as well as the electoral process. Both the internal life and work of groups and their external activity, especially their lobbying, are treated. The necessity to stop short of every question and every useful treatment was inescapable though frustrating, but a substantial range is presented.

The interest group scene is a dynamic one, of course. Changes occur much faster than research can keep up with, and some of the specific substance of these readings will be out-of-date. Thus fair trade laws have been largely undercut by discount houses since Joseph Palamountain wrote about the National Association of Retail Druggists and their campaigns for fair trade protection. And Samuel Huntington wrote about inter-service rivalries before Robert McNamara's tenure as Secretary of Defense (1961–1968) modified them. David B. Truman wrote about labor before the AFL and CIO had reunited and A. H. Raskin, writing more recently, was still unable to foresee Walter Reuther's withdrawal of the United Auto Workers from the federation. My hope is to achieve an appropriate balance of relevant and timely substantive discussion of important groups and of useful illustration of theoretical propositions. If that design is successful, each student will be able more effectively to make his own observations and understandings current.

One final note should be expressed, in part by way of an apology. Most of the selections in this volume have been edited, some rather severely. My strategy has been to eliminate nearly all of the footnotes which refer to published material and thereby gain additional space for substantive material. If students lose some ease of access to the sources of additional data as a consequence, I hope they will find compensation in the range of studies presented. And I hope, also, that they will be encouraged to look around them, intrigued, at the current interest group scene.

1

THEORY
AND APPROACH

It sometimes has seemed that more scholarly energy has been devoted to the problems of whether and how to study interest groups than to the study of groups themselves. Part of this disputatious literature has concerned the question of "the interest group approach" to the study of politics generally, but that is not the focus of the selections presented here. Rather, they are addressed to the matter of how to think about interest groups themselves. Organized groups are treated as phenomena of interest to political scientists, and Mancur Olson and Robert H. Salisbury both discuss ways of theorizing about these phenomena.

Mancur Olson is an economist and brings the analytic tools and perspectives of an economist to bear on the discussion of interest groups. In the first selection he reviews two of the major group theorists, Arthur F. Bentley and David B. Truman. He goes on to develop his own interpretation of interest groups in the second reading. Robert H. Salisbury's approach builds upon Olson's and considers a number of the problems of developing a comprehensive theory of interest groups in American politics.

Orthodox Theories of
Pressure Groups

MANCUR OLSON, JR.

The most important of the "modern" or "analytical" pluralists was Arthur F. Bentley, for it is his book, *The Process of Government*,[1] that has inspired most of the political scientists who have followed the "group approach." His book, probably one of the most influential in American social science, is partly an attack on certain methodological errors that had troubled the study of politics, but mostly a discussion of the dominant role that pressure groups play in economic and political life.

The economic aspect was very important to Bentley. He had previously written about economic history, and considered himself for much of his life an economist. Wealth, he thought, was the main source of group division in society. Apparently he turned to the study of pressure groups primarily because of his interest in economic affairs. "I will say," he wrote in *The Process of Government*, "that my interest in politics is not primary, but derived from my interest in economic life; and that I hope from

Excerpted by permission of the publishers from Mancur Olson, Jr., *The Logic of Collective Action*, pp. 118–125. Cambridge, Mass.: Harvard University Press, Copyright, 1965, by The President and Fellows of Harvard College. Also reprinted by permission of the author. Most footnotes are omitted.

[1]Arthur F. Bentley, *The Process of Government* (Evanston, Ill.: Principia Press, 1949). Although this book was first published in 1908, and thus is contemporaneous with many of the original or "philosophical" pluralist writings, its approach is completely in harmony with modern political science.

9

this point of approach ultimately to gain a better understanding of economic life than I have succeeded in gaining hitherto."

His idea that group pressure was the basic force was not, however, confined to the economic sphere, though that was apparently the most important. "The great task in the study of any form of social life is the analysis of these groups," he contended; "when the groups are adequately stated, everything is stated. When I say everything, I mean everything." It was group *interests*, moreover, that were basic. "*There is no group without its interest*. An interest, as the term will be used here, is the equivalent of a group." These group interests were to be found by empirical study. Bentley thought that no "interest" could be considered to exist unless it manifested itself in group action.

Whereas group interests were everything, individual interests were nothing. What mattered were the common interests of groups of people, not the losses and gains to single individuals. "The individual stated for himself, and invested with an extra-social unity of his own, is a fiction. But every bit of the activity, which is all we know of him, can be stated either on the one side as individual, or on the other side as social group activity. The former statement is in the main of trifling importance in interpreting society; the latter statement is essential, first, last, and all the time." Just as the idea of the individual interest was a fiction, so was the idea of the national interest. All group interests pertained to groups comprising only a part of a nation or society. "Usually we shall find," wrote Bentley, "on testing the 'social whole,' that it is merely the group or tendency represented by the man who talks of it, erected into the pretense of a universal demand of the society." This situation was logically necessary in Bentley's model, since he defined groups in terms of their conflict with one another, and thought that "no interest group has meaning except with reference to other interest groups."

By defining group interests in terms of their conflict with one another, thereby excluding the idea of an interest of society as a whole, Bentley was then able to say that the resultant of the group pressures was the one and only determinant of the course of government policy. "Pressure, as we shall use it, is always a group phenomenon. It indicates the push and resistance between groups. The balance of group pressures *is* the existing state of society." Government in Bentley's theory, was "considered as the adjustment or balance of interests." Now the outline of the model is evident. By assuming that there are no effective individual interests, that every group has its interests, that these always result in group action, and that there is no one group interest that includes everyone in society, Bentley was able to claim that all things involving government, all things great and small, are determined by the conflicting group pressures[2] This was the key to understanding government in general and economic policy in particular.

Not only was the resultant of all the group pressures always the determinant of social policy, but it was also, in Bentley's mind, for the most part a reasonably just determinant. Groups had a degree of power or pressure more or less in proportion to

[2]Bentley went all the way with his model. Everything that mattered in the control of social and economic policy could fit into the model of conflicting group pressures. Differences in the quality of political leadership? This was mainly the result of different group patterns. If a group leader was weak, it meant that there were quarreling subgroups within the group he was attempting to lead. The type of government? Group pressures would triumph, whether there was dictatorship, constitutional monarchy, oligarchy, or democracy. Even the most powerful dictator was a mediator among groups, the army, the church, the landowners, or whatever; even the slaves' interests had their effect on the outcome. The separation of powers? Group pressures would determine the outcome however the government was organized, though each different agency or part of the government was itself a group with an interest of its own which would in turn affect the balance of pressures. Even the judicial decisions could be understood in terms of pressures. The extent of the franchise? A group would have power whether or not it had the vote. Whether women were enfranchised mattered little, for if they were not they would still affect the resultant of group pressures through the family, an important subgroup.

their numbers. The larger, more nearly general, interest would usually tend to defeat the smaller, narrower, special interest. He considers a situation in which a relatively small group of team owners with heavy wagons are tending to damage the public roads in a town to the detriment of the majority of the taxpayers and citizens in the town. Bentley asserts that eventually the interest of the larger number will win out over the special interests of the minority: the mass of taxpayers is "bound to win" eventually and require wider tires for the teamsters' wagons, despite the fact that many in the majority may not even be aware of the controversy. This result was typical. "The greater proportion of the detail of government work . . . is composed of habitual actions which are adjustments forced by large, united weak interests upon less numerous, but relatively to the number of adherents, more intense interests. If there is anything that could probably be meant by the phrase 'control by the people' just as it stands, it is this." Legislatures, he concedes, were at times working quite imperfectly, but when special interests got too large a hand, a hue and cry arose against them. The logrolling of special interests was not to be feared: it was an excellent, efficient device for adjusting group interests.

For all his emphasis on the importance and beneficence of group pressures, Bentley said very little about *why* the needs of the different groups in society would tend to be reflected in politically or economically effective pressure. Nor did he consider carefully what it is that causes groups to organize and act effectively. Or why some groups are important in some societies and other groups important in other societies and periods. Bentley's disciples, however, have attempted to fill this gap in his thinking.

David Truman, in his well-known book *The Governmental Process,* has given particularly careful attention to this lacuna in Bentley's book. Essentially Professor Truman tried to develop a variant of the sociological theory of voluntary associations to show that organized and effective group pressures will emerge when necessary. As a society becomes more complex, Truman argued, and its group needs become more numerous and varied, it will naturally tend to form additional associations to stabilize the relationships of the various groups in the society. With more specialization and social complexity, more associations are needed, and more will arise, because it is a basic characteristic of social life that associations emerge to satisfy the needs of society.

> With an increase in specialization and with the continual frustration of established expectations consequent upon rapid changes in the related techniques, *the proliferation of associations is inescapable* [italics mine]. So closely do these developments follow, in fact, that the rate of association formation may serve as an index of the stability of a society, and their number may be used as an index of its complexity. Simple societies have no associations (in the technical sense of the term); as they grow more complex, i.e., as highly differentiated institutionalized groups increase in number, societies evolve greater numbers of associations.

This "inescapable" increase in the number of associations will inevitably have its impact on government. The associations will acquire connections with the institutions of government whenever government is important to the groups in question. This tendency for associations to arise to fill the needs of the groups in society is especially evident in the economic sphere.

> There are, undoubtedly, a number of reasons for the prevalence of associations growing out of economic institutions . . . There has been a series of disturbances and dislocations consequent upon the utopian attempt, as Polanyi calls it, to set up a completely self-regulating market system. This attempt involved a policy of treating the fictitious factors of land, labor, and capital as if they were real, ignoring the fact that they stood for human beings or influences closely affecting the welfare of humans. Application of this policy inevitably meant suffering and dislocation—unemployment, wide fluctuation in prices, waste, and so forth. *These disturbances inevitably produced associations—*

*of owners, of workers, of farmers—operating upon government
to mitigate and control the ravages of the system* through tariffs,
subsidies, wage guarantees, social insurance and the like. [Italics
minc.]

Truman then appears to contend that "suffering," "dislocation," and "disturbance" will almost inevitably result in *organized*
political pressure. Those disadvantaged groups that need an organization will in fact come to have an organization. But the
facts of recent political life do not necessarily substantiate this
view. By Truman's standard, more associations should have been
formed during the industrial revolution (when there was a great
deal of "suffering" and "dislocation"). But, as he points out, the
rate at which associations have been formed has been highest in
recent years (which have been mainly prosperous and stable).

Apart from this attempt to amend Bentley's theory (by adding an explanation of why group needs and interests would result
in organized political pressure), Truman tended to follow every
twist and turn in Bentley's account. Truman, like Bentley, neg-
lected individual interests; group interests, group attitudes, and
group pressures were the only things that mattered.[3]

Truman not only shared Bentley's belief that group pressures
alone determined the final equilibrium position of the social system, but was, if anything, even less qualified in his belief that this
group equilibrium tended to be just and desirable. There were
two main reasons for Professor Truman's benign view of the results of pressure-group politics. He thought, in the first place,
that most pressure groups would be weak and divided in those
circumstances in which they asked for too much from society,
since their members also had "overlapping" memberships in
other groups with different interests and would thus tend to op-

---

[3]Truman also resembled his master in his neglect of the all-inclusive social
or national interest. "In developing a group interpretation of politics," he
commented on p. 51, "we do not need to account for a totally inclusive
interest, because one does not exist."

pose excessive demands. Tariff-seeking manufacturers were also consumers, churchmen, and so on, so that if the manufacturers' association went too far it would alienate some of its own members. Moreover, in the second place, there were "potenial groups" that would arise and organize to do battle with the special interests if the special interests got far out of line. If the tariff proposed was excessive, presumably the consumers would organize a lobby that would oppose it. And the very existence of these potential groups, and the fear that they would organize, keeps the organized interests from making excessive demands.

> Thus it is only as the effects of overlapping memberships and the functions of unorganized interests and potential groups are included in the equation that it is accurate to speak of governmental activity as the product or resultant of group activity . . . To assert that the organization and activity of powerful interest groups constitutes a threat to representative government without measuring their relation to and the effects upon the widespread potential groups is to generalize from insufficient data and upon an incomplete conception of the political process.

So confident was Professor Truman of the generally salutary effects of group pressures that he belittled almost all attempts to improve the system of legislation and lobbying.

By-Product and Special Interest Theories

MANCUR OLSON, JR.

The common characteristic which distinguishes all of the large economic groups with significant lobbying organizations is that these groups are also organized for some *other* purpose. The large and powerful economic lobbies are in fact the by-products of organizations that obtain their strength and support because they perform some function in addition to lobbying for collective goods.

The lobbies of the large economic groups are the by-products of organizations that have the capacity to "mobilize" a latent group with "selective incentives." The only organizations that have "selective incentives" available are those that (1) have the authority and capacity to be coercive, or (2) have a source of positive inducements that they can offer the individuals in a latent group.

A purely political organization—an organization that has no function apart from its lobbying function—obviously cannot legally coerce individuals into becoming members. A political party, or any purely political organization, with a captive or compulsory membership would be quite unusual in a democratic political system. But if for some nonpolitical reason, if because of some other function it performs, an organization has a justification for having a compulsory membership, or if through this other function it has obtained the power needed to make membership in it compulsory, that organization may then be able to get the resources needed to support a lobby. The lobby is then a by-product of whatever function this organization performs that enables it to have a captive membership.

An organization that did nothing except lobby to obtain a collective good for some large group would not have a source of rewards or positive selective incentives it could offer potential members. Only an organization that also sold private or noncollective products, or provided social or recreational benefits to individual members, would have a source of these positive inducements.[1] Only such an organization could make a joint offering or "tied sale" of a collective and a noncollective good that could

---

[1] An economic organization in a perfectly competitive market in equilibrium, which had no special competitive advantage that could bring it a large amount of "rent," would have no "profits" or other spare resources it could use as selective incentives for a lobby. Nonetheless there are many organizations that do have spare returns they can use for selective incentives. First, markets with some degree of monopoly power are far more common than perfectly competitive markets. Second, there are sometimes important complementaries between the economic and political activities of an organization. The political branch of the organization can win lower taxes or other favorable government policies for the economic branch, and the good name won by the political branch may also help the economic branch. For somewhat similar reasons, a social organization may also be a source of a surplus that can be used for selective incentives.

An organization that is not only political, but economic or social as well, and has a surplus that provides selective incentives, may be able to retain its membership and political power, in certain cases, even if its leadership manages to use some of the political or economic power of the organization for objectives other than those desired by the membership, since the members of the organization will have an incentive to continue belonging even if they disagree with the organization's policy. This may help explain why many lobbying organizations take positions that must be uncongenial to their membership, and why organizations with leaders who corruptly advance their own interests at the expense of the organization continue to survive.

stimulate a rational individual in a large group to bear part of the cost of obtaining a collective good. There are for this reason many organizations that have both lobbying functions and economic functions, or lobbying functions and social functions, or even all three of these types of functions at once. Therefore, in addition to the large group lobbies that depend on coercion, there are those that are associated with organizations that provide noncollective or private benefits which can be offered to any potential supporter who will bear his share of the cost of the lobbying for the collective good.

• • •

The labor union is probably the most important single type of pressure-group organization and accordingly deserves first place in any discussion of large lobbying organizations. Though the opponents of the labor unions are exaggerating when they claim that the Democratic candidates in industrial states are merely puppets of labor leaders, it is quite clear that the Democrats in these states are normally very friendly to labor, and that the Republicans usually treat labor unions as the major source of enemy strength. The membership of the AFL-CIO is *several times larger* than the membership of any other lobbying organization. The labor unions have, moreover, an impressive organizational network to match their numbers: there are about 60,000 to 70,000 union locals in this country. Labor leaders have claimed that they could influence about 25 million voters. Their purely political expenditures are measured in the millions. In 1958 some candidates may have been elected as a result of the large labor vote brought out by "right-to-work" proposals on the ballot in some industrial states. In Michigan the Democratic party came out of the doldrums as labor organization grew. There were about 200 unionists who were either delegates or alternate delegates to the 1952 Democratic national convention. . . .

Just as there can be little doubt that labor unions are a significant political force, neither can there be much question that this political force is a by-product of the purely industrial activities that unions regard as their major function. . . . [I]t was only when labor unions began to concentrate on collective bargaining with employers and abandoned the mainly political orientation of the earlier American unions, that they came to have any stability or power. It was only when the labor unions started to deal with the employers, who alone had the power to *force* the workers to join the union, that they began to prosper. It is, moreover, hard to see how the labor unions could have obtained and maintained the "union shop" in a democratic country like the United States if they had been solely political organizations. Labor unions came to play an important part in the political struggle only long after they had forsaken political action as a major goal. It is worth noting that the Wagner Act, which made organizing a union with compulsory membership much easier, and which led to the greatest increase in union membership, was passed *before* labor unions came to play a really important role in politics. The experience of Great Britain also shows that a democratic nation is often happy to overlook compulsory membership in organizations that engage in collective bargaining, but hesitant to make membership in a political organization in any degree automatic. Although . . . it has long been taken for granted in Britain that unionists will often not work with nonunion men, there has been a great deal of bitter controversy over whether union men should "contract in" or "contract out" of a contribution to the Labour party. (The vast majority of the members of that party, incidentally, are a by-product of the trade unions' activities; all except a small minority belong through the trade unions.) If, then, it is true that a democratic nation would not normally want to make membership in a purely political union compulsory, and that compulsion is essential to a stable labor movement of any size, then it follows that the political power of unions is a by-product of their nonpolitical activities.

PROFESSIONAL LOBBIES

Many of those who criticize organized labor because of the coercion entailed in labor unions are themselves members of professional organizations that depend upon compulsion as much as unions do. Many organizations representing prosperous and prestigious professions like the law and medicine have also reached for the forbidden fruits of compulsory membership. There is in fact a pervasive tendency towards compulsion in professional associations generally. . . . The guild form of organization is often adopted not only by the ancient and learned professions, but also by undertakers, barbers, "beauticians," "cosmeticians," plumbers, opticians, and other groups interested in professional status. This adoption of the guild form of organization is evidence for the by-product theory of large pressure groups, for compulsory membership has always been . . . "the first rule" of the guild system.

The self-regulating guild with compulsory membership has reached its furthest degree of development in many state bar associations. Many state legislatures have been induced to require *by law* that *every* practicing lawyer must be a member of the state bar association. These bar associations have closed shops enforced by government, and thus should be the envy of every labor union.

The modern professional associations or guilds are moreover coming to resemble "miniature governments." They have "all the types of power normally exercised by government." State governments often give the professional groups authority to govern themselves (and to a degree their clients) and to discipline any members of the profession that do not maintain the "ethical" standards the profession finds it expedient or appropriate to maintain. It follows that, even when membership in these associations is not a legal requirement, the individual in professional practice knows that he has an interest in maintaining membership in good standing with the professional association.

The advantages of maintaining membership and good relationships with a professional association may be illustrated by the fact that it was not found expedient to release the name of a doctor who had written to a congressional committee to argue that "the central organization of the AMA in Chicago has no idea what the average physician wants his patients to have." Oliver Garceau, author of the classic work on the American Medical Association, has argued that the recalcitrant doctor in trouble with organized medicine may face "a genuine economic threat." When the American Medical Association blocked the Denver city council's program for Denver General Hospital in 1945, a Denver councilman, according to *Time* magazine, was driven to exclaim: "Nobody can touch the American Medical Association . . . Talk about the closed shop of the AFL and the CIO—they are a bunch of pikers."

The role of coercion, even in its subtler forms, in the American Medical Association is, however, probably less important as a source of membership than the noncollective benefits the organization provides its membership. According to Garceau, there is "one formal service of the society with which the doctor can scarcely dispense. Malpractice defense has become a prime requisite to private practice." One doctor who had founded a cooperative hospital, and lost his membership in his medical society, discovered that not only had he lost his chance to have other doctors testify in his behalf during malpractice suits, but that he had lost his insurance as well. The many technical publications of the American Medical Association, and the state and local medical societies, also give the doctor a considerable incentive to affiliate with organized medicine. The American Medical Association publishes not only its celebrated *Journal,* but also many other technical periodicals on various medical specialties. Since the nineteenth century the *Journal* alone has provided a "tangible attraction for doctors." The importance of this attraction is perhaps indicated by a survey conducted in Michigan, which showed that

89 per cent of the doctors received the *Journal of the American Medical Association,* and 70 per cent read a state society journal, but *less than 30 per cent* read any *other* type of medical literature. The *Journal* has been, moreover, the "prime money maker of the organization." Much of the organization's revenue, according to Garceau, comes from drug companies' advertisements— advertisements which Garceau believes helped companies obtain the AMA seal of approval for their products. The conventions of the American Medical Association and many of its constituent organizations also provide technical information needed by doctors, and thus give the member a "direct return in education" for the investment in dues, just as the medical journals do.

In short, by providing a helpful defense against malpractice suits, by publishing medical journals needed by its membership, and by making its conventions educational as well as political, the American Medical Association has offered its members and potential members a number of selective or noncollective benefits. It has offered its members benefits which, in contrast with the political achievements of the organization, can be withheld from nonmembers, and which accordingly provide an incentive for joining the organization.

The American Medical Association, then, obtains its membership partly because of subtle forms of coercion, and partly because it provides noncollective benefits. It would have neither the coercive power to exercise, nor the noncollective benefits to sell, if it were solely a lobbying organization. It follows that the impressive political power of the American Medical Association and the local groups that compose it is a by-product of the nonpolitical activities of organized medicine.

It is interesting to ask why no organization of college professors has acquired anything like the political power of the American Medical Association. Probably the most important factor is that, in the academic profession, the learned societies are independent of the political association. If the American

Association of University Professors could usurp the functions of the learned societies, it could rival the AMA. If subscriptions to the scholarly journals, and attendance at the conventions of the learned societies, were restricted to members of the AAUP, professors would probably be as well organized and as powerful as doctors. If the AAUP published as many technical journals as the American Medical Association, almost every faculty member would have an incentive to join, and the AAUP membership would presumably rise above its present level, and dues and participation could perhaps also increase.

• • •

The most striking fact about the political organization of farmers in the United States is that there has been so little. Farmers have not on the whole been well organized, except perhaps in recent years. And what organization the farmers have had has tended to be unstable. Many farm organizations have come and gone, but only a few have come and stayed.

There was no lasting, significant farm organization or lobby in this country until after the Civil War, though farmers were the largest group in the population throughout the early history of the country. The first farm organization worth mentioning was the Grange—the Patrons of Husbandry. The Grange was started in 1867, and in the first few years of its life it spread like a prairie fire across the plains of the country. It had very soon acquired an impressive membership and a considerable amount of power. But the Grange soon collapsed as fast as it had grown. By the 1880's it was already insignificant. The Grange has survived with a small membership to the present day, but has never regained the power and glory of its youthful years. Indeed, the precipitous decline it suffered apparently affected the spirit as well as the body of the Grange, for since then it has generally avoided controversial economic or political issues. It has become to a great degree a social organization, and is no longer an aggressive pressure or lobbying organization, though it does some low-keyed lobbying.

The remarkable achievement of the Grange is that it has managed to survive at all, when so many other farm organizations formed since it began have passed away. The Farmers' Alliances, the Greenback movement, the Free Silver movement, the Agricultural Wheel, the Gleaners, Populism, the Equity, the Brothers of Freedom, and other such organizations died within a few years of their birth. This indeed has been the general pattern.

The Farmers Union and the Farm Bureau are the two distinct exceptions to that pattern. But these two organizations also have had their difficulties. The Farmers Union, the older of the two, was started in Texas in 1902. During its early years it acquired a significant membership in the South. This membership was lost after the First World War and the organization nearly succumbed to this tragedy. The organization began a new life in the Great Plains states during the interwar years, but its membership in this period was very small. In the late 1930's and in the 1940's the Farmers Union built a firmer base of support in the states of the Missouri Valley, however, and it is from this region that it presently draws most of its strength.

The Farm Bureau, which is now the largest of the farm organizations, and the only one with a nationwide membership, was from the beginning completely different from other farm organizations. For the Farm Bureau was created by the government. The Smith-Lever Act of 1914 provided that the federal government would share, with the states, the cost of programs for providing what have come to be called "county agents," who furnish farmers information on improved methods of husbandry developed by the agricultural colleges and agricultural experiment stations. Many of the state governments decided that no county could receive any government money for a county agent unless it organized an association of farmers that would be evidence of an interest in getting more information on modern agricultural methods. These county organizations came to be called "Farm Bureaus." They were the beginning of the Farm Bureau movement that exists today. There were, it is true, a handful of these county Farm Bureaus a year or two before the government started providing money for county agents, but these were so few in number that they were totally insignificant, and they were in any case like the county Farm Bureaus started by the government in that their purpose was simply to obtain better information on agricultural methods.

The expenditure of government funds for "extension work," that is for the county agents, increased greatly during World War I, so the number of county Farm Bureaus naturally increased *pari passu*. These county Farm Bureaus, normally under the guidance of the county agent (who often had to maintain the Farm Bureau in his county or else lose his job), soon combined to form statewide Farm Bureaus. These state organizations in turn formed a national organization, the American Farm Bureau Federation, in 1919.

Up to this time the Farm Bureau was, first, a quasi-official organization, set up in response to financial incentives provided by government, and second, an organization that provided individualized or *noncollective* benefits to its members. The second point is especially important. The farmer who joined his county Farm Bureau got technical assistance and education in return. The farmer who joined was normally put on the mailing list for technical publications: the farmer who did not join was not. The farmer who joined had first call on the county agent's services: the farmer who did not, normally had last call, or no call at all. A farmer thus had a specific incentive to join the Farm Bureau. The dues he had to pay were an investment (and probably a good investment) in agricultural education and improvement.

Under the stimulus furnished by the increasing government

expenditures on agricultural extension work, the membership of
the county and state Farm Bureaus, and therefore of the American Farm Bureau Federation, increased very rapidly. By 1921,
the Federation had a membership of 466,000. In the next year,
however, the membership was considerably less, and it continued to fall more or less steadily until 1933, by which time
it was only 163,000.

• • •

There was, meanwhile, one state in which the Farm Bureau
was developing important new organizational techniques, and
in which it was making its best progress. These organizational
techniques, which have since been widely copied, have unfortunately never been explained or analyzed in any single publication, and as a result the problems of the farm organizations
in general, and the Farm Bureau in particular, have often been
misunderstood. Throughout the thirties and forties the Farm
Bureau in Illinois was coming to have more and more membership in relation to the other major agricultural states. The Illinois
Farm Bureau (which strictly speaking should be called the
"Illinois Agricultural Association") had a tenth fewer members
than the Iowa Farm Bureau (the most nearly comparable organization) in 1925, but it had twice as many members by 1933
and an even bigger lead over the Iowa Farm Bureau by 1938.

The progress of the Farm Bureau in Illinois was due to
the extensive system of cooperative business organizations it had
set up in that state. But these cooperatives were not the "Roch-
dale" type of cooperatives normally found in this country, but
rather a new type, which is appropriately called the "Kirkpatrick" type of "cooperative," because it was designed by
Donald Kirkpatrick, the general counsel for the Illinois Agricultural Association. The "Kirkpatrick" cooperatives differ from
other cooperatives, first of all, in that they are controlled, not
by their patrons, but by a legally separate organization. All of

the voting stock in the cooperative business and mutual insurance companies associated with the Illinois Agricultural Association is held, not by their patrons, but by the Illinois Agricultural Association itself—the political or lobbying organization. The cooperative marketing, supply, and insurance companies associated with the Farm Bureau in Illinois are run, then, by an organization that is legally completely separate, and which has legislative and lobbying objectives rather than the business or economic objectives cooperatives and mutual insurance companies normally have. The system was set up in such a way that the business purposes of the purely economic parts of the system would *always* be completely subordinate to the political part of the system. As an official pamphlet on the history of the Farm Bureau insurance companies in Illinois points out, "men of vision were drafting policies and *systems of control* that placed the insurance companies *forever* under the direction of the parent organization." [Italics mine.]

The proof that the interest of the political arm of the Farm Bureau is important even in the management of the business side of the movement is found in the fact that *some of the business enterprises are not allowed to sell their product to anyone who is not, and will not become a member of the political organization.* This is true primarily of the mutual casualty insurance companies. The marketing and farm-supply cooperatives controlled by the Farm Bureau in Illinois will normally do business with anyone, but *they generally will not pay a "patronage dividend" to anyone who is not a member of the Illinois Agricultural Association.* This means many farmers find that, if they do not join the Farm Bureau, they lose patronage dividends or other noncollective business benefits amounting to far more money than the Farm Bureau dues; thus it would cost them money, sometimes a lot of money, to stay out. So the Farm Bureau dues often come indirectly out of the earnings of Farm Bureau business enterprises. Obviously, arrangements of this kind do not exist primarily for business reasons. The requirement that the benefits from patronizing a Farm Bureau business organization should normally go only to Farm Bureau members is maintained in the interests of the political organization. The publications of the organization admit this. For example: "Still another avenue of vision and hope was being explored in the field of commercial services with the thought that offering them through the state association would bring about greater membership participation . . . Thus, in looking into the possibilities of establishing commercial services to be offered by the state association, it was in the hope that such services would be confined to Farm Bureau members only."

The Kirkpatrick type of cooperative, then, is distinguished from other cooperatives, first, in that it is controlled by a lobbying or legislative organization, and second, by the fact that it generally restricts the benefits of trading with it to members of that lobbying or legislative organization. This Kirkpatrick plan has worked very well indeed in Illinois. In recent years the membership of the Illinois Agricultural Association has come to include almost every farmer in the state (as well as a sizable number of nonfarmers who have dealt with its business organizations). It is sometimes said (though this is no doubt an exaggeration) that it is economically almost impossible to operate a farm in Illinois without patronizing some Farm Bureau business and therefore becoming a member of the Farm Bureau. The Farm Bureau businesses in Illinois deal in a vast variety of products. By 1951 the Illinois Farm Supply Company, which is only one of the Farm Bureau business organizations, had paid out (along with its local affiliates) over 41.5 million dollars in patronage dividends. The Country Mutual Casualty Company, another Farm Bureau company in Illinois, had 337,000 insurance policies in force. Since there are not nearly that many farmers in the state, some farmers must have more than one policy and many nonfarmers must have dealt with the company. These policies obviously have brought a good proportion of the farmers in the state into the Illinois Agricultural Association. The membership in this organization has grown *pari passu* with the expansion of its business affiliates.

The success of the Kirkpatrick type of business organization in Illinois bred imitation by state Farm Bureaus throughout the nation. By now Farm Bureau business organizations of one kind or another are operating in almost every state. These organizations are generally, but not invariably, patterned in the exact image of those in Illinois. They are normally controlled by the state Farm Bureaus and generally restrict their benefits to Farm Bureau members. They have normally been quite profitable. This profitability often owes something to the favorable tax treatment given cooperatives, but that is not the only explanation. The Farm Bureau has created an especially large number of automobile insurance companies, and these may have profited from the fact that their clientele was largely rural, and thus at times probably less apt to drive in congested areas and be involved in traffic accidents. It is interesting that the two largest automobile insurance companies in the nation, State Farm and Nationwide, both started out selling insurance to farmers in affiliation with the Farm Bureau.

As the Kirkpatrick type of business organization has been adopted by state Farm Bureaus all over the nation, the membership in the Farm Bureau has increased manyfold. The membership in the American Farm Bureau Federation was 163,000 in 1933, 444,000 in 1940, 828,000 in 1944, and 1,275,000 in 1947, and since 1953 has been in excess of a million and a half. The growth in membership has followed the expansion of the business organizations that tend to restrict their benefits to Farm Bureau members. The American Farm Bureau Federation now has what no farm organization in America has ever had before: a large, stable, nationwide membership.

The size and relative stability of the American Farm Bureau

Federation, then, has been the result of two factors. One is that for a long while it was the natural channel through which farmers could get technical aid and education from the government; the other is that it controls a vast variety of business institutions that normally provide special benefits to Farm Bureau members. The Farm Bureau is of course also a lobbying organization—one of the nation's largest. But there is almost no evidence that the lobbying the Farm Bureau has done accounts for much of its membership. The fluctuations in its membership clearly cannot be explained by any changes in its legislative policies, or in the popularity of its policies. On the contrary, the Farm Bureau seems to have grown very rapidly in periods when, if the results of polls and elections can be believed, its policies were the least popular. The theory of latent groups would suggest that the lobbying activities of an organization as large as the Farm Bureau would not provide an incentive that would lead rational individuals to join the organization, even if they were in complete agreement with its policies. Therefore, large pressure-group organizations must derive their strength as a by-product of some nonpolitical functions. The lobbying strength of the Farm Bureau seems, then, to have been a by-product of the county agents, on the one hand, and the Farm Bureau business organizations, on the other.

The Farm Bureau is not, however, the only farm organization whose political power is a by-product of its nonpolitical functions. The Farmers Union, which had such a troubled and unstable existence until the late thirties, has now found a stable, solid membership in the Great Plains, and it has got this stability through the farm cooperatives and insurance companies with which it is associated. The Farmers Union has sponsored some mutual insurance companies which are like the Farm Bureau insurance companies in that they normally do business only with those who are or will become members of the political branch of the movement. In addition, it has arrangements with a number of farm cooperatives which further increase its strength. Those farm cooperatives associated with the Farmers Union normally "check off" membership in the Farmers Union—that is to say they simply subtract the dues to the Farmers Union from the patronage dividends the farmer earns by patronizing the cooperative. In addition, these cooperatives normally pay five per cent of their earnings to an "Educational Fund" which is spent by the Farmers Union for lobbying, organizational work, and the like.

Because of the recreational and social benefits the Grange provides for its members, and because of the limited character of its lobbying activities, the Grange probably has less need for business enterprises than the Farm Bureau or the Farmers Union. Yet it, too, has a considerable variety of business organizations associated with it, and many of these businesses also provide an incentive for membership in the Grange.

There is one farm organization that has tried not to use business institutions or governmental agencies to obtain membership. This is a new and small organization—the National Farmers Organization. It has advertised that the "NFO insures your income instead of your car," thereby implicitly criticizing the business activities of the Farm Bureau. But it has had a great deal of trouble getting members, and this policy may be changing. Significantly, the National Farmers Organization has so far failed in its "holding actions," or strikes, to withhold farm products from the market. The failure of these strikes was exactly what the theory of latent groups would have led one to expect. Should the National Farmers Organization some day succeed, without using violence or other selective incentives, in maintaining farm prices by getting farmers to withhold some of their output from the market, that would tend to refute the theory offered here.

An Exchange
Theory of Interest Groups

ROBERT H. SALISBURY

In one of those apparently casual passages into which enormous significance may be read David B. Truman remarks that "the origins of interest groups and the circumstances surrounding their orientations toward the institutions of government [are] . . . among the factors most relevant to a description of group politics." He goes on to suggest or imply some fragments of general theory concerning group formation which remain largely undeveloped, either by Truman or by other students of interest groups. Issues of major theoretical relevance are raised in these fragments, however, and we propose to examine them closely to see whether they, and the data concerning interest group formation, may lead to some fuller theoretical understanding of interest group phenomena.

We shall focus much of our attention on the development of American agricultural groups. In part, this focus is the product of convenience and ready accessibility of illustrative data. In part, however, this sector of American group development is especially apt for the testing of extant theories of group formation. In addition to farm groups we shall refer to other types of groups sufficiently often to indicate the range of application of the argument. It should be noted at the outset that the argu-

From *Midwest Journal of Political Science,* Vol. XIII, No. 1 (February, 1969), pp. 1–32. Reprinted by permission of the Wayne State University Press. Most footnotes are omitted.

ment presented here has many close links to an intellectual focus now attaining major stature in other social sciences; namely, exchange theory. This paper represents an effort to contribute to that development by applying its terms to, and reinterpreting them in the light of, interest groups in politics.

Briefly, the argument is that interest group origins, growth, death, and associated lobbying activity may all be better explained if we regard them as exchange relationships between entrepreneurs/organizers, who invest capital in a set of benefits, which they offer to prospective members at a price–membership. We shall compare this approach to others in an attempt to explain the data of group origins and elaborate its terms to explore the implications of the argument for other facets of group activity.

One other prefatory note should be entered. Our concern here is with organized interest groups or, in Truman's term, formal associations. We wish to explain how such associations come into being, the conditions affecting their growth or decline, their internal structures of action and their role in the political process. We do not wish to develop an interest group theory of politics, à la Arthur F. Bentley. That is quite a different intellectual enterprise and one that is largely unrelated to the present analysis. This is an effort to develop a theory of interest groups, not an interest group theory of politics, and its hoped that any disputation which might center on the latter issue may be avoided.

THEORIES OF PROLIFERATION AND EQUILIBRIUM

One fragment of extant group formation theory we may call the proliferation hypothesis. It argues, in effect, that as a consequence of various processes of social differentiation, especially those linked to technological change but including others as well, there is within a given population more and more specialization of function. Increasingly specialized sets of people are observed engaged in a growing range of particular economic activities or specific social roles and from this specialized differentiation of role and function comes greater and greater diversity of interests or values as each newly differentiated set of people desires a somewhat different set of social goals.

For example, it may be argued that American farmers became increasingly specialized in terms of the commodities raised in a particular area or by particular farmers and also in terms of that corollary of specialization—interdependence with other segments of the economy; banks, merchants, railroads, and the like. Ever since the Civil War, it is quite clear farmers have grown more and more differentiated as technological innovations, such as mechanical combines and cotton pickers or refrigerated transport, combined with other factors, such as the increased use of less flexible, arid land, and changing demand patterns in both peace and war, to induce each farmer to concentrate his resources on the commodity he could produce to greatest advantage rather than try to supply himself with a wide range of necessary foods and fibers. In short, the full scale commercialization of agriculture, beginning largely with the Civil War, led to the differentiation of farmers into specialized groups with specialized interests, each increasingly different from the next. These interests had to do with such questions as prices and market shares for the farmers and also for those with whom the farmers dealt in the market place. The interdependence which accompanied the specialization process meant potential conflicts of interests or values both across the bargaining encounter and among the competing farmers themselves as each struggled to secure his own position.

The proliferation hypothesis now simply adds that as a "natural" social response among these conflicting specialized groups formal associations are created, or emerge, to represent the conflicting claims of each differentiated set of interested parties. The association articulates the interest, and by organizing its adherents provides more effective bargaining power vis-a-vis other groups. It may be, as Bentley put it, "mere technique" since the association is seen as a kind of automatic fruit of the process of social differentiation, but it has an independent effect upon the political processes in which the group may be concerned. Thus unorganized groups, i.e., people with differentiated but unarticulated values, are presumed to be weaker than organized groups. The questions of whether truly differentiated interests will actually languish for long in unorganized circumstances is a matter which remains unclear in the theoretical fragments we have to work with. It does seem that, taken over time, such interests are expected to achieve organizational expression even though the specific processes by which formal organizations are generated are nowhere examined and seem rather generally to be regarded as inevitable consequences of differentiation itself. In any case, for our purposes, the salient points concerning the proliferation hypothesis are three: (1) associations are products of differentiated sets of values or interests, (2) over time there will appear more and more different, diverse, specialized groups in the political arena as the processes of social fission continue, and (3) it is to the processes by which values are altered that one must look for an explanation of group formation.

A second proto-theory, so to speak, of group formation may be referred to as the homeostatic mechanism hypothesis. This argument places much less emphasis on the processes of social differentiation and the generation of "new interests" thereby. Rather it assumes a certain differentiation and suggests the following sequence as typical of group origins. A putative equilibrium among social groups is disturbed as a consequence of such socially disruptive factors as technological innovation, war, transportation or communications changes, and such macrosocial processes as major population movements, business cycle fluctuations, and industrialization. The disequilibrium will evoke a response from the disadvantaged sectors as they seek to restore a viable balance. A principal way of doing so is by organizing a formal association because, as Truman points out, this not only improves bargaining power but it also helps to stabilize and strengthen relationships within the group by increasing the mutually supportive interaction among members and thereby the range and salience of their shared values. Notice that the organization is seen as a more active agent in this approach than from the proliferation perspective. Its operations contribute directly, if only marginally, to the changing of member values and it is thus much less dependent on underlying social processes to show the interest direction the group should pursue.

Truman observes that "the formation of associations . . . tends to occur in waves" because once a group organizes in order to reassert a satisfactory equilibrium it may inspire counter-organization among rival groups in a kind of dialectical process. Presumably there is an equilibrating tendency underlying this process, however, so that once a set of social group bargaining encounters has been organized on all sides there is an end to the group formation process and a stability to the associational activities. In this respect the homeostatic mechanism hypothesis differs from the proliferation hypothesis since the latter predicts the continuing development of new interest configurations and hence of new associations.

We may well have read distinctions into remarks which were intended for less intensive exegetical use, but the two theoretical sketches outlined above do occasionally appear in the literature. The two approaches differ in emphasis and in certain of their assumptions, but they are not mutually exclusive. The critical question is which hypothesis gives the better empirical return or, if neither is adequate, is there a superior alternative? Attention to the formation of agricultural groups in the United States leads us to find congenial elements in both hypotheses, but there are disquieting elements as well. Let us examine, albeit briefly, the relevant data.

By either of our hypotheses the growth of politically relevant farmer organizations would be expected in the post-civil war period. On the one hand, the spectacular rise of the Grange from 1867 until about 1875 is a sufficiently prominent datum that no theory of group formation would be likely to miss it. At the same time, it is clear that agricultural technology changed dramatically in the direction of mechanization during this period. The dislocations of war and the railroad-assisted post-bellum westward expansion contributed, as did the growth of corporate industrial power, to the transformation of the farmer's circumstances. In large measure, it appears that the proliferation hypothesis has somewhat the better case for the immediate postwar period in its stress upon the generation of new interest and value configurations as a consequence of social differentiation. Clearly, it was not simply a matter of older groups coming into a new situation, for, outside the South, there had never before been large groups of commercial farmers with such dependence on the market and so vulnerable to its vicissitudes.

But it is also clear that for nearly half a century farm groups did not proliferate into more and more organizations, each with its specialized concerns. At least until after 1900 the overwhelming bulk of farm organizations which were formed were aggregated under the comprehensive embrace of few, though often loose, organizational structures. Thus the Grange was followed by the Farmers Alliance in the 1880's, the Populist Party in the 1890's, and the Agricultural Wheel, the Farmers Union and finally the Farm Bureau in the first part of the twentieth century. Although each of these organizations was composed of a large number of local and state units, and in the case of the Farmers Alliance there were several distinct regional components which were partly or wholly autonomous, no real evidence can be found of a fission-like process. Rather a rapid series of

local organizational successes was followed by official aggrega-
tion under a broad group banner and then, until this century,
by the equally rapid demise of the organization, in its power if
not, as usually happened, in its very existence.

This sequence of organizations may seem to disconfirm the
proliferation hypothesis, but it does not readily fit the homeostatic mechanism theory either. The rapid rise and fall of actual
farm associations in a period, 1867–1900, which was one of consistent market disadvantage for most farm groups could hardly
be construed as conducive to the reassertion of a viable equilibrium. It may be argued that whether they were successful or
not the groups were certainly organized in order to reassert just
such an equilibrium, and of this there can be little doubt. The
rhetoric of farm protest groups has consistently stressed the
postulate that a primeval state of grace had been violated by
this industrial revolution and public policy should work toward
the restoration of Eden. But rhetoric which evokes Arcadia may
be distinguished from empirical social theory, and neither proliferation nor the homeostasis hypotheses seem adequate to
explain the succession of organizational failures among people
who, it has generally seemed, were in considerable distress and
needed political and organizational help. Both our theories seem
to assume that under such conditions organized groups will
emerge and in some sense succeed. Yet the empirical landscape
is cluttered with abandoned farm group vehicles, and effective
theory must deal with the relics as well as the survivors.

Another set of data with which extant theories do not satisfactorily cope relates to organizational membership figures. The
proliferation hypothesis implies not only that the number of
organized groups will increase over time but also that total
membership will probably grow. This might follow for such
social psychological reasons as that the more groups there are
the more opportunities for a given person to participate actively
in one and the more inducement therefore to join. It might also

follow from the expectation that the greater the specialization the greater or more wide-reaching the self-consciousness of group involvement and hence the greater the likelihood of formal group membership.

Homeostasis theory, on the other hand, implies a cyclical pattern of membership. If groups are formally organized as a response to bargaining disadvantage, so their membership would be expected to rise in conditions of adversity and, probably, to decline or at least stabilize when adversity was overcome. So long as the organization's existence remained essential to the new equilibrium the membership might not fall off precipitately but it would still follow a kind of cycle over the course of the fluctuating fortunes of the group involved.

Group membership data are generally rather elusive and sometimes a bit suspect too. For some groups, especially those of a professional and technical occupational character, there appears to be a slightly uneven but generally rather steady growth in membership.[1] In some groups there is a rapid surge, often followed by a precipitate decline even to disappearance of the group altogether. In two socio-economic sectors, however, agriculture and labor, the data are reasonably complete and follow similar curves; namely, they show a growth of membership in times of comparative prosperity and a decline during economic recession. For example, in the first decade of the twentieth century, a decade of relatively favorable farm prices and income after thirty-odd years of almost unbroken decline, farm group membership increased five hundred per cent! The

[1] In the ABA and AMA membership shows rather a rapid early growth, averaging more than ten per cent per year until up to one-fourth of the potential members were enrolled. Thereafter growth has averaged approximately three per cent per year. There are very few periods of absolute decline, however, with 1933–34 being much the worst. Membership in the NEA, an organization of more ambiguous professional status and with a less well-defined market, has fluctuated much more widely.

Grange, by then politically quiescent, more than doubled. The Farmers Union and the American Society of Equity were formed and each quickly attracted one hundred thousand members. Numerous commodity groups were organized at this time, and finally, still under relatively favorable economic conditions which extended until about 1919, the local and state farm bureaus were organized, to be federated in 1919 in the American Farm Bureau Federation.

Once the happy times for farm prices of World War I were over, prolonged farm depression set in and lasted until about 1926. During this period farm group membership generally declined. In the mid-western heartland of the Farm Bureau membership fell by almost one-fourth between 1920 and 1925. The Farmers Union lost forty percent of its strength between 1915 and 1933. Efforts to organize new farm groups out of the disequilibrium conditions of the early 20's uniformly failed. Decline in membership again was noticeable in the early Depression years of the 1930's, but this was followed by a spectacular recovery and growth between 1940 and 1950. In this decade, which was again one of greatly increased prosperity, the three main general farm organizations, the Grange, the Farmers Union, and the Farm Bureau went from a combined total of 866,224 family memberships to 2,108,849. Since 1950 a slow growth has continued despite the continuing decline in farm population.

Broadly, a similar pattern may be observed in the labor movement with substantial union growth during the prosperous periods of high employment, such as both World Wars, and decline in periods of recession. Additional variation is introduced by such factors as the passage of legislation like the Wagner Act, and changes in industrial technology, but the point remains. In these areas, at least, organized group membership varies directly with the relevant portion of the business cycle, going up with good times and down with bad, and this is exactly the opposite of the expectations derived from the homeostasis hypothesis.

Although the proliferation hypothesis is vague with respect to expected patterns of group membership over time, it clearly does not lead to a cyclical pattern linked to the business cycle. This hypothesis fares much better, however, especially in the period of the last thirty-five years, regarding the number and variety of distinct organizations. More or less paralleling the enormous infusion of science into agriculture has been a very striking growth in the number of specialized commodity associations. Cotton and tobacco organizations like specialization in the production of these crops, are older, dating from around 1900. But wheat, corn, cranberries, turkey broilers, and several dozen other groups have been formed more recently as an undoubted consequence of the proliferation of farming interests.[2]

Yet as we consider the appearance of, say, the National Corn Growers Association in the mid-1950's one cannot seriously regard it as any kind of an organizational manifestation of the differentiated corn growers partly because corn growers had been differentiated for years and partly because they have not joined the group in appreciable numbers. The NCGA seemed much more a kind of letterhead organization which might, if its founder's dreams materialized, someday speak for a sizeable portion of the corn growers but it had hardly yet begun to climb toward such eminence. It was still a small, struggling business enterprise, and the example suggests a very important modification required of the proliferation thesis—to establish

[2]In 1957 and 1958 some thirty-seven regional and national farm commodity organizations joined the National Conference of Commodity Organizations, an organization attempting to build program agreement among the disparate interests of commodity groups. NCCO had brief success in 1958 but shortly foundered.

some analytical distance between the technological and other social forces, on the one hand, and the emergence of organized interest groups on the other.

Before we pursue this theme, however, let us again consider the implications of the cyclical pattern of group membership. There appears to be a fairly straightforward, one might almost say simple-minded, explanation for this pattern. It is simply that in times of prosperity potential group members are much more likely to have the dues money and be willing to spend it for membership, while in hard times group membership may be one of the first luxuries to be sacrificed. Thus union membership regularly declines in the face of unemployment, and it is clear that for some portion of the members membership itself is a very marginal investment. At the same time, however, group leaders, faced with declining membership in hard times, may step up the tempo of agitation, both to hold on to their organizational membership and to alleviate the underlying group distress. Farm group leaders undoubtedly increased their public militance in the early 1930's, as did unions, while their organized strength was shrinking. But leadership vigor cannot therefore be treated as an unambiguous indicator of group emergence or strengthening. Again, the point is that group strength, insofar as it implies or involves either weight of numbers or the formation of new groups, is generally greater in prosperity than in times of trouble, and thus a significantly revised theory of group origins is required.

ENTREPRENEURS/ORGANIZERS

We find congenial a conceptualization of interest groups which regards them as benefit exchanges. Let us think of them in the following way. Entrepreneurs/organizers invest capital to create a set of benefits which they offer to a market of potential customers at a price. If, and as long as, enough customers buy, i.e., join, to make a viable organization, the group is in business. If the benefits fail, or are inadequate to warrant the cost of membership, or the leaders get inadequate return, the group collapses. *All* interest groups are conceptualized within this frame; it follows therefore that only "organized" groups, in the sense of entrepreneured exchange relationships, whether formally self-identified as organizations or not, are observable. The frame is inclusive and, it is argued, encompasses all cases without altering its basic terms.

It should immediately be noted that the conceptual scheme employed here is closely akin to an analytical frame which presently is of burgeoning interest to sociologists and represented especially in the work of Peter Blau and George Homans. At the same time, there are major identities of thought as well as language with economic theory where, after all, exchange behavior is the heart of an economist's world. Indeed, a partially parallel argument about interest groups has already been presented by economist Mancur Olson, Jr.

Many of the substantive hypotheses to be suggested here are rather direct transfers from simple economic models, and there is every reason to suppose that more elaborate and complex formulations can also be exchanged among disciplines as clarity increases respecting just how much alike our conceptual apparatuses are. The point should hastily be added, of course, that a significant residue of hypotheses in the present work is derived from distinctively political problems of types which other social scientists seldom if ever are compelled to face.

Let us now consider the core meaning of our crucial terms. These are four in number; entrepreneur/organizer, benefits, group member, and exchange. In several ways the notion of entrepreneur/organizer is particularly central to the argument. The entrepreneur in any organizational situation is the initiator of the enterprise. Behaviorally, it is always true that he must make the first move if any exchange activity is to occur. Economics is not simply adopting a useful fiction when it singles out capital formation and investment as critical to economic development and entrepreneurs as the behavioral units involved in putting capital to work. In fact, that is what happens. Entrepreneurs use capital to generate goods or services, which, they hope, will be valued enough to be wanted; people desiring to satisfy wants, will work and save, and a growth spiral is set in motion. And unless the valued goods and services are offered no latent demand can be observed, only postulated. Capital formation processes must, to be sure, come before the entrepreneur can begin to work, but in terms of any specific organized economic exchange the entrepreneur is the starting point.

If we are to apply this analogy to the phenomena of interest groups, it will be necessary for us to identify specific entrepreneurs whose activities constitute the first visible signs of every particular organized group. It will also be necessary to identify some sort of capital which is invested to launch a group enterprise. If we can meet these tests, we will then also wish to inquire concerning such questions as the sources and processes of recruitment of interest group entrepreneurs.

It would be helpful to have a systematic array of group origins data to work from, but for the moment we must be content with illustrative cases to buttress the assertion that in no instance does an entrepreneurial theory of group formation fail to apply. Again the history of American farm groups demonstrates the point. The first big group to be organized was, of course, the Grange. It was initiated by Oliver Hudson Kelley who, by dint of considerable personal sacrifice and some generous friends, managed to survive until his organizational dream began to take hold. Similarly Newton Gresham, having failed as a newspaper publisher, fed his family on credit and neighbors' largesse for more than a year until his Farmers Union began to attract enough dues-paying members to sustain him. There is evidence of personal investment, though less dramatic, on the part of leading organizers of more recent groups such as the

Farmers Holiday Movement, the National Corn Growers Association and the National Farmers Organization. And clearly a great many contemporary interest groups active in such fields as civil rights or foreign policy are headed by persons who have made heavy personal investments in their respective organizations.

Several of the early, large, farm groups were begun by publishers of small newspapers or periodicals serving primarily rural markets. The new organization was partly conceived as a circulation building mechanism and members received an immediate tangible benefit in the form of a subscription. In addition, the publication gave publicity to the group and in various ways capitalized its formation. It should be noted that these publisher-organizers may have had quite diverse *reasons* for establishing their groups. Conceptually, however, the reasons are less significant than the behavioral patterns.

A considerable number of farm groups were subsidized by other, older, groups. In part, of course, the Farm Bureau was organized and long sustained by subsidies, some from federal and state governments and some by local businessmen. The expectation that the Bureau would be a supportive group, economically and perhaps politically, no doubt underlay these subsidies, but similar expectations must usually inform the subsidizing of one group by another. The organizing of sub-units under subsidy from the parent organization may be thought of as a variation on the same theme, though the latter is so "normal" and "legitimate" an aspect of organizational growth that it occasions no comment from observers. Inter-group subsidy, however, is very often regarded with suspicion by observers who somehow expect someone to be corrupted in the process.

In any case, it is clear that both capital costs and specific entrepreneurs have often come from other, older, organizations. This seems to be particularly significant as a source of entreprenurial recruitment, at least in the case of farm groups, but perhaps for others too. Not now as a form of subsidy but rather as a training ground and example of the possibility of establishing viable organizations of farmers, the early Grange provided the first real organizational experience for an enormous number of people. Many organizers of the Farmers Alliance had had experience in the Grange. In turn, Newton Gresham had been a zealot with the Alliance, allegedly organizing some fifteen hundred sub-alliances, before he attempted to establish the Farmers Union. Contemporaneously, other former Alliance and Grange organizers, such as Issac McCracken of the Brothers of Freedom and Harvie Jordan of the Southern Cotton Growers' Association, were at work organizing their new enterprises. Saloutos is able already to refer to Jordan as a "professional farm organizer and lobbyist."

What seems to have occurred is that once the Grange had set the example of a viable organization of farmers, a large number of people, especially those with direct experience in the prototype group, were attracted by the prospect of establishing farm groups of their own. One might follow as another collapsed. They might be differentiated by region or by crop or both. They might stress somewhat different combinations of material or political or rhetorical objectives. But in a broader sense they were all in the same line of business, and many of these businessmen came to constitute a rather specialized and self-sustaining subset of farm organizers. It seems warranted to suggest that a large portion of labor organizers have come from backgrounds closely associated with the union movement, or that both right and left wing group organizers tend to have long careers in that kind of activity—as *organizers*, not necessarily as heads of any particular group.

One important point which is suggested by the foregoing discussion is as follows. If groups must be organized by organizers investing capital, and if very often these organizers and this capital are derived, either as a subsidy or a legacy, from older organizations, then the emergence of extensive organized group life in a political system will tend (a) to be a gradual process, partially dependent on the spread of the organizational experience to socialize and recruit organizers, and (b) will depend upon the accumulation of social capital sufficient to invest in the formation of durable organizations. To the extent that the capital required is material, group formation requires, and must largely wait upon, industrialization. This is in no sense a novel conclusion, of course, but the argument by which it is reached is quite different from most.

THE NATURE OF "BENEFITS"

We turn now to our second key concept. It should be understood at the outset that we do not attempt to assess "real" or "true" benefits. Rather we assume that people do or pursue those experiences and things which they value, for whatever reasons, and *in this sense only* may be regarded as rational. We assume that people mainly do or seek, subject to periodic evaluation and correction, whatever brings them a positive balance of benefits over costs. (It may be simpler to think only of positive and negative benefits since the latter is really what the notion of costs mean.) Notice that this is a conceptual assumption which is useful in thinking about certain kinds of behavior and of no necessary relevance either to normative theories of behavior or to motivational analysis.

How then shall we conceptualize benefits? A useful beginning point is the threefold distinction suggested by Clark and Wilson with reference to organizational incentives.[3] They distinguish among material, solidary and purposive incentives. By

---

[3]See Peter B. Clark and James Q. Wilson, "Incentive Systems: A Theory of Organizations," in *Administrative Science Quarterly*, Vol. 6 (September 1961), pp. 129–166. Clark and Wilson are concerned more generally with organizations than with interest groups *per se*, but their analysis is generally relevant even when only implicitly so. Some of their hypotheses are similar to those suggested here, some are not. For example, they suggest that organizations will stress purposive incentives in the formative stages. We argue the contrary for farm groups and many others.

material incentives they mean the tangible rewards of goods or services or the means, such as a job, by which goods and services may be obtained. Material incentives—or, in our terms, benefits—are always extrinsic to the parties involved in the transaction and are typically instrumental toward more fundamental values such as deference or well-being. Solidary benefits, on the other hand, are intrinsic to the parties. They are experienced directly and within the self. Clark and Wilson suggest that solidary values "derive in the main from the acts of associating and include such rewards as socializing, congeniality, the sense of group membership and identification, the status resulting from membership, fun and conviviality, and so on."

Purposive benefits or incentives consist of the realization of suprapersonal goals, goals of the organization or group. Although, of course, the benefits of such achievement may accrue to particular individuals they are not ordinarily divisible into units of value allocated to specific persons or charged against unit costs. Nor can purposive benefits always be confined to the parties seeking them. Thus "good government" or "peace" or "states rights" or "civil liberties" are all desired by individuals and benefit individuals, but the benefits cannot readily be cost analyzed and they accrue to all sorts of people who took no part in the efforts to secure them. Blau employs a related concept when he discusses "expressive" social actions, as distinguished from instrumental actions. Expressive actions are those where the action involved gives expression to the interests or values of a person or group rather than instrumentally pursuing interests or values. Presumably one cannot *express* material values; one must pursue them and achieve them. Similarly, one can only enjoy solidary benefits by having them. But one can often derive benefits from expressing certain kinds of values. Opposition to war or poverty and affirmation of free speech or civil rights are contemporary examples of values many people wish to express and, what is of critical importance for our purposes, they are willing to join groups which provide mechanisms for the public expression of those values. Whether the expression is instrumentally relevant to the achievement of the values in question is, for the moment, not at issue. The point here is that important benefits are derived from the expression itself.

We prefer here to use the notion of expressive benefits rather than Clark and Wilson's term, "purposive." They were dealing only with intra-organizational incentives and consequently were untroubled by whatever complexities might appear regarding transactions between an organization's leaders and other groups. Clearly, however, some interest group leaders lobby for suprapersonal organizational goals—price supports, let us say, or a tax cut—which are purposive in Clark and Wilson's sense but also material in their explicit anticipated consequences. Material, solidary and expressive benefits would seem to constitute mutually exclusive categories at the conceptual level, though the difficulties of empirical specification and measurement can hardly be exaggerated.

Our argument is that the group entrepreneur invests his capital to create a set of benefits, composed of some combination or mix of the types mentioned, which he offers at a price to a market. The price is group membership, which may cost as little as a supportive signature or as much as the heavy dues attached to some trade association memberships. The market is whatever range of people the entrepreneur chooses to try to attract. This leads us to an examination of the implication of our three-fold typology of benefits for the entrepreneurial activities of group organizers. We then shall consider group members and potential members as sets of markets with demand patterns or preference schedules and see what implications this angle of vision may have.

What benefits are in fact offered by the entrepreneur/organizer to potential members of his group? It is clear that in a high proportion of cases the benefits initially offered are largely material. In the case of the early farm groups, for example, beginning with the Farmers Alliance and continuing through the Farmers Union and the Farm Bureau as well as a host of smaller groups, the initial exchange centered around some form of economic cooperation, for buying or selling or both. Cooperatives were sometimes promoted by stressing their ideological virtues, but in every case they were also expected to return direct economic benefits to those who joined. Obviously the same has been true of labor unions and also of most business trade associations.

To observe the initial stress on material economic benefits in so many groups is to call attention to a closely related phenomenon which any theory of group formation and functioning must take into account. This is the phenomenon of organizational failure. No extant theory of interest groups seems to recognize the evident fact that a great many specific organized groups go out of business. Turnover is extremely high. Now if groups are organized through benefit exchange, it follows that they will dissolve whenever the benefits are inadequate to warrant continued support of the group. If the organizer fails to maintain the flow—if, for instance, the cooperative fails—the members will quit. So will they if they can no longer afford the cash dues. And this is precisely what happened to numerous farm groups and sub-groups during the latter nineteenth century. What were essentially small business operations failed; often because of bad management, but in several cases because of the special adversity of recession, as in 1893.

Not every group is organized around material benefits, of course. The early local agricultural societies probably flourished on the basis of solidary benefits derived from membership, and it has long been standard to attribute much of the success of the Grange to the high solidary benefits resulting from the semi-secret rituals and Grange Hall-centered fraternal activities of the group. From the point of view of an entrepreneur, however, solidary benefits are often difficult to sell unless the market has special characteristics. An organizer can build a clubhouse but he cannot easily guarantee it will be worthwhile to go there. The solidary benefits may develop but the entrepreneur is especially dependent on his customer to help him create his product. Furthermore, it is not clear that for most people sociability is valued highly enough to persuade them to join a new group to get it. They may do so if there are no other alternatives—if the market is genuine virgin territory regarding group association as the post bellum farming frontier largely was. Or people may join solidary benefit groups which provide a generous admixture of other types of benefits too. A typical mix is solidary benefits mixed with rather a specialized type of expressive benefits. For example, cell-based organizations, which certainly have structures conducive to providing solidary benefits, tend also to be linked to extremist ideologies, often fraught with conspiratorial theses. In the small group situation of the cell, "the enemy" can be denounced enthusiastically and thereby maximize both expressive and solidary benefits of membership. Nevertheless, we tend to regard those interest groups which stress solidary benefits as "fringe" groups, unlikely to have much impact on public decisions, perhaps precisely because so much of their membership satisfaction is provided within the group itself.

It is probably the case, however, that we do not concern ourselves with solidary groups, or, for that matter, with material exchange groups either, unless there is also some kind of politically relevant expressive content to the group's internal exchange. Thus we care about the Grange not because of its fraternal rituals but because of the political relevance of the values and interests expressed by its leaders through its various official mechanisms. Still, it is one thing for, say, a material benefits group to acquire an overlay of expressive benefits and quite another to organize a group around the exchange of expressive values to begin with. The latter is a frequent phenomenon but one of special characteristics.

For the entrepreneur it is comparatively easy to essay establishing an expressive group. It requires little capital to articulate a cause and go about promoting the nascent group as guardian of that cause. On the other hand, this type of group presents especially high risks too. The cause may be a popular one without there being any persuasive reason for people who believe in it to join the particular group whose organizer claims to be the *true* defender of the faith. Moreover, it is likely that expressive groups are especially vulnerable to slight changes in circumstances, including many over which the group has no control. For example, America First and the Committee to Defend America by Aiding the Allies were wiped out organizationally by Pearl Harbor. More broadly, for most people the act of joining an expressive group—contributing dues to ACLU or signing a Viet Nam protest petition—is a marginal act. The benefits derived from value expression are seldom of great intrinsic worth. Consequently, even if civil liberties remain equally endangered, a slight change in the member's resources or social pressures may lead to his failure to renew his membership.

Two points of quite general political relevance follow from this line of analysis. On the one hand, expressive groups, being cheap to organize, will abound in a political system to whatever extent there may be entrepreneurs available to organize them, but they will tend to be highly transient. They will be easily established and as easily disappear. They will utilize communications media, especially the mail, more than face-to-face contacts; they may alter their expressed position to meet changing "market conditions." But above all they are unstable organizations. The corollary point is that expressive group organizers may be expected to infuse other types of benefits into the group in order to give it stability. They may attempt to enlarge the solidary benefits, for example, through the use of direct action protests. Whether a group moves from expressive toward solidary or the other way is an empirical question, but our analysis has suggested that a group originally stressing one type will tend to add the other in order to increase its stability as an organization.

We observed earlier that political scientists take notice of groups only if there is some politically relevant expressive content to the groups' activities. But, we have argued, strictly expressive groups are unstable and transient. At the same time, stable groups such as those based on viable economic benefit exchanges may not have any politically relevant values. Must our concern with groups be only sporadic, incorporating them only when they enter the political arena and ignoring them otherwise? It would appear that, in fact, this is what we have done and it has led us to assume a durability and politicization of interest groups far in excess of reality. The theoretical posture adopted here, which deals with organized groups as generic phenomena, not simply in their politically relevant aspect, leads to the conclusion that most group activity has little to do with efforts to affect public policy decisions but is concerned rather with the internal exchange of benefits by which the group is organized and sustained. But surely, one may argue, some significant fraction of the universe of groups is established *in order to affect* and with the consequence of affecting policy outcomes. To consider this question properly we must also consider the work of Mancur Olson, whose argument is in many ways parallel to this one.

Olson is concerned with the question of why people maintain membership in interest groups. He demonstrates that in most familiar group situations it is not rational for any member to be part of an interest group in order to support a lobby, even though he genuinely desires the goals toward which the lobbying is directed. The argument hinges primarily on the distinction between what Olson calls *collective benefits*—those which accrue to people in a particular situation or category regardless of their organizational affiliations—and *selective benefits*—those which accrue only to members of the association. Thus the Farmers Union may lobby for price supports; i.e., collective benefits, but its members will receive the benefits of price supports whether they stay in the Union or not. Olson shows that therefore its members would not stay if they rationally balance the cost of membership against its benefits insofar as these benefits are collective. But cooperatives and cheap insurance may be available only to members. They are selective and may be entirely sufficient to induce continued membership.

Thus far Olson's argument differs little from the present one except that it is less clearly couched in exchange terms and thus does not explicitly examine the entrepreneur/organizer as a functionally distinct role from that of group member. Olson does not contend that all group members are rational, but only that to the extent that they are they will not normally join organizations in order to seek collective benefits. Two main exceptions are noted: where the members are philanthropic and seek through group membership to obtain benefits for others; and where membership is coerced, as in a union operating under a closed shop agreement. Yet the broadened conception of benefits we have employed, including the notion that costs, e.g., of coercion, are the same as negative benefits, allows us to subsume these exceptions under the same headings as in the central argument. Moreover, as we noted earlier, we can assume that rationality in the sense of purposiveness or goal-orientation is characteristic of such a preponderance of behavior that any observed exceptions will not affect the main contentions.

There are two critical points in Olson's argument, both of them points of omission, with which we must take issue. Olson does not examine how groups are first organized but assumes a going system. As a consequence he does not adequately deal with group development through time. If one looks at group formation, however, one finds that some organizations such as the Farmers Alliance were indeed organized around the exchange of selective benefits but that others, such as the Grange, were organized initially, at least in significant part, in order to alter public policy; i.e., to secure collective benefits. Granted that many of the groups in the latter category may later have introduced selective benefits in order to hold the members, we must still account for the initial appearance. And Olson's argument does not hold for this situation. Is it relevant for farmers to join together in order to bring about policy change? Does organization improve their bargaining power? Political lore and science agree on the affirmative. How many farmers must join before this power is sufficient to secure any collective benefits through policy change? The answer is, within very broad limits, indeterminate. Accordingly, it may be entirely rational for any potential member to join until the benefit is achieved as long as his costs in joining are exceeded by his anticipated benefit from the collective good. Once the latter is a reality, however, the indeterminacy disappears and Olson's analysis comes into play; the member ought rationally to withdraw unless selective benefits are introduced. Thus a sizable array of organized groups *may* appear on the political scene to lobby for collective good but, lacking selective benefits, their mortality rate is likely to be high.

Olson's second omission is any explanation of the phenomenon of lobbying. We shall deal with this whole subject in greater detail below, but it should here be noted that Olson's argument accounts for the maintenance of groups without regard to their impact on public policy but does not explain why groups lobby or how lobbying is related, if it is, to the dynamics of intra-group relationships. Nevertheless, Olson has performed an important service in destroying the comfortable myth of an interest group behaving in a simple representational way, seeking public policy goals because these goals are desired by the group's members.

GROUP MEMBERSHIP

We must now consider a very tricky but important component of our conceptual structure, the matter of consumer, or member, preferences. It seems fair to say that at bottom extant interest group theory assumes that group members have public policy-related interests, values, or preferences which (1) antedate the existence of the organized association, (2) are the rational basis for joining and remaining as members of the association, (3) are articulated and heightened by virtue of the associational interactions, and (4) are represented through the association to the policy-making arenas by virtue of lobbying activities. As we have seen, Olson undermines the logical plausibility of points 2 and 4 and, in a sense, renders point 3 beside the point for explaining interest group phenomena. But there are additional difficulties even in the first item. How do we know that a particular array of interests exists? Conventionally we have approached the issue in two very different ways. We may impute interests to categories of people—workers, farmers, etc.—on the basis of some theory about how individual values are derived and ordered, say Marxism or its variants. Thus we conclude that factory workers desire policies which raise wages, or give authority to unions, or the like. Alternatively, we may infer preferences from observed behavior. Thus some types of workers join unions more readily than others and are presumed therefore to place a different valuation on union membership. Most behaviorally derived preference schedules look far more diverse than do those imputed on the basis of more abstract theories about how values are formed. One might therefore suppose that empirical inquiry into preference schedules ought to be urged to test competing analytic strategies. But here one runs into the problem that inter-subjective comparisons of utility schedules are, in virtually all cases, impossible. Without examining the large body of literature on this point, we may apply this conclusion to our situation in the following manner. Preferences and their orderings may be established for any set of people only on the basis of their behavior. Although he may make a reasonable estimate in advance, say on the basis of some kind of market research, the only way a producer really determines what consumer preference schedules are is by offering a good at a price, or at varying prices, and observing the differential demand schedules. Similarly, the only way empirically to determine the existence of an interest is to articulate a position (expressive benefits) or offer material or solidary incentives at one or more price levels and to observe the incidence and distribution of support—membership, votes, money, or whatever else is valued political currency. Price, a behaviorally derived result of exchange activity, resolves the dilemma posed by the noncomparability of inter-subjective preferences. And this means that interests of a group or class of people may be observed *only* by examining exchanges between political entrepreneurs and consumer/member/voters.

The analytic problem is thus, *a fortiori,* resolved by conceptualizing interests and interest groups in terms of exchanges of benefits between entrepreneurs/leaders and consumer/followers. This point does not, however, affect the relevance of individual preferences or of questions concerning how those preferences are formed or changed. Thus one may still argue that technological changes affecting the structure of economic activity may alter the preference schedules of many persons. These new schedules may constitute a promising potential market for political entrepreneurs or, indeed, they may adversely affect a particular entrepreneur's market. Variables affecting market potential are relevant to an understanding of group formation and development. But, as we have stressed, they are never a sufficient explanation of interest activity and their aggregate structure cannot be more than guessed at in the absence of group organizing activities.[4]

THE EXCHANGE

It follows from what we have said that the "potential group" or market is a matter of great uncertainty from the point of view of

---

[4]The discussion here of potential markets, a familiar enough notion in economic analysis, would seem to incorporate the principal meaning of Truman's oft maligned concept of potential group. Truman imputed a political impact to potential groups, however, which is quite absent from any understanding one might have of potential markets. Again, the latter are truly fallow until cultivated by entrepreneurs.

the group organizer. The latter, having invested his capital in an array of benefits, offers these benefits at a price—membership in the group—which he hopes will attract members and also maintain a viable organization. Entrepreneurs/organizers generally appear to select their markets on the basis of their own experiences and contacts or by emulating other, similar, organizational efforts, as when they purchase or borrow mailing lists of similarly inclined groups or publications. Farm organizers are closely affiliated with farmers, labor organizers with workers, rightists with rightists, and so on, and seldom do group entrepreneurs seem to cross over from one field to another. Thus, they have some expectation concerning the probable demand curves of the market they seek to reach, but they must be unsure whether the response will be sufficient to sustain the organization. And in order to sustain a group organization, it is necessary to maintain an adequate flow of benefits both to members *and* to the organizers themselves. In short, there must be a mutually satisfactory *exchange*.

Now what kinds of benefits are derived from these group organization exchanges by the entrepreneurs? The economists have no difficulty with this question, which they assert is answered by the notion of profits. If, in addition to profits, an entrepreneur derives other types of job satisfactions, profits remain the key requirement for continuation of the enterprise, and in abstract economic models of entrepreneurial activity the profit must approach some optimal return on the capital investment or the investment will be transferred to some other, more promising, enterprise.

It may be that many kinds of group organizing capital are not as easily transferred as straight money capital; a prosperous labor union probably will not subsidize other enterprises randomly nor will a farm organizer equally well defer his spending in order to organize in the urban ghetto. The *tendencies* would surely be for investment to go toward expressively supportive organizations, cognate markets and relatively familiar territories, geographical and functional. Yet we can cite numerous examples to show that even this capital is transferred from one enterprise to another within quite broad limits. Let us, therefore, consider what is implied by the notion of profit in respect to political entrepreneurs.

As a minimum we may assume that, so long as the entrepreneur desires to maintain the organization as a going enterprise, he must get a sufficient return in the form of membership support to enable him to continue to provide the benefits which attract members. Over some initial period of time the benefits may be more costly than membership will pay for, but, unless the enterprise is permanently subsidized, the returns must ultimately match the cost of providing the benefits. Where the benefits to members are material, of course, the membership must also provide material rewards in exchange. But even in solidary and expressive groups the entrepreneur must derive enough material return to pay the overhead costs *and* keep him sufficiently satisfied so as not to shift his energies to some other enterprise. Conceptually, the entrepreneur's reward may be viewed as profit. Thus: Entrepreneurs provide benefits to members whose membership must entail a return sufficient to pay the costs of the benefits received plus some profit to the entrepreneur.

What form does group organizer profit take empirically? A common form is that of the salaried executive. In some groups the organizer may be chosen president of the group he develops and paid a salary. In other cases he may occupy the position of executive secretary or its equivalent. In either situation he must maintain an adequate flow of benefits to members or lose his position, either because the enterprise goes bankrupt or because he is dismissed somewhere short of organizational catastrophe. If the organizer does not desire or cannot obtain a paid position from his entrepreneurial activities, he may nevertheless persist in them if they have sufficient expressive value for him, and many expressive groups probably are developed in this fashion as avocational or philanthropic concerns substitute for entrepreneurial "profit motives." Even here, however, organizing is costly, and there must be subsidies drawn from other extra-group sources to sustain the activity or the group will shortly be bankrupt. The great difficulty experienced by many civil rights groups in keeping their leadership afloat illustrates the point.

I do not wish to argue that group organizers are classic "economic men" whose conscious motives are to secure the largest possible financial return. Indeed, although there surely are examples of such motivation among extant interest group entrepreneurs, taken as a whole their conscious intentions are undoubtedly very diverse. The point is rather that "profit" to the leadership is a necessary part of the exchange with the members and without it the leaders cannot continue.

One implication of the foregoing discussion is that any *election* of leaders by members, or of representatives by constituents, may be regarded in terms familiar to economic analysis of the firm. Thus the minimum return required on investment is reelection to office, and office must provide sufficient resources to motivate and to maintain the flow of benefits to members/constituents. Dissatisfied members of a voluntary group may quit or switch to a rival group; dissatisfied constituents may be expected to switch to a rival candidate. But the logical and conceptual relationship is the same. It is an exchange which must satisfy both parties.

Now, let us go an additional step. It may be observed that large numbers of organized interest groups do go bankrupt in some sense. They fail as enterprises. Their organizers/leaders must find some other line. But large numbers of groups survive over long periods of time. Moreover, it is characteristic of many relatively stable groups, especially those involving primarily material benefits exchanges, to exhibit great stability in their paid leadership personnel. Further, it may be suggested that the "profits" accruing to this leadership from providing members with selective benefits, available only to group members, very often exceed by a comfortable margin the minimum requirements of sustaining the enterprise. How may we think about this "surplus"?

From the standpoint of the entrepreneur, whose decision it is to dispose of his "surplus profits," there may be a number of options. He may, for example, enlarge the benefits available to members in order to restore the balance between his costs and his profits. Or he may spend his profits in various private, but personal, activities—higher salary, extra-group activities, or whatever. Perhaps he builds a fancy new building as an organizational headquarters. But, if his enterprise is internally prosperous, he may spend some of his "profits" in public activity. He may, for example, lobby for legislation which *he* thinks desirable and do so quite independent of any views his members have on the question. When he does so, he cannot expect his members to agree with him, but, as long as his organization survives and he with it, it does not really matter. He takes his policy positions and invests what he has in the way of profit in promoting them not because his membership demands that he do so but only because his membership makes it possible for him to pursue his private desires by providing him a profitable exchange. Now it may be that his desires are not incongruent with those of his members. It may also be that he seeks legitimation and support for his desires by asserting that they conform to those of his members. But it may also be that those whom he attempts to persuade to his views are unimpressed by his claims of membership support, and his success must then be achieved by other bargaining tactics. Applying this same conception to a legislator we often say that he has a considerable number of "free votes" on which constituency demands are absent or conflicting or vague and which he casts according to bargaining criteria which he derives independent of constituency pressure. Yet unless he satisfies the minimum constituency expectations of benefits he will not survive in office long enough to spend his profits in his "free votes."

It is not argued that "profit consumption" is the sole explanation of lobbying or influencing activity or that all such activity is equally well explained this way. It is contended, however, that a significant portion of what we observe to be lobbying activity by group leaders may result not from a mandate derived from membership demands but from the personal choices and values of the group leaders. This conception would fit and make sense of a broad spectrum of data which show group spokesmen taking public policy positions at variance with the apparent views of their members and still suffering no reprisals. Indeed, as Milbrath among others has pointed out, a major focus of lobbying is not the policy-makers at all but the group members themselves. If lobbyists were simply reflecting membership demands, they would not spend so much time "farming the membership."

Moreover, we may in this way more easily make sense of the reported disregard of lobbyists, or at least extremely uneven response to them, by policy makers. And, finally, we may thus square the lack of logical necessity for lobbying by group spokesmen, which Olson shows, with the obvious fact of extensive lobbying in the observable world.

There remains a significant portion of lobbying activity which may be regarded as instrumental to the benefit flow and exchange of the group and it would be wrong to ignore this portion. As we noted in criticizing Olson's argument, the problematic but presumably positive relationship between group strength and activity and the achievement of public decisions providing collective good makes it rational, within broad limits for individuals who value the good to join a group which proposes to lobby for it. Moreover, many collective goods are provided in discontinuous or, at least, recurrently renegotiable form so that simply because an act is passed providing a given level of farm subsidies for three years does not guarantee it will be renewed or, if renewed, maintained at the same level. Group lobbying may often, therefore, be instrumental in securing or maintaining the flow of collective benefits, and, while not all those affected by the benefits will join the group, or join for that reason, some may do so and press the entrepreneurs to act accordingly.

In addition, for some groups potential public policy decisions constitute a significant source of the selective benefits by which the group's internal exchange is sustained. This would be true, for example, of a significant portion of the licensing regulations applicable to professional groups who secure the legal authority to control entry to the profession, and, having such authority, make it attractive thereby for prospective practitioners to join the association. Or for a labor union, policy decisions involving picketing, antitrust applications to union activities, yellow-dog contracts, and the like directly affect the ability of the union leadership to provide selective benefits to its members through favorable contracts. Whenever this is the case, it is obvious that lobbying by the entrepreneur leaders requires no additional conceptual trappings for satisfactory explanation.

CONTINUITY OF GROUP LEADERSHIP

In the analysis we have presented the focus has been mainly on the initial organizer/entrepreneurs of the group. There are good reasons for this emphasis. It reminds us that existing organizations such as unions or major farm groups, which sometimes seem to be permanent features of the political landscape, have quite specific origins and originators. Moreover, it has been useful to examine those origins and the individuals who played the key entrepreneurial roles in establishing the groups. But one need not rely on state of nature assumptions in the analysis of contemporary groups. A large proportion of the extant roster of politically relevant groups are durable enterprises with origins which may or may not shed light on their present affairs. Implicit in our argument, however, is the view that all groups may be approached in the same terms. If the entrepreneur/organizer is easier to identify through examining group origins, his role is conceptually identical with that of the leader of a going group concern. It is, therefore, group leadership generally that we are discussing in a framework of benefit exchange. The entrepreneurial role is generically identical with that of leader; the leader is perforce an entrepreneur.

We will not repeat what has already been said of the entrepreneur in order to make clear its application to leadership generally. Nor is it possible here to do more than assert that the argument may be transferred *in toto* to the consideration of leadership generally, not simply group leadership. Suffice to say that although we begin with an attempt to develop an empirically valid and logically secure theory of interest groups we find ourselves with a formulation of truly general proportions.

Let us here add only one additional point of substance derived from our general argument. We have already noted that among material benefit groups leadership tenure has generally been very secure. There are, of course, some notable exceptions, but most union or farm or business group leaders have had long careers, seldom challenged. On the other hand, what we have referred to as expressive groups are frequently characterized by bitter schisms. Does our formulation contribute to an explanation of this phenomenon? We indicated earlier that expressive groups are cheap to organize but fragile. If they are cheap to organize, they are also cheap to factionalize. A rival to the leadership needs only a membership list and a better line to support a factional fight. The fruits of victory may be great or small, depending on what the faction leaders value and how prosperous or prestigious the group is. What are the potential costs of attempting a factional fight? The ultimate cost is expulsion. But seldom is an expressive group the sole guardian of expression of a value. If one is kicked out of CORE or the John Birch Society one is not thereby denied the opportunity to express one's position but probably only of whatever solidary values the group conferred on its members.

On the other hand, consider a comparable situation in a union or a farm organization. In order to mount a serious effort to unhorse the leadership, factional leaders must, in effect, assemble enough capital, perhaps from anticipated profits, to promise enough increased benefits to attract support for themselves and away from their rivals. This is typically very difficult to do partly because the capital to organize a factional drive is hard to assemble, partly because the existing leadership faced with factional opposition may often reinvest more of their profit into membership benefits, and sometimes may simply coopt potential factional leaders into the existing leadership cadre. Moreover, uncompromising factional rivals may be met with exclusion from the group which in turn may mean exclusion from a substantial array of material benefits available only to group members. For all these reasons then factional efforts in established material benefits groups are comparatively rare and often came to grief. And this is true even though the profits available to material benefit group leaders are often substantial and hence might be expected to attract rival entrepreneurs. But the capital requirements to capture control of the UAW or set up a rival union in the same employment markets would surely not be much less difficult to manage than capturing control of, or establishing a rival to, General Motors. Finally, material benefit interest groups have been successful as have business firms in coopting potential factional leadership into an orderly hierarchy with sufficient profits derived from the group's exchange structure to sustain the full cadre.

CONCLUSION

In concluding a paper of this kind one is tempted simply to restate the core of the argument, recognizing that for the most part the usefulness of the kind of conceptual orientation presented here depends upon its plausibility and suggestiveness as a heuristic model. In the main it is neither true nor false but to be tested by its intellectual utility. Nevertheless, the utility of such a scheme must ultimately rest on whether one can imagine ways by which to derive reasonable empirical applications which are amenable to testing against data. One such application has been illustrated here in the discussion of farm group origins, and our conclusion was that an entrepreneurial exchange hypothesis both fits and explains the data better than alternative hypotheses. It has also been suggested that this formulation accounts for the high incidence of schism among ideological or expressive groups and the low incidence of severe factionalism among material benefit groups. One must recognize, however, that in the latter explanation the data are largely impressionistic since they assume more knowledge than we have of the kind of benefits exchanged in the two categories of groups. In principle, however, such data could be obtained by inquiring of group members, and of people solicited to join who decline, what benefits they derive from membership and determining the points at which, under various conditions, marginal costs equate with marginal benefits or utility.

Another empirical test might be undertaken by examining closely and systematically the behavior of group leaders over time. It was argued that much lobbying activity by group leaders may be understood as a form of personal consumption of profit derived from their intragroup exchanges. If this is correct, it would follow that when their membership declines or is threatened with decline such profit is reduced and the lobbying for policies that are non-instrumental to the group's exchange structure would also decline. If, that is, UAW membership declines, Walter Reuther should spend more time on contract bargaining and union-related instrumental lobbying and less time on policy issues of a more personally expressive character. Without gainsaying the difficulties of making such observations, one may suppose that they are possible and would constitute an empirical test of the theory.

Finally, and whatever the empirical outcomes of the specific inquiries proposed or of others which might be imagined, we must assert the crucial importance of developing systematic empirical theory, of interest groups as of other politically relevant phenomena, to bring greater order and clarity to the extant array of literary theory. Nearly two decades ago David Truman demonstrated extraordinary imagination in assembling a vast array of fragments into a richly suggestive fabric of commentary and insight. Ironically, his accomplishment was so complete that remarkably few political scientists have worked ahead with the tools he sought to fashion. By employing a more generic conceptual orientation to examine interest group phenomena, perhaps we may at least hope to revive the substantive investigation into their characteristic properties and more systematically relate them to other facets of the political system.

2

MEMBERS, LEADERS, AND ORGANIZATIONAL STRUCTURE

Since shortly after World War II, political scientists have slowly but steadily shifted their attention from a preoccupation with legal institutions and philosophical ideas to a concentration on the ways in which people actually behave. This "behavioral revolution" has had many variants and off-shoots of its own, but there would seem to be one commitment which all behavioral social scientists share; a commitment to look at the evidence, the tangible evidence, of what people do rather than simply at their rhetoric. This, in turn, has forced us to be more careful in using terms which are really abstractions representing large and often diverse numbers of people. We cannot blithely assert that "The Republican Party is . . . ," or "organized labor believes . . ." We must recognize that such phrases are often the crudest sort of shorthand for describing the richly complex behavior and belief patterns of millions of people. We need shorthand expressions, of course, in order to aggregate and summarize what would otherwise be more complexity than we could comprehend. But we need also to look at the individuals.

The selections of this part consider first the members of organized groups. Who belongs and, at least by inference, why? These are the questions Charles R. Wright and Herbert H. Hyman address. Next, Paul Jacobs and Saul Landau describe the origins, appeals, and beliefs of the Students for a Democratic Society. SDS has played such a prominent role in contemporary university affairs that analysis can hardly keep pace with reality. But it is important to recognize that SDS and all the other organizations which these days so dramatically cross a student's vision are part of the interest group universe. John H. Bunzel and Richard Dudman focus attention on group organizers, reminding us again that real people are responsible for putting interest groups together.

The final selection is drawn from David B. Truman's classic work, **The Governmental Process.** In this section Truman discusses variations among organizational structures which interest groups may display and probes the consequences of these various forms. In one sense, Truman here harks back to an older political science tradition as he looks closely at formal institutional arrangements. But what he takes to be interesting about these formal rules and structures is how they do, or do not, affect patterns of behavior within and among groups. Thus Truman displays the essence of the behaviorists' concern: What difference does it make for what people do? And in the process of this discussion as throughout his book Truman summarizes a grand array of descriptive material including such classic examples as the American Legion and the American Medical Association.

Voluntary Memberships of American Adults: Evidence from National Sample Surveys

CHARLES R. WRIGHT AND HERBERT HYMAN

. . . Through good fortune, a number of nationwide and local surveys conducted by the National Opinion Research Center have contained one or more questions on voluntary association memberships. These items provide substantial information on the actual magnitude and pattern of voluntary association membership of the American people and of subgroups within the general population. Secondary analysis of these surveys can also provide evidence about numerous sociological determinants of membership, which have figured in past speculative discussions but have seldom been supported by much empirical data, for example, the effect of urbanization upon membership. In addition, the surveys often contain data on possible determinants of membership which have rarely been treated, either speculatively or empirically, in past writings. Thus data are available on various situational factors which might facilitate or impede membership and participation, such as parenthood, residential mobility, travel time to work, and the like. For many of these latter analyses, it is necessary to consult sample surveys which were conducted on local rather than national populations, but here too all the in-

From the *American Sociological Review*, Vol. 23, No. 2 (June, 1958), pp. 284–292. Reprinted with permission of the authors and the American Sociological Association.

quiries have the merit of being based on large samples drawn by a probability design. Therefore, though limited to the cities or counties involved, they still constitute reliable evidence concerning hypotheses based on representative sampling. Finally, by secondary analysis tabulation of voluntary association membership is possible, not only by hypothesized determinants, but also by the customary questions asked in such surveys about attitudes, opinions, interests, conduct, and so on. In this manner, some empirical perspective can be obtained on the fundamental question of the functions of organizational membership for citizens in a democratic society.

Admittedly there are serious limitations to such secondary analysis. Foremost among these is the reliance put upon questions not primarily designed for the study of voluntary association memberships. Since data on such memberships were only incidental to the primary purposes of the surveys, the questioning in this area is not as thorough as would be desired. Furthermore, the wording of questions about membership varies from study to study, hence complicating the analysis. Nevertheless, we believe that these inherent limitations of secondary analysis are more than offset by the gains which have been outlined above.

The bulk of the analysis to be presented is based on two national probability samples of the adult, non-institutionalized population of the United States, over 21 years of age. The first sample contains 2,809 men and women, and the second 2,379. The studies were conducted in the years 1953 and 1955. In addition to the national data, findings on voluntary association membership were available for representative samples from NORC studies of the following localities: a large metropolitan area (New York metropolitan area represented by a probability sample of 1,053 cases drawn in 1951); a medium sized Western metropolis (Denver represented by a probability sample of 920 cases obtained in the spring of 1949); a small city and surrounding county (Findley and Hancock County, Ohio, represented by 535 cases drawn in May, 1952). The local findings on magnitude of membership and its social distribution are not presented in detail, although, where confirmation or contradiction occurs, some brief reference will be made. They will be used to examine hypotheses about particular variables, however, which are not demonstrable on a national scale.

FINDINGS

Memberships of Americans

Data from the national surveys confirm the conclusions drawn by previous researchers based on local studies, which showed that a sizeable group of Americans are not members of any voluntary associations and that only a minority belong to more than one such organization. Table 1 presents data from two surveys, one of which inquired about the voluntary association membership of *any* member of the family, the other survey pertained to activities of the respondent himself. Calculated either way, voluntary association membership is not a major characteristic of Americans. Nearly half of the families (47 per cent) and almost two-thirds of the respondents (64 per cent) belong to no voluntary associations. About a third of the families (31 per cent) and a fifth of the respondents belong to only one such organization. Only about a fifth of the families (21 per cent) and a sixth of the respondents (16 per cent) belong to two or more organizations. These findings hardly warrant the impression that Americans are a nation of joiners.[1]

[1]To some extent, the open-ended form of the questions in the national studies might have reduced the proportion of memberships reported insofar as respondent recall might be faulty. There is some indication, however, that the impact of question format was not great in this instance. In the Denver study a card listing several types of organizations was handed to the respondent before he reported memberships. Under these conditions, 36 per

TABLE 1. *Membership in Voluntary Associations for Two National Cross-Sections of American Adults, 1953 and 1955*

Number of Voluntary Associations	Percentage of Families Whose Members Belong to Organizations as Indicated (1953)[a]	Percentage of Adults Who Were Themselves Members of the Organizations, as Indicated (1955)[b]
None	47	64
One	31	20
Two	12	9
Three	5	4
Four or more	4	3
Unknown	1	0
	100%	100%
Total	(2,809)	(2,379)

[a] "Does anyone in the family belong to any sort of club, lodge, fraternal order, or union with ten or more members in it?" If *yes*, "What organization? Any other?" (SOURCE: NORC Survey 335.)

[b] Union membership is *not* included in these data because the interviewing on organizational membership during this part of the survey concerned associations other than union. The question was, "Do you happen to belong to any groups or organizations in the community here? If *yes*, "Which ones? Any other?" (SOURCE: NORC Survey 367.)

cent of the Denverites reported that they belonged to no organizations, including unions. In the 1953 national survey, which used an open-ended question, 39 per cent of the urbanites living in large cities (1,000,000 or more) and 42 per cent of those living in any sizeable city (50,000 or more) reported no organizational memberships, including unions, for anyone in their family.

Obviously, primary research on voluntary association membership would require more and different questioning in this area, including check lists of organizations, investigation of the meaning of "belonging" to the respondent, etc. The data used in the current secondary analysis, however, were obtained from studies in which information on membership was only

Data on the types of organizations to which Americans belong are also revealing. In the 1953 survey, which contained an account of organizations to which any family member belonged, only two (unions and fraternal or secret societies) have relatively large memberships, 23 per cent and 19 per cent respectively. Next in order are neighborhood-ethnic-special interest groups (8 per cent), veterans' organizations (7 per cent), civic organizations (5 per cent), church sponsored organizations (3 per cent), youth organizations (2 per cent) and professional and learned societies (2 per cent). These findings provide national perspective on the data recorded by former studies of local populations . . . in which unions and fraternal organizations also accounted for more of the citizens' voluntary memberships than any other type of association.

Racial and Religious Subgroups

Table 2 presents figures on the membership patterns for two types of subgroups within American society: racial and religious. Comparison of Negro and white respondents shows that voluntary association membership is somewhat more characteristic of whites than Negroes. Less than half (46 per cent) of the white families and 63 per cent of the white respondents belong to no associations in contrast to 60 per cent of the Negro families and 73 per cent of the Negro adults. And nearly a quarter (23 per cent) of the white families belong to two or more organizations in contrast to only 11 per cent of the Negro families.

---

incidental to the primary purposes of the surveys, for which the open-ended questions sufficed. Confidence in the interpretation of the findings as indicative of low membership among Americans is increased through the use of data from *several* national and local surveys, which support one another, in general, despite variations in the wording of questions.

Of course, this is not to dispute the fact that, from a *comparative* point of view, Americans may be more prone to such membership than other national groups. Such a mode of analysis is illustrated, for example, by Arnold Rose, *Theory and Method in the Social Sciences*, Minneapolis: The University of Minnesota Press, 1954, pp. 72–115.

TABLE 2. *Voluntary Association Memberships of Racial and Religions Subgroups Based on National Samples*

| (A) Family Data (1953) | Per Cent of Family Whose Members Belong to: | | | |
	No Organization	One	Two or More	N (100%)
Race[a]				
Negro	60	29	11	279
White	46	31	23	2,472
Religion[b]				
Jewish	31	37	32	99
Catholic	44	34	22	579
Protestant	49	30	21	1,992

(SOURCE: NORC Survey 335.)

| (B) Respondent Data (1955) | Percent of Respondents Who Belong to: | | | |
	No Organization	One	Two or More	N (100%)
Race[c]				
Negro	73	18	9	229
White	63	20	17	2,139
Religion[d]				
Jewish	45	25	30	71
Protestant	63	20	17	1,701
Catholic	69	17	14	519

[a] Figures exclude 58 cases of other races or of unknown race.
[b] Figures exclude 139 cases who report some other religion or none at all.
[c] Figures exclude 11 cases of other races.
[d] Figures exclude 88 cases who report some other religion or none at all.
(SOURCE: NORC Survey 367.)

Differences in rates of membership also distinguish the major religious subgroups of the population. Whether measured on a family or individual basis, the highest rate of membership is found among the Jews. On a family basis, the next highest participants in voluntary associations are the Catholics (56 per cent), and the least active are the Protestants (51 per cent). Data on individual memberships, however, are different, with a higher percentage of Protestants than Catholics belonging to any organizations.

Interesting comparisons with national data on memberships of religious subgroups are available from the local studies of New York City and Denver. In both cities the ordering of memberships agrees with the national sample on individual memberships: the rate of membership is highest for Jews, next for Protestants and lowest for Catholics. In New York, 64 per cent of the Jewish respondents reported membership in at least one voluntary association, 54 per cent of the Protestants and 37 per cent of the Catholics. In Denver, the membership rates were 77 per cent for Jews, 65 per cent for Protestants and 55 per cent for Catholics. Thus the Catholic membership rates in these urban settings appear lower than those of the Jews and Protestants, as in the 1955 national survey.

Social Stratification and Membership

On the local level, several studies have demonstrated a relationship between the social status of the respondent, as measured by a variety of indices, and membership in voluntary associations.

• • •

Data from the national samples support the correlation between social status and membership. Table 3 presents data on the membership of the 1955 sample classified by five indices of social status: family income, education of respondent, interviewer's rating of family's level of living, occupation of head of household, and home ownership. Whichever index of status is used, an appreciably higher percentage of persons in higher status positions belong to voluntary associations than do persons of lower status. For example, fully 76 per cent of the respondents whose family income falls below 2,000 dollars do not belong to any organizations in contrast to only 48 per cent of those whose income is 7,500 dollars or more. Furthermore, there is an increase in the percentage of persons who belong to *several* organizations as social status increases. For example, only 7 per cent of the lowest income group belong to two or more associations in contrast to 30 per cent of the highest income group. Similar findings are obtained from inspection of the data on education, level of living, occupation, home ownership, as examination of Table 3 reveals.[2]

One set of findings warrant special mention. The pattern of voluntary association membership among different occupational levels indicates even less participation among blue collar workers than had been noted in previous local studies. For example, from 68 to 87 per cent of the blue collar workers belong to no organizations (not counting union membership), in contrast to 59 per cent of the white collar workers and 47 per cent of the businessmen and professionals. The higher rate of voluntary association membership among businessmen and professionals is clearly documented by the national data, which show that 29 per cent of these two occupational categories belong to two or more organizations, in contrast with only 5 to 13 per cent of the blue collar workers. These data extend to the national level a relationship noted by Komarovsky in her New York study, namely that it is only in the business and professional classes that the majority is formally organized.

[2]Data from the 1953 sample on family participation in voluntary associations generally corroborated the findings presented above and hence are not reproduced here. In addition, several of the local studies contain data in support of the relationships described. For example, home ownership data were available in Denver and provided an opportunity to examine the influence of this factor within an urban setting. Here, as on the national level, home owners were more likely to be members than were renters, 67 per cent versus 59 per cent respectively. And in New York, families employing domestic help were more likely to be members than those without help, 73 per cent versus 45 per cent.

TABLE 3. *Indices of Stratification and Voluntary Association Membership, 1955*[a]

| | Per Cent Who Belong to: | | | |
	No Organization	One Organization	Two or More	No. of Cases (100%)
A. Income level				
Under $2,000	76	17	7	385
2,000–2,999	71	17	12	304
3,000–3,999	71	18	11	379
4,000–4,999	65	21	14	450
5,000–7,499	57	22	21	524
7,500 and over	48	22	30	328
B. Education				
0–6 years	83	12	5	348
7–8 years	73	17	10	522
9–11 years	67	20	13	495
12 years	57	23	20	610
1–3 yrs. of college	46	24	30	232
4 yrs. college or more	39	25	36	170
C. Level of living (Interviewer's rating)				
Very low	92	7	1	125
Below average	81	14	5	580
Average	61	22	17	1,318
Above average	43	25	32	288
Very high	18	18	64	44
D. Occupation				
Professional	47	24	29	259
Prop., mgrs., officials	47	24	29	294
Farm owners	58	28	14	265
Clerical and sales	59	21	20	240
Skilled labor	68	19	13	447
Semi-skilled labor	77	14	9	492
Service	73	18	9	142
Non-farm labor	79	16	5	155
Farm labor	87	13	0	54
Retired, unemployed	77	11	12	35
E. Home ownership				
Owns home	57	22	21	1,407
Rents	75	16	9	968

[a] Data exclude union membership.
(SOURCE: NORC Survey 367.)

Urbanization and Voluntary
Association Membership

Voluntary associations customarily have been identified as characteristic of the urban way of life, and membership in such associations has been assumed to be more common for city residents than rural people. Recent observers, however, have noted that the spread of urbanization in America is reducing such differences between city and country. . . .

From the 1953 national survey it is possible to determine the number of associational affiliations of family members living in counties of varying degrees of urbanization, taking the size of the largest city in the county as a crude index of its degree of urbanism. Three types of counties can be examined: (1) highly urbanized counties, those with at least one city of 50,000 population or more; (2) moderately urbanized, with at least one city of 10,000 to 50,000 population; and (3) least urbanized, having no city of 10,000 or more. Examination of the memberships of residents of these three types of counties reveals that only 57 per cent of the families who live in highly urbanized counties have members in at least one voluntary association, 53 per cent of those in moderately urbanized counties, and 41 per cent of those living in the least urbanized or predominantly rural counties. Thus some correlation appears between the degree of urbanization and voluntary association membership, although the difference between the most urban and least urban counties is not great.

But the type of county is only a crude index of the social atmosphere within which the citizen lives. Within each county, for example, there are areas of more *and* less urban nature. Therefore a finer breakdown is desirable in order to determine more precisely the relationship between urbanism and membership in voluntary associations. Table 4 presents data on membership according to urban, rural non-farm, and rural farm residences within each type of county.

TABLE 4. *Urbanism and Voluntary Association Membership, 1953*

	Place of Residence								
	Metropolitan Counties (with City of 50,000 or More)			*Other Urbanized Counties (with City of 10–50,000)*			*Primarily Rural Counties (Have No Town of 10,000)*		
Per Cent of Families Whose Members Belong to:	*Urban Residence*	*Rural Non-farm*	*Rural Farm*	*Urban*	*RNF*	*RF*	*Urban*	*RNF*	*RF*
No organization	42	40	67	46	46	53	54	52	70
One organization	33	37	21	36	34	28	27	24	21
Two or more organizations	25	23	12	18	20	19	19	24	9
Total	100%	100%	100%	100%	100%	100%	100%	100%	100%
Cases	1,394	193	48	294	115	134	110	264	252

(SOURCE: NORC Survey 335.)

Several interesting findings emerge. First, it appears that, with one exception (rural farm residents in moderately urbanized counties) the relationship between urbanization of county and membership in voluntary associations persists. That is, more of the residents of highly urbanized counties belong to organizations than do persons living in similar types of neighborhoods but in less urbanized counties. For example, only 42 per cent of the urbanites in highly urbanized counties belong to no organization, in contrast with 46 per cent of the urbanites in moderately urbanized counties, and 54 per cent in the least urbanized.

Secondly, within each type of county, rural farm residence is more closely associated with non-membership than is either rural non-farm or urban residence. For example, within highly urbanized counties 67 per cent of the rural farm residents belong to no voluntary association, in contrast to only 40 per cent of the rural non-farm residents and 42 per cent of the urbanites.

Third, there is *no* appreciable difference between the membership rates of urbanites and rural non-farm residents within any type of county. This finding, in connection with the second, suggests an interesting hypothesis about the spread of urbanism into American suburban and rural areas. If the countryside were becoming urbanized then one might expect that rural-urban differences would be minimal in counties which contained large cities and maximal in counties still rural. Such is not the case, at least with respect to voluntary association membership. True, the urban pattern of membership prevails in rural non-farm areas but it does not extend to rural farms. Furthermore, an anomaly (requiring further substantiation) appears in that rural farm persons living in *moderately* urbanized counties resemble their urban and rural non-farm neighbors more than do ruralites in either highly urbanized or heavily rural counties. Perhaps this finding means that rural-urban differences in general are polarized—being greatest in both highly urban and highly rural counties and least in partially urbanized areas.

Some Situational Determinants
of Membership

In this section some data from the Denver survey are examined to clarify certain situational factors which might be presumed to affect urban participation in voluntary associations. Specifically, data are presented on the effect of length of residence in the community, length of residence at the same address, type of residence (for example, single family dwelling versus apartment), travel time to work, and family status (for example, single, married with children or without children). The presumed influence of such factors is illustrated by the hypothesis that long-time residents in the community or in the neighborhood are more likely to be involved in formal organizations. Or, persons living in apartments might be expected to participate less in voluntary associations than those living in single family dwellings. Persons who spend less time commuting to work, it may be argued, should have more time to devote to organizations and therefore should show a higher incidence of membership. Similarly, single men and women, who are unencumbered by children, might have more spare time and hence be more apt to belong to voluntary groups. Table 5 presents data which fail to support several of these arguments.

None of the residential factors shows a systematic relationship with the incidence of affiliation with voluntary associations. For example, persons born in Denver are hardly more likely to belong to voluntary associations than those who have arrived recently. Apartment dwellers are slightly more likely to be voluntary association members than persons renting houses. Commuters who spend more than 45 minutes getting to work are about as likely to belong to organizations as are those people who have to travel only 25 minutes or less.

Only two of these situational factors—home ownership and family status—seem related to voluntary association member-

TABLE 5. *Some Situational Determinants of Voluntary Association Membership: Evidence from Denver Survey*

	Percentage of Each Type Who Belong to Voluntary Associations	No. of Cases in Base
A. Residential history		
Born in Denver or lived there at least 20 years	65	504
Lived in Denver less than 20 years	62	404
Lived in Denver at present address over 20 years	63	200
Lived at present address for 5 to 20 yrs.	67	346
Lived at present address less than 5 yrs.	60	358
B. Residential mobility		
Moved to Denver from place of under 2,500 population	61	272
Moved from place of 2,500 to 25,000 population	60	205
Moved from place larger than 25,000	64	281
C. Type of residence		
Single family house rented	57	81
Multiple family dwelling, rented	59	165
Apartment building, rented	60	117
Owned, all types of dwelling	67	512
D. Travel time to work		
45 minutes or more daily	60	81
35–44 minutes	70	185
30–34 minutes	64	256
25–29 minutes	66	192
Less than 25 minutes	57	205
E. Family status		
Men: Not married	66	79
Married, no children under 18 yrs. old	74	182
Married, with children under 18 yrs. old	82	162
Women: Not married	51	149
Married, no children under 18 yrs. old	53	174
Married, with children under 18 yrs. old	56	174

(SOURCE: Denver Community Survey, NORC-12B.)

ship. Home ownership as a determinant of membership, as brought out above, is related to social stratification. The data on family status show that married persons are more likely to be members of organizations than single persons; and that men and women with children are more likely to be members than childless couples. One might hypothesize that children—and perhaps the expectation of children—draw adults into participation in the voluntary associations in the urban community. This finding corroborates that of Janowitz in his study of Chicago residents in which he notes that neighborhood involvement often centers around activities connected with the rearing of children in a metropolis. As Janowitz remarks, on the neighborhood level, "children are not only the best neighbors in the community but they lead their parents to neighborhood community participation and orientation."[3]

Civic Involvement of Voluntary Association Membership

In this final section, data from the Denver Survey are presented which demonstrate psychological and behavioral differences between citizens who are members and those who are not members of formal organizations. Admittedly the data do not indicate that such differences can be attributed solely to the respondents' patterns of associational membership. Clearly several factors already established as correlates of membership (for example, high socioeconomic status, occupation, place of residence) may also account for differences in political interest, voting and charitable acts of members and non-members. The authors feel, however, that comparison of members and non-members without controlling these associated factors is proper insofar as the purpose is

[3]Morris Janowitz, *The Community Press in an Urban Setting*, Glencoe, Ill.: The Free Press, 1952, p. 124. Janowitz's remark is made in connection with family structure as a determinant of readership of the community press, but its import extends to other forms of involvement in community activities.

solely to *describe* the differences between persons who are or are
not members of voluntary associations, regardless of the ultimate
causes of such differences.[4] Hence Table 6 presents simple comparisons between the formally organized and unorganized, concerning their interest in political topics, voting records, and contributions to charity.

TABLE 6. *Political Interests and Behavior Associated with Voluntary
Association Membership: Evidence from Denver Survey, 1949*

	Persons Who Were Members of:	
	No Organizations	One or More Organizations
A. Per cent who said they take "a great deal" of interest in:		
Presidential elections	73	84
Unemployment in the U.S.	53	57
The Denver public schools	33	50
City planning in Denver	31	50
Labor relations	31	45
The situation of Denver Negroes	23	35
B. Per cent who voted in each of the following elections:		
1944 Presidential	36	40
1946 Congressional	27	36
1947 City Charter	15	24
1948 Primary	24	34
C. Per cent who report making a contribution to the Community Chest in Denver	56%	72%
Total cases	335	585

(SOURCE: Denver Community Survey, NORC-12B.)

[4]For a discussion of the differential demands of descriptive vs. explanatory
analysis see Herbert Hyman, *Survey Design and Analysis: Principles, Cases
and Procedures,* Glencoe, Ill.: The Free Press, 1955, especially pp. 121–124.

Several measures of interest in public affairs (including presidential elections, unemployment, labor relations, minority problems, public schools, and city planning) indicate that persons belonging to voluntary associations are more concerned with such topics than are non-members. For example, fully 84 per cent of the Denverites who belonged to any voluntary association said they took a great deal of interest in presidential elections, in contrast with only 73 per cent of the non-members. And members were more likely than non-members to be interested in city planning, 50 per cent to 31 per cent respectively.

Political interest is backed by participation in the political process, insofar as participation is measured by voting. Data on behavior in four elections—the 1944 Presidential, 1946 Congressional, 1947 City Charter, and 1948 Primary—indicate in every instance a greater percentage of voting among Denverites who were members of voluntary associations than among non-members.

Finally, in the non-political sphere of community life, charity, 72 per cent of the persons belonging to associations reported having made a contribution to the Community Chest in Denver, in contrast to 56 per cent of the non-members.

Thus three separate measures—interest in social issues, voting, and support of community charities—show that voluntary association participants are more involved civically than the non-members. Further research might fruitfully be addressed to such questions as the following: (1) to what extent does the citizen's interest in public affairs lead him to join voluntary associations; (2) to what extent do the voluntary associations contribute to their members' interest in public affairs; (3) to what extent is membership in one or more voluntary associations functional for the citizen who has a great deal of interest in public affairs. Questions of this order, however, fall beyond the scope of this secondary analysis.

SUMMARY

A secondary analysis of two national and several local surveys provides evidence on the topics: the pattern of membership in voluntary associations of Americans in general and of such specific subgroups as class and religion; some possible determinants of membership, for example, socio-economic status; and certain correlates of membership which relate to civic participation, for example, interest in public issues and voting.

The major findings are listed below in abbreviated form. In each case, the major source of data, that is, national or local survey, is indicated in parentheses. Subject to the qualifications noted above, the major findings are:

(1) Voluntary association membership is not characteristic of the majority of Americans (National).

(2) A relatively small percentage of Americans belong to two or more voluntary associations (National).

(3) Membership is more characteristic of the white than Negro population (National).

(4) Membership is more characteristic of Jewish than Protestant persons, and of Protestant than Catholics (National).

(5) Membership is directly related to socio-economic status, as measured by level of income, occupation, home ownership, interviewer's rating of level of living, and education (National).

(6) Membership is more characteristic of urban and rural nonfarm residents than of rural farm residents (National).

(7) Membership does not appear to be related to a variety of situational factors, for example, length of residence in the community, length of residence at the same address, type of dwelling unit, commuting to work (Denver).

(8) Membership is related to family status, being higher for couples with children than without (Denver).

(9) Membership is accompanied by a greater interest in such public affairs as unemployment problems, city planning, and public schools (Denver).

(10) Membership is associated with voting in Presidential, Congressional, and local elections (Denver).

(11) Membership is associated with support for local charities (Denver).

Students for a Democratic Society

PAUL JACOBS AND SAUL LANDAU

In June 1965 between four and five hundred young people gathered at a camp in Upper Michigan for the fourth convention of Students for a Democratic Society. By car and bus they came from all over the country, although the Eastern contingent was larger than those from the West and South. All SDS projects were represented at the convention, and other left groups—including the League for Industrial Democracy (LID), the uneasy and unhappy ex-parent of SDS—sent observers.

Most of the delegates—college students, college dropouts, graduates, and graduate dropouts—were relaxed and eager to talk. They exchanged comradely greetings, although some had met only once before. Everyone referred to "The Movement" rather than to SDS. They spoke of their allies, SNCC, as the "Snick kids."

Living conditions at the camp were primitive: sleeping bags were crowded together in small rooms or on the cold ground outside. The food was cheap, badly cooked, and insufficient to feed the crowd. But no one expected anything better. Despite the lure of the lake, the warm sun, the empty tennis courts, most of the people spent their energy in workshops, discussing the issues that had brought them to the convention: program, policy, and strategy, the election of officers and the exchange of information.

From *The New Radicals*, by Paul Jacobs and Saul Landau, pp. 27–41. © Copyright 1966 by Paul Jacobs and Saul Landau. Reprinted by permission of Random House, Inc.

The exchange of information was probably the most important function of the week-long convention, for although SDS has printed pamphlets about its work, the primary source of information among the members is conversation. And since they travel about the country continually to regional and national meetings or talk to each other by phone, they and their SNCC allies are very well informed about The Movement's activities. They pass on to each other whatever they have learned about community organizing, the dos and don'ts of working in the South, the why and how of setting up a campus chapter, the tactics and theory, or non-theory, of their movement.

"Theory" or even "ideology" are uncomfortable words. Most SDS members are anti-ideological, not so much because they have learned and rejected ideology, but because they are suspicious of it before they know it. In conversation they "put down" the generations of the thirties, forties, and fifties, not for what they did, for that is unknown to them, but for what they didn't and don't do.

In the formal sense SDS is a direct descendant of the Student League for Industrial Democracy (SLID), organized in 1930 by the League for Industrial Democracy, a Fabian group closely linked to the Socialist Party. During the thirties, SLID had been a Socialist opposition to the Communist-dominated National Student Union (NSU). SLID and the NSU merged to form the American Student Union, which died a few years later, torn apart by an internal struggle between the Socialists and Communists.

After the end of World War II, SLID was revived, under the leadership of James Farmer, who later became national chairman of CORE. But the new SLID suffered from the deadening effect of McCarthyism on the campus, and by the end of the fifties its membership had dwindled. It was revived by the new activist radicals, mostly from the University of Michigan campus, who took it over in 1960 and gave it an action orientation.

SDS maintained a formal but steadily weakening link with the SLID, for purposes of tax exemption and for an aura of respectability, not from any common ideology, but on January 1, 1966, there was a break. SDS is a new radical group with few ties to any of the older left groups in America. In the view of SDS, LID, once an active and vital socialist education organization, is now dominated by aging trade unionists whose anti-Communism outweighs old commitments to socialism. In turn, SDS's radical critique of American policy goes too far for most of the LID board, especially since SDS does not frame its analysis from an anti-Communist premise.

The majority of the newer SDS members, unlike the founders, are not well read in Marxism or in other radical literature. Most of them—middle-class born and bred, not oriented toward careers—are moved to action primarily by events in their own lives, and they see themselves as active public men.

Few relate themselves to the Soviet Union, China, or even Cuba, although they would probably give visceral support to the Cuban Revolution, without knowing too much about it. The SDS founders recall the Bay of Pigs and the missile crisis, and their critique of American foreign policy was stimulated in part by those events.

For many members and leaders SDS is more than an organization; it is a community of friends. Both the national office staff and the local campus and community chapters stress openness in their personal lives and in their political roles. They try to understand the motives for their actions, although this often results in parlor psychologizing. "But how else do you get to know each other?" asked a Chicago SDSer. There is no "criticsm and self-criticism" in the Leninist tradition, but particularly at the community projects some discussions resemble group therapy. Meetings as therapy are not rejected, for self- and group-knowledge enhance relationships on all levels. Personal relationships are often inseparable from political life, since the community projects involve group living in the same house, sharing the experiences and matériel of sustenance. Movement marriages and Movement divorces are not uncommon; love affairs abound, but they are unfrivolous and usually involve a deep commitment. For many SDS staff the distinction between marriage and relationship is questioned: "Why do you need a legal sanction for a relationship?" asked the West Coast SDS organizer.

The SDS attitude is "anti-cool," for the essence of their activity is serious commitment to other people, in the community, in the project houses, and in campus chapters. Their response to questions about marijuana and promiscuous sex is that if the interviewer understood them, the questions would not be asked. While all agree that marijuana smokers should not be penalized, many feel it pitiable that people need artificial stimulants to "turn on." Sex should be linked with love, and many SDSers, both men and women, state emphatically that they cannot accept sex without a deeper commitment to the other partner.

Their vocabulary reiterates words like "initiate," "participate," "community," "hang-ups," "movement," and, especially, "people" (poor people, middle-class people). Those who work in community projects develop an almost oversimple speech. "How many blank stares and 'What does that mean?' does it take to make an organizer realize that the shorthand he learned in college won't do in the poor community?" asks an SDS official.

The vocabulary and community life are part of the SDS style. Many staff members talk more than they read, but this is not necessarily anti-intellectual. It is partly a result of the new experiment: living in a communal project while trying to organize a poor community around social and economic issues.

In Cleveland, where an SDS community project is more than a year old, the organizers are considering leaving their communal house and moving into small apartments in the neighborhood. The urban *kibbutz* produces great satisfaction for young people whose quest for community is answered by SDS projects: there is security in a community and intimacy in the friendships that develop. But new people are often more attracted by the group's communal life than by their neighborhood activities. This places the SDSers who live in the project house in the position of being exclusionist when they allow or refuse someone entrance to their *kibbutz*.

They are aware of this, and at group meetings their openness is apparent. They exhibit great tolerance, and no speaker is silenced, no matter how irrelevant or repetitious. And it is difficult to single out those who hold authority. Leaders, elected or *de facto*, hem and haw when they are called leaders, for traditional authority and arbitrary decision-making are incompatible with the values of the SDS staff.

Leaders mean organization, organization means hierarchy, and hierarchy is undemocratic. It connotes bureaucracy and impersonality, said one of the speakers at the plenary session of the Kewadin, Michigan, convention. He described his project, in Hoboken, New Jersey, as a non-project. One of his speeches, about forty-five minutes long, was an example of a kind of spasmodic sincerity, an inarticulate, highly gesticulating presentation which emphasized "gutting with people." For him, and for many in his audience, the fine line between leader and organizer must remain clear: an organizer does not impose his ideas on the community.

Leadership *per se* is viewed with apprehension. Tom Hayden, past SDS president, writing in *Studies on the Left*, warned of "maintaining a dependency on fixed leaders, who inevitably develop interests in maintaining the organization (or themselves) and lose touch with the immediate aspirations of the rank and file."

True leadership, in the SDS ethos, must avoid imposing ideas and values on the people. If there was to be a transformation in values, the spokesman for the Hoboken non-project felt, it had to come through personal relationships. Throughout his speech he spoke of alienation, the quality of human life produced by the bureaucratized society. It was not Marxist alienation, however, since it did not relate directly to the economic structure.

SDS approached economics more through the eyes of C. Wright Mills than Karl Marx. Some early SDS members with Marxist backgrounds contributed a kind of reality to SDS politics and analyses. Nevertheless, the labor metaphysic, a belief that the working class had a historic mission to transform capitalism into socialism, was rejected. In the Port Huron Statement of 1962, in which SDS outlined its ideals, the largest section analyzed the economy, but in terms of elites, not classes.

It was SDS that injected economics into the early civil rights movement, and underlined the role of private American capitalism in supporting foreign as well as American racism. To demonstrate this point SDS led pickets on the Chase Manhattan Bank, which had large investments in South Africa. In its community organizing and education programs SDS stressed employment, control of anti-poverty funds, and even conversion from wartime to peacetime industry. But in the Port Huron Statement there is no talk of workers' power. Rather, the SDS vision is "the establishment of a democracy of individual participation governed by two central aims: that the individual share in those social decisions determining the quality and direction of his life; that society be organized to encourage independence in men and provide a medium for their common participation."

What SDS founders were groping for in their early statements and pamphlets was a theory or narrow ideology that could simultaneously encompass their ideals of democracy and serve as a guide for social change. The rejection of Marxism, the only ideology that revolutionaries have had for a hundred years, placed an enormous burden on the shoulders of young men like Al Haber, Tom Hayden, Robb Burlage, and Dick Flacks.

Just as SDS injected some concept of economics into the civil rights movement, so too did it begin ideological discussion among the young intellectuals. But the majority of SDS members, then and today, are anti-ideological, and are in SDS because that's where the action is. In 1962 and 1963, however, the staff and leadership began to debate whether SDS's analysis was developed enough to go into the community, where the ideology would grow from experience, or whether the answer was to be found in universities and libraries.

In 1966 SDS is still uneasy and undecided about an ideology. An SDS member from the University of Texas chapter expressed this in a mimeographed communication: "Someone said, 'ideology disunites, action unites.' And there is a good deal of truth in this. I also recognize the desire of SDS to stay away from rigid dogma. However, it has been my experience that, to persons not intimately connected with radicalism, a lack of ideology in some form is misleading."

In fact, SDS has several partially developed ideologies, but they converge around the importance of the individual and his ability to make meaningful decisions. In turn, this assumes that individuals must have the resources, other than empty forms of institutions parading as democratic, to make these decisions.

Within this over-all concern for the individual SDS leaders and members differ over how to achieve the good society, in which the individual will be able to function freely. At this point choices must be made among agencies of change, and these choices in turn involve an analysis of society, a theory of how it works, where it is going, and who will bring it there.

SDS now has two major sections reflecting its continuous internal debate: one deals with the campus and related work around education and political issues; the other, Economic Research and Action Project (ERAP), involves community organizing, mainly of the poor. ERAP began with a $5,000 grant from the United Auto Workers in 1963. The most active community project in 1964–65 was in Newark, and it was directed—although the word would be rejected—by Tom Hayden, past president of

SDS and the drafter of the Port Huron Statement. Hayden is the most articulate spokesman for a strong position in SDS. His charisma and energy attract people, and of all the activists in community organizing he has the most coherent ideology.

To this group the enemy is "corporate liberalism." Existing institutions, from Cold War to home welfare, have been framed and are administered by political liberals who assume that the large corporation is the most desirable unit for organizing social and economic life. These liberals try to effect a smooth and efficient meshing of all levels of society by distributing enough rewards to keep even the lowest segments from disrupting the harmonious balance. But because this cannot be done, argue SDS activists, large numbers of poor people remain. Therefore, the revolutionary thrust toward restructuring society should be through organizing the poor, for they are the force that shakes up all institutions.

In this SDS view the leadership of the liberal community is responsible for all the barbaric aspects of American society: Southern segregation, the war in Vietnam, and to some extent apartheid in South Africa. (The largest depositor in the Chase Manhattan Bank, whose interests in South Africa are enormous, is the ILGWU, claims an SDS publication.) In addition, this SDS group is convinced that these liberals do not want to help young radicals, but rather wish to hold them back as they did the Mississippi Freedom Democratic Party at Atlantic City by urging a compromise of principles, or as they opposed the recent SDS March on Washington, where ideological disputes over Communists and the contents of posters drew strong criticism.

In addition, says this SDS faction, the corporate liberals seek to "keep the lid on local insurgency" to prevent an alliance developing between the poor and the workers that might defy the existing trade union or civil rights leadership. According to this group, the traditional liberal leadership always takes into ac-

count the needs of the President as chief representative of the
national interest, and gives these needs the highest priority.

To this large segment of SDS barbarism and war are at the
very center of the nation, supported by the liberals who have
helped merge respectability with pseudo-fascism and have played
a large and conscious role in defending the barbarism. At one of
the workshops at the Michigan convention Tom Hayden explained: "My own disenchantment with the U.S. didn't really
come because of its failures in Negro rights and foreign policy,
but with the realization, which has grown within the last year,
that responsibility for these things lies with the most respectable
people in society . . . people in the North with connections with
the foundations, corporations and banks and the Democratic
Party, who parade in their own suburban communities as liberals,
but who happen to own, lock, stock and barrel, the major enterprises in Mississippi."

Hayden's thesis, then, that the politics of the poor is the way
to revolutionary change, relates to his critique of liberalism. The
poor have no organization, not even the forms, and since they
are outside the pale of organized liberalism, not only because of
the failures of the social and economic system, but often because
of designed exclusion, they are the forces who, with allies, can be
organized with their own ideology and values. In this perspective organizing the organized working class and middle class are
not excluded, but the middle-class alienated professionals must
discover that their salvation also lies with organizing the poor.

Obviously, the poor must be organized around and for something. To meet these needs, not just tactically but philosophically, the ideas of "counter-organization" or "counter-government" were developed. And because means and ends must not
be separated in SDS's good society, the concept of "participatory
democracy" has evolved, where every man has an equal voice in
decision-making. With "participatory democracy" the poor can

achieve political realignment, but from the bottom up, not from the liberal middle class that imposes conditions: "If we support you, you must promise to do such and such, or not to do it." Hayden explained:

> The emphasis in the movement on "letting the people decide," on decentralized decision-making, on refusing alliances with top leaders, stems from the need to create a personal and group identity that can survive both the temptations and the crippling effects of this society. Power in America is abdicated by individuals to top-down organizational units, and it is in the recovery of this power that the movement becomes distinct from the rest of the country and a new kind of man emerges.

"Counter-community" was discussed at a spring, 1965, ERAP meeting, but many felt Hayden's notion was not developed enough to use. According to past SDS President Paul Potter, a community organization must develop "to a point where it has enough strength and cohesiveness to withdraw support and respect from existing government agencies." The counter-organization, perhaps a clearer term than counter-community, opposes and challenges the established organizations, for example "the building of a free university to confront the existing university structure." The counter-organization is both a tool for challenge and a demonstration of an alternative that hopes to attract or win people away from passive commitment to established forms.

The SDS counter-organization would allow the poor to participate in the control of their own lives. Because these SDS activists are convinced that the important needs are personal, the immediate goal in organizing among the poor is to help each person feel his own sense of dignity and worth. Before the poor can achieve political independence and act as an insurgent force they must have a sense of independence, a sense of identity, a sense of being able to make decisions in a nation of bureaucracies that has usurped all decision-making. The men who administer these bodies are part of a system that regards the poor as unqualified to make their own decisions. SDS projects often begin organizing around such issues as housing and urban renewal, or jobs and welfare, or school lunch programs, taking on local governing bodies.

In political terms, this loose SDS faction thinks a new kind of independent politics should begin in Northern cities, but not related to the traditional third party which runs candidates before it has a constituency. Instead, independent politics means finding a Northern parallel to Southern freedom politics, so that the Northern poor have a real means of political expression, a means of choosing their own representatives to challenge the Establishment at local levels.

Such new politics means organizing perhaps a parallel to the Mississippi Freedom Labor Union in or out of the AFL-CIO, or even some type of business that would support a "counter-society." It might mean attempting to control the anti-poverty allocations, the economic resources, in the community. This search is for a form through which a constituency can be developed based on a radical program and analysis.

Since the Establishment, through its official and unofficial control mechanisms (trade unions or many civil rights groups, for example), will not recognize the organized poor's claim, a counter-government might be set up, in Hayden's words, "to compete with the existing structure for legitimacy." This legitimacy only comes, however, when the counter-government becomes a real threat or gets enough allies, when large numbers lose their respect for "law and order."

The ideas of this grouping in SDS attempt to bypass the concepts of reform versus revolution, or realignment versus independent political action. It is Hayden's belief that the support for the new politics, like the MFDP, must come from "local people's movements elsewhere," or else, as the failure of the MFDP to win its Challenge showed, it will have to depend on the liberal reformers and the Democratic machines. Even a realigned Party that would bend more to the demands of the poor would be "committed still to elite domination of politics, industry and war."

Thus it is not the far right that poses the great threat, but the broad liberal consensus that has developed present American society into the most "flexible of totalitarianisms," paralyzing human activity by its dependence on welfare capitalism and the Cold War.

These SDSers believe that the new movements are still in their infancy and that a great amount of work has to be done at the base. Hayden and most of the ERAP workers are not deluded by articles in *Life* or the left-wing *National Guardian* about the strength of the insurgencies. The war in Vietnam continues despite marches and draft card burning; Southern civil rights workers are murdered despite vigils and challenges. They hope that the civil rights movement, plus riots in Watts, will expose the limits of the American political and economic systems' ability to provide social justice and democratic participation. Yet talk of breaking all ties with liberal Establishment institutions is meaningless because at times such groups are needed, with the result that no "choice" of political alternatives really exists: in civil rights, SCLC needs SNCC and vice versa, and both need the NAACP. Nevertheless, Hayden and others in ERAP and on campuses believe real tensions can be created inside the Democratic Party which would be helpful for new movements and perhaps for those liberal Democrats who could accept meaningful realignment. In Hayden's view, "The new movements . . . *are* realigning the Democratic Party even though they often work outside the Party and their values go far beyond those of the Democratic leadership." For example, SNCC did more to realign the Democratic Party than the coalitionists could hope to do.

The real task visualized by this group, a vision which most of the SDS shares, is to gain freedom from the "one-dimensional society" which controls by terror, welfare, and vested interests.

Almost all SDS members are convinced that in order to survive the might of the Establishment, the emphasis of new politics must be on letting the people choose, on decentralizing decision-making. Thus, the citizen will recover his power and emerge as a civic person who will not be lured from his responsibilities. Concomitantly, in their concept, the movement must differ from older left and liberal ones in retaining a long-range commitment from its rank-and-file members, so that no organizational shells with only leaders develop. The old left is irrelevant to them largely because they believe it is rendered ineffective by Communist-anti-Communist arguments, is committed to overly bureaucratic organizing, and is limited by its adherents' family ties and jobs. For some of the militants in ERAP it is all or nothing: work full time for The Movement if you wish to be accepted by the committed revolutionaries on a personal basis.

Always, while organizing the poor, the belief that the poor must lead themselves is uppermost in the organizers' minds, with all decisions to be made democratically, and not just in the formal sense. An organizer, for example, might organize but has no right to make decisions for those he organizes. His job is to help them make their own decisions, even though in practice this does not always work. The organizer must reach people, talk to them, involve them in action which would radicalize them. The young college graduate must communicate to poor people that they are worthy, potentially powerful, and capable of fighting for rights and ideals. It is understandable that many SDSers cannot accomplish this formidable task.

SDSers do feel rewarded when they influence people and enlarge the social consciousness, but theory or even long-range strategy is a fuzzy notion to them. The question of how to link the various projects is unanswered, not only by SDS but by all the new radicals. A radical political movement does not necessarily mean socialist to them, for only a few of them could explain what "socialist" means. They have faith that through sincere and determined organizing the people's essential goodness will transform itself into effective politics. That faith remains with them, despite the frustrations and hardships endured in many projects, and despite the internal conflicts between the SDS members who worked so closely on a day-to-day basis. Typically, Judy Bernstein of the Chicago project replied to the question of whether she believed that all this activity would get anything done, with: "I have to believe it. . . . I want to eventually go back to school . . . but I will end up talking to students about how to organize a community."

Another trend in SDS does support involvement with the institutionalized labor movement and liberal reformers. The goals of this group, centered in New York and deriving from a more traditional left background, are increased material benefits and a greater share of the national income for the poor. For them human dignity and decision-making are dependent upon better material rewards and can be accomplished through a modification of pacifist Bayard Rustin's idea of a coalition with unions, religious groups, and the liberal political forces.

Another faction feels the middle classes can be organized and that they too can form a change agency, not from material stress but because they are the most alienated. According to this group, the middle classes can be shown that they are able to control their own lives and that the sham of affluence, symbolized by conspicuous gadgets and services, is less meaningful than experiencing more profound human feelings and needs. It is an offering of the possibility of joy or even sorrow in place of fun, fun, fun.

Combinations of these approaches exist in SDS, too, as does a group of "leaders" who feel it essential to develop a new political philosophy that can encompass the general need for social justice with concern for the individual. This philosophy calls for "existential humanism" in personal life and behavior coordinated with the social goal of a "radical transformation" in society.

The two sections of SDS, the campus and the poor neighborhood, organized the twenty-five-thousand-man March on Washington in April 1965 to protest the war in Vietnam. The role of SDS in stimulating and organizing anti-war sentiment, especially at the universities, has been given wide attention by the press and government. Newspapers have reported and analyzed SDS's role, while right-wing columnists have labeled them Reds. After the October 15–17 protests Senate speeches abounded, and the Attorney General and the FBI promised an investigation. SDS membership rose rapidly, and there are now chapters in most states.

It has been SDS's emphasis on foreign policy, particularly on Vietnam and the Dominican Republic, that has gained them new supporters from the campuses, the center of SDS strength. Often the new recruits become interested in the community projects, and after working on campus for a semester, move into a project house.

The national teach-ins were organized at Michigan, the birthplace of SDS, and much of the impetus for the teach-ins came from SDS. Strong chapters developed at Swarthmore, the University of Texas, Johns Hopkins, and in the Boston colleges. Some SDS campus chapters have singlehandedly begun anti-Vietnam movements, while at other campuses like Berkeley, where SDS is weaker, they have either joined or worked with existing organizations.

The SDS community projects, linked in the loose organization of ERAP, have had more difficult experiences than the campus chapters. Even the successful ERAP projects in Newark, Chicago, New Haven, Boston, and Cleveland, some in existence for more than a year, have gone through a very trying period. The Baltimore and Oakland projects have gone out of existence, despite the enthusiasm with which they began. SDS leaders believe the failures are due to the organization having over-extended its staff resources; in some of the projects the staff had great vigor but little knowledge, while in others no clear conception existed of the project's role in the community.

It is amazing that the SDSers did possess the determination to carry on in the face of the difficulties they confronted, and did succeed in organizing some communities, in Newark, Cleveland, and Boston, both on issues and around ideas. Changes in the lives of the communities did take place which would not have occurred without ERAP and SDS: in Newark, an urban renewal plan that was in effect Negro removal was defeated by a solid organization that included local people as organizers. Community services around welfare, schools, and legal aid have been provided by other projects, and some of the poor have become involved in attempting to direct their own lives, even in communities where projects have failed.

Many who have been active in SDS for a sustained period see an urgent need for The Movement to develop an effective new politics based on a sound ideology; this need has become the main concern of some of the older leaders, all in their late twenties or early thirties. Paul Pipkin of the Texas chapter wrote: "It is time to stop fearing ideology and lay the basis for a new one, more suitable for our times, as well as a more stable guide for our own policies. This is what C. Wright Mills was working towards at his death, and I feel that the task falls to us."

So it is that perhaps SDS in its short life has come almost full circle. Created partly as a response to the lack of radical ideology in America, some segments of it then attempted to carry out operations based on an ideology of simple activism, of getting people in motion; but now, once again, the question is being asked: Motion toward what?

Paul Potter analyzed the experience of the last two years of SDS as an experiment in which organizing strategy was substituted for program. But it was discovered that the mere rejection of old ideologies, such as social democracy or Bolshevism, did not provide a new one that could effectively destroy Cold War and welfare liberalism and also serve as a guide for future alternatives and programs.

SDS came into existence, according to Potter, "because of a concern for the lack of ideological thinking in the developing civil rights movement and out of a reaction to the anti-ideological ideology of the universities and the society. Initially, its founders hoped SDS would fill the vacuum of thought for the new left movements." It then moved into activism, and according to Potter, "The experience . . . particularly in the communities has shaken people loose from their once facilely constructed analytic constructs," forcing them to think anew. Many in SDS now feel they must get back into the habit of reading and writing so that they can confront the university not with anti-intellectualism, as many have, but with radical scholarship and sound polemics that can be transformed into action. In the minds of these SDSers, it is their obligation to show broad segments of American society that the misery suffered by the domestic poor is part of a system of over-all deprivation that threatens the individuality and potential of most Americans; that American foreign policy is hindering world peace rather than building it.

The National Federation of Independent Business

JOHN H. BUNZEL

The National Federation of Independent Business was founded by Mr. C. Wilson Harder in 1943 in a small town on the Peninsula south of San Francisco. A former manager of an automobile agency and member of the United States Chamber of Commerce, Mr. Harder understood the difficulties of unorganized small businessmen struggling for survival in a highly organized society and felt the need for a national association operating solely in their behalf. From its beginning the purpose of the Federation has been "to promote and protect our system of private business, with equal rights for all" and to give small business "a greater voice in laws governing business and our nation." It was hoped that a national organization of independent business and professional people might be able to maintain direct lines of communication and build a better understanding between the "folks at home" and their representatives in Washington. The call went out to people whose stores, offices, warehouses, and manufacturing plants dot the Main Streets and industrial areas in the thousands of towns and cities across the country, from the mom-and-pop grocery outlets to the drug wholesaler, from the country doctor to the medium-sized aircraft parts manufacturer. In the early days of the Federation

From *The American Small Businessman*, by John H. Bunzel, pp. 69–83. © Copyright 1962 by John H. Bunzel. Reprinted by permission of Alfred A. Knopf, Inc. Most footnotes omitted.

the only employees were Harder, his wife, and two children. Using the den of their home as an office, they took care of the mailing and kept the books. Today, as it has been since 1947 when it was incorporated under California law as a non-profit corporation, the Federation is run by the original proprietor, President Harder.

By 1945 the Federation, now quartered in a single-room office, had grown to a membership of about 8,000, each member paying annual dues of about ten dollars. A year later the membership grew to 40,000 and has steadily increased to its present size of over 100,000. Today Mr. Harder has a spacious and comfortable office in the Federation's own building in Burlingame, with some twenty-five people in his employ. In addition, he has hired fifteen other men to work out of the Cincinnati, New York, and Washington offices, plus 150 salesmen located throughout the United States. The Federation has a Public Relations Division in Cincinnati, a full-time lobbyist in the nation's capital, and a legislative researcher who prepares the *Mandate*, a tear-off, self-mailer ballot that is the cornerstone of its activities. From a shoestring operation when it first began to a going concern today, the Federation epitomizes the same entrepreneurial, shoulder-to-the-wheel philosophy it espouses.

Unlike the system of hierarchy and bureaucratic procedures which characterizes large business organizations, the internal structure of the Federation has no rigid pattern. Mr. Harder is responsible to a ten-man board of directors of which he is the permanent chairman. It meets once a year, usually in June, when it reviews the activities of the past year and discusses Mr. Harder's ideas for the coming twelve months. There is no strict budget or tightly planned program since Mr. Harder feels the Federation must be able to respond immediately to problems as they arise. Thus the control of the Federation's funds is in the hands of one man. He can seek approval for any proposal he has in mind by simply calling together a quorum (5) of the board, something he can easily arrange since four of them live in the immediate area and the fifth can be quickly reached by telephone. Having founded the Federation himself, Mr. Harder has made certain that the authority and responsibility for its direction have remained in his hands. None of the board members objects, many of them serving only because they are personal friends of Harder and sympathize with his feelings about small business. They recognize that he is a dedicated man and that the Federation is still his show.

Membership in the Federation is limited to small businessmen who own and operate an independent business that is not dominant in its areas of operation. There is no limit as to size, which means both the corner merchant and Armstrong Tire (whose sales exceed $60,000,000) may belong. This definition gives the Federation a degree of flexibility regarding membership which some definitions of "small business" would not permit. The type of membership is widely diversified: one random district includes doctors, lawyers, accountants, garages, gas stations, banks, insurance companies, electric appliance stores, grocers, and drugstores. Gas stations appear to be the only form of business which constitutes a distinguishable percentage of the total membership; on a regional basis, a significant percentage of members are bankers or owners of independent oil companies who have come from Texas.

In order to build its membership the Federation operates a sales department, with a small group of district sales chairmen and approximately 150 salesmen. Paid on a strict commission basis, the salesmen recruit new members by trying to make a certain number of "sales" a week. The art of salesmanship, so important in a wide variety of small business ventures, is put to careful use in building up first the "customer's" goodwill and then his faith and confidence in the "seller"—the Federation. In much the same way that any salesman learns how to deliver the "pitch" which hopefully will sell his product, the Federation's salesman uses an approach on the prospective member that follows a time-tested formula. There are seven basic steps: (1) the salesman tells the businessman that he is interested in getting his personal opinion on five separate public issues: (2) he then encourages him to vote on the issues and promises to send the ballot to his Congressman; (3) he proceeds to explain the purposes and program of the Federation; (4) he shows him some statements of Senators and Congressmen which are favorable to the activities of the Federation and points out that the national vote of the Federation's membership has been quoted on the floor of the Senate and the House; (5) the salesman then goes on to deliver the first part of his "clincher":

> All of this proves one thing: that Congress will listen to you businessmen providing you can shake just as big a fist as your labor unions, farm groups, big chains and other pressure groups that are working day and night because they have an axe to grind at your expense—and I believe you will agree this is the only way we can hope to get this reduction in business taxes, reduce all of this paper work forced on us . . .

(6) Here the salesman interrupts himself long enough to mention some of the local businessmen who are supporting the Federation and then continues:

> If we each vote on the laws of our land in a concerted action every month, we can put our country back on a firm foundation. This does show that regardless of party or politics or types of business that small business is no longer just standing on the side lines but is taking some very definite action and doing something about it. These men realize like you that it's only by taking action that independent business can have decent take home profits and can build a sound national economy.

(7) In closing the deal he informs the small businessman that it will cost him between a minimum of twelve dollars and a maximum of $100 a year to become a Federation member and goes out of his way to explain that the limit is justified because

the Federation refuses to be controlled by any single financial group or power. Usually the salesman tells the story of how Joseph Howard Valentine, who died in 1955, willed the Federation 10,000 shares of stock in his refinery in Salt Lake City, which then had a par value of $.25 per share and one year later rose to $45, only to have Mr. Harder refuse the offer of stock because of the $100 limit on contributions. The entire sales pitch is supported by a variety of visual aids, including elaborate reference to the *Mandate*, a chart showing the district chairman depositing the member's ballot in a pipeline which runs directly to the Capitol, and a picture of the Federation's lobbyist reading the results of their national poll to a Congressional committee.

The general entrepreneurial outlook of small business is clearly the guiding philosophy of the Federation in its approach to new members and, for that matter, in all of its activities. The appeal is made on a face-to-face basis, and the individual businessman, whether laundry operator or local banker, is given the feeling that his support of the Federation is a personal act of real importance. One thing is certain: there is nothing that smacks of the confidence and finesse of a big business organization. The whole philosophy behind the sales technique, as the following paper sent to the district sales representative makes clear, is strictly Main Street, not Wall Street:

> In about eight cases out of ten your new salesmen will not understand that, in order to successfully sell a Federation membership, the appeal MUST be made to the EMOTIONS of the prospect— and that there is nothing unethical or wrong in so doing. Our interview time is short, and no salesman could present, or any prospect understand more than a tiny part of the underlying economic principles which create the necessity for the Federation and its program—*nor is it desirable that either completely so understand it.* . . . You must in all your training and retraining continually stress the need to "pour the sales talk into the prospect's own place of business."

One of the assumptions implicit in the statement above is that the independent businessman is fully aware of his own problems and position in our industrial society. For this reason the Federation does not concern itself with selling the "idea," but rather sells a tool of action. Mr. Harder firmly believes that if independent businessmen are brought together at a convention to establish a policy and program, they will succeed only in producing chaos and conflict. They would never be able to agree on anything. Take them aside individually, however, and ask them for their own opinion on any issue—this tactic will lead to a high degree of unanimity.

The Federation reached a plateau in 1951 when the membership was between 75,000 and 100,000. In the last ten years the number of members has fluctuated around this figure or increased slightly, but the over-all growth has declined sharply. In 1957, for example, the Federation took in some 24,000 new members but renewed only 70 per cent of the ones who were contacted, thereby resulting in a loss of membership of approximately 5,000. The problem of renewals is important to the Federation and has been receiving increasing emphasis over the years. There has been a steady turnover in the sales force since 1951, necessitating the constant training of new salesmen which, in turn, has reduced sales efficiency. Some seventy salesmen, or about 50 per cent of the total sales force, devote full time to renewals. Experience has shown that 40 to 50 per cent of the renewals are automatic; the other 20 or 25 per cent are retained through the strenuous art of salesmanship. A businessman is not removed from the membership or mailing list until he has been contacted by a salesman who cancels the renewal. Placing great stress on stabilizing and expanding the sales force, the Federation would ultimately like to have a salesman in each Congressional district. Like all sales campaigns where the individual with the highest totals is rewarded, the Federation has its own incentive program as well as an internal publication called the

Spotlight, which gives recognition to the fifteen leading sales-men each week. The *Spotlight* also includes hints for better sales techniques and provides the salesman with fresh arguments to be used against big business or big government.

To Mr. Harder the activity perhaps most vital to sales success and the future expansion of the Federation is a vigorous program of public relations. Again the contrast with big business organizations, which are more likely to turn to Madison Avenue for the newest promotional schemes, is striking. The Federation has one man, its vice president, Edward Wimmer, who devotes his time and energy to selling the public on the virtues of small business and in boosting the work of the Federation. He is, in effect, the idealist who gives his life to the Federation because he believes wholeheartedly in its purpose. His is a thirty-year crusade for the small businessman, whose plight he feels personally.

> I was engaged in candy manufacturing in 1932, when the depression wiped out so many. I launched an educational program designed to awaken the people to the values of the family farm, the independent business enterprise, and the local bank; to point out as well as could be done at that time, the disastrous effects of economic power in the hands of the few—one of those effects being the crash of 1929.

In 1932 Mr. Wimmer founded the Forward America Publishing Guild, Inc., in Cincinnati, Ohio, and for sixteen years published and distributed papers, booklets, and circulars. In the latter part of 1946 he joined the Federation, taking on a number of duties designed to promote the work of the Federation and the cause of small business. He has lectured throughout the United States, has appeared on radio and television, and for many years has written a weekly column for the *Cincinnati Enquirer.* He is also a frequent guest speaker at national and local conventions of various trade associations such as the Retail Druggists, Automotive Wholesalers, and Independent Bankers. His mission is constant and clear.

On Main Street America, newsboys, farm hands and low-wage
earners rose from rags to riches; bankers rubbed elbows with
fruit and vegetable wagon operators; merchant princes, statesmen, editors and clerks won fame and fortune. The real name of
this Main Street was Freedom of Opportunity and not until the
"Father & Son" signs start going up again on the Main Streets of
America will Freedom of Opportunity in this country be assured.

The "public relations" activities of the Federation are
carried on by Mr. Wimmer with a zeal that saturates all of its
advertising and propaganda. Mr. Wimmer's role, as he sees it,
is to awaken the people to what is happening in this country, to
stir up concern and excitement about the "chisel age" in which
we live, when Main Street has become Chain Street. Calling
himself a radical, Mr. Wimmer observes that "a radical is a man
who intellectually goes to the bottom of all problems. Dante
said, 2000 years ago"—a slight error—" 'The hottest places in hell
are reserved for those who in a period of crisis maintain their
neutrality.' " Far from being a neutral observer, Mr. Wimmer
is a passionate and angry critic of the contemporary American
scene.

The key to the Federation's activities is the *Mandate*, a
special device for polling the members to learn their opinions
on a variety of domestic and international issues. In order to
determine which issues should be placed before the membership,
the Federation's Washington representative informs the home
office about the bills currently before Congress which pertain to
small business. Five issues are selected for the *Mandate*, each
of which is accompanied by a supporting and an opposing argument. The *Mandate* is then printed and mailed to all of the
members, who in turn vote on the separate issues and send the
votes for his district and sends the ballot, plus one copy of the
ballot to the Federation's district chairman. He counts their
tabulation, to his Congressman, with a carbon copy also going
to the Federation's home offce in California. Mr. Harder and
his staff proceed to tabulate the national result based on the

returns from the 2,500 or so district chairmen, and the national total is then forwarded to each member of the House and Senate, plus selected members of the executive branch of the government. Congressmen are also sent the results of the vote within their own district, thereby saving them the trouble of doing the counting. Actually the Congressmen and Senators are only given percentage figures—that is, the per cent voting For, Against, or No Vote—and thus there exists considerable discrepancy between the Federation's claim that it represents 100,000 independent businessmen and the fact that only about 25 per cent of the members participate in the balloting. The Federation leaders are sensitive to this situation and therefore are not eager to make public the percentage of returns of each *Mandate*. An administrative assistant to a prominent Senator has written that as far as his office is concerned the Federation has been "of no importance" and that "their national polls have absolutely no influence at all on decisions either for or against legislation." He pointed out that the Senator for whom he worked has "no way of determining the Federation's qualifications with respect to any specific bill, or whether the views it may express really do reflect those of its members." He went on to say, in a candid manner often more characteristic of administrative assistants than Senators themselves: "I hope you will believe that the foregoing represents an attempt at a frank statement and not simply a protestation of virtue."[1]

The most important member of the Federation politically

---

[1]There are, of course, comments more flattering to the Federation, although they sometimes have the air of a public testimonial rather than a private appraisal. Congressman Abraham J. Multer, for example, wrote that the Federation and its lobbyist "are among the most effective national groups working in Washington. They are on the job all the time, trying to improve the conditions of the small businessman. Not only do they sponsor and urge the enactment of legislation that is helpful to the small businessman, but they also work against legislation that is bad for that important segment of our economy." Letter dated February 19, 1958.

is its Washington lobbyist and vice president, George Burger, Sr. Like others who have gone to work for the Federation, Mr. Burger has come up "through the ranks" of small business. With only a grammer school education and some work experience as a traveling bill collector for United States Motor Company (which later became the Chrysler Corporation) he established his own business in New York in 1911, retailing automobile tires and accessories. Ten years later he became first president of the Greater New York Tire Dealers Association and then president of the National Association. In 1929 he was one of the founding members of the United Tire Stores of America, an organization designed to give "tire independents" the benefit of mass purchasing power to help them meet the competition from Sears, Roebuck's arrangement with the Goodyear Tire and Rubber Company. Mr. Burger began his own consultant service for independent tire dealers in 1941, acting as a lobbyist in their behalf. In 1946 he became a member of the board of directors of the Federation and in two years was elected vice president in charge of the Federation's legislative activities.

As a lobbyist Mr. Burger's major objective has been the preservation of small business through consistent and vigorous enforcement of the antitrust laws. This concentration of purpose, however, has not prevented the Federation from being concerned with all phases of government policy. Among Mr. Burger's claims for his twenty years of lobbying is the establishment of the Senate Small Business Committee as a permanent committee in 1950. It is difficult for any organization to lay claim to the sole responsibility for the passage of important legislation, but it is not unusual for its representatives to try, if for no other reason than to promote their own special group and salute themselves. Mr. Burger is no exception.

> . . . as far as trade association activity, it was probably our exclusive handiwork that brought about the acceptance of Congress in the creation of the Small Business Administration, which agency

as you know, its main function is to make loans to small business. And, the recent action of the House in proposing this Agency be made a permanent agency, it may be found that in the First Session of the present Congress, we played no minor part, and I repeat no minor part in having the House vote this legislation 393 for and 2 against. We are striving right at this moment to have concurrent action taken by the Senate.

In 1947, the writer, then a few months later joined in by the National Federation of Independent Business, by our exclusive handiwork was able to bring about action under the Robinson-Patman Act invoking a section of that law as applied to the rubber tire industry, namely the Quantity Discount, for the sale of rubber tires. This case is not concluded as yet and if finally validated, it will act as a guinea pig for all other industries to follow where monopoly or concentration is rampant within a particular industry.

The Federation also takes credit for helping to repeal the Basing Point Bill and the passing of the Celler-O'Mahoney-Kefauver Act of 1949, which plugged up a loophole in the antimerger laws by amending Section 7 of the Clayton Act.

Mr. Burger's techniques as a lobbyist reflect the general attitude of many small businessmen in their own dealings as independent proprietors. The art of selling is given the same importance in influencing legislators as it is in persuading customers.

Lobbying is no different than salesmanship. In other words, it is my belief that in salesmanship a good salesman is successful for himself or in his own business only after he builds up in the first instance the customers' goodwill, faith and confidence in the seller. . . . Carrying out this principle to the fullest degree, you gain the respect and confidence of members of Congress and Federal agencies. This does not mean that they will always concur but they will respect your sincerity for an honest objective.

The activities of a lobbyist are multifarious. In giving the position of the Federation Mr. Burger spends a good part of his time testifying before Congressional committees. A typical presentation by Mr. Burger would proceed along the following lines.

I am George J. Burger, Vice-President in charge of legislative ac-
tivities of the National Federation of Independent Business. . . .
Our national headquarters are located in Burlingame, California.
We also maintain division offices at New York, Cincinnati, and
Chicago.

Mr. Chairman, no officer or group of officers is permitted to
speak for the Federation prior to the direct nationwide vote of
our entire membership. I make this statement so that I will qual-
ify under the mandate of our nationwide membership.

Mr. Burger will go on to show that the Federation's membership is above 100,000 and will offer an explanation of the
Mandate and how it operates. Frequently he will invoke the
results of past or present Federation polls to support his testimony and will often have the arguments on both sides of a
specific issue read into the *Congressional Record* to impress the
Congressmen with his fair-mindedness. Occasionally he feels
called upon to talk about his own experiences and difficulties
in his "40 years as an independent tire dealer." He usually concludes his remarks by thanking the members of the committee,
pointing out that his association with the Federation has endured
for so many years because it has never failed to live up to its
professed goals, and, finally, making a plea for the "little guy"
in our country.

For their own part the members of the committee first
inquire about the over-all operation of the Federation in order
to establish its basic integrity as a pressure group and then
turn to the more immediate issues under consideration. More
often than not the committee is concerned with solutions to
antitrust measures, the operation of the Anti-Trust Division or
perhaps the Federal Trade Commission, and questions arising
over the many problems of monopolistic practices in the economy. Because of Mr. Burger's knowledge of the tire industry,
his opinions in this area are especially sought. In 1953 the
Senate Select Committee on Small Business prepared a report
which drew heavily on Mr. Burger's own Tire Consultant Service
for information which later became the basis of its recommenda-

tions. Mr. Burger has been particularly effective and articulate in his defense of the independent tire dealer, and it is not surprising that the Federation itself has a special interest in the independent gas and tire dealers among its members.

Another political function of Mr. Burger is to appear before the platform committees of both major parties prior to their national conventions and present the demands of small business. In 1956, according to one Federation publication, Mr. Burger and Mr. Harder were the only representatives of small business to appear at the platform-drafting hearings of both the Democrats and the Republicans. The Federation has repeatedly asked both parties to commit themselves to vigorous enforcement of the antitrust laws, tax reduction for incorporated and unincorporated smaller firms, higher tariff laws, measures to protect small business from labor unions, withdrawal of commercial activities on the part of the government which compete with small business, a reduction in the federal paperwork burden on independent businessmen, and continuation of the Small Business Administration with its responsibility fixed solely to Congress.

Although the Federation has not been directly responsible for a good deal of Congressional legislation, it has nonetheless met the requirements of an active interest group seeking to promote the welfare of small businessmen.[2] It has a sizable membership, its financial condition is healthy, and it conducts a conscientious operation in its *Mandate*. Its lobbyist in Washington is vigorous and hard-working. Unlike the associations which

[2]There are many small business pressure groups but most represent a particular type of small business. The Federation has one other important competitor, the National Small Business Men's Association. In 1957 the expenditures of the Federation amounted to $32,161.97 as over against $27,268.31 for the NSBMA. The Federation ranked 22nd in total expenditures out of a total of 133 business lobbies and was among the top five lobbying groups concerned with small business. See the *Congressional Quarterly Weekly Report*, XVI, No. 6 (Washington, D.C.: 1958), p. 151.

speak the professional language of big business, the Federation is without polish in its dealings with people and issues. But what it lacks in sophistication as an organization it more than makes up in dedication to its chosen mission of representing the hard-pressed small businessman. More important than anything else, however, the Federation is run much like a small business, with its original and only proprietor, Mr. Harder, still minding the store.

Entrepreneurs of the Right

RICHARD DUDMAN

. . . The best single action-group organizer on the far right today is a former communist by the name of Marvin Liebman. When a full-page advertisement for a right-wing cause appears in the *New York Times,* the chances are it came out of Liebman's office on the ninth floor of 79 Madison Avenue.

Liebman, now thirty-eight, was a member of the Young Communist League and the Communist Party of the United States from 1938 to 1945. He quit the party after leaving the Army because he thought its expulsion of Earl Browder was unfair. In subsequent years, he kept learning the fine points of organizing pressure groups. Among his adventures was a voyage to Palestine on a ship of the Irgun Zvai Leumi, the Jewish terrorist group, which ended with internment on Cyprus. One of the men he admired most was "Beanie" Baldwin, publicity man for Henry A. Wallace's Progressive Party campaign for the Presidency in 1948. Liebman still looks back in awe at Baldwin's success with the "sea of green," in which he asked an audience to hold up bills, "so I can see a sea of green," and then passed the hat.

In 1951, when Liebman was working for the International Rescue Committee, he suddenly came to see the Soviet Union as a world danger, he says. In 1952, he helped to set up an

From *Men of the Far Right,* New York: Pyramid Books, 1962, pp. 144–150. Reprinted by permission from the publisher.

organization called Aid to Refugee Chinese Intellectuals, which drew support from liberals as well as conservatives.

His biggest operation began in 1953, when he helped start the Committee of One Million against the Admission of Communist China to the United Nations, which now raises $70,000 a year to carry on its continuing campaign. Liebman says it took from October, 1953, to June, 1954, to get the first 1,037,000 signatures for that cause. He says it took only five months last year to get 1,250,000 more signatures at half the earlier cost. To show the breadth of the organization's support, he points out that the three largest contributions last year were only $1000 each—from Henry R. Luce, Eli Lilly and J. Howard Pew of the Sun Oil Co.

The building directory on his floor has listings for Liebman's suite, No. 909, that include "Marvin Liebman Associates, Inc." and the "Committee of 1,000,000" as well as some of his later efforts—"American-Asian Educational Exchange, Inc.," "American Committee for Aid to Katanga," and "McGraw-Edison Co. Committee for Public Affairs." Last summer, the list also included the "Greater New York School of Anti-Communism," Fred C. Schwarz's project, which was operated out of Liebman's office.

His organizations come and go, and in a sense they are not organizations at all. He has a list of about 300 persons who are prepared to contribute $100 each when he needs money for a newspaper advertisement and will be willing to lend their names to a cause when they see his name and those of the *National Review* crowd among the principal sponsors. His public relations firm can buy the newspaper space—$6,000 for a full-page advertisement in the *Times* and additional amounts for whatever other newspapers he selects—and the firm is repaid later from pledges already obtained or from contributions in response to the advertisement.

The Katanga organization lasted only a few months and

now is dead, or at least quiescent. Its debts are paid, it has only $100 left in its bank account, and it will remain inactive unless there is another flare-up in the Congo and its seems advisable to run another advertisement.

A later appeal was for a committee to aid Chinese refugees arriving at Hong Kong last summer. Liebman was able to attract two prominent liberals as sponsors for that campaign—Senator Paul H. Douglas of Illinois and Associate Justice William O. Douglas of the United States Supreme Court. An advantage of having many separate organizations is that some persons who would not have anything to do with one are happy to sponsor another.

Liebman's experience with Senator Everett M. Dirksen of Illinois showed the kind of headaches that sometimes plague the organizer of such groups when he deals with politicians. When the Katanga advertisement appeared, Dirksen was listed as one of the 69 sponsors. President Kennedy telephoned Dirksen in Chicago as soon as he saw the Senate Minority Leader's name on a statement attacking the United States foreign policy and calling Katanga "the Hungary of 1961." Dirksen's Chicago office promptly issued a statement saying the use of his name was without authorization.

But Liebman was able to produce a telegram from Dirksen agreeing, not merely with the sentiments in the advertisement as it appeared, but with an earlier, stronger statement, which called for private American contributions to send arms to assist the "Katanga Freedom Fighters" in their conflict with the forces of the United Nations. Dirksen was not immediately available to clarify his position.

As if anticipating the trouble, Dirksen had written to retired Admiral Ben Moreell a week before the Katanga episode urging that right-wing groups get together on a unified program. Dirksen complained that the movement was splintered into many factions, competing for attention by taking stands each a little wilder than the other. It was hard for a conservative politician to know whom to treat as friends.

Another Liebman offshoot is Young Americans for Freedom, a rather puerile organization that makes projects out of heckling pacifist pickets in front of the White House and the like. The YAF put on a big and successful "conservative rally" in Madison Square Garden last spring, marred only by the withdrawal of Senator Thomas Dodd and the disinvitation of former General Edwin A. Walker. Other meetings tend to be lackluster affairs at which the standard far-right themes are discussed by young persons already thoroughly sold on them. At a recent meeting in Washington, a young woman member was heard to say to a friend, "Honestly, if I have to see 'Operation Abolition' once more, I think I'll *scream*."

YAF now publishes a well-printed monthly magazine, *The New Guard*, which provides space for additional discussions of the same themes and encouraging notes to chapters of the organization operating on college campuses around the country. An occasional success or near success in local elections has given the YAF hope that it can become an effective political force against the liberal Republicans.

Those in Liebman's circle feel a kinship with the John Birch Society, but being political realists, say little about it. They know that Welch's extreme and ridiculous statements have given the organization a bad name. Privately, however, many leaders of what can be called the sane right-wing praise the Birchers as good citizens seeking a reasonable means of political self-expression and Welch himself, for all his shortcomings, as the one man who saw a way to mobilize ultra-conservative frustrations into a tightly organized action movement. Most of the Birchers, these persons insist, are perfectly nice people, who "wouldn't think of calling a librarian up in the night to harass her."

Liebman's various lists of sponsors have some overlap with

the known John Birch Society membership. Other action groups contain so many Birchers among their leadership that they can be considered little more than front groups for the Birch Society, in much the same way that the communists set up left-wing front groups.

One of these is the Citizens Foreign Aid Committee. The national chairman, retired Brigadier General Bonner Fellers, the legal counsel, Clarence E. Manion, and at least one-third of the 47 members of the national committee are all Birchers. The founder and honorary chairman is Walter Harnischfeger, board chairman of the Harnischfeger Corporation of Milwaukee. He also is a director of Merwin K. Hart's National Economic Council, which the Buchanan lobby investigating committee in the Eighty-first Congress accused of disparaging its opponents by "appeals to religious prejudice, often an ill-concealed anti-Semitism."

The Citizens Foreign Aid Committee shares offices, officers and office force with For America, a right-wing lobby organized in 1954 as a post-war revival of America First to combat "super-internationalism and interventionism." It was hardly surprising that Fellers's testimony before the Senate Foreign Relations Committee this year was a proposal to cut the foreign aid authorization from a requested $4.9 billion down to $1 billion.

Two Birchers in New Orleans, a husband-and-wife team, Kent and Phoebe Courtney, operate the Conservative Society of America and put out a bi-monthly newspaper, *The Independent American.* Their paper was one of the first to give prominence to Robert Welch, carrying a photograph of Welch and William F. Buckley, Jr., editor of the *National Review,* as speakers at a meeting in Chicago in 1959.

Kent Courtney, publisher of the paper is a former airline pilot, public relations man and unsuccessful political candidate. He is a devoted segregationist and has been active in his local White Citizens Council. He calls the Conservative Society of

America a political action organization that "picks up where the John Birch Society leaves off."

His wife, whom *Look* magazine has called the "tigress of the far right," is editor of the newspaper and helps put out a stream of other publications, including "Tax Fax" pamphlets, attacking the Common Market, the proposal for a Department of Urban Affairs and federal aid to education. She would withdraw from the UN, end all foreign aid, repeal the income tax, impeach Chief Justice Earl Warren and expose Reds in government. She "loved" Joe McCarthy, and when she orders steak for dinner, she wants it "communist blood red."

The Courtneys have been trying since 1959 to weld the far right into an effective third party. Kent Courtney ran for the Louisiana governorship on a States Rights ticket in 1960, polling less than 3 per cent of the vote. They returned to the Republican Party briefly in 1960 to organize a "Goldwater for President" rally in Chicago on the eve of the Republican convention, with Robert Welch as one of the speakers. But they soon were disillusioned. Phoebe Courtney wrote in January, 1961, that Goldwater was shifting to a "middle-of-the-road philosophy" and suggested he was making a deal with Nelson A. Rockefeller for 1964. Her husband later said publicly that Goldwater "has been tainted by socialism." More recently, the Courtneys have been looking to former Major General Edwin A. Walker, whom Phoebe Courtney called "one of the foremost leaders of the rising conservative movement."

The Courtneys are closely linked with Willis E. Stone's National Committee for Economic Freedom, one of several groups devoted to abolishing the federal income tax by a Constitutional amendment. Kent Courtney is a state chairman of Stone's organization in Louisiana. It held joint national conventions in 1959 and 1961 with the Courtney's Independent American Forum. The repeal-the-income-tax movement seeks resolutions in 34 states, the two-thirds necessary to force Congress to act. It has already been successful in five—Wyoming, Nevada, Texas, Louisiana, and Georgia. Among other groups working in this campaign are the Organization to Repeal Federal Income Taxes, Inc., and the American Progress Foundation, both headed by D. B. Lewis, of the company that sells Dr. Ross Dog Food.

These are only a few of the many action groups that send out a steady flow of right-wing literature with greater or less effect. Others include the Watch Washington Club of Columbus, Ohio; the Network of Patriotic Letterwriters of Pasadena, California; Defenders of the American Constitution, Inc., of Ormond Beach, Florida; the Four Freedoms Study Group, Inc., of Kirkwood, Missouri; the Southern States Industrial Council, of Nashville, Tennessee; the old Committee for Constitutional Government, Inc., still operating out of New York, and so on.

They preach against the UN, disarmament, the income tax, proposed social legislation such as federal aid to education or health care. Their literature usually carries a special low price for bundle lots, accounting eventually for a substantial quantity of the mail that goes to Senators and Representatives.

Forms of Organization: Myths and Realities

DAVID B. TRUMAN

. . . We are all familiar with declarations that begin with such phrases as "Business expects . . . ," "Doctors protest . . . ," "Labor demands . . . ," "The veteran insists . . . ," and the like. Even when such declarations are, or can be made, meaningful, they involve certain hidden assumptions, assertions, or conclusions about the political life—and particularly the unity—of the interest groups designated by such labels. These are at best shorthand expressions, simplifications, which avoid the awkward or embarrassing tasks of indicating which individuals are included under such terms as "business," "farmers," "labor," and the like in a concrete situation and of stating which of them are doing how much insisting, protesting, demanding, and so on. In effect such expressions take it for granted that the degree of cohesion in these groups is perfect. But such an assumption is unrealistic, for the degree of cohesion is of critical importance in determining the effectiveness with which the group operates. It is a product, in large measure, of the dynamic relations existing within the group—of its internal political life. An analysis of the patterns of politics within groups is, therefore, of commanding importance in understanding the role of these groups in the life of the nation.

THE SIGNIFICANCE OF FORMAL ORGANIZATION

It is appropriate to begin an exploration of these internal relationships by discussing certain features of formal organization. We must, of course, guard against the danger of mistaking the asserted for the real, of overlooking those very dynamics that are the heart of political relationships. We must not take descriptions of organizational forms at their face value. Nevertheless, a grasp of formal organization is essential to the understanding of a group's internal political life, just as a familiarity with the Constitution of the United States is essential to, though not sufficient for, an appreciation of the country's politics.

The formal organization of interest groups is of particular importance for several reasons. In the first place, formal organization is usually a consequence, and therefore an index, of a fairly high frequency of interaction within a group. . . . For instance, the activity of collecting postage stamps may be very widespread without leading to much interaction among the participants. Even rather frequent interaction within this potential group may remain informal. But when a philatelic society is formally organized, such interaction usually has greatly increased, and the group has achieved a degree of cohesion sufficient for certain purposes, such as making special arrangements with postal authorities for securing specimens of new stamp issues. The degree of a group's cohesion is frequently indicated in its formal organization. For example, although the writing and adoption of the Constitution of the United States indicated an increased measure of cohesion among at least certain elements in the population of the young nation, the provision in Article V guaranteeing equal representation in the Senate, the inclusion of the Tenth Amendment, and other features indicated, at least in general fashion, the limits of that unity.

Secondly, the existence of formal organization in a group suggests a measure of permanence or at least an expectation that the arrangement will be a continuing one. A degree of stability in a group pattern, as we have seen, usually precedes formal organization, and the regularization of such arrangements implies the expectation that they will continue at least as persistently as the circumstances that give rise to the group.

In the third place, formal organization necessarily presupposes acceptance by the participants of a particular division of labor—forms of leadership, distributions of responsibility, and methods of determining policy.

Finally, a particular type of formal organization is in a sense a precipitate of the values shared by the group, at least at its inception. Such values are a function of the personalities and experiences of the participants; but their expression in the form of group organization is affected by the organization and political techniques of other groups. As in military conflict, so in the political process the organization, strategy, and tactics of one combatant in part determine the organization, strategy, and tactics employed by the other. Within this context these values— embodied in agreed procedures—constitute a mold by which the dynamic activities of the group are formed and into which only certain kinds of action can safely be cast. Around these forms, moreover, develop habits of behavior that, like those in institutionalized groups, are resistant to change and that may persist long after their usefulness as a means of guiding group activities has disappeared. These habits may so stifle dissenters within the group—restive because they cannot achieve expression through the habitual pattern—that they invite disunity or revolt.

All these factors—degree of cohesion, expectations of permanence, internal division of labor, and formalized values— intimately affect the survival and influence of the group. If they can be stated even partially through an examination of formal organization, that scrutiny is essential.

One further caution with respect to formal organization

should be emphasized if this feature of the process of group politics is to be seen in proper perspective. Organization is merely one aspect of the process. For . . . when we speak of the organized dues-paying members of a group, we are not necessarily stating its outer limits. All interest groups have their "fellow-travelers" who may or may not be eligible for formal membership, but who act or interact with actual members with a frequency that in certain types of political situations may be of considerable importance. For example, the American Association of University Professors, which functions as an interest group to defend standards of academic freedom in institutions of higher learning, has never included more than a small fraction of the nation's professors in its formal membership. The unenrolled professors, however, may sympathize with and support particular efforts of the association by refusing to accept an appointment at an institution blacklisted by the organization. Alumni and other interested citizens not eligible for membership may form judgments and even take action concerning a college on the basis of the A.A.U.P.'s recommendations. To the extent that they do, they may be regarded as functional members of the group for the time being.

• • •

STRUCTURAL TYPES

Any discussion of the broad types of organization found among political interest groups must necessarily be confined to certain general tendencies. So great is the diversity of types and forms and so imperceptibly do they merge into one another that they almost defy generalization. This state of affairs is not astonishing if one bears in mind the fact that, although all these groups have certain political functions in common, they may also carry on a congeries of related activities, some of them of basic importance to the group, that assume a variety of organized forms. Some of these activities, such as the promotion of craft skills by trade unions may have been of primary importance only at an earlier stage in the organization's history; yet their impress upon the organizational structure of the group may continue. Vested interests and habits of action grow up around this structure and resist displacement, as anyone familiar with efforts at governmental or corporate reorganization will recognize. Younger organizations, appearing under a different set of competitive circumstances but performing similar basic functions, are more or less free of such group habits. They will frequently assume forms differing in significant detail from older groups of the same kind. Thus, even in a single limited field, such as organized labor, structural forms showing general similarity prove, upon close examination, to be greatly varied.

Perhaps the most useful distinction that can be applied to political organizations in the United States is that between federated and unitary forms. The first is, generally speaking, an organization of organizations, in which powers or functions are divided, formally, at least, between the constituent groups, on the one hand, and the more inclusive organization, on the other. Membership in the larger group may be direct or may be indirect—that is, derived from membership in a constituent group—although significant fusions of these patterns occur in some instances. The second is a single organization that may, and usually does, have subdivisions to carry on various functions or stages of functions. Membership is directly in the parent group, and derivative participation in the activities of subdivisions depends upon geographical location, occupational specialization, and so on.

An example of the federated form is, as its name implies, the American Federation of Labor. It is primarily an organization of national and "international" unions, in turn made up of local unions in which the individual holds his membership. The majority of national and regional trade associations can be cited as illustrations of the unitary type. For the most part these are made up of individuals or firms, the difference being of slight significance, who belong directly to the trade association. These groups may, however, be subdivided on a temporary or permanent basis into groups making or selling the same product or units primarily concerned with a specialized phase of trade association activity, such as product standardization or technical research.

The importance of this distinction between the federated and unitary forms of organization may be seen in their influence upon the cohesion, or unity, of the group. Federations tend to have much less cohesion, especially with respect to functions whose importance increases after a distribution of powers is agreed upon. The tendency is strikingly apparent, of course, with respect to activities that have long been the prerogative of the constituent groups but that the logic of events suggests should be assumed by the more inclusive organization. As in the case of government itself, the defense of local autonomy in such circumstances is likely to clothe in the vestments of principle a partially acknowledged desire for inaction on the matter at issue, as well as hostility toward any diminution of the perquisites of a local officialdom. Under these conditions any organization, whether strictly governmental or not, is forced to feel out a dangerous course between, on the one hand, debilitating inaction or localized actions that are self-defeating because mutually inconsistent and, on the other, centralized action that may invite dissolution or an embarrassing nonconformity.

• • •

Many examples indicate that even where constitutional powers permit, action may produce an embarrassing refusal by constituent units to conform. The American Medical Association, which for a variety of reasons has suffered from the diseases of federation less than many groups, has had to countenance open defiance of its policy against compulsory health insurance programs by various State societies and even by some county societies. The national organization once was reduced to petulant complaints that it was not permitted to state its position in the pages of the California Medical Association's journal. The monumentally impressive American Farm Bureau Federation has had similar difficulties. Its Ohio affiliate, a notable example, not only has refused to conform to this federation's policies from time to time, but has even sided with the rival Farmers' Union.

Of the many recent examples that could be cited, one is provided by the Utility Workers' Union, C.I.O., which has openly refused to support the national C.I.O. policy of pressing for the extension of publicity owned power projects in the Tennessee, Missouri, and Columbia river valleys and has for this purpose allied itself with the interest groups of the private utility companies.

The fundamental reason for the tendency toward disunity in federated organizations is not obscure, although its ramifications may be highly complex. By acknowledging in formal terms certain spheres of local or constituent autonomy, a federated organization establishes and, as it were, sanctifies subcenters of power. The functions that are assigned as of right to the constituent units, although they may conform to realities at the time the division is agreed upon, become the focus of interaction for subgroups whose interests (or the interests of whose leaders) may not always be in harmony with those of the national group. Where changed circumstances make advisable a centralization of responsibility and a consequent diminution in the power and prestige of subgroup leaders, these formally recognized subgroup interests resist change. Under these circumstances the federated organization may in fact be no more unified than a league of sovereign states unable to act except upon the unanimous agreement of the constituent units.

The A.F. of L., as earlier comments suggest, provides an excellent, though by no means unique, example of this situation.

It is a very loose federation of autonomous unions. The chief governing body in fact, though not under the terms of its constitution, is the Executive Council, consisting of the president, secretary-treasurer, and from thirteen to fifteen vice-presidents. Although this body has considerable discretionary authority, its members are, before anything else, established leaders of their own national or international unions, and as such, they exercise a *liberum veto* on any proposals tending to limit their autonomy. This veto power rests on an implied or expressed threat to withdraw a union from the federation, a threat that is by no means an empty one, especially when made by the larger organizations. Since members of the Executive Council are likely to have consolidated their positions within their own unions prior to their service on the Council, any attempt to go over their heads to the rank and file—a procedure not sanctioned by A.F. of L. rules— would be futile. . . . This inability of the A.F. of L. to adjust to changed circumstances was crucial in the split that led to the establishment of the C.I.O.

Although this tendency toward low cohesion is a common feature of federated structure, it should not be exaggerated or overgeneralized. For one thing . . . a number of such groups have achieved a very high measure of unity, partly through the skillful use of a variety of offsetting controls. For another, subcenters of power rivaling that of the larger group may develop even in nominally unitary types of organization. Long enjoyment, by subordinate units, of delegated powers and a sphere of *de facto* autonomy can as easily produce resistance to unified central action as can a constitutional distribution of functions. This situation is well illustrated in the sphere of government by the stubborn independence of counties, municipalities, and school districts—legally merely creatures of the State governments—in the face of efforts toward consolidation and redistribution of functions.

• • •

ORGANIZATIONAL ELEMENTS AFFECTING COHESION

Given the general tendency of federated organizations to lack cohesion, we may ask what determines whether or not a particular federation will display this tendency. . . .

. . . [T]he problem of cohesion almost invariably arises where the constituent units antedate the federal body, as is usually true. In this situation the very fact that organization assumes a federated rather than a unitary form indicates that the interests associated with the individual units are so strong that the inclusive organization cannot absorb the units, but can only take over those functions that they can be induced to relinquish.

On the other hand, as has been noted above, this resistance to central control may be grounded in social facts outside the particular groups. Under the Constitution of the United States, for example, the federal system, especially before the early 1930's, left to the State governments a very large sphere of action. The activities of local and State-wide interest groups were early focused upon the State governments, and, to the extent that these governments still exercise significant power, there is basis for the claims of autonomy by the constituent units of federated groups. That State powers are still important influences upon the cohesion of interest groups is illustrated by the experience of the movement, between 1943 and 1947, for permanent national legislation on fair employment practices. "Co-operating" State committees frequently relegated the financing and prosecution of the campaign for national legislation to a position secondary to the securing of legislation from the various State governments. Yet the effort to operate simultaneously on both the State and the national governments does not necessarily lead to lack of unity. The Anti-Saloon League in its heyday encountered no such difficulties. Though its constituent units were constantly working on prohibition legislation in State and local areas and though a considerable amount of latitude was permitted these for purposes of experimentation, they were subject to close control by the national officers. The League was federal in form, but unitary in operation.

A reason for subunit independence is provided in the case of various occupational groups, notably labor unions, by the structure of an industry—the heterogeneity in the conditions under which various firms operate, the character and extent of competition within the industry, and so on. Recognition of these hard facts of localism and decentralization by the founders of the A.F. of L., it is generally agreed, was crucial in facilitating the association of highly independent unions in a single national organization. It is equally apparent that the freezing of these arrangements has in recent years weakened the A.F. of L. as a national group. By way of contrast it is significant that the C.I.O., a number of whose major constituent units had little or no independent existence prior to their association with the newer federation, has achieved a far more compact and powerful national leadership than its older rival.

• • •

In some federated interest groups, notably the American Medical Association, some of the constituent units antedate the federation, while others are of later origin. The A.M.A's organization is somewhat different from that of many federated groups, since doctors who belong to the constituent units are eligible for membership in the A.M.A. *as individuals.* (The pattern thus resembles in many ways that of the Chamber of Commerce of the United States.) The governing arrangements, however, are federal in character; all but a few members of the House of Delegates are elected from the constituent societies, beginning at the county level. Although a large number of the State medical societies considerably antedate the A.M.A., the county organizations originally developed through the efforts of the State societies to unify their memberships. It is not astonishing, therefore, that although both State and national groups have experienced difficulties with recalcitrant units lower in the hierarchy, the centralized powers of the State societies in such situations are more extensive and more effective than those of the national body. Timing is not the only influence in such a situation, but it is ordinarily an important one. . . .

A second influence upon the degree of cohesion in federations is the basis upon which their constituent units are organized. This may either recognize and formalize the potential lines of cleavage within the group or utilize some form of association that instead cuts across such lines. The first basis usually involves organizing each unit on the basis of function or specialization, whereas the second utilizes a geographical area as its starting point. Though potential cleavages of major importance within a group may exist along geographic lines, as will be noted below, organization according to function especially tends to encourage interaction growing out of specialized subinterests. Because leadership at the lower levels of the structure is necessarily caught up in these subinterests, the problem of reconciling these potentially conflicting elements is delayed until it reaches the middle or top levels of leadership. The situation is roughly comparable to the one that would develop in the government if legislators were elected by occupational (functional) groups rather than by geographically defined constituencies. Adjustment under such conditions is made more difficult because those assuming responsibility for it are removed from regular contact with the concerns of the rank and file. On the other hand, the nonfunctional, or geographical, basis of organization tends to settle the task of adjusting conflicting subinterests upon the entire leadership at all levels by emphasizing interaction based on more inclusive shared attitudes. This sharing of the responsibility for compromise will occur unless the subinterests follow geographical lines—a situation that is becoming less and less common in the United States.

We must remember, however, that adoption of one of these

bases of federation is not altogether a matter of choice. The organization of groups, as we have previously noted, grows out of more or less durable patterns of interaction that necessarily determine the basic structural forms. The choices of founding fathers are confined within relatively narrow limits. This proposition is well illustrated by the A.F. of L., which also typifies the problems emerging from the functional basis of federation. . . . It is apparent that in the 1880's the only basis for a viable national labor organization lay in loose federation of national trade unions, especially those built upon common skills. The successive failures of the Knights of Labor, the I.W.W., and the movement for One Big Union in 1919–20 testify to the absence of any genuine choice.

. . . The precarious position of even this form of unification is neatly summarized in the remark: "For the first fifteen years of its life the Federation consisted chiefly of Samuel Gompers and a series of annual conventions." Although the organization has gradually achieved a greater degree of unity than this situation suggests, its Executive Council is still limited in the exercise of its extensive powers by the fact that it consists of the ambassadors plenipotentiary of a series of "sovereign" units. The primary loyalties of the hierarchies within the international unions, moreover, are focused on the extension and preservation of these units.

• • •

. . . [T]he American Farm Bureau Federation [is] a federation of geographic units, county and State [but] it has avoided many, though not all, of the disunities associated with that form. In its early years there was some discussion of the desirability of establishing it as a federation of commodity organizations, such as wheat growers, live-stock raisers, fruit growers, dairymen, and the like. This possibility was never a serious one, however, and there are evident explanations for the fact. The promotional-educational work of the county agents, out of which the units of the national movement grew . . . necessarily produced patterns of interaction based on areas rather than on commodities as such. Leaders aspiring to use these patterns as elements in a national structure had no choice concerning basic forms. Since these forms had developed out of a program of aiding a large number of commercial farmers throughout the various counties, it was not astonishing that the leaders of these groups at all levels emphasized the interests that farmers could be expected to share regardless of the crops on which they specialized for the market. The period of the 1920's, during which the American Farm Bureau Federation was getting its start, was an auspicious one for this line of development. The uniformly depressed state of agriculture, affecting all the major commodities, made it easier to fuse the problems of all commercial crops into a generalized picture of the plight of "the farmer." The interests of specialized producers have been organized in independent groups such as the National Co-operative Milk Producers' Federation, the American Soy Bean Association, the American National Livestock Association, and the like. Nevertheless, many commercial farmers find it quite feasible to maintain memberships in both the Farm Bureau and one of these commodity associations.

Although there are great advantages accruing to the Farm Bureau from federation on the basis of geographical area rather than of crop specialization, the differences should not be exaggerated. In the first place, areas, especially in agriculture, often have their particularized interests. These may stem not only from crop specialization but also from such factors as relative proximity to markets or the availability of cheaper modes of transportation. Whatever their source, they involve the possibility of disunity in a national organization that includes such rivals. In the second place, although federation of units organized according to geographic area facilitates emphasis upon nonspecialized agricultural interests, it is obvious that in agriculture geographic area may correspond closely to commodity unit. Not all farmers in the Corn Belt specialize in corn and hogs, nor are there none but wheat farmers on the eastern Great Plains, but these crops are the primary concern of a great majority of farmers in the areas. County and State farm bureaus in these areas can be expected, therefore, to display some of the characteristics of commodity organizations. In view of the concentration of membership in the American Farm Bureau Federation . . . it is not astonishing that the interests of the corn-hog farmers of the Middle West have been served by the national organization with more than ordinary solicitude. Organization by geographic units reduces the emphasis upon the claims of such factions, but the difference from a federation of commodity units is necessarily one of degree.

• • •

. . . A threat to cohesion frequently occurs where certain of the problems with which a group is concerned cease to be primarily local or regional in scope and become predominantly national. Under such circumstances, an increased measure of centralization in the group is normally required, but resistance to an alteration either in the distribution of powers between the federal body and its constituent units or in the basis of federation may assume threatening proportions. Although the attachment of local or subordinate officials to the perquisites of their accustomed positions may be a cause of this lag in adjustment, as we have suggested previously, it is important to look at the factors that facilitate and support their objections. A shift in the scope of a group's problems is ordinarily not sudden and complete, but gradual and partial. Thus at any given point in time the functions of the subordinate unit may still be of considerable significance in the lives of the membership. It is the continuing importance of such local activities, and the consequent degree of intimate, face-to-face interaction, that affords the basis of resistance to centralization. Conflicts of loyalties resulting from such circumstances are the setting for disunity and hesitant inaction.

• • •

THE DEMOCRATIC MOLD

Formal organization, as we have noted earlier, indicates the existence of significant values or attitudes within a group, at least at the time of its creation. These attitudes mold the formal structure, which in turn sets channels and limits for the group's activities. Some of these formative attitudes may be peculiar to the group—for example, those regarding craft autonomy that so sharply affected the structure of the American Federation of Labor. Others, however, may be so widely held in the society of which a given group is a part that they are in effect imposed on an organized group from without as well as demanded from within. Such widespread attitudes, in fact, are indicative of potential, or even actual, interest groups that may, or do, exert claims for conformity upon other groups in the society.

Prominent among attitudes of the latter type in our society are those that can be subsumed under the general heading "democratic." The attitudes themselves are vague, but they usually involve approval of such devices as periodic elections of key officials, broad participation by the membership in the group's policy making, either directly or through a system of elected representatives, written constitutions, and the like. These, in fact, become elements without which an organization cannot achieve "respectability" and "legitimacy" in the community. No matter how solidly the rank and file of a labor union may stand behind their leaders, if the latter do not submit to regular elections and periodic "legislative" conventions, they invite censure from other groups and guilt feeling among the membership that may destroy their cohesion. The elaborate efforts of some corporations to give an impression of large attendance at, and active participation in, annual stockholders' meetings provide another example.

Within limits that we will examine later, the organizational structure of political interest groups in the United States has been molded in conformity with the "democratic" expectations of the community, including, of course, most of their members. Some representative examples will illustrate the point.

Taking first the two national labor federations, we find the clearest instances of "democratic" structural formalities. Both place the formal control of the groups in an assembly of delegates, primarily drawn from the international unions. A typical constitutional provision is the following: "The convention shall be the supreme authority of the Organization and except as otherwise provided in the Constitution, its decisions shall be by a majority vote." Membership in the annual assemblies is based upon rather elaborate systems of representation. In the C.I.O. each international union is entitled to from two to ten members, in proportion to paid-up membership. On a roll-call vote, the internationals cast one vote for each paid-up member. The directly chartered locals and the Industrial Union Councils cast one vote each. The A.F. of L. arrangement is similar. Both organizations show the dominant position of the internationals in the federal structure, the C.I.O. somewhat more sharply than the A.F. of L. if voting arrangements alone are considered.

The annual conventions themselves, at least formally, dispose of a considerable authority. They elect (usually re-elect) the respective presidents, secretary-treasurers, and vice-presidents who make up the governing boards that operate between conventions, called the Executive Committee by the C.I.O. and the Executive Council by the A.F. of L. In addition they elect the members of the convention committees, in which the most important business is initially transacted; this selection, however, amounts to a formal ratifying action, since the president's recommendations for these committee posts are made in advance of the convening of the electoral body.

Such formal arrangements as these are clearly the product of the values and practices of representative democracy, whatever may be the actual operation. They imply broad participation in the affairs of the group, regular answerability to the rank and file by means of annual elections, and some measure of delegate control of the purse strings. The parallel is less clear in financial practice, as the almost hallowed practice of legislative appropriations is not followed. In both federations the governing boards authorize expenditures. Nevertheless, in both groups the taxes on individuals and units—the primary source of the groups' revenue—are fixed in the constitution, and, as is customary in such cases, auditors' reports are submitted to the annual conventions, though they are not challenged.

The peculiarities of financial control in these federations are in part the result of the conflict situations in which these groups have operated, particularly in their early years; these arrangements thus illustrate the molding effect of external circumstances on the organized expression of group values. Because these circumstances are often close to warfare, in which exact knowledge of the group's resources would be a tactical advantage to opponents, individual unions and the federations have been cautious about publicizing finances. The following observations by Philip Murray early in 1940 illustrate the problem as it applies to individual unions:

> The United Mine Workers of America, of which I am vice-president, is one of the older and well established unions. It has virtually every coal operator under contract. . . . Its position is recognized as invulnerable. As a result, every six months the United Mine Workers makes public its financial accounts. The S.W.O.C. [Steel Workers' Organizing Committee, now the United Steelworkers of America] is a new union, still violently opposed by a minority of the steel employers. It does not give out a public financial statement because of the obvious reason that its enemies

would distort its meaning and significance for the purpose of maligning and harassing the S.W.O.C.[1]

The limitations on "democratic" control of the purse strings are not peculiar to the labor federations, nor are they most sharply illustrated by these groups. In varying degrees they appear in almost all large modern associations. In this respect and for much the same reasons, as will be noted in the next section, such associations have adopted some of the forms of the modern business corporation, which has been characterized as "an arrangement by which many men have delivered contributions of capital into the hands of a centralized control." These practices are implicitly in conflict with some of the "democratic" forms, as others have noted.[2] The exigencies of operation, the dominance of attitudes reflected in business control patterns, and other factors have given these groups the appearance of a mixture of differing elements. It is almost possible to rank associations and other groups on the basis of the extent of adoption of "corporate" forms. Such is the pervasiveness of the "democratic" preferences in our society, of course, that even the corporation shows their influence, as the semiritual of the annual stockholders' meeting suggests.

Illustrative of an almost balanced mixture of these elements, and of the conflicts that it creates, is the American Medical Association. Like the labor federations, the A.M.A. structure places formal control in an annual assembly, designated in this case the House of Delegates. The house is made up of approximately 175 members, all but a handful of whom are elected for a two-year term by the State societies, the number allotted to each State being proportional to its medical population. Reapportionment

---

[1]Quoted in [Joel] Seidman, *Union Rights and Union Duties* (New York: Harcourt, Brace & World, 1943), pp. 191–2.
[2]Adolf A. Berle, Jr. and Gardiner C. Means, *The Modern Corporation and Private Property* (New York: The Macmillan Company, 1932), p. 127.

takes place every three years, and each State is guaranteed not less than one representative. The remaining delegates are drawn one each from the scientific sections of the society, the medical corps of the military services, and the United States Public Health Service.

The powers of election exercised by the House of Delegates are impressive on paper. It elects the A.M.A.'s president (one year term), president-elect, and vice-president. Although it also elects the secretary, general manager, and treasurer, these normally receive repeated re-elections for a considerable period of years. The house elects a speaker and vice-speaker as its presiding officers, as well as the members of its standing committees. Finally, it elects for five-year terms the nine members of the board of trustees.

This nominal power of election is evidence of the strength in the organization and in the community of "democratic" interests. These are to be seen also in some of the rules of election procedure. A standing rule of the House of Delegates provides that "the solicitation of votes for office is not in keeping with the dignity of the Medical profession, nor in harmony with the spirit of this Association, and . . . such solicitation shall be considered a disqualification for election to any office in the gift of the Association." The rule is apparently observed largely in the breach, and, as will be noted later, its effect may be the reverse of its apparent intent. But the "democratic" expectations of the community that it embodies remind one of the myths surrounding the New England town meeting, or, even more appropriately, the Quaker meeting, since it is assumed that the House of Delegates can reach a consensus on competing candidates without any electioneering by the latter.

tion is perhaps best illustrated by the board of trustees, which is

The tendency to follow corporation practice in the associa-
charged with the powers conferred by law upon a corporate

board of directors. The board exercises, without direct control from the House of Delegates, complete authority over the property and finances of the organization. Such vestiges of control of the purse strings as remain to the house are further limited by the participation of the trustees in its deliberations, though without vote. The extent of the trustees' discretion is highlighted, moreover, by the fact that no more than half the association's revenues is normally derived from dues, the remainder coming from investments and the profits of its publishing ventures.

The extent of the conflicting patterns in the A.M.A. is not completely indicated by the control over finances. Nominations for many of the elective positions whose incumbents are nominally chosen by the House of Delegates are made by the officers. The treasurer falls into this category, as do the standing committees of the house, candidates for these positions being nominated either by the president or by the trustees. The purely appointive power in the hands of the officers is also impressive. The trustees appoint all members of the A.M.A. staff, including the members of the important Bureau of Medical Economics, the Bureau of Legal Medicine and Legislation, the editor of the A.M.A. publications, and the business manager. The speaker of the House of Delegates, who is ex-officio one of the trustees, has complete appointive control over the reference and special committees, in which the main business of the house is actually conducted. He has, moreover, almost unlimited discretion in assigning matters to the various committees. Finally, the deliberations of several of these bodies are influenced by the officers through ex-officio membership by members of the standing committees and the paid staff. Thus the reference committee on amendments to the constitution and by-laws includes all five members of the powerful Judicial Council, "supreme court" of the A.M.A., whose members are elected for a five-year term on nomination by the president. The reference committee on legislation and public relations similarly includes the director of the Bureau of Legal Medicine and Legislation.

The conflicts of interest that inevitably intrude upon and occur within the association have become involved in these contradictory tendencies of the organization's structure. Resistance to changes in policy has been facilitated by the restraining character of the "corporate" tendencies, and the obvious inconsistencies between the two tendencies have permitted the critical and the rebellious to verbalize their efforts in terms of "democracy" against "oligarchy."

If associations in the field of business and industry are examined, clearer evidence appears, as might be expected, of the preponderance of "corporate" practices, though they are somewhat softened by tendencies that appear also to satisfy the claims of "democracy."

This situation is particularly well illustrated by the trade association. Although virtually all such groups hold one or more meetings of the membership each year, the effective as well as much of the legal power in the organization rests with the officers, boards of directors, and the paid staff. Where the general membership plays a contributing part in policy making, it does so largely through committees. . . . The elected officers and boards of directors are in a peculiarly strategic position in the setting of policy, since they exercise the formal authority of the group (especially when the association is incorporated, as more than half are). The influence of the officers is further enhanced by their relations with the staff and particularly the paid executive.

The key importance of the paid executive of a trade association has been suggested in forthright terms:

> The selection having been made, the executive can, to no inconsiderable degree, determine the direction and emphasis of the association's program; and the executive in some instances probably has been quite as much a factor in determining the character of

the association's program of activity as the nature of the industry, the size of the membership, and other circumstances . . .[3]

His freedom of action, however, is subject to control by the directors, whose influence is increased in a large number of instances by the fact that the executive holds his position only from year to year. Among or behind the directors, moreover, may stand a few large financial contributors whose preferences and recommendations will carry special weight. The T.N.E.C. survey found that nearly half of the national and regional trade associations in 1937–38 received 40 per cent or more of their income from their four largest contributors. This situation is due largely to the common practice of apportioning dues by some measure of size or volume of business. It is worth noting that, although size of financial contribution may be a clue to the actual lines of influence, the formal patterns usually conform to the "democratic" mold. Nearly 90 per cent of the trade associations surveyed by the T.N.E.C. indicated that their formal voting arrangements permitted only one vote per member regardless of size or amount of contribution. Only 14 per cent alloted votes on some other basis.

The same kind of pattern emerges from an examination of the national business organizations. In the case of the Chamber of Commerce of the United States nominal policy control rests in the annual national convention. Delegates to this meeting are apportioned among the organization members, the individual and firm members having no direct voice. This body elects some two thirds of the members of the board of directors, which is the locus of effective control in the association. The board is supplemented, however, by a national council made up of one representative for each organization member, which formally assists in planning the convention and advises and takes part in nomi-

[3] U.S. Temporary National Economic Committee, *Trade Association Survey*, p. 38.

nating members of the board of directors. With nearly three thousand organization members in the chamber, this body is not materially more significant than the annual convention itself.

The position and functions of the board of directors of the Chamber of Commerce are clearly of the "corporate" type. This body, numbering about fifty, elects the president and other officers of the organization, designates an executive committee from among its own membership, and appoints the principal officials of the headquarters staff. In addition, the board of directors passes upon all applications for membership, screens proposals submitted for action by the annual convention, and maintains close control over the organization's finances.

The importance of the last-named function is enhanced by the circumstance that the formal sources of policy-making authority are not identical with, nor even representative of, the major sources of financial support. This situation is similar to that in the American Medical Association, but it is more striking. Not only does the chamber, like the A.M.A., derive a sizable income from its publishing ventures, but also . . . its income from dues is derived from two different classes of members. The organization members, upon which the representative system in the annual convention is based, supply a relatively small proportion of the chamber's annual income, probably a good deal less than 10 per cent. This situation is the result of a deliberate policy, for the chamber's leadership has felt for a good many years that contributions from individuals and firms provide a firmer financial base than do those from the constituent commercial associations, whose own financial positions are often weak and subject to wide fluctuation. The chamber has thus concentrated its promotional efforts on potential individual and firm members. Although these members must also belong to one of the organization members, they will perhaps display interests divergent from those of the organization members, since they are men and firms financially strong enough to pay dues to at least two associations. To the extent that they do hold different interests, such individual and associate members are more directly, though not formally, represented in the key policy-making units than the constituent associations, whose continued support is less necessary on financial grounds. Such financial structure makes the financial powers exercised by the board of directors of more than ordinary significance.

The Chamber of Commerce thus illustrates sharply the symptoms of "centralized control" characteristic of modern large-scale business organizations, though many features of its formal organization show the impress of the democratic mold. One further feature that conforms to the latter pattern is of particular interest—the referendum. This device is also included in the formal organization of a number of the State medical societies, though it is virtually a dead letter. It is a permissive device in the organization of the National Association of Manufacturers and some labor unions, but is rarely used in either. Its use by the Chamber of Commerce is comparatively active. Decision to hold a referendum on a policy issue is taken by the board of directors, which appoints a special committee to look into the issue and make recommendations. A ballot on the issue, together with the committee's findings and a statement of the arguments counter to those supporting the committee's proposals, is sent to the organization members, each of which has as many votes as it is entitled to in the annual convention. The usual response is a large majority in favor of the committee's suggestions. Whatever may be the functional significance of the device, its existence is a striking instance of the impact of widespread community practices and values upon a group's formal organization.

Turning to a final example, the National Association of Manufacturers, we find, not unexpectedly, the clearest case of concentrated control, both formal and actual. Even here, however, the influence of "democratic" demands is apparent. Like the associations previously described, the N.A.M. holds its annual convention (called the Congress of American Industry). The policy-making functions of this body are limited, as is illustrated by the fact that its sessions, with few exceptions, are open to members and nonmembers alike. This limitation is further evidenced by the absence of any representative system for the annual convention. Presumably all of the membership—currently claimed at sixteen thousand—could participate directly in its deliberations. This body elects roughly two thirds of the members of the board of directors, which numbers approximately 150, the exact number varying according to the size of the underlying membership. The most direct connection of the association's members with policy formulation, however, is through roughly a dozen standing committees—appointed by the board of directors —which submit recommendations to the board and its policy committees. About four fifths of the elected board members are chosen by a form of geographic proportional representation, the remainder being elected at large by the membership as a whole.

Despite these arrangements, centralized control is rather explicitly provided for in the organization. The board of directors, which has "full authority to effectuate the purposes and policies of the association," exercises the most extensive powers. It elects the president of the organization, chooses its own chairman (by custom the past president), and appoints an executive committee of about two dozen, whose chairman is usually the past chairman of the board. It elects the other officers of the association, appoints the principal members of the paid staff, makes changes in the bylaws, exercises complete authority over the budget, and approves changes in the constitution before they are submitted to the membership.

The nonelected members of the board are the officers, serving ex-officio, and a dozen to sixteen appointees. Among the latter are representatives of the National Industrial Council, a satellite organization of manufacturers' associations whose exact relations with the N.A.M. have never been entirely clear. (The parent group supplies staff and headquarters facilities, and the chairman of the N.A.M. board is chairman of the N.I.C. This offshoot appears to have little or no influence on N.A.M. policy, functioning largely as a channel for spreading the parent organization's views among manufacturers not directly numbered among N.A.M. members.) The elected members of the N.A.M. board are chosen from a slate presented by a nominating committee appointed by the president, who also appoints members of the board to the policy committees, which sift proposals coming to the board and the executive committee.

In summary, the significance of the "democratic mold," which affects all associations and to some degree almost all organizations in our culture is of fundamental importance in the process of group politics. It has a profound relationship to the problem of unity—not only the cohesion of the particular association, but as well the unity of the society of which it is a part Associations in our culture are expected to be "democratic." This expectation, moreover, represents a sort of hostage to other elements in the community. That is, to the extent that these "democratic" expectations have vitality, they constitute interests. These interests are expressed through groups or, more commonly, are represented by potential groups, the membership of which cuts across that of the associations of narrower compass. Thus, when a conflict occurs within or between groups of the latter sort, a conflict in which the broad "democratic" interests appear to be violated, cleavages within the affected associations may be accentuated. That is, interaction may occur on the basis of these "democratic" interests, and the potential group may become actual and operative. The situation is well illustrated by Garceau's observation concerning the American Medical Association: "It is . . . probable that the official interpretation of medical politics is so dogmatically democratic, not out of conviction, or personal preference, but rather to meet the emotional issue as framed by the economic protest group."[4]

Depending upon the intensity of the supposed violations, the cohesion of the affected associations may be reduced, their influence in the society jeopardized, and their continued existence threatened. These possibilities are a part of the setting of the internal politics of interest groups, which is the primary concern of the next chapter. Before turning to that subject, however, it is appropriate to examine somewhat more closely the origins and character of those tendencies that operate outside the "democratic mold," that furnish an occasion for cleavage and disunity, and that define the problem of interest group leadership. What precisely are these contradictory tendencies? Why do they develop?

THE ACTIVE MINORITY

Tendencies toward minority control are not confined to the political interest groups used here for illustration, nor are they peculiar to this type of group. Writers of the most diverse political views and using the most widely variant methods of observation have called attention to the existence in almost all groups of an active minority—identified by such condemnatory terms as "oligarchy" and "old guard" or such approving ones as "public spirited citizens" and "civic leaders." The late Lord Bryce put the situation in these words:

> In all assemblies and groups and organized bodies of men, from a nation down to the committee of a club, direction and decisions rest in the hands of a small percentage, less and less in proportion to the larger and larger size of the body, till in a great population it becomes an infinitesimally small proportion of the whole num-

[4]Reprinted by permission of the publishers from Oliver Garceau, *The Political Life of the American Medical Association* (Cambridge, Mass.: Harvard University Press, 1941), p. 28.

ber. This is and always has been true of all forms of government, though in different degrees.[5]

It is unnecessary here to examine all the varied formulations of this proposition. However, one of these, a book by the Italian Swiss sociologist, Robert Michels, has peculiar relevance to the discussion of political interest groups. Studying the European socialist parties prior to 1914, Michels found that these groups, above all others attached to the "democratic" principle, showed unmistakable evidence of control by an active minority. His central conclusion, stated by him in somewhat flamboyant language as "the iron law of oligarchy," can be summarized in his words as follows: "The appearance of oligarchical phenomena in the very bosom of the revolutionary parties is a conclusive proof of the existence of imminent oligarchical tendencies in every kind of human organization which strives for the attainment of definite ends."[6]

Because of some serious limitations in his method, Michels derived from his evidence a series of implications concerning political leadership that are largely untenable and that do not adequately explain the complicated phenomenon of leadership. They need not be dealt with here. In isolating and stating some of the causes of the "oligarchical tendency," however, Michels performed a lasting service. With some modification his formulations will help to answer the question of this section: Why do interest groups develop an active minority in apparent contradiction of the "democratic mold?" Part of the answer has been mentioned in earlier paragraphs; it will be restated in more complete form now.

---

[5]James Bryce, *Modern Democracies* (New York: The Macmillan Company, 1921), Vol. II, p. 542.
[6]Robert Michels, *Political Parties: A Sociological Study of the Oligarchical Tendencies of Modern Democracy,* translated from the Italian by Eden and Cedar Paul (London: Jarrold & Sons, 1915), p. 14. This translation was republished in 1949 by The Free Press, Glencoe, Illinois.

As Michels has suggested, the fact of formal organization is itself basic to an explanation of the existence of the active minority. Organization, viewed as a standardized, habitual pattern of interaction, implies varying degrees of participation by the membership in the process of decision making. These variations stem in part from the fact that it is virtually impossible for any considerable body of people to solve directly all the problems that may confront it. They represent the fact of delegation, explicit or implicit, of what we may call authority. Thus formal organization creates or recognizes various roles in a group, some of which involve more intimate and direct participation in the solution of the group's problems than do others. It acknowledges at least the rudiments of an active minority.

By way of illustration, the American Medical Association fairly early found that a general meeting of its members was too unwieldy a body for policy determination. Its present House of Delegates was a partial solution. That even this smaller body could handle only a limited segment of the association's delicate external and internal problems was acknowledged in the creation of the board of trustees, the committees, and the paid staff. "If the general meeting could not manage these affairs, no more could the House of Delegates."[7] The same observations can be made about any other such group.

The importance of formal organization in fostering the active minority is increased as the group increases in size of membership or variety of functions performed. Trade associations provide a good example. In the manufacture of electric refrigerators there are not many more than a dozen producers in the United States. In the trade association that includes these firms no elaborate formal organization is necessary. Three or four men or firms

[7]Reprinted by permission of the publishers from Oliver Garceau, *The Political Life of the American Medical Association* (Cambridge, Mass.: Harvard University Press, 1941), p. 19. See also p. 15.

may act as a leadership group for limited purposes, and a small number of others may function similarly for other purposes, but the differences in participation among all members of the group are not great at any time. The association secretary performs some delegated functions, as do committees of the membership, but he is easily subject to a continuing check. Those dealing with the group can almost as easily reach the whole membership as they can the secretary. In the National Retail Dry Goods Association, however, which includes thousands in its membership, the general manager performs quite different functions. No effective approach to the group is possible except through him and the association's officers.

Berle and Means have called attention to the same situation in the development of minority control in the modern corporation. Their essential thesis, in fact, is that as ownership of corporations has been more widely dispersed, a separation of ownership and control has tended to develop.[8]

Those at the upper reaches of a large organization develop a remoteness from the rank and file that, buttressed by the special managerial skills usually necessary in such positions, approximates insulation from the stresses that may operate at lower levels. This situation has been noted frequently in studies of labor groups. Thus the long tenure of many officers of international unions, as compared with local officials, is ascribed primarily to their being "better insulated from rank-and-file pressure." Their performance is not so directly apparent to the local membership. This remoteness, combined with the discretionary power implicit in delegation, is illustrated in unchallenged efforts by the well-situated minority to take action that does not conform to the decisions or preferences expressed by the rank and file or by their elected representatives. For example, in discussing the role of the American Legion's National Executive Committee as a

[8]Berle and Means, *The Modern Corporation and Private Property*, pp. 69 ff.

formulator as well as an executor of policy, Gray cites the fact that in 1943 this body reversed a vote of the previous national convention that had censured Hamilton Fish, one of the founders of the Legion, for his alleged assistance to elements deemed hostile to the best interests of the United States.

Two words of caution should be emphasized in discussing the connection between formal organization and the active minority. In the first place, the authority of the active minority as fostered by formal organization is stated as being a matter of degree. It is an error to assume, as Michels and others implicitly do, that delegation is necessarily complete, that it necessarily involves complete renunciation of power by the rest of the group. Although in some groups, under appropriate circumstances, some of which will be discussed in later paragraphs, nearly complete power may be delegated to an oligarchy, in no organization do we consistently find a sharply defined "mass" who merely obey and an equally definite minority who always command. The extent to which this sharp differentiation is approached is a matter for precise determination for individual groups in varying circumstances and not one for easy generalization. One may find, as Garceau has, that as a partial consequence of formal organization one can discern in the American Medical Association the rough outlines of an active minority exercising delegated functions that are extensive and highly discretionary. All initiative, whole and entire, does not, of course, necessarily rest in such minority hands. The interaction that defines the group puts limits on the monopoly of initiative.

In the second place, in order not to overemphasize the influence of formal structure, it is important to bear in mind the suggestion at the beginning of this chapter that formal organization represents a stage in the frequency of interaction of a group. The delegation it necessitates creates opportunities for the exercise of greater authority by leaders, but it also recognizes the authority that has already developed. That is, although formal organization facilitates leadership, leadership precedes this stage of interaction, for differential powers also exist at a stage where the frequency of interaction does not produce formal organization.

Consequent upon organization and influential in fostering the growth of an active minority are the managerial skills that are acquired by those who occupy in the organization positions through which the delegated authority is exercised. Because men in such positions know the "system" and have learned some of the special skills that it demands, and because such posts in most organizations involve some measure of discretion, the occupants enjoy corresponding advantages over the rank and file. They are in possession of manipulative skills and tools not available to the uninitiated. Managerial position is itself a form of power, as many observers have noted. . . .

The effects of occupying managerial positions—whether elective or appointive—may be quite varied. They stem, however, from the specialization, the "know-how," necessary in key positions in a hierarchy. Anyone who has observed a legislature in action will have noted how important to the effectiveness of a bloc is a knowledge of parliamentary tricks. The newcomer in such a setting is almost powerless unless he too learns how to operate the machinery. Tenure of such positions not only permits a tactical manipulative advantage but gives such individuals some control over the flow of ideas to the rank and file.

The effects on the development of an active minority of acquiring managing skills are particularly well illustrated by labor groups. Even at the local union level "the development of a bureaucracy seems almost inevitable irrespective of the philosophy or political outlook of the leadership," and local union leaders enjoy a wide discretion in matters of policy. At the more inclusive level of the international unions, the situation is more striking. . . . Such officials and their immediate associates, through their greater familiarity with the organization's affairs, through their power to name the membership of key committees, and through other advantages derived from their position, play a disproportionately large role in determining policy. The situation is similar in a federated national group like the A.F. of L. The Executive Council of that organization determines the major business to come before the annual convention; such business is largely transacted in committees led by members of the active minority. Millis and Montgomery indicate as fairly typical a convention of the A.F. of L. in which the chairmen of thirteen out of fourteen convention committees were either A.F. of L. vice-presidents or other major officers. They sum the matter up in the following terms: "Thus it is for the most part the voice of labor as interpreted by the Executive Council that becomes articulate in the legislation of the A.F. of L. The policies of the Federation are essentially those of the official class."[9]

In the National Association of Manufacturers the paid staff constitutes only a segment of the active minority, but they are reported to have more than a little to do with molding objectives and formulating policy, owing to such factors as long tenure in office and knowledge of the affairs of the association. A key figure of this sort was the late James A. Emery, who was counsel and chief legislative representative of the N.A.M. for thirty years; the late Walter B. Weisenburger was executive vice-president for nearly fifteen years; Noel Sargent has occupied various administrative positions, including that of manager of the industrial relations department and secretary of the association, since 1920.

In the American Medical Association, as in the N.A.M., the active minority is made up partly of long-term holders of various elective and appointive positions and partly of its salaried administrators, many of whom have been in the same positions for long periods of time. Dr. Morris Fishbein, who in the eyes of many laymen was the A.M.A., served as the editor of its principal pub-

[9]From *Organized Labor* by [H. A.] Millis and [R. E.] Montgomery (New York: McGraw-Hill Book Company, 1945), p. 308.

lication for nearly thirty years. The implications of such arrangements are fairly obvious.

> For such men, work for organized medicine is a large part of their life, and for some it is their only career. . . . Secretaries, editors, and technicians develop skills which are useful primarily in "organized medicine" as such. It is natural and not wholly unrealistic that, to some commentators, they should appear themselves to be "organized medicine."[10]

The functions and power of such minorities become most apparent when they are used, not necessarily without reason, to resist either a change in long-established policy or the inclusion of new elements in the minority, or both. For example, a struggle has been carried on in the American Legion since 1945 over the inclusion of veterans of World War II among the major officers. Attempts to make a younger man National Commander have taken place at every postwar convention. One influential legionnaire has been quoted as saying: "After all, this Legion is a billion dollar corporation. You don't just throw something that big over to a bunch of inexperienced boys." Despite the voting strength of the "boys," the elected National Commander is invariably the man groomed and named for the position by the active minority, known in Legion parlance as the king-makers.

In many groups the defensive efforts of those with managerial "know-how" stem from the indirect effects of acquiring such skills. Although those who over the years have learned how to manipulate the elements of a group's organization have thereby gained a means of exercising power, they may also have incapacitated themselves for gaining a satisfactory livelihood by any other means. The doctor who has given all of his time for a decade or more to the activities of organized medicine is in no position to return to active practice. The union leader who for

[10]Reprinted by permission of the publishers from Oliver Garceau, *The Political Life of the American Medical Association* (Cambridge, Mass.: Harvard University Press, 1941), p. 49. See also p. 25.

years has not been a factory worker, who has not used the tools of his trade and has become accustomed to the forms and perquisites of union leadership, has disqualified himself psychologically, if not technically and physically, for work at the bench or lathe. To a lesser degree, perhaps, the business man who has spent years as a trade association secretary is not prepared readily to resume a career that he has all but forgotten. Under such circumstances it is not astonishing that some members of an active minority should tenaciously use their skills to perpetuate policies and methods with which their personal fortunes are literally identified.

Other examples could be given at length. In his New Jersey study McKean found in all the groups he studied that control lay in the hands of a small group of officers, among whom the paid officials were an important element. About fifteen directors actually governed the New Jersey State Chamber of Commerce; control of the Manufacturers Association of New Jersey was in the hands of its secretary and the other officers; an executive secretary controlled the New Jersey Taxpayers Association, allegedly with support from the railroads. The position of the paid executive in many trade associations has already been alluded to. It is well summarized in a statement by the general manager of one such group to the effect that less than a dozen association secretaries "can very largely control the general thought and action of employers' associations of the country." The board of directors and the paid staff are the principal source of program and policy for the Chamber of Commerce of the United States. Even in the Board of Temperance, Prohibition, and Morals of the Methodist Episcopal Church, Herring noted some years ago: "The pronouncements of a few men in a central office are . . . able to direct the thought and actions of a large church body."[11]

---

[11][Pendleton] Herring, *Group Representation Before Congress* (Washington, D.C.: The Brookings Institution, 1929), p. 211.

A third influence upon the development and maintenance of an active minority is the financial structure of the group. In the groups that Michels studied, he did not encounter this as a major element. Yet he noted that in the socialist parties that needed the contributions of their more affluent members this dependence tended to give such contributors a disproportionate influence in a party's affairs.

The influence of financial structure is far more noticeable in the interest groups examined here, though it is not characteristic of all of them. It is not easily isolated in any group, but in some it is indicated by the close correlation between tenure in key positions and the ability to pay. In the National Association of Manufacturers, for example, 125 corporations, constituting less than 5 percent of the total membership, between 1933 and 1946 held an overwhelming proportion of the key positions: 63 percent of the positions on the board of directors, 88 percent of the positions on the executive committee of the board, 79 percent of the finance committee posts, and 52 percent of the major executive positions outside of the paid staff. This inner group represented primarily large, financially strong firms, and they accounted for a large proportion of the organization's funds. In 1936, for example, approximately 5 percent of the membership contributed just short of half the N.A.M.'s funds. Moreover, although the organization has asserted that more than four fifths of its members employed less than 500 workers, none of the 125 in the active minority was so small a firm, and nearly two thirds of them employed more than 2,500 workers. If organizational structure in the N.A.M. in a sense defines the key posts occupied by an active minority, the financial structure measurably influences what elements are to occupy them.

Other examples are numerous. In the case of the New Jersey State Chamber of Commerce, the officers have been drawn from firms representing a considerable proportion of the State's corporate wealth. The Manufacturers Association of New Jersey employs a system of choosing its directors from those firms that employ relatively more workers and that have given the organization major financial support. Similar tendencies in many national and regional trade associations have been mentioned in another connection.

Care should be taken to avoid any superficial explanation of this phenomenon, such as the common suggestion that the influence wielded by those who give major financial support indicates a sort of conspiracy on their part. A trade association secretary whose budget is heavily dependent upon the contributions of four or five firms will simply avoid situations likely to offend such members. The more or less continuous representation of these firms in the key policy positions, moreover, will minimize the chances of mistakes of this kind. In some instances the needs of financial strength and stability will indicate solicitous concern for the large contributor. Such considerations have encouraged the Chamber of Commerce of the United States to avoid soliciting chambers of commerce in small cities as organization members, to promote individual firm memberships over organizations, and among firms to solicit primarily those whose credit ratings indicate a capacity to pay dues in significant amounts.

In some situations, finally, the financial structure of a group may operate to strengthen the position of an active minority within it in a manner unrelated to the money contributions of the minority element. In a good many labor unions, for example, the inability of locals alone to support adequate strike funds and research facilities has meant the movement of control to the financially stronger national unions. This movement has strengthened the hands of those in control of such top machinery. Then, too, where the entire national union is none too strong financially, cost considerations may necessitate the weakening of some controls on the active minority, such as conventions. Although the annual convention of a labor union or other association is not a profoundly important means of restraining leadership elements, it does afford some opportunity for protest and challenge. Since such meetings are expensive, a financially weak union may be able to stage them only at fairly long intervals. In the interim the freedom of action of those in the key positions is appreciably strengthened and protected.

Financial structure, therefore, may account in various ways for the development and continuance of an active minority within an interest group.

A fourth cause, less important than those already discussed but related to the second and third, is the fact that leadership is time-consuming and only a few can afford to spend the necessary time without remuneration. Michels found the emergence of paid, professional leadership one of the signs of developing minority control; and, in part, this professionalized leadership is a product of the managerial skills, already discussed, that it develops. But these manipulative skills seem to be also a consequence of the professional leader's continuing preoccupation with the affairs of the organization. Even unpaid, nonprofessional leaders acquire such skills as a consequence of spending more time upon, and gaining greater familiarity with, the group's activities than can the rank and file. Professionals can give most of their time to the group because they are paid for it. The non-professional leader gives the time that he can spare from the activities by which he secures his livelihood.

In many groups only those with personal financial security and success in the institution to which the association is peripheral can afford the time required of unpaid leaders. In many instances the consequence is a highly conservative leadership, since, because of their status, the leaders have most to lose by any change in existing arrangements. Thus in the Chamber of Commerce of the United States and the National Association of Manufacturers the segment of the active minority that is not included among the professional leaders and staff is quite naturally drawn from among men whose jobs permit their devoting considerable time to the activities of these groups. Indeed, major corporation executives, from the very nature of the positions they occupy, may find it desirable to engage in the activities of such associations. The leaders of most large corporations today carry an extensive responsibility for managing the company's relations with various outside groups, of which labor unions are only one example. Remembering the functions of the association in stabilizing such relations for individuals and subgroups similarly situated, we can understand why the heads of large companies can afford time for extensive participation in these associations.

The influence, in the American Medical Association, of the fact that unpaid leaders must be men of some leisure has been spelled out in considerable detail. A study of the principal elective bodies of the A.M.A. over a period of fifteen years, and of several of the State societies, has indicated that specialists from the more urbanized areas have held positions of power in numbers out of all proportion to their numbers in the medical population as a whole. Those with long tenure (eight years or more) in their positions were especially likely to fall into this category. In accounting for this characteristic Garceau observes:

> A man must have some margin of wealth and leisure to leave his practice and attend conventions, to say nothing of serving on active operating committees, with trips to the state capital or to Chicago. Politics and the public office that goes with it take time; less it is true, in associational politics than in the politics of the state, but too much for a man in active general practice where substitutes are rivals and there may often, in fact, be no one to care for the community if the doctor goes off on a junket.[12]

The American Legion provides another illustration. As in the A.M.A., so in the Legion, membership on key committees tends

[12]Reprinted by permission of the publishers from Oliver Garceau, *The Political Life of the American Medical Association* (Cambridge, Mass.: Harvard University Press, 1941), p. 54. This mobility and leisure afforded by a favorable financial situation help to define the active minority in the American Library Association also. See Garceau, *The Public Library in the Political Process* [New York: Columbia University Press, 1949], chap. 4.

to fall disproportionately to those who can afford the leisure necessary for frequent participation in group actions. The necessity for such leisure favors city specialists among the doctors; in the veterans' organization it encourages higher military officers, both active and retired.

A fifth influence in the formation of an active minority may be found in qualities peculiar to leaders as persons. We must avoid the implication that the existence of the active minority can be accounted for entirely on the basis of elements outside the personalities of the particular leaders. This is not the place for a thorough discussion of the psychology of leadership; suffice it to say that the matter of leading is better viewed as a relationship between individuals than as a quality that some individuals "have." Nevertheless, it must be recognized, as Gordon Allport emphasizes in his discussion of differential participation, that "talents differ." It then becomes entirely reasonable to suggest that a few members of a group may adequately represent the attitudes and aspirations of the rank and file. Michels discusses the influence of leaders' personalities, though in rather loose terms that associate it primarily with such elements as formal learning and personal prestige. The general point can be illustrated by Garceau's observations on the American Medical Association. He points out that the city specialists who dominate the group's active minority are men already set apart from their constituents by personality and energy. Not that organized medicine provides rewards exactly corresponding to merit, but the successful city specialist is likely to exhibit high energy and differentiating talents of various sorts. Those talents, whether strictly professional or not, that lead to a successful practice are likely also to prove useful in the hierarchy of the organized group, if only because they make their possessor a more skillful spokesman for the group's claims upon other elements in the society. The practice of medicine, moreover, although it is a demanding, and in many cases completely absorbing, enterprise, is for many of its devotees not a complete means of satisfying individual psychological needs. Talent for management in its many forms, and drives for prestige, can be expressed by achieving influential positions in the group. If such men tend to cling to the positions thus acquired and if they persistently defend a system that has been the apparent means of their advancement, one should not be astonished. By so doing, in fact, the active minority may most effectively represent, except in periods of rapid change, the attitudes and aspirations of their constituents, both those who have similar but as yet unrecognized talents and those whose personalities do not require the satisfactions of leadership.

Assent to these representative qualities by the rank and file except in periods of rapid change suggests a sixth influence sustaining an active minority, the influence of custom. As Michels has noted, the holding of an office tends to become a customary right, and an individual will "remain in office unless removed by extraordinary circumstances or in obedience to rules observed with exceptional strictness." These "extraordinary circumstances," moreover, may be long postponed if the official appears to advance the group's interests sufficiently to make his continuance in office a gesture of decent gratitude on the part of his constituents or at least sufficiently to forestall intense dissatisfaction. . . .

Such gratitude is unquestionably one of the keys to the power of the active minority in the American Legion, since these leaders are able not only to champion veterans' benefits in general but also to facilitate the settlement of the individual claims of members. Many a veteran has found a pending claim against the government mysteriously expedited upon his joining the Legion. A similar situation can be noticed in trade associations. For example, the successful promotion of anti-chain-store legislation in the 1930's placed the director of the National Association of Retail Druggists in an almost invulnerable position with his constituents. Edward A. O'Neal, President of the American Farm Bureau Federation from 1931 to 1947, was elevated to the position of a demigod as a consequence of his successful leadership of the organization during these years that produced so marked a change in the economic position of farmers.

In many labor unions gratitude for services presumably rendered supports a customary re-election of officers. On the other hand, although opposition in union elections is exceptional whether they are held in convention or are conducted by referendum, unsuccessful leadership is often as likely to be supported by custom as is one that has gained marked advantages for its group. Taft points out that success in strengthening the union was a poor explanation for the tenure of the officers of the United Mine Workers in the 1920's and suggests as a more likely cause the decline of the older union districts with the shift of the industry and the consequent movement of the union into areas where the miners had little memory of autonomous locals undominated by the national officers. High membership turnover, in fact, has been noted by many observers as promoting the customary stability of leadership in a variety of groups.

The nature of the strategic position of a group in relation to other groups in the society suggests a seventh influence that, under appropriate circumstances, may facilitate the development of an active minority, just as it may affect the character of formal organization. That is, where a group finds itself in more or less open conflict—not necessarily involving violence—with other groups, the need for quick maneuver and discipline will, as Michels observed concerning his socialist parties, promote the influence and authority of the few. This pattern is a familiar one in the operation of the government itself, for the executive acquires almost dictatorial powers in time of war or serious domestic crisis. It is further illustrated by the discretionary power exercised by the makers of a nation's foreign policy and by the secrecy that necessarily surrounds much of their work, even in a period in which a fetish is made of hostility to secret diplomacy. Interestingly enough, groups attempting to influence the making of foreign policy may be similarly affected by the dynamics of the situation in which they find themselves. A study of interest groups operating on foreign affairs in the United States in the two years prior to Pearl Harbor indicates that "events transpired so rapidly that the initiative was in the hands of a small controlling leadership" in all such groups.

The influence of conflict upon labor groups has been referred to in a slightly different connection earlier in this chapter. Labor unions are a peculiarly appropriate example, since, as many students of the subject have observed, the operation of such groups is closely analogous to war and diplomacy. To gain its ends, whether economic or political, a union must give considerable authority to its leadership, the amount varying with a multitude of circumstances affecting the strategic position of the group.

3

INTERESTS, VALUES, AND GROUP CONFLICTS

Central to the analysis of interest groups is the notion of "interest." What do leaders and members of the group want? What are they after, and of particular relevance to the political scientist, what are they after in the arenas of government. It has sometimes been argued, most notably by Arthur Bentley, that the words "groups" and "interest" are interchangeable; that there is no group without interests, and that one indeed identifies and defines a group by the goals or values it pursues. These goals are often quite complex, however. Those groups which political scientists generally study often pursue a considerable range of interests and may also display a good deal of internal disagreement over what public policies are deemed most appropriate and what tactics and strategies are most likely to work. Furthermore, we are not content simply to know the policy platform of an organized group. We want also to know why one set of interests is preferred over another. We wish to explain the sources and, if we can, forecast the future direction of policy interests. Why does one farm group differ in its objectives from another? How does an organization of teachers develop and adapt its interests in governmental programs? These are the issues with which the selections in this part deal.

James H. Laue describes some of the most notable groups active in the civil rights protest movement and notes the variations in their program, strategies, and sources of support. In this rapidly changing area of group activity his assessment may already be outdated in some respects, but his attention to differences within "The Movement" has continuing relevance. John P. Heinz performs a similar function regarding farm groups, and his discussion is closely linked to some of the material presented in Part I. A. H. Raskin discusses the situation of the merged AFL-CIO, and points out the especially difficult tensions present in a group that is really an organization of organizations. Nicholas A. Masters, Robert H. Salisbury and Thomas H. Eliot examine the efforts of the Missouri State Teachers Association to accommodate the diverse values within its membership and, at the same time, adapt to the circumstances of the state political arena within which the group must compete for support.

The Changing Character of Negro Protest

JAMES H. LAUE

In 1955, most Americans had not even heard of most of the organizations whose reports are included in this section. Yet today, just ten years later, the desegregation movement in America has reached its highest peak of energy and effectiveness, largely through the efforts of thousands of Negro and white Americans working through these six groups—the National Association for the Advancement of Colored People (NAACP), the National Urban League, the Southern Regional Council (SRC), the Congress of Racial Equality (CORE), the Southern Christian Leadership Conference (SCLC), and the Student Nonviolent Coordinating Committee (SNCC).

Many Americans ten years ago probably could have named the NAACP as one organization working for desegregation, mainly because of its long history of legal action culminating in the 1954 United States Supreme Court decision banning segregation in the public schools. The other five groups, however, were either little known or nonexistent ten years ago. Today, most of them are familiar to anyone who reads a newspaper—a good indication of how rapidly the character of Negro protest is changing.

From the *Annals of the American Academy of Political and Social Science*, Vol. 357 (January, 1965), pp. 120–126. Reprinted by permission of the author and the publisher. Most footnotes are omitted.

FROM PROFESSIONALISM TO PERSONAL MILITANCY

These changes may be summarized by comparing the basic means of protest today to those of even a few years ago. For most of the twentieth century, most American civil rights supporters were willing to contribute financially only to organizations like the NAACP, whose staff professionals carried through the front lines activity. The crucial difference today is the active personal participation of thousands of persons who are willing to risk their jobs, social status—and, in some cases, their lives—to protest segregation. In short: "Year by year and month by month, Negroes have been growing more militant, more immediatist, more fed up with limited successes and tokenism."

This change from an attitude of professionalism to one demanding personal commitment—"putting your body on the line," as student sit-inners put it—has had three important correlates:

(1) *The transfer of initiative for change from the hands of a relatively few civil rights professionals, religious leaders, and "white liberals" to the broad backs of militant individuals of every color and calling.* Prior to 1954, the approach of desegregation strategists was basically legal and educational. Low educational levels, lack of economic and political power, and the resulting scarcity of articulate Negro leadership necessarily had kept the drive for equal rights in the hands of a few skilled professionals. Discrimination was rigidly institutionalized, and change was generally slow and piecemeal.

But almost overnight after the Montgomery bus boycott of 1955–1956, the initiative for change shifted to average citizens whose segregation-bred frustration had been spilling over into action at an ever-increasing rate. Organizations and their leaders were still important, to be sure, but their role was becoming one of channeling and structuring the energy for change which was releasing itself among growing numbers of citizens. "Hurry up so we can catch up with our followers!" has become a common feeling among civil rights leaders.

(2) *The development in the last ten years of a full-scale social movement for desegregation.* Sporadic protests against racism in America have been going on since the first Africans jumped overboard rather than be sold into slavery some 400 years ago. But not until the Montgomery bus boycott and its catapulting of Dr. Martin Luther King, Jr., into nationwide prominence was the final groundwork laid for development of a widespread desegregation movement. Montgomery dramatically showed Negroes a new technique—nonviolent direct action—which had won immediate gains in a hard-core segregationist area of the Deep South. More importantly, Dr. King was a *person* (not an organization or a court decision), a living symbol of achievement with whom Negroes could identify in their strivings for self-fulfillment. So it was that nonviolence was added to legalistic and educational approaches to desegregation.

The sense of movement crystallized in 1960 when the lunch counter sit-ins among Southern Negro college students attracted immediate response from students and organizations throughout the nation. Dr. Leslie Dunbar, Executive Director of the Southern Regional Council, has observed that, almost from the beginning, the sit-ins were referred to by both participants and observers as a "movement," but that no one ever spoke of the "school desegregation movement." From 1960 on, this new-found sense of movement and direction has, among other things, increased the tempo of desegregation, led to the birth of new civil rights organizations and the revitalization of existing ones, and hastened the national political confrontation with the problem which culminated in the comprehensive civil rights law of July 1964.

(3) *The growing importance of organizational structures in channeling and co-ordinating the energy generated by the emergence of the desegregation movement.* Movements cannot live by charisma alone—and the current desegregation drive is no exception. Ours is an organizational society, so while laymen and their mass militant activism have become a major source of initiative

for change, this energy can be effective in the long run only if it is appropriately organized and directed. Efficient organization has become increasingly important as segregationist community leaders learn to deal with direct action demonstrations, and organizations like the White Citizens Council retaliate with stronger economic and political sanctions. All in all, these conditions have helped to hasten the growth of militancy in the desegregation movement among religious and labor leaders as well as the formal civil rights leadership.

THREE TYPES OF PROTEST

It is in this context of changing participation and leadership, I believe, that the strategies of the six major organizations should be viewed. There have been three basic methods employed in the desegregation effort, which we shall label legal, educational, and activist. The civil rights groups may be distinguished on the basis of which one of these strategies makes up the major part of their approach to the problem: (1) *legal*—appeal to law through filing suits, court litigation, encouraging favorable legislation, and the like (NAACP); (2) *educational*—appeal to reason through researching, informing, consulting, persuading and negotiating with political and economic leaders (Urban League, Southern Regional Council); (3) *activist*—appeal to morality through direct personal confrontation of the enforcers and tacit bystanders of the segregated system, usually through nonviolent direct action in the area of public accommodations (CORE, SCLC, SNCC).

While the major approach of each organization can be characterized by one of the three terms in this typology, it should be noted that (1) most of the groups today employ the other two strategies to some extent and (2) the relative emphasis on the three techniques varies within each organization over time, often depending on the external situation. Using the same framework, the history of protest in the twentieth century may be viewed as an accumulation of effective strategies, beginning with the basically educational approach which the NAACP and the Urban League followed upon their founding in 1909 and 1910, respectively, adding the turn to effective legal means of the NAACP in the 1930's and the Southern Regional Council's area educational function in the 1940's, and including, finally, the growing importance of direct action with CORE (1942), SCLC (1957), and SNCC (1960).

Two essentially educationist strategies have been used in varying degrees by all of the organizations: publications and the sponsoring of workshops and conferences. All the groups publish regular newsletters in addition to issuing special releases and pamphlets. Publications as a means of fund-raising are becoming increasingly important for all the groups, with the exception of the Southern Regional Council and the Urban League, for whom more stable foundation support is a major source of income. Another important form of communication—the workshop or conference—has been a major activity of the educationists and an important part of the programs of all the organizations. Such meetings generally have been of two types: (1) to bring Negroes and whites together for intergroup experiences not provided in a segregated society,[1] and (2) to train leaders and supporters in the philosophy and techniques of the organization.

The role of each of the groups now may be assessed in terms of the general typology of protest techniques, and changes in four important dimensions of group life—goals, strategies, leadership and membership/support.

[1]This type of workshop is, of course, more frequent with the educationist organizations. A number of other groups have sponsored such meetings since the 1940's, the most important of which are the American Missionary Association—annual Race Relations Institute at Fisk University in Nashville; the Fellowship of Reconciliation; the War Resisters League; the Southern Conference Educational Fund; the National Student Association; the Anti-Defamation League; and the National Conference of Christians and Jews.

THE LEGALISTS

National Association for the Advancement of Colored People (1909)

Goals: To end racial discrimination and segregation in all public aspects of Amercan life.

Strategies: Educational activities important—especially in voting—but legal and legislative techniques have been major approach since the 1930's, when courts began consistently upholding unconstitutionality of public segregation. Approach has expanded considerably since 1960, when rapid success of sit-ins spurred more direct action.

Leadership: Board determines policy, but effective leadership at executive level from Roy Wilkins, Executive Secretary since 1955—and with the organization for thirty years. Grassroots leadership shared by local executive secretary and president of chapter in larger communities.

Membership and Support: Dues-paying membership of more than 400,000 in 1,600 chapters throughout the United States. Effectively utilizes structure of Negro church, with many clergymen as branch presidents, especially in South.

THE EDUCATIONISTS

National Urban League (1910)

Goals: "Opportunity, keynote of American freedom, has been the theme of the National Urban League since its founding."

Strategies: Social work and community organization emphasis. Educational, consulting, and persuasive activities designed to convince employers and government officials that equal opportunity is economically as well as morally right. Important programs include youth talent search and training, promoting com--

pliance with federal equal opportunity regulations, research on Negro-white demographic differences, and wide distribution of findings in such pamphlets as "Economic and Social Status of the Negro in the United States."

Leadership: Highly trained national staff, full-time professional local directors. Increasing militancy since Whitney M. Young, Jr., became Executive Director in 1961—reflected in Young's proposal for a "Marshall Plan for Negro Americans" and his full participation in the March on Washington.

Membership and Support: Nonmembership organization, supported largely by foundation grants. Some 8,000 volunteers and staff members throughout the nation.

Southern Regional Council (1944)

Goals: "To attain, through research and action, the ideals and practices of equal opportunity for all peoples in the South."

Strategies: Maintenance of a reputation for careful and objective research makes SRC a respected spokesman on Southern economic, political, and social problems. It has done much through this role to legitimate the ideal of desegregation in the South. Not an activist organization; therefore has unique access to the media, business leaders, educators, religious leaders, and government officials, and is able to serve as mediator between activist groups. Organization and service of state and local human relations councils. Wide circulation of journal, *New South,* and numerous releases, reports and pamphlets. Representative examples: "What the Supreme Court Said" (1955); "The Economic Effect of School Closing" (1959); "Integration and Industry: What Price Tag for 'Massive Resistance'?" (1960); "The Federal Executive and Civil Rights: A Report to the President" (1961); and "The Price We Pay [for Discrimination]" (1964).

Leadership: Professional staff trained in political science, law, economics, sociology, journalism, governed by Board of

Directors. Rapid staff growth with new programs since 1960. Executive Director is Dr. Leslie W. Dunbar, widely respected as knowledgeable on race relations and the South.

Membership and Support: Nonmembership organization, supported largely by foundation grants. Volunteers and some staff in state and local human relations councils. Several thousand academicians, agency personnel, religious, educational, and economic and political leaders subscribe to publications.

THE ACTIVISTS

Congress of Racial Equality (1942)

Goals: To abolish racial discrimination through application of the Gandhian philosophy and techniques of nonviolent direct action.

Strategies: Pioneered nonviolent direct action demonstrations with sit-ins, stand-ins, wade-ins, in the North in 1940's and 1950's; Journey of Reconciliation to test interstate bus facilities in Middle South in 1947; supplied intensive leadership training for sit-inners in 1960's; led Freedom Rides in 1961. Like other activists, approach is basically moral, confronting society's sense of right and wrong directly instead of working through law or reason. Recent leader in organizing voter registration and community centers in Deep South.

Leadership: Small, action-trained national staff including field workers; volunteer leadership on National Council and in local chapters. National Director since 1961: James Farmer, a founder in 1942, has gained position of major leadership in civil rights movement in short time.

Membership and Support: Small active membership organized in approximately 50 local chapters; required commitment to continuous direct action on local level keeps active membership small. Rapid growth in local chapters and all phases of program since sit-ins began in 1960. About 10,000 financial supporters in 1960, now well over 60,000.

Southern Christian Leadership Conference (1957)

Goals: "To achieve full citizenship rights, and total integration of the Negro in American life . . . to disseminate the creative philosophy and technique of nonviolence . . . to secure the right and unhampered use of the ballot for every citizen . . . to reduce the cultural lag."

Strategies: Founded to spread techniques of Gandhian nonviolence which brought desegregation on Montgomery's buses, SCLC remains basically direct actionist in approach. Educational and legal work often implemented through direct action. Most important contribution to strategies of movement: highly professional citizenship education and voter-registration schools, training indigenous leaders from throughout the South.

Leaders: SCLC was formed as an organizational embodiment of *the* major symbol of direct action in America—Dr. Martin Luther King, Jr., who is President. Day-to-day policy and implementation under leadership of Executive Director Reverend Andrew J. Young, who succeeded Reverend Wyatt Walker in 1964. Rapid expansion of office and field staff since 1961, including Directors of Citizenship Education and Voter Education; nonprofessional local leadership—mostly clergymen.

Membership and Support: Approximately one hundred affiliates—church groups, civic organizations, and the like—in some thirty states, mainly engaged in fund-raising. Budget increased ten times from 1960 to 1964 with expanding program in direct action and voting. Major fund-raising source: Freedom Rallies with Dr. King speaking in all parts of the country, sponsored by affiliates.

*Student Nonviolent Co-ordinating
Committee (1960)*

Goals: In 1960, to build "a social order of justice permeated by love." In 1963, to build "an interracial democracy [that] can be made to work in this country."

Strategies: Formed to facilitate communication among sit-inners in 1960, SNCC worked primarily in mass nonviolent direct action for first year. Significant change in 1961: decision to take the movement into rural Black Belt through voter-education work. SNCC field secretaries, living on close to subsistence salaries, are more consistently on the rural front lines than any other group. Organized first large voter projects in rural Georgia and Alabama, and laid groundwork for the now extensive voter work in Mississippi. Major strategic contribution: building indigenous leadership through field secretary-led projects in Deep South.

Leadership: Co-ordinating Committee of representative sit-in groups in 1960 became full-time staff of fifteen leave-of-absence students in 1961; grew to more than 200 field secretaries in 1964. Policy-makers James Forman and Robert Moses envision program designed to revolutionize Deep South political and economic caste system.

Membership and Support: "Not a membership organization, but rather an agency attempting to stimulate and foster the growth of local protest movements." Financial support from voluntary contributions, aided by foundations in voter work, Northern Student Movement, and various Northern Friends of SNCC groups.

A GENERALIZATION: CRISIS BRINGS CHANGE

The major generalization deriving from these data is that in virtually every case of desegregation in the United States, change has come only after the development of a crisis situation which demanded rapid resolution by a community's leadership structure. It may have been a legal mandate which had to be met, or the loss of business due to demonstrations, or the fear of school closings—any situation defined by the decision-makers as a severe enough crisis to demand solution.

This Crisis-Change model provides the framework for understanding how the three strategies have worked together in the desegregation process. A crisis arises whenever a significant number of elements in the social structure deviate from expected patterns enough to threaten the system's equilibrium. In terms of our typology, such threats to the status quo may come from court cases and equal-opportunity legislation (legalist), or through some form of mass protest (activist). In either case, crisis within a community must be resolved ultimately through face-to-face negotiation (educationist). Or: Activists may test the constitutionality of a law, be bailed out and defended by the legalists, while the educationists help the community adjust if the case produces a new legal definition of the situation.

THE POLITICIZING OF THE PROTEST MOVEMENT

Though strategies differ, the emerging goal of all the civil rights organizations seems to be social and economic self-help within a framework of equal opportunity.[2] All the groups reflect this orientation in their growing concern for development of indigenous leadership.

But social and economic self-help and equal opportunity are only possible within representative political institutions.

[2]Note that the stated goals of the legalists and educationists are phrased strictly in secular terms, while all of the activist groups have said that they are striving toward goals with definite philosophical (that is, Gandhian) or theological (Judeo-Christian) bases.

Thus, it is not surprising that the Negro protest is already well into an essentially political phase. There are numerous indications already: citizenship education, voter registration, the Mississippi Summer Project, and the Mississippi Freedom Party's challenge at the 1964 Democratic National Convention. The real measure of things to come, however, was begun early in 1962: the massive—an initial three-year grant of more than $500,000— Voter Education Project sponsored by several foundations, blessed by the federal government, co-ordinated by the Southern Regional Council, and carried out by the other five organizations plus many more. In its first two years, the Project had, among other things, registered more than 550,000 new Negro voters in the South.

The increasing reliance on political means will call for still greater commitment and organizational skills. It must, in fact, combine the best of the three strategies discussed here in order to succeed. Assuming this trend, we may conclude with several predictions about the course of the protest in the next few years:

(1) The need for greater technical sophistication—in interpreting and defending provisions of the civil rights law, or in behind-the-scenes consulting with community leaders through crisis periods, for instance—may produce a trend to a new kind of professionalism, but at a much broader and more militant level than the pre-1954 variety.

(2) In the North, civil rights advocates and community leaders will work more closely together for equal opportunity in housing and jobs in an effort to avoid more ghetto riots like those of last summer.

(3) In the South, the activists will necessarily gain increasing support from legalists and educationists as they continue to challenge local custom and thereby demand enforcement of federal law—and protection of their very lives.

(4) Finally, we can expect to see more of the trend to co-operation manifested in the Council of Federated Organiza-

tions,[3] the National Conference on Religion and Race,[4] the March on Washington, and the formation of the United Council on Civil Rights Leadership. In short, the civil rights groups will be putting aside past differences over strategy as the growing sophistication of segregationist resistance—North and South— makes continued re-integration of the movement itself a practical and moral necessity.

[3]"COFO," a united project of the NAACP, CORE, SCLC, SNCC and other groups.
[4]Attended by 600 representatives of all major faiths in America in Chicago, January 1963.

The Political Impasse in Farm Support Legislation

JOHN P. HEINZ

THE POLITICAL CONTEXT

Classically defined, a political interest or interest group is men, formally organized or not, who desire to obtain advantages through government, and who thereby come into conflict with other men. Conflict results either because the same advantage is desired by both groups, and is scarce, or because the second group would be at a relative disadvantage if the first group obtained its desires. This definition emphasizes groups because an individual cannot generally be a significant factor in governmental politics unless other individuals join with him. It requires no formal organization of groups because even unorganized groups can be effective political forces. And it uses the terms interest and interest group interchangeably because the present existence of a group is not required, but only the present existence of a common interest which could become an effective political force if that interest became the subject of political controversy.

Since agricultural price-support laws are a form of economic regulation, the groups concerned with them are usually based on economic interests. Rational, objective economic self-interest

From the *Yale Law Journal*, Vol. 71 (April, 1962), pp. 954–970. Reprinted by permission of the Yale Law Journal Company and Fred B. Rothman & Company. Footnotes omitted.

is not the sole determinant of political behavior; such behavior reflects the totality of the experiences of each of the participants. For example, a strong commitment to individualism rooted in religious beliefs may lead a farmer to place a higher value on goals other than maximum economic advantage, or may even shape his perception of the direction in which his economic interests lie. It is generally true, however, that farmers align themselves in accordance with identifiable economic interests and make political demands which would advance those interests. Consequently, it is important to determine what those patterns of alliance and conflict are.

INTER-CROP CONFLICTS

Competing Crops

Where different crops compete for the same market, conflict may occur. To the extent a law benefits one crop, it puts others at a competitive disadvantage. There are two major conflicts of this type. Since soybeans, corn, cottonseeds, dairy fats, and lard from meat animals are alternative sources for many fats, oils and shortenings, bills which benefit producers of one meet opposition from producers of the others. Likewise, corn interests oppose bills which would make wheat competitive with corn as a source of feed. At present, artificially high wheat prices maintained by the government preclude this use.

Supplier-Consumer Relation

Where some crops are consumed in the production of other agricultural commodities and the consumers do not themselves produce substantial amounts of these crops, their interest will conflict with the suppliers' interest. Livestock producers generally oppose any program which would increase their costs by raising feed grain prices. Since the demand for any given meat is highly elastic, livestock men believe they cannot increase prices to cover the increased feed costs without substantially reducing their sales. But there are some exceptions. Where farmers raising livestock also grow feed grains, they are less likely to oppose grain supports. Hog and dairy farmers fall into this category. Similarly, where the demand for livestock products is highly inelastic as in the case of fluid milk, these producers have less to fear from increased costs because they can raise prices with little effect on sales. And where periods of gestation and maturation differ among livestock, producers of animals with short periods such as hogs may be more fearful of lower feed prices than producers of animals with longer periods such as cattle. Since this difference in gestation and maturation periods causes the cattle market to respond more slowly than the hog market to an increase in grain supplies, hog producers have a more immediate fear that their own market will be glutted.

"Diverted Acres"

Even where two crops do not compete for the same markets, government programs favoring one may have a detrimental effect on the other. When acreage allotments are placed on a crop to reduce its supply and raise its price, the acres diverted from the production of that crop may be used to grow another. The increased supply of this second crop will depress its price, injuring those who had been producing it. When acreage controls were imposed on cotton and wheat producers, many of them diverted some of their acres into production of feed grain, increasing its supply and decreasing its price. Since climate, terrain, legal impediments, or the lack of expertise and capital may make it difficult for old feed grain producers to compensate for their decreased income by going into production of other crops, they opposed these controls. The use of diverted acres would create conflicts between a large number of crops which might be controlled, and a large number of other crops which might be grown in their place.

Agricultural Budget Allocation

Further conflicts may develop in the process of allocating the agricultural budget among different crops. Since the amount of funds that can be secured for price support programs is limited, and especially since legislators have perceived this to be the case, all crops may compete among themselves to maximize their individual shares of the available funds.

INTRA-CROP CONFLICTS

New Areas v. Old Areas

When it becomes profitable to produce a crop in a new area, the interests of those who historically have grown the crop may conflict with the interests of the new producers. This conflict has occurred in both cotton and wheat. In an attempt to raise cotton prices, Congress restricted cotton acreage during the 1930's. Growing privileges were allotted to individual farms on the basis of what land had produced on the average in several prior years. During World War II Congress dropped these restrictions. Increased wartime demand combined with technological innovations to stimulate new cotton production in the western states. Since the war, the old cotton South has attempted to stem this movement by supporting reinstatement of high support programs with acreage restrictions based on past production. This interest collides with that of the new producers. The latter group desires freedom to expand production. Since they can grow cotton more efficiently, lower prices have less impact on their profit margins. Moreover, lower prices may allow these growers to expand sales in foreign markets and even to capture the domestic markets of the old growers by driving them out of business.

Similarly, old wheat producers have sought to limit new sources of wheat. Government programs have raised wheat prices to attractive levels. Although these programs include history-based production restrictions, many Corn Belt farmers with no history of wheat production have been able to take advantage of the guaranteed, high wheat prices because the law has permitted any farmer to grow at least fifteen acres. Since this exemption has benefitted these new wheat producers but has hurt old producers by glutting their market, the exemption has become the subject of political controversy.

Proximity to Markets

When commodities are perishable, and historically have been produced near consumers, differences in proximity to markets provide another basis for conflict among producers. Farmers near markets argue for controls which will insulate their historical markets from more distant suppliers. But to the extent technological innovations allow the more distant suppliers to sell profitably in these markets, they oppose such controls. This conflict has been especially intense in the determination of so-called "milkshed" areas surrounding large milk-consuming centers.

Competing Varieties and Grades

As with different crops, different varieties and grades of the same crop which compete for the same markets may conflict over programs which would give one a competitive advantage over others. This conflict occurs only where the differing varieties cannot be grown on the same land; otherwise disadvantaged producers could switch to the favored variety. Arguing that their particular variety was not in surplus, but that in fact their crop's special attributes caused more demand for it than could be filled under existing acreage restrictions, producers of certain types of wheat have secured special, more favored treatment in wheat legislation. Growers of other, more abundant varieties opposed such treatment because buyers who were unable to get enough of the preferred variety of wheat had been buying the more abundant variety as a substitute. Similarly, in seeking to have parity computed with long-staple cotton as the base, the newer, long-staple cotton producers seek advantages over the older, short-staple producers. Since in free markets the higher quality long-staple cotton would bring higher prices, and since relative price differences among varieties are maintained under the parity system, this method of computing parity accords all cotton relatively low prices, a goal sought by the newer, more efficient, long-staple, western growers and resisted by the older, less efficient, short-staple, eastern growers.

THE INVERSE

Where none of the conditions previously discussed are met, conflicts are not likely to occur. Tobacco price support programs, for example, have not engendered inter-crop conflicts. Since no other crop can be used as a substitute for tobacco, there is no inter-crop competition. Tobacco is not consumed in the production of other agricultural commodities. There have been relatively few acres diverted from tobacco to other crops as a result of acreage controls. Since small decreases in tobacco supplies increase prices significantly, tobacco programs have required little government subsidy, decreasing the likelihood of conflicts over budget allocation. Moreover, there has been little conflict *within* tobacco. Different varieties of tobacco do not compete; they each have distinct uses. Since each variety can be grown in only a few well-defined areas, these areas are substantially immune from competition from any new areas. Moreover, differences in proximity to markets are not crucial in tobacco. Therefore, each of the reasons for conflict enumerated above is not present in tobacco, and the tobacco programs have, in fact, proved particularly non-controversial in Congress.

POLITICAL VARIABLES

The shape that these inter-crop and intra-crop economic conflicts take in Congress may be conditioned by other, political factors. Some crops have superior access to key points in the legislative process. For instance, the Chairmen of the House and Senate Agriculture Committees are spokesmen for tobacco and rice interests respectively. This not only gives those crops valuable support, but also discourages other interests from opposing them lest they should alienate such important legislators. Conflict is further minimized if the crop interests are small, wealthy businesses. The relative size and wealth of truck farmers, for example, enables them to exert pressure on Congress while attracting a minimum of public attention. The kind of program advocated bears also on the degree of conflict generated. Compare, for example, "marketing order" programs with price support programs. Proponents of a marketing order need not request Congress to review the details of a plan and vote subsidies to support it, but only to authorize the Secretary of Agriculture to enforce the marketing restriction plans designed and approved by the growers. And once established, marketing order programs are rarely reconsidered in Congress since they do not require periodic appropriations. Thus, the growers of many, smaller, more specialized crops—because of procedures which attract little attention thereby minimizing political controversy, and because of the limited amount of government activity involved—have been able to secure beneficial legislation with relative ease.

BROADER INTERESTS?

The conflicts discussed so far have been based on individual crop interests or on interests within a crop. But do larger groups, each of which includes several crop interests, play significant roles in agricultural policy-making? The importance of two kinds of larger groups—the political party and the national farm organization—should be considered.

Political Parties

Since farm policy is one of the few major issues in American politics on which the Republican and Democratic platforms clearly differ, and since roll call votes in Congress look partisan, party membership appears to be an important determinant of politicians' behavior on farm price support bills. If, however, the makeup of the parties is examined, this behavior can be as easily explained on the theory that crop interests are the dominant forces. The congressional delegations representing each crop tend to be found in one party or the other. A survey of the party affiliation of Congressmen representing districts ranking in the top twenty in the production of each of several crops indicates the following pattern:

Crop	Democrats	Republicans
Rice	20	0
Peanuts	20	0
Cotton	20	1
Tobacco	17	3
Wheat	7	14
Dairy	4	16
Corn	2	18

Most rice, peanut, cotton, and tobacco producers have in common the desire for programs of production restrictions and price supports. The Democratic Party, with which they are affiliated, espouses these programs. Similarly, many dairymen and corn-hog farmers favor fewer controls, and embrace the Republican Party, which advocates this approach. Moreover, although there are conflicts among the crops within each party, the differences in crop interests between the two parties are greater. For example, some Southern (Democratic) crop interests conflict with Midwestern (Republican) interests because their products compete. Party regularity on congressional votes is, therefore, often consistent with the following of constituency interests.

Indeed, the nature of the particular crop interests within each party probably determines the party's agricultural policy. The case of wheat is instructive. Although one would expect wheat farmers to be aligned with the Democrats because wheat has a chronic problem of oversupply, of the 20 wheat districts, 14 have Republican Congressmen. However, these Republicans are a substantial portion of those few party members who occasionally stray from the official party position and vote for the Democrats' programs. Furthermore, the Democrats have been making substantial gains in wheat districts in recent years. In wheat therefore, the crop, not the party interest seems dominant. The two available studies on the problem support a generalized statement of this conclusion. A study of several roll calls on price-support bills during the period 1949–1955 found that Congressmen followed constituency interests to a greater degree than party. And a more recent study concludes that the pull of party as compared with constituency influences is even less strong in congressional committee maneuvering than it is in final roll call votes on the floor. In the agriculture committees, where most of the important compromises between crop interests must be worked out if a bill is to succeed, the unifying effect of party discipline is weaker, and loyalty to narrow crop interests is greater. There the impasse in agricultural policy-making has its roots.

National Farm Organizations

National farm organizations represent broad segments of the farm population, and therefore each includes many crop interests. The oldest and largest of these organizations are the American Farm Bureau Federation (AFBF), the National Farmers

Union (NFU), and the National Grange. More recently the National Conference of Commodity Organizations and the National Farm Organization have been formed. The two organizations most influential politically, the AFBF and the NFU, have consistently been at odds on agricultural policy. But, as with the two parties, this conflict may be explained in terms of crop interests. Most crops affiliated with the AFBF—livestock, corn-livestock, and big cotton—would be benefitted by Republican free market policies, while the dominant crop interest in the NFU—wheat—depends on price support programs advocated by the Democrats. The conflicts among crops within each organization are less pronounced than the crop-based conflicts between the two organizations. Paradoxically, consistency in the policy positions expressed by the leaders of each organization may be a result of the multiplicity of internal conflicts. Since none of the many factions are strong enough to challenge the national leadership, entrenched organization spokesmen are usually able to disregard with impunity the objections of individual crops. While the dissidents are free to resign their membership, they rarely do so because of fringe benefits such as cheap insurance, cooperative buying and marketing, and social and educational programs.

As in those even larger conglomerations of interests, the major political parties, there is much evidence that the pronunciamentos of the national offices of the major farm organizations carry as much weight as the particular crop interests that they benefit, and no more. State Bureaus of the AFBF often appear at congressional hearings to oppose the position of the national organization when it conflicts with the interests of crops in their own states. But, even stronger evidence of the importance of particular crop interests as opposed to the organizational entity can be found in the experience of the National Conference of Commodity Organizations (NCCO). The NCCO, a confederation of existing single-crop organizations such as the

National Milk Producers Federation and the Association of Virginia Peanut and Hog Growers, was formed in 1957 in reaction to the impasse on farm legislation. The idea was that through a series of compromises by the member crop organizations, a single bill, agreed to by all, could be presented to Congress in 1958. Many of the interests of member crops, however, conflicted with each other. Since each member got less than it wanted, all had a general reluctance to press the final bill on the Congressmen with whom they had special influence. The bill failed, as did the NCCO a year later, demonstrating not only the dominance of narrow crop interests, but also the intensity of conflict among them.

ECONOMIC AND POLITICAL CHANGE

The politics of agricultural policy-making has not always been so complex a process of particularized, but vigorous conflict among many small, but adamant farm interest groups. In 1921, Congressmen representing a broad range of agricultural interests, and including members of both parties, joined together in the "Farm Bloc," a formally organized group bent on securing federal laws to alleviate the agricultural depression which had followed World War I. In spite of some conflict within the bloc, it functioned with increasing success. In the early '20s it achieved the passage of several laws designed to loosen farm credit, and lower the freight rates for transporting crops to market. Later, with the McNary-Haugen bills, the bloc attempted to secure more direct support for low farm incomes. This movement culminated in the passage of the first Agricultural Adjustment Act during the early New Deal. In the later '30s and early '40s, farm bills continued to sweep through Congress, with the bloc managing to secure favored treatment for agricultural commodities in the Price Control Act of 1942—even in the face of opposition from a wartime President who had party majorities in both houses.

Today, however, there is no farm bloc. Instead, there is intense conflict among farm Congressmen, reflecting the concerns of the presently dominant, narrow, particularized interests. Two reasons for this change are suggested.

First, the original goals of the bloc were modest and conservative—perhaps even palliatives designed to head off the more radical demands of some farm groups. And its early successes were facilitated by the non-controversial nature of the bills. As the depression became even more widespread and severe, common privation created near consensus on the necessity of doing *something*. After Congress had responded to these relatively non-controversial demands by adopting a program of production control and price support, and after increased income had made many crop interests less desperate, the relevant issues concerned how individual crop, variety, or area interests would be treated in subsequent legislation. When all interests are losing money it is comparatively easy for them to unite, but as their condition improves they may begin to feel they can afford the luxury of internal conflict.

Second, the rapid technological change in agriculture in recent years has also contributed to the change in the pattern of conflict in farm politics. Chemists have provided improved fertilizers, dusts, and sprays; biologists have developed new hybrids, serums, and artificial insemination techniques; and engineers have designed new machines and irrigation methods. Although natural conditions of terrain, climate, soil type, and access to markets lead different areas to specialize in different crops to some extent, these recent technological innovations have accelerated the process of specialization. Since it is expensive, and usually inefficient for a farmer to acquire the machinery and skills necessary to raise each of several crops, the farmers in each region have concentrated on the few crops best suited to that land, adopting only as much of the new technology as those crops require. Therefore, any given region is now likely to contain fewer crop interests than was the case when agriculture was less specialized. Since political representation is allocated geographically, each Congressman now has fewer interests in his district than formerly. This limits his concern to a narrower range of interests. Moreover, the localization of particular crops means that there is less overlap of interests among the several congressional districts. Consequently, less common ground exists among the Congressmen to form a basis for compromise, and all the economic conflicts within agriculture are able to obtain political expression. In addition to specialization, dividing the old farm bloc into many narrow factions, technological innovation has also changed the configuration of farm interests by creating several entirely new interest groups, not previously contained by the bloc. Such new interests may occur through the introduction of a new crop or variety, which changes the interest of an old farming area, or through technological changes which open a new area to agriculture. Thus, in its several ways, technological change has produced a proliferation of farm interests.

IMPASSE

This proliferation of interests within agriculture has created a stalemate on farm policy. Congressional procedures are such that a concerted minority interest can usually block action distasteful to it through various obstructive tactics, if the interest has sufficient access to strategic points in the legislative process. Many farm interests have access through the agriculture committees, without whose approval no farm bill is likely to be adopted. The proliferation of interests has meant that there are now many groups, each trying to obstruct the others' programs. The sum of all these obstructionist tactics has been impasse. . . .

AFL-CIO: A Confederation or Federation? Which Road for the Future?

A. H. RASKIN

When the American Federation of Labor and Congress of Industrial Organizations (AFL-CIO) merged in 1955, John L. Lewis of the United Mine Workers, then in majestic self-exile from both groups, pronounced the new entity a "rope of sand." It was a characterization borrowed—without acknowledgement—from Samuel Gompers, who had used precisely the same phrase to describe the formation of the AFL nearly three-quarters of a century before.

Lewis intended his description as pejorative, Gompers as compliment; but essentially they were saying the same thing. The AFL was a co-ordination of autonomous international unions, each confirmed in its own sovereignty by the terms of the federation's constitution. Lewis, contemptuous of the merger he had no part in welding, insisted that the AFL's successor would be torn apart by rivalries among the leaders of its huge affiliated organizations, all using union autonomy as a shield for power grabs and disruption.

Eight years of living in the same house have made it plain that autonomy in the AFL-CIO is not what it was in the old

From the *Annals of the American Academy of Political and Social Sciences,* Vol. 350 (November, 1963), pp. 37–45. Reprinted by permission of the author and the publisher.

AFL. The merged organization has constitutional powers that give it an authority Gompers would have considered unthinkable. Not only has it exercised those powers with vigor but it has repeatedly gone beyond them with the support of the affiliates which once would have fought and bled against such "usurpation" of authority. As a result, the central federation is more than the sum of its parts. It is no longer as true as it was in premerger days that "we have strong unions but a weak labor movement"—the private estimate repeatedly made by union chiefs in the era of division. Nevertheless, there remains room for serious doubt that the national federation has all the authority that would be desirable in a period when rapid technological change is changing unions most of all.

Gompers never wavered in his stress on the federation as a voluntary association of independent organizations, subject only to moral suasion, and usually not much of that. In what amounted to a final testament shortly before his death, he told the 1924 AFL convention that the federation had "no power or authority except of a voluntary coming together of unions with common needs and common aims." Out of a feeling of mutuality, in his view, had developed "a stronger bond or union than could be welded by any autocratic authority."

"So long as we have held fast to voluntary principles, and have been actuated and inspired by the spirit of service, we have sustained our forward progress and we have made our labor movement something to be respected and accorded a place in the councils of our Republic," Gompers declared. "Where we have blundered into trying to force a policy or a decision, even though wise and right, we have impeded, if not interrupted, the realization of our aims."

Gompers' basic philosophy on this point was fully shared by his successor, William Green. But the concept of autonomy was substantially reshaped by President Franklin D. Roosevelt's New Deal and by the advent of the CIO in 1935. The extent

to which union destiny was determined by legislation governing collective bargaining, wages and hours, unemployment compensation, and other equally basic subjects made it obvious that
there would have to be much more centralization of labor's
activities in the political and legislative realms.

However, it was the cleavage between the forces of craft
unionism and industrial unionism that provided the decisive push
away from simon-pure Gomperism. The industrial unionists, led
by Lewis, formed a committee within the AFL to promote the
unionization of the mass-production industries. The craft unionists, in command of the federation's convention and executive
council, branded the move as dual unionism.

When the CIO group rejected an executive-council demand
for its dissolution, anticompromise elements within the federation pushed through the council a motion to suspend the ten
founding unions of the CIO. This action was taken in the face
of strongly expressed opinions within the council that the AFL
constitution provided no legal foundation for ousting an affiliate,
except by two-thirds vote of a convention.

To the dominant forces in the federation, the protection
of the autonomous right of each affiliate to sole possession of
its technical field of jurisdiction was more important than the
invasion of autonomy involved in investing the executive council with a suspension power whose justification in AFL law
was virtually undefinable. Thus one concept of autonomy dealt
a crushing blow to an even more fundamental one. The CIO,
cast adrift—to the evident satisfaction of both Lewis and his
enemies in the craft camp—was, from the start, far more of a
top-down organization than the federation from which it sprang.

The rigid boundaries of jurisdiction that fettered the AFL
and that had been principally responsible for the split were
almost unknown in the CIO's initial assault on the citadels of
the open shop. It established broad organizing committees in
such fields as steel and textiles. And even where it functioned

through international unions, as in automobiles, rubber, maritime, and electrical manufacturing, the important thing was to organize. The worry about jurisdictional lines of assignment could come later.

The great bulk of funds and organizing personnel came from the United Mine Workers, although the Amalgamated Clothing Workers and the International Ladies Garment Workers Union (ILGWU) also contributed heavily in men and money. Overshadowing everything, as symbol and source of strength, was the personality of John L. Lewis. Millions of workers flocked into union ranks without knowing anything about the unions except Lewis' name.

The CIO, under both Lewis and Philip Murray, grew in the image of the mine union. National headquarters exerted a role of influence that frequently represented dominance in all the affairs of the unions that made up the CIO. However, the trend toward centralism was sharply arrested in the internal feuding that followed Murray's death in 1952. Indeed, one of the elements that impelled the CIO to welcome a merger was the fear that the United Steelworkers of America and other unions cool to the leadership of Walter P. Reuther might switch to the AFL without waiting for an organizational alliance embracing all the CIO affiliates.

THE ERADICATION OF CORRUPTION

In the AFL, after the New Deal and the formation of the CIO, the most potent single push toward a reassessment of traditional concepts of autonomy came with the election of George Meany to succeed Green as president—a change almost simultaneous with Reuther's takeover in the CIO. Meany, himself a product of the emphasis on legislation and lobbying brought by the New Deal, started with the thesis that labor had to be heavily involved in politics to safeguard the gains it won at the bargaining

table or to win them in the first place. He was also increasingly
impatient of the notion that autonomy should provide armor
for irresponsible elements to discredit the entire labor movement.

The evolution of this attitude and the way it has reflected
itself in both the constitution and the operating policies of the
AFL-CIO under Meany's presidency are perhaps best reflected
in an appraisal of the stand taken by the old AFL toward
racketeering, as against that which has prevailed since merger.

A good time to begin this comparison is 1940, not because
that was the start of racket infiltration of organized labor but
because that was when the issue of federation policy was first
presented in dramatic form. The International Ladies Garment
Workers Union had just reaffiliated with the AFL after having
been a charter member of the CIO. One of the conditions it
had set for coming back was that the federation revise its constitution to give its executive council more authority to force a
cleanup of corruption in unions that failed to act with sufficient
vigor to purge their own upper echelons of crooked leaders.

The AFL high command held to the traditional view that
it could do nothing about the internal practices of its unions,
short of expelling them from continued affiliation. It was made
plain that this remedy would not be exercised, even in the face
of evidence that some unions had become captives of the under-
world. The ILGWU pressed its demand on the floor of the
AFL's 1940 convention in New Orleans. It submitted a resolution that would have empowered the federation to remove corrupt officials of affiliated organizations where the organizations
themselves were derelict.

The reply was twofold. The AFL executive council informed
the convention delegates that it deplored gangsterism in unions
but that it would be contradictory for the federation to confer
on its unions "full and complete power to administer their own
affairs" while at the same time assigning to the central body

"the right to exercise dictatorial control" over their administrative policies or their choice of leaders.

The second reply was a good deal blunter. It came from the fists of Joseph S. Fay, a vice-president of the International Union of Operating Engineers, who was later to be sentenced to a long jail term in New York for extortion. Fay assaulted David Dubinsky, president of the garment union in the lobby of the convention hotel. The assault was preceded by a long harangue on the villainy of the Dubinsky resolution for driving crooks out of union office.

The national outcry occasioned by the attack forced the AFL leadership—in which Meany then served as secretary-treasurer—to back away from its original intention to shelve the resolution entirely. Instead, a watered-down version was put on the floor and passed. It made the eradication of corruption the primary responsibility of the individual unions, but it added a stipulation that, where the AFL council had "valid reason" to believe that a union official was guilty of racketeering and his union evaded its obligation to remove him, the council "shall be authorized to apply all of its influence to secure such action as will correct the situation."

For more than ten years the resolution was treated as a dead letter, buried deep in the federation's files. When an attempt was made to utilize it as the basis for AFL intervention in a dispute involving the return to office of a convicted extortionist in the Brooklyn District Council of the Brotherhood of Painters and Decorators, Matthew Woll, as special investigator for the federation, reported that the resolution conferred "no compulsory or disciplinary power" on the parent body.

Meany's Accession

There the matter rested until Meany's accession to the presidency at the end of 1952. He was installed in the middle of the inquiry by the New York State Crime Commission into the fetid conditions on the New York waterfront. The investigation disclosed, to the satisfaction of almost everyone, including Meany, that the International Longshoremen's Association (ILA) had become the mask of a union, so infiltrated was its leadership with corrupt elements.

Dubinsky, in his capacity as an AFL vice-president, sent Meany a letter asking whether the 1940 resolution did not give the federation a legal warrant for proceeding to demand a purge of crooks in the ILA. Meany agreed that it did. The result was an ultimatum by the executive council to the ILA—get clean or get out. In a letter dated February 3, 1953, the council said it had no intention of "changing the traditional position of the American Federation of Labor in regard to freedom and autonomy of its affiliated units," then added:

> However, no one should make the mistake of concluding that the American Federation of Labor will sit by and allow abuse of autonomy on the part of its affiliates to bring injury to the entire movement. The exercise of autonomy by affiliated units in an organization such as ours presupposes the maintenance of minimum standards of trade union decency. No affiliate of the American Federation of Labor has any right to expect to remain an affiliate "on the grounds of organizational autonomy" if its conduct, as such, is to bring the entire movement into disrepute. Likewise, the cloak of organizational autonomy cannot be used to shield those who have forgotten that the prime purpose of a trade union is to protect and advance the welfare and interests of the individual members of that trade union.

When six months of missionary effort failed to produce the desired transformation of the ILA, Meany and the executive council called on the AFL convention in St. Louis that September to expel the ILA and to establish a rival union to drive it from the piers. The expulsion was carried through but the hope of breaking the union's hold on the waterfront was not.

Despite the AFL's disappointment at the defeat of the union it had chartered to dislodge the ILA, there was no weakening of Meany's resolve to utilize the maximum power of the federation to fight corruption in all of its unions. This resolve was equally strong in the CIO. It had never been afflicted with the problem of gang penetration to anything like the extent to which it had bedeviled the AFL, but the CIO had moved in vigorously whenever signs of taint appeared. "The CIO does not recognize any autonomous right of crooks and racketeers to use the good name of the CIO as a cloak for their corruption," was its philosophy, as enunciated by Walter Reuther in a speech to the 1954 CIO convention.

Self-Policing

The joint determination of both groups to make self-policing a duty of the central organization was embodied in the AFL-CIO constitution. It laid down as a basic principle of the merged body that "it must be and remain free from any and all corrupt influences." The executive council is empowered, on motion of any of its members, to investigate any situation "in which there is reason to believe that any affiliate is dominated, controlled or substantially influenced in the conduct of its affairs by any corrupt influence. . . ."

The anticorruption section goes on to authorize suspension of any union found guilty of violating its ethical standards. A two-thirds vote of the council is sufficient for suspension. This remains in force pending an appeal to the convention, the highest deliberative element in the federation structure.

Acting under this grant of power, the AFL-CIO expelled in 1957 its biggest and most powerful affiliate, the 1,500,000-member International Brotherhood of Teamsters. Also expelled were two smaller unions—the Bakery and Confectionary Workers and the Laundry Workers. This represented the most forceful exercise of centralized authority in the history of American labor.

Unfortunately, despite the courage and high-mindedness the

action reflected, the consequences have been such as to diminish substantially any enthusiasm within the AFL-CIO for repeating its stand for moral rectitude in terms that would entail equivalent decisiveness or willingness to make substantial sacrifice in the interest of probity.

The AFL-CIO Ethical Practices Committee, which prepared the cases against the ousted unions and which is the keeper of the federation's conscience in the administration of its ethics codes, has not even had a meeting since 1958. Indeed, it is all but dismantled, even though it still nominally exists.

The reasons for this decline in crusading zeal are disturbing in their implications for the exercise of the broader powers the AFL-CIO is likely to need if organized labor is to move forward, not backward, in the next decade. One factor that discouraged the federation from vigorous implementation of its cleanup rules after 1957 was the increasing conviction among its leaders that expulsion was an ineffective weapon. Once a union was outside the fold, it could go about its affairs, immune even to the moral suasion of the AFL-CIO.

When the union was as strong and as strategically well-situated as the Teamsters, it became a disturbing question as to which was more hurt by a cutting of ties—the federation or the Teamsters. The evidence over the years tended to provide considerable support for the boast of Teamsters President James R. Hoffa that his union could get along better without the federation than the federation could without the Teamsters. The orders the AFL-CIO gave its affiliates to shun any alliances with the exiled Teamsters were widely ignored; the truck union was just too vital to other unions in strikes and organizing campaigns.

Government Action

Equally damaging to the ethical-practices drive was the torpedoing of the AFL-CIO belief that Congress would not impose excessively restrictive laws on unions generally if labor demonstrated that it was making a sincere effort to enforce high ethical standards within its own house through its own efforts.

Here again labor's ideas had undergone a substantial revision from pre-New Deal days. The concept that government should stay out of union affairs—once so rigorously held that the old AFL had objected to the passage of laws for unemployment insurance or a federal minimum wage—was obviously untenable in a period when many unions owed their birth to the legislative protection provided by Section 7a of the old National Industrial Recovery Act and to the even broader props supplied by the Wagner Act and other Roosevelt innovations.

The result was that the AFL under Meany swung to an acceptance of the idea that Congress had both a right and a responsibility to adopt regulatory legislation to prevent abuses in labor-management welfare funds. The CIO, as a child of the New Deal era, needed even less persuading on this point. After the merger, with the McClellan Committee investigation creating a clamor for tight legal curbs on corruption and undemocratic practices in unions, the AFL-CIO made it plain that its worry was about the kind of curbs, rather than about whether there should be any.

Meany and the bulk of the AFL-CIO leadership readily acknowledged that, inasmuch as labor had no subpoena powers of its own, it was dependent on government for the investigative machinery necessary to discover where corruption had obtained a foothold. At a meeting of the federation's council in February 1958, in Miami Beach, Dubinsky urged that it record itself in favor of a bill that would empower the government to investigate union racketeering and impose sanctions where abuses were discovered. He warned that the alternative to such a measure was punitive legislation of a kind that would bear adversely on all unions, including those untouched by corrupt influences.

However, the prevailing sentiment in the council was that any support for specific legislation would simply provide a springing-off point for more drastic restraints on labor and that the best policy was to fight any general laws imposing new controls. Meany took a less negative position but the split in approach became so apparent that labor's friends in Congress were left baffled as to how to proceed. With the McClellan revelations reinforced by strong pressure from President Eisenhower for a tough law against union malpractices, Congress finally gave its approval to the Landrum-Griffin Act of 1959—a law that went well beyond anything anyone in labor's upper echelon considered either helpful or warranted.

The upshot is a feeling that keeping unions clean is now a government responsibility, and the brave effort at self-policing is a somewhat bitter memory for most of those who were once its most dedicated partisans. The teamsters are still outside the fold, but, if Hoffa were out as president, the welcome mat would be on the AFL-CIO doorstep almost at once. The ILA has purified itself sufficiently to be welcomed back already, even though the Waterfront Commission of New York Harbor is still patrolling the docks.

COMMUNISM, JURISDICTIONAL DISPUTES, AND CIVIL RIGHTS

In other fields, there has been a consistent movement toward the exercise of more centralized authority without the full-circle turn that stopped the clean-union drive. Communist influence is virtually no problem in the AFL-CIO, and constitutional machinery is available to make sure it does not become one. In areas ranging from international affairs to community services, funds and personnel on a large scale are made through the federation.

Perhaps the most impressive progress toward assumption of leadership has been in the handling of jurisdictional disputes—

the issue that underlay the original split in 1935 and that seemed likely through most of the merged organization's early years to split it again. At the 1961 convention in Miami Beach, the warring craft and industrial unionists agreed to a constitutional change that has taken most of the heat out of this perennially troublesome issue.

It provides a system of mediation and arbitration on conflicts over which union is entitled to do what work, with final power of decision vested in the executive council. Elmer Brown, president of the International Typographical Union, cautioned the delegates that the plan represented "seven pages of sugar-coated demands that you surrender your autonomy." But this appeal to the revered shibboleth of autonomy had little persuasiveness for the convention. It approved the change overwhelmingly. Now the executive council, which used to spend 90 per cent of its time holding hearings on jurisdictional battles—with few ever settled to the satisfaction of either side—has few such disputes carried to it. Nevertheless, some building and maritime unions remain unhappy with the machinery and are determined to wreck it.

In the battle for greater civil rights, Meany and the central federation have also taken a role of leadership. This has stopped short of expelling any union for violating the AFL-CIO's constitutional ban against racial discrimination—a procedure Meany has ruled out as impractical and unjustified. But there has been increasingly intense pressure from Meany to make real the guarantees of equal opportunity for Negros. There has also been a strong federation position in favor of a federal fair-employment-practice law to apply sanctions against Jim Crow unions or employers. Unhappily, the fatuous decision of the executive council to withhold support from the mammoth civil-rights march on Washington last August has obscured the generally strong upper-echelon push for racial equality.

UNION ORGANIZATION

The places where the concept of federation is still far too weak are those which in many ways will be most determinative of organized labor's future vitality and influence. These have to do with organizing the unorganized, merging unions now active in the same or kindred fields and helping to shape basic policy in industries where strikes or economic demands impinge directly on the national health and safety.

If there is to be a genuine breakthrough in union organization, after fifteen years of stagnation, it will have to be through the emergence of new techniques and approaches to replace those that have proved so sterile in the postwar period. But the chances for success will be slim if the AFL-CIO cannot play in the implementation of such techniques the same dynamic role that was filled by the CIO in the late thirties. It must be co-ordinator, spur, and image—both for its affiliates and even more for the community.

The initial hope when the twenty-year war between the AFL and CIO ended was that the fused organization would make sensational forward strides in organizing. Some of its founders even envisaged a doubling of total membership within a decade. But the authority it had for conducting co-ordinated organizing drives, cutting across the lines of established affiliates, went almost unexercised until 1963.

Just as in the old AFL before the breakaway of the industrial unionists, unions that were doing virtually nothing to organize the unorganized in their fields blocked the entrance of the AFL-CIO by refusing to waive their paper rights or to agree to an outside determination—by the AFL-CIO or by an umpire—of who should get unorganized workers when and if they were organized.

This roadblock was finally pushed aside in Los Angeles

where all the federation unions—outside the distributive field— agreed to a co-ordinated organizing drive with the direct participation of the national federation. The enrollment of 7,000 new members was reported at the end of the first four months. This was a modest figure when considered against a potential of a half-million unorganized in the Los Angeles area, but at least it represented a thaw in the long impasse. Similar drives are now getting under way in the Baltimore-Washington area and a few other districts.

It would be delusive, however, to pretend that campaigns of this kind offer any substantial promise of over-all union growth in a period when automation is chopping away the traditional foundations of union strength and the percentage of organized workers in the total labor force is eroding. Without an assumption of primary responsibility by the AFL-CIO on a national basis, the road ahead for labor membership is mostly downhill.

A sense of priority would require more than the assignment of more money and manpower—or even than the creation of a labor university to train organizers and to develop organizing concepts calculated to convince professional and white-collar workers that unionism has something beneficial to offer them. The structure of unionism is out-of-date. It is becoming as archaic in the new technology as it was when the AFL formula for unionizing General Motors or United States Steel necessitated respect for the hegemony of scores of craft affiliates.

Purity of jurisdiction in the classic sense is no longer a problem; the line between craft and industrial unionism has become increasingly fuzzy. But the expectation that the merger would be paralleled by a considerable movement toward the voluntary amalgamation of unions with duplicating or related jurisdiction never was realized. Only a few minor groups have entered into mergers, usually as tributaries of the giants in their fields. But the big unions have not combined, even where their fields were virtually identical. At the founding convention, announcement was made by a pleased George Meany of the pro-spective merger of the Amalgamated Meat Cutters and the United Packinghouse Workers. Today these groups remain apart —mute symbols of the general ineffectuality of the movement toward one-unionliness.

In industry, however, the trend has been just the reverse. Big companies get bigger by merging with other big companies. They diversify into fields that bear no visible relation to their original fields of business. In this environment, only a fused organizational effort, spearheaded by the AFL-CIO and sub-divided in a dozen or fewer major organizing units, promises headway against the factors of apathy, even hostility, that now stand between labor and the unorganized.

PUBLIC-POLICY POSITIONS

A much more assertive role for the AFL-CIO also is necessary in the formulation of labor's position on matters affecting public policy. This means a much greater involvement in political activ-ity and a much clearer articulation of political goals. The fight for full employment and the conquest of poverty are so impera-tive to the survival of a strong labor movement that they are entitled to precedence over every activity except organizing— and even there they must have coequal status.

The most pressing threat to labor lies in the probability that the army of youngsters flooding into the job market will begin to identify union seniority and job-security programs as walls of exclusion, preventing them from finding a productive outlet for their talents. In their contracts with employers, unions under-standably give first attention to devising protections for the workers already on the job. Thus, the favorite defense against technological displacement is an attrition clause, under which no present employee will be jolted out of employment by the advent of more efficient technology. If the result of such clauses is to convince youngsters on the outside looking in that the union is conspiring to keep a solid grip for its own members on a dwindling total job roster, labor will find itself under an attack even more compelling than that which Negroes mounted to break down Jim Crow barriers in the building trades.

The obvious remedy lies in the creation on a national basis of brighter job opportunities for everybody. That is why the legislative aims and accomplishments of labor must assume an importance far beyond any present dimensions. The federation has become a major factor in political fund-raising and in getting out the vote, but the extent to which it has become a White House political appendage, rather than a vigorous initiator of independent policy, has stripped it of any notable effectiveness on Capitol Hill.

Labor's political image will depend inevitably on its success in curbing economic clashes that seem to pit labor against the community welfare—especially inasmuch as all of its political program is geared to the concept of labor as the most dedicated battler for legislation serving the total good. This is a particularly delicate field, because there is no area in which autonomy is more cherished by any union than the determination of its own bargaining and strike policy. Yet the long controversy over railroad work rules and the legislation President Kennedy felt obliged to recommend to head off a strike indicate how adversely all labor can be affected by the conduct of unions in a pivotal industry.

Interestingly, in the rail dispute, the brotherhoods made Meany their unofficial spokesman in presenting to Congress their proposal for averting a tie-up through extended time for collective bargaining under the eyes of a congressional watchdog committee. Meany also served as a presidential fact-finder in one phase of the dispute—a role he has been called on to play with increasing frequency. In fact, in the conflict between flight engineers and pilots over the third seat in the cockpit of jet planes, the President designated the AFL-CIO head as an arbitrator.

It is not unthinkable, in a period when the effectiveness of the strike weapon is coming more and more into question in some key industries, that the federation chain of command might be altered in ways that would give its top leaders more voice in the peaceful adjustment of disputes that might invite reprisals against all labor. This thesis of interdependence underlies the constitutional clauses covering corruption, communism, and other issues in which the federation is made the custodian of the good name of labor generally. Perhaps one outcome of the bitter railroad battle will be the adoption of a somewhat similar approach to issues of economic warfare.

The School Men in Missouri

NICHOLAS A. MASTERS, ROBERT H. SALISBURY, AND THOMAS H. ELIOT

If you ask an insider how public school policy is made in Missouri, the answer will go something like this: there isn't much conflict on school questions. In the legislature nobody can be against the schools. Besides, the school people have one of the strongest lobbies in the state. They can get most anything they ask for—provided there's enough money to pay for it. The speaker may feel that he has described the process fully enough to satisfy any reasonable inquiry. But although the statement is accurate as far as it goes, it requires much elaboration to provide a full picture of how education policy is made in Missouri. Who are "the school people"? Why are they so influential? Indeed, how influential are they, if they must work within the limitations of the available money?

In 1959, Missouri ranked forty-ninth in public school revenue from state and local sources as a percentage of personal income. The state ranked eighteenth in per capita income but thirty-eighth in per capita expenditure for local schools. Missouri has no state-wide teacher tenure protection. The politics of public schools includes what is not done as well as what is.

The following analysis attempts to demonstrate that an ap-

From *State Politics and the Public Schools: An Exploratory Analysis,* New York: Alfred Knopf, 1964, pp. 12–39. Reprinted by permission of the authors. Some footnotes omitted.

parent paradox is nevertheless a valid picture of education policy-making; that the Missouri school men are indeed influential, though their achievements seem unimpressive when compared with Michigan and many other states.

In Missouri, the school men are organized in one major group, the Missouri State Teachers Association (MSTA), which defines Missouri's school needs and presents them to the state legislature. However, the proposals MSTA makes to the legislature are adjusted to the state's political traditions. The Missouri political system militates against large state expenditures and high service levels. It is what we shall call a low-pressure system. Within such a system, the MSTA can get what it asks for only if it does not ask for too much. This chapter describes the MSTA and its operations, explores the political system within which MSTA functions, and finally considers some specific cases involving education issues both of local and state-wide importance.

THE SCHOOL MEN IN MISSOURI

The Missouri State Teachers Association holds a virtual monopoly over the process of articulating the policy demands of the public school professionals. This group alone presents demands to the state legislature and presses for their passage. For example, in Missouri, teachers colleges do not play as direct or prominent a role as they do in some other states, notably New Jersey. The University of Missouri's College of Education, the several state colleges, and the private universities of the state rarely become involved in legislative struggles over elementary and secondary school policy. Whatever influence these professional educators have on school policy is exerted through their contacts with MSTA, which we discuss below. Moreover, the process of seeking legislative support for higher education in the state is

quite different from that in which the public schools are involved; different interests are active and different legislators are
concerned.

School administrators and school board officials do not constitute *major* separate interests in Missouri as they do in Michigan and Illinois. The administrators belong to MSTA, which represents them and in effect controls them. The officials have their
own association, but rarely try to change policy through independent action. Instead they devote most of their efforts to supporting MSTA proposals.[1] Nor do the various lay groups interested in education—such as the PTA's[2] or the State League of
Women Voters—act as innovators.[3] Finally, the State Board of
Education and the Department of Education it governs carefully
avoid *direct* contact with the legislature's pending policy matters.

The teachers union is not as yet a significant participant in
the state political arena. Since 1961, however, it has gained membership, particularly in St. Louis. MSTA leadership is concerned
about the growing union strength and the possible threat it poses
to MSTA hegemony. Nevertheless, since most state education

---

[1]The Missouri Association of School Boards was organized in 1936, and
since 1953 has employed a full-time secretary. The association attempts to
provide services—handbooks, in-service training, conferences, etc.—for school
boards. It has not attempted to influence policy except as a supportive
group for MSTA proposals.

[2]The Missouri Congress of Parents and Teachers consists of over 2,000 units
with a membership of nearly 200,000. Its office is located in the MSTA
building in Columbia, and its political efforts are similarly linked.

[3]Private citizens' groups were very instrumental in generating enthusiasm
for a state-supported junior college program in 1961. This program did not
attract much direct interest from existing school groups, however, and so an
unusual citizen effort was required in order to make any political headway.
In other words, there were no important professional teacher groups with a
stake in developing a junior college program. If the program was to get
support, it had to come from lay groups. Public elementary and secondary
school programs *do* attract constant and intense interest from professional
school men, and this leaves little opportunity for lay groups to exercise
influence.

decisions still are directed primarily at outstate school systems, where MSTA remains strong, the challenge of the union is minor. Perhaps its principal effect is to nudge MSTA leaders into more vigorous action in behalf of state aid.

To some extent, all these groups may be important in feeding information into the policy-making system. The University of Missouri College of Education conducts studies that may eventually be translated into policy demands. School men in the various localities do not ignore laymen's interest in the schools. They are important as supportive interests, backing up MSTA demands and giving them a broader base. MSTA sometimes adjusts its demands to assure this broad support, too, but there is no discernible pattern of overt influence leading from these groups to the MSTA and thence to the legislature. Rather, the MSTA serves as *the* agency which articulates the policy demands of the school people *ab initio* and presents these demands to governmental policy-makers. Insofar as a separate role in the process can be identified for other groups, it consists of contributing to the climate of education opinion—within which MSTA develops specific policy demands. Thus any discussion of the "school men" in Missouri state politics leads almost exclusively to a discussion of the MSTA.

The MSTA and Its Strategy

The Missouri State Teachers Association was founded in 1856. Its first constitution proclaimed its purposes "to promote the sacred interests of education by uniting the different members, advancing their mutual improvement, and elevating the profession to its just intellectual and moral influence in the community." This organization grew slowly until after the turn of the century, but between 1907 and 1923 the membership jumped from 667 to 21,303. In recent years, virtually all public school teachers and professional school administrators in the state have joined, and it now has more than 30,000 members.

From the beginning, the MSTA has sought to influence legislation and to work for constitutional amendments of advantage to public school development. The short official centenial history of MSTA points with pride to and claims at least partial credit for a substantial list of accomplishments. Some of the principal items may be noted:

the establishment and support of state normal schools and of the College of Education at the University of Missouri;

the establishment and improvement of certification requirements for teachers;

the development of compulsory school attendance legislation and lengthening of the school year; the extension of kindergarten, junior college, and adult education programs; programs for physically and mentally handicapped; and free textbook legislation;

the reestablishment of the office of county superintendent after its abolition in 1874 and the raising of its standards of performances;

the development of legislation to encourage larger school district units;

the establishment of an appointed bipartisan state board of education, replacing the elected state superintendent of schools;

increased financial support for education at the state level and support for measures making it easier to finance schools at the local level; provision for retirement benefits for teachers; provision for continuing contract law to give some degree of job security to teachers.

Some of these programs may not owe their approval solely to the efforts of the MSTA, but the organization, except perhaps in the area of teacher welfare, has had an impressive record of legislative accomplishment.

MSTA influence in Missouri stems partly from the organization's ability to adapt its demands and its tactics to the political context in which it operates. (This context will be examined in detail at a later point.) In addition, however, the organization's effectiveness results in part from internal cohesion. Its internal structure and operation are therefore significant.

The basic units of MSTA are the 278 community associations composed of groups of 25 or more teachers and administrators in particular districts or groups of districts throughout the state. These community associations attempt to maintain cohesion among the various groups associated with public school problems at the local level and are the basis for sending delegates (one for each 25 members or major fraction thereof) to the state Assembly of Delegates.

The Assembly of Delegates is the official policy-making body of the MSTA. As with any large group, however, a relatively small nucleus of members makes policy decisions and exerts influence. A part of this nucleus is the Executive Committee, which is composed of the annually elected president and vice-president plus one representative from each of ten districts. The district members are nominated by district associations, of which five are organized around the state teachers colleges, with St. Louis, St. Louis County, Kansas City, St. Joseph, and South Central Missouri forming the other five. The district associations are otherwise autonomous from the state organization but their activities are coordinated through the state office of MSTA.

The Executive Committee is the administrative agency of MSTA, issuing publications, controlling expenditures and membership, assisting local community associations, serving as a committee on teacher welfare, appointing all other standing and special committees, receiving their reports and passing them on to the Assembly of Delegates. The Executive Committee thus occupies a crucial position in shaping the MSTA's policy recommendations. Through its appointment of a legislative committee and special committees for major public policy questions such as the foundation program, it helps to energize the campaigns of the MSTA.

A substantial portion of the concrete recommendations for legislative action emerge from the work of the committees which the Executive Committee appoints. They reflect the diverse local experience of the members and work closely with the Executive

Committee, the MSTA staff, and educators in the state colleges and universities. These committees are the formal mechanism through which more or less standard professional education recommendations, adapted to the Missouri scene, are prepared.

The Executive Committee also appoints the staff of the MSTA. The staff is another major locus of influence within the organization. Four professional staff members plus an office staff occupy the MSTA headquarters across from the University of Missouri campus in Columbia. The professionals are all products of Missouri, taking their formal training at Missouri universities and acquiring teaching and school administrative experience entirely in outstate—or rural—Missouri. All four have long experience in their present positions, ranging from fourteen to twenty-three years of service. Indeed, since 1915 when the first full-time executive secretary of MSTA was appointed, only three men have held that position. The present incumbent has served in this capacity since 1941.

Continuity in office and the completeness of identification with Missouri contribute greatly to the success of the MSTA staff in getting legislative results. For while the Executive Committee and the MSTA membership generally participate in formulating policy demands, it is inevitably the full-time professional staff that carries on the day to day legislative work. That the legislators regard the MSTA as the most effective lobby in the state is due in no small measure to their feeling that Everett Keith, Executive Secretary of the MSTA, is the most skillful lobbyist.

What are the bases of Keith's and the MSTA's influence? What is his role; how is it defined? What are its limits? Certainly one basis is the considerable influence the school people are able to muster with respect to individual legislators. The MSTA officials are well situated to contact the teachers and administrators, school boards, PTA's and others interested in education in each county of the state, alert them to school issues, and successfully exhort them to contact their representatives. Members and friends of MSTA are typically persons of prominence and influence in their local communities and legislators naturally treat their views with respect. The deference given their views on education issues is partly that accorded to leading citizens actively concerned with the issues before the legislature. MSTA's supporters are not simply composed of leading citizens, however. The school people have a special tactical advantage which most lay education interest groups do not possess. They have a direct interest in school legislation, not merely an altruistic concern. Accordingly, they are given a more respectful hearing by legislators. It is an observable fact that legislators are usually more sympathetic to "realistic" (i.e., self-interested) claimants to public funds than to groups which they regard as do-gooders.

More than that, the school people are professionals, and their claims for legislative support are made in a context of professional expertise. Over the years MSTA has worked to develop a professional reputation for teachers and public school officials, and consequently, MSTA legislative recommendations are regarded as based on expert opinion in the public school field. The MSTA staff works closely with the University of Missouri College of Education, the State Department of Education, and other professionals to assure that MSTA proposals embody the common thinking of all the professional educators. MSTA is a part of the National Education Association, and its proposals usually follow the national pattern of professional educators' views, thus reinforcing the appearance of expertise.

Nothing would be more damaging to MSTA's standing as an expert than to have rival experts appear on the legislative scene. Therefore, unity among the various educational groups—school boards, county superintendents, PTA's, etc.—is a high priority objective for the MSTA. MSTA leaders take great care to avoid actions that will result in divisions in the education lobby. As we shall see later, in 1961 MSTA shied away from taking stands that might alienate school boards or county superintendents. Indeed it seems fair to say that a major reason Missouri has no teacher tenure or minimum salary laws is that MSTA has not wished to alienate its school board supporters in behalf of its classroom teacher constituency by recommending such proposals to the legislature. Unity strengthens MSTA's bargaining position, but also imposes limits on its objectives.

Avoiding local issues and local quarrels is another rule which governs MSTA's legislative objectives. We shall explore below the process of resolving local education issues in the state arena. We should note here, however, that MSTA stays away from these issues as much as possible. MSTA has adopted the position that local issues may involve local factional quarrels, and if the organization were to take a position, siding with one faction against another, it might jeopardize its state-wide activities. The quest for unity among educational interests thus requires MSTA to confine itself to state-wide issues only. Unity enables the MSTA to present its recommendations as the products of detached, objective study, supported by all the professional experts in the state, and in addition, supported by a large organization which, if necessary, can mobilize considerable grass-roots pressure on individual legislators.

This strong bargaining position is further reinforced by MSTA's great symbolic advantage: namely, its position as spokesman for improving the public schools. Few legislators feel secure enough to challenge that symbol directly. "Who can be against the schools?" said one legislator. "That's like opposing motherhood or the flag." During the 1961 legislative session, Republicans frequently vied with Democrats in House debate to see which party could establish the greater reputation as champion of the schools. After one morning's partisan debate, for instance, one legislator laughingly expressed it this way: "Well, another hard morning fighting for the kiddies."

No one opposes schools openly. No one in the legislature

opposes improving them. Thus no one openly resists MSTA. No one in the legislature opposes the *idea* of increasing state financial support for public schools. However, public money is in short supply in Missouri as elsewhere, and its scarcity constitutes the strongest limitation on MSTA effectiveness.

"Where is the money coming from?" is a frequent negative reaction to many legislative proposals. When public school issues involve state expenditure, MSTA is faced with its most demanding legislative task. Broadly, the organization and its leaders respond in two ways to the problem of money.

First, MSTA scales down its demands for support to "reasonable" levels, hoping to minimize conflict over school issues. Keith and his associates are fully conscious of the gap between the Missouri school aid level and that of, say, neighboring Illinois. (Keith also points out that by comparison with other neighboring states—Arkansas, Oklahoma, or Nebraska, for example—Missouri's record is much more impressive.) Nevertheless, rather than press for state aid at an abstractly desirable level, MSTA has sought to pitch the formula for aid at the highest level that present or immediately prospective state revenues will support, assuming no *major* shift in existing patterns of allocation of state money. Missouri's political culture includes a powerful tradition against asking for more money than the revenue picture comfortably allows. This means that one agency should not seek money at the expense of another. It also means that an agency or interest group should ordinarily wait for additional revenue to be available rather than try to lead its own campaign for tax-increase proposals.

The two-step increase in the foundation program exemplifies how this norm constrains MSTA, Missouri's most powerful lobby. Having secured authorization for increased state aid in 1959, MSTA attempted to finance the increase through an earmarked boost in the sales tax. This failed, however, and MSTA was forced to wait until 1961 when, from a variety of sources, increased revenue was available to finance the Foundation Program increase.

A second response of MSTA to the problem of money is to support all gubernatorial requests for tax increases. Almost all of the requests for increased taxes that have any serious chance of legislative passage are presented by the governor. MSTA has supported all such proposals in recent years as a matter of policy. As Keith put it, "We'll take any live (tax) program," and the governor's program is the only one "alive." In Keith's judgment, this approach is the best MSTA can do to maximize the chances of having enough revenue to finance an increase in state aid. In 1961, for example, the status of the governor's revenue program was described at the head of each MSTA Legislative Bulletin, and the importance of these tax measures to full financing of the authorized state aid increase was regularly noted. Moreover, MSTA agreed to delay pushing certain other legislative requests until after passage of the governor's revenue measures was assured.

The MSTA's policy of supporting all of the governor's proposals for increased taxes is a critical factor in its relationships with other major interest groups in the state. Whenever MSTA supports a sales or cigarette tax boost, labor groups oppose it. If, as in 1961, MSTA backs a proposal to begin withholding of state income taxes, business groups oppose it. Partly as a result of these variations, MSTA does not have any strong durable alliances with nonschool groups. Keith does not regard these groups as enemies. None of them would or could risk the stigma of being anti-school. But MSTA's dependence upon increasing state revenues by whatever means are most readily available requires the organization to retain its freedom of action. Hence it forms no lasting alliances on a *quid pro quo* basis.

The MSTA's self-imposed policy of not attempting to obtain more money for schools unless it is apparent that increased revenues are forthcoming, does not preclude its seeking objectives that require positive legislative action, which may eventually cost substantial amounts of money. This means that Keith and his associates are often trying to buck the system. Missouri is a low tax, low service state in almost every area of state activity, and to change this substantially, in education or any other policy area, requires skillful handling. The policy is to capitalize on any opening the political system offers for increased appropriations. True, Keith and the MSTA might choose to fight the inertia and fiscal conservatism of the system in a direct frontal assault, utilizing the newspapers and the other mass media in an effort to mobilize such massive public backing that demands for educational policy would be irresistable. But the only time in recent years that they adopted this strategy was in the campaign for the foundation program in the period from 1952 to 1956. MSTA organized a citizen's committee and undertook a broad public campaign to mobilize extensive popular support to increase financial aid for public education.

The situation is different in Missouri when the desired legislative result involves a more modest change; and resistance, while present perhaps, is not so strong nor so strategically located as it was in 1953, when the governor himself opposed the MSTA's program. In such circumstances, Keith and MSTA mobilize their own specialized grass-roots support but do not try to extend that support very far beyond their own membership. Legislative Bulletins to MSTA members, phone calls to counties whose representatives are wavering, speech materials to legislators and other political figures, and other similar tactics are employed for this kind of campaign. In these circumstances, unity within the school men constituency is of special importance. MSTA relies heavily on school administrators, school board members, and county superintendents as contacts in communicating constituency sentiments to individual legislators. In order to maintain these contacts in good order, MSTA must and does avoid exerting itself on behalf of some recommendations which the classroom teachers or college educators might regard as obvious articles of faith. Teacher tenure and proposals to eliminate the office of county superintendent of schools are good examples.

Although MSTA uses both the general public campaign and the more limited grass-roots pressure, the most characteristic way in which Keith and MSTA seek legislative support is by working *with* the Missouri political system rather than against it. "Quietly" is the key to this process. Keith does not usually try to pressure legislators. He does not buttonhole them in the corridors, nor cajole and flatter them in the hotels. He does not testify at committee hearings (although MSTA officers and MSTA-designated experts often do). Instead he uses a more subtle approach. He sits in the back of the committee room, or at the rear of the legislative gallery, or in the offices of the most important legislators, talking with those whom he feels can help the most. He and his staff draft in bill form four or five of their key proposals at each session, and they provide technical data and advice on many other bills. MSTA often serves as an informal staff to the education committees of the legislature.

Keith's contacts with individual legislators are highly selective. He makes no attempt to get broad coverage and rarely tries to persuade the uncommitted or to convert opponents. He relies primarily on the devoted supporters of MSTA objectives, who hold such key positions as chairman of the House Education Committee. Keith's friends are, for the most part, outstate Democrats. The MSTA does not reject Republicans; its key legislation always has bipartisan sponsorship. But in the last several years there have been so few Republicans, relatively, that no group is likely to expend great effort cultivating their support. Moreover, on the whole, Democrats are regarded as somewhat more sympathetic to most MSTA objectives than are Republicans. Such hard-core opposition to public expenditure as there is in Missouri —and this means opposition to MSTA—is largely among outstate Republicans.

Keith makes little effort to cultivate support among metropolitan representatives either. MSTA is less influential in the urban areas and could bring less effective grass-roots pressure on urban legislators. The urban districts have less need of state aid and so give less support to MSTA recommendations. Moreover, there is some degree of suspicion that, if aroused, metropolitan representatives might be more responsive to parochial school interests than to MSTA. We found no evidence of attempts by parochial school groups to influence the legislature on major public school questions, but the high proportion of Catholics and Lutherans in the large cities makes MSTA chary of working up interest in state school issues in St. Louis and Kansas City. Keith is content to prevent serious overt opposition from the cities, while seeking his active proponents outstate.

In this posture and in the quiet tactics employed to implement it, Keith and his colleagues adhere fully to the norms of the Missouri political culture. Ae we noted earlier, the MSTA staff is entirely drawn from outstate Missouri experience. It is not surprising that they have chosen primarily to try to get what they can with a minimum of agitation or conflict rather than attempt broader public campaigns in behalf of larger objectives. The latter strategy would surely require MSTA to hire new personnel in place of Keith and his associates, for they are as much a part of the culture as the legislature they work with so closely.

"THE INTERESTS" AND PUBLIC SCHOOL POLITICS

We have suggested that the tactics of moderation in behalf of limited objectives characterize MSTA activity in Missouri. This mode of activity seeks to minimize conflict over education issues and thereby get legislative results. A *priori* judgment might seem to indicate that other groups in the state would be embroiled in more severe conflicts. Specifically, an urban and rural cleavage of some sort might be anticipated, since these interests are so often thought to engage in constant battle; rival economic groups, each staking out claims and vigorously competing with each other, would fit the expected pattern. If such conflicts occurred with any frequency in Missouri, they would surely affect public school policy, but the relationships of these putative groups and education issues are not what we might anticipate. Let us consider each of them to see why.

Urban-Rural Splits and the Local Unity Norm

In many states, including Missouri, it is often alleged that rural interests dominate the state arena to the disadvantage of urban interests. Specifically, St. Louis newspapers often attribute the defeat of bills proposed by the St. Louis School Board to unsympathetic rural legislators. Statistical and qualitative analysis alike have shown that this myth does not account for much that occurs or, at most, grossly oversimplifies situations where outward appearances suggest rural domination. The myth assumes that rural interests are substantially united in opposition to equally unified urban interests, whereas in fact neither grouping ordinarily exhibits the assumed unity. Legislators themselves stoutly deny the validity of the myth. Rather, in Missouri, the norm to which legislators insist they conform calls for legislators to support the request of a local delegation when it unites in support of a legislative proposal affecting only the local area. If the local group is not united, the other legislators will not approve the requested change, refusing to get involved in local quarrels. A variety of local public school issues is dealt with according to the norm of local unity.

Most local proposals emanate from the large urban areas: St. Louis City, St. Louis County, and Kansas City. However, almost any area of the state may have a special problem requiring special treatment of some kind or other, and it is this potential need for reciprocity which gives the norm such force in the legislature. It follows from the norm that all urban problems which are framed into legislative requests by the St. Louis or Kansas City administrations are treated as *local* problems, not *urban* problems. Thus, if the urban delegation agrees on the proposal, outstate legislators will support it. Precisely what "unity of the local delegation" requires is somewhat hazy. It does not require unanimity; the defection of an intransigent representative or two can be ignored. It does not require bipartisan agreement; a Republican dissenter in a predominantly Democratic delegation cannot kill the bill. Local disagreement can sometimes be minimized, too, through an intensive campaign beyond the local area by the proponents of a measure. But the norm does generally govern. Local interests lose when they are divided, win when they are united.

Traditional reliance on the local agreement formula serves to minimize overt urban-rural dichotomies. "If the St. Louis delegation can agree on a bill, we'll pass it," is a sentiment that has been voiced in Jefferson City for nearly a century. It does not, of course, eliminate all country-city conflicts. There remains a distinction in perspective and value between the modal urban legislator and the modal rural legislator. They are concerned with different problems and look to different bases of support. City legislators are regarded, accurately for the most part, as primarily interested in two kinds of questions, those involving labor and those affecting the city's party organizations to which city legislators owe their election. Neither interest is of much concern to outstate representatives. The latter are concerned by the general lack of local resources in outstate Missouri and the consequent dependence upon state programs of aid for highways, schools, welfare services, and the like.

This difference in interests is reinforced by differences in ethnic and religious background—as well as speech patterns and oratorical flourishes. Each grouping views the other with a certain suspicion, a presumption that "the country boys" will not understand city problems and vice versa. For instance, school men inside the legislature and out feel that wealthy St. Louis County has little sympathy for state programs that aid rural schools with funds raised largely in urban areas. St. Louis newspapers, on the other hand, often blame the defeat of local St. Louis bills on rural opposition.

To summarize, it seems fair to say that rural interests practically never unite to oppose united urban interests. Rather, there is a kind of presumptive urban-rural difference which must frequently be negotiated away in order to enact urban legislation. The local unity formula assists this negotiation by providing an automatic basis of alignment for rural interests: pro when there is unity among the affected urban legislators; anti when there is not.

We have already noted that MSTA stays out of local issues. The local unity formula also has a conservative effect which reinforces the general Missouri system. If urban legislative proposals require urban unity, then a substantial area of public policy cannot be materially altered except by first achieving broad agreement. If the change is a major one, for example, broad expansion of local financial resources, it will take much time and energy to achieve the necessary local unity. This slows down change in public policy and it may sometimes appear in roll call votes as rural opposition to the programs retards enactment, for the bulk of the votes against the measure will come from outstate. Clearly, rural legislators could have voted for the proposed changes, and greater rural resistance to urban programs cannot entirely be ignored. On the whole, however, in Missouri conservatism or inaction with respect to urban problems is based on intra-urban disputes rather than urban-rural conflicts. The outstaters too have local matters for which they will seek legislative approval and invoke the same local agreement norm.

Thus, although a certain amount of mutual suspicion may be present between urban and rural representatives, this will rarely blossom into overt urban-rural conflict over public school questions. We will consider some examples below.

St. Louis and Kansas City

Most of the "local" school issues that develop in Missouri have to do with two major cities in the state, St. Louis and Kansas City. As we have noted, the internal politics of the local area determines the outcome of these local proposals in the legislature, so we must look briefly at the intra-urban conflict in the two cities.

Both cities have developed political systems in which the party organizations are largely separated from the policy-making administrative leaders of the city governments. The local politicians concentrate their attention on the patronage offices of the city, or in the case of Kansas City, the city and county. Their concern with policy matters is marginal. They rarely succeed in controlling the policy-making offices of mayor or, in Kansas City, city manager. Both cities have home rule charters which help insulate the policy-making offices from the pressures of patronage demands by providing for merit system protection of municipal employees and, in Kansas City, by establishing the city manager system. Neither home rule provision, however, controls the so-called "county offices." In St. Louis these offices—recorder, license collector, collector of revenue, etc.—are required and governed by state statute, even though St. Louis is not part of any county. In Kansas City, the county offices are part of the Jackson County governmental structure. In both cases they are the primary sources of patronage for the local party organizations.

In both cities, especially St. Louis, quite different social groupings have come to cluster around the two sets of offices. The policy-making agencies are associated with the daily newspapers, downtown business interests, and the middle-class citizens, while, in keeping with urban political tradition, the ward politicians draw their support from locally active labor groups, Negroes, and other lower income strata.

The politician-party organization grouping in the cities is intensely interested in participating in the state arena, where decisions are made concerning the salaries and other perquisites of the jobs which are their lifeblood. Moreover, the state offers supplements to the meager patronage available locally, including the legislative seats themselves. On the other hand, the policy-making agencies of the cities are less interested in state affairs. They decide locally, under their own charter authority, many of the issues which concern them most. The federal authorities make other substantial decisions.

For example, the state makes few decisions as important to the city of St. Louis as those which Washington makes on urban renewal. To be sure, on occasion a city administration has important policy objectives that can only be achieved with state legislative help, and both city administrations present legislative programs embracing both major and minor items to each session of the legislature. When they approach the legislature, however, the city administrations are in the position of any other respectable interest-group claimant. They cannot assume the support of the city legislative delegation and must bargain for whatever support they receive. With greater interest in the arena and control over the machinery of nomination and election, the politicians dominate the selection of state legislators, and the latter have a primary obligation to represent the party organization interests in Jefferson City. In the same way, state executive officials pay closer heed to party groups with votes than to policy-oriented city officials who have no direct control over blocs of votes in primary contests. Of course, policy-makers and politicians do not inevitably disagree with each other. On many issues harmony prevails. Yet there are always differences: in interest, in base of support, and in personal values; and these differences must be negotiated away before urban unity can be achieved.

Thus it is relatively unusual to have an urban interest that really unites the city delegation with the city administration. The latter can usually get city representatives to introduce and speak for its measures, but it is likely to find indifference at best and often resistance emanating from local interests that oppose the request. Even opposition of modest local strength, provided it has contact with the politician grouping, may be able to kill the measure by splitting the city delegation and thereby evoking outstate opposition—in keeping with the local unity norm. The local unity norm is the standard mechanism on which the legislature relies to resolve local issues requiring state legislative action. This category includes a considerable number of public schools issues, especially issues affecting St. Louis or Kansas City. Let us look at some examples from the 1961 session.

A relatively simple example of the local unity rule in relation to education occurred in 1961 with House Bill 671 and Senate Bill 197. Both bills revised the procedures for annexing territory to the Kansas City school district. The first specified that territory to be annexed must be adjacent to the Kansas City district. The second specified "adjoining," not "adjacent." The latter bill would have permitted somewhat easier annexation. The two versions reflected a controversy between the Kansas City school district and one nearby. House Bill 671 was sponsored by a representative whose district included an area adjacent to Kansas City, and he hoped to forestall Senate Bill 197 with his bill. This demonstration of disagreement among Jackson County Democrats was enough to kill both bills.

Senate Bill 96 was designed to improve the St. Louis City public school retirement system as recommended by the St. Louis Public School Retirement Board. It had no opposition within the city and the city legislators all supported it. It passed both houses unanimously.

A group of bills and constitutional amendments affecting both St. Louis City and St. Louis County also received unanimous approval eventually. The major one of these proposals authorized St. Louis County to levy a tax of $1 per $100 assessed valuation, with the revenues to be apportioned among the county's 27 school districts on the basis of number of students in average daily attendance. This equalization tax was regarded as a step toward boosting the resources available to the poorer and more crowded suburban districts. The legislators from St. Louis County had met several times before and during the early stages of the session and were all in agreement. They all accepted the equalization tax as a way of helping poor or overcrowded suburban districts without giving up local school-district autonomy. Some of the outstate legislators who were especially cognizant of school problems resented the proposed tax measure. One said:

> These rich St. Louis County people never want to help rural Missouri, and here when they could go ahead and reorganize [into fewer, larger districts] and get the same result, the way we have outstate, they won't do it. Hell, we wanted to keep our little districts too but we combined. Why can't they? Then they wouldn't need this tax and it would be cheaper all around. But it's their money, I guess.

So the norm of local unity prevailed. The resolution calling for a vote on the constitutional amendment required for equalization passed the House unanimously.

In the Senate two other amendments were added to make a package. One of these raised the levy which the St. Louis City Board of Education could raise without a referendum from $.89 to $1, thus placing the city on a par with other districts in the state. St. Louis City legislators were not enthusiastic about combining their proposal with those of the county, but they finally agreed. A second proposal provided for an increase from $.35 to $.50 in the basic levy which St. Louis County might raise for general operating purposes. County representatives had developed the required agreement on this measure early in the session and had no objection to combining it with the school tax. The final package won unanimous approval in both the Senate and the House.

Several bills affecting the St. Louis City school system illustrate the relationship among the school board there, the political divisions in the city, and the state legislative arena. We have spoken of the division in St. Louis between the policy-making offices and the political offices and the socio-economic groups associated with the offices. Some of the potential for more direct conflict which this division of interest contains has been realized with respect to control of the St. Louis Board of Education. The St. Louis school system, like that in Kansas City, is governed directly by state law rather than under home rule charter provisions. This has meant that through state legislative influence, the politicians in St. Louis could use the school system as a source of patronage. They did so by keeping the building and maintenance department separate from the instruction program and using the former for patronage purposes, leaving educational policy decisions largely to the professional staff. Control of the school board was essential to maintain the patronage control, but until recently the ward organization had had little trouble in dominating the nonpartisan, at-large election of board members.

Periodically during the past decade, the metropolitan papers and other policy-oriented interests have agitated against politician control of the school board. The central theme of this agitation has been unit control, placing building and maintenance functions under control of a single superintendent, thus eliminating the administrative separation that was viewed as the major protective covering of the patronage opportunities.

With unit control as the battle cry, blue ribbon tickets were formed on several occasions to compete with the politician slate for board of education posts. After several defeats, the blue ribbon group won enough seats so that by April 1961, they controlled a majority of the board and it was, for the first time, actively committed to unit control. The board hired a lobbyist, himself a former legislator, and sought more eagerly than in other years to get favorable action on its proposed bill.

The board had another advantage over former times. Many of the city ward leaders had concluded that whatever patronage had been gained in the building and maintenance department was not worth the effort. The concentrated fire of the newspapers, grand jury investigations of board members (one member was convicted for exploiting school employees for private purposes), and otherwise tarnished reputations had convinced many political leaders in the city that for them the administrative independence of the building and maintenance division was a wasting asset.

The bill for unit control was sent to the House Committee on Governmental Organization rather than the House Education Committee. Three influential St. Louis representatives served on this committee, whereas only one city member was on the Education Committee, and he was completely inactive. Thus local unity could be tested more accurately in the former committee's action. The committee voted 5–4 to recommend that the bill not pass, with the three St. Louisians joining two other Democrats against it. The reasons for rejecting the bill were more than the traditional desire to protect patronage. As we have noted, the legislators were losing enthusiasm for the jobs involved. They did fear, however, that the blue ribbon board would drastically change the present non-teaching personnel. The board was characterized as "Republican." It might attempt to oust all Democrats and replace them with deserving Republicans. Actually the recently elected school board, though chosen as a nonpartisan ticket, contained one acknowledged Republican and some others whose political affiliation was held suspect by Democratic leaders.

This fear was reinforced by the proposed unit control bill which affirmed the principle of merit system protection for nonteaching employees but did not spell out the procedures for implementing it. The city legislators and the public school employees union wanted the tenure of these employees protected by legislation, not left up to the "Republican" board. Consequently, they opposed the unit control bill. Instead they backed a separate bill to provide merit protection for nonteaching personnel similar to the tenure law for teachers in St. Louis. After differences between the union and the school board had been compromised, this bill passed the legislature almost unanimously. A last-ditch effort was made to get the reorganization bill through by introducing it in the Senate. This bill did come out of committee successfully, but not until June 9, much too late to get through the rest of the legislative process by the constitutional deadline of June 30, even if the St. Louis legislators had all supported it.[4]

These examples illustrate something of the nature of urban interests in the state legislature as they are related to public school questions and suggest the ways in which other legislators respond. Urban residents do not present a united grouping with the voting potential to exert substantial power in the state arena. Instead, they are divided into two distinct groupings with different sets of interests. Sometimes they are in direct conflict, but even when there is no incompatibility, they must negotiate and renegotiate whatever agreement they may reach on any given

[4]After losing the legislative battle over unit control, the St. Louis Board of Education decided they could achieve most of their intent by administrative action. The board designated the superintendent of instruction as the chief officer of the school system and required other officials, including the head of the building and maintenance department, to report to him. This action, combined with the act providing tenure and merit system protection for nonteaching personnel, may be expected to eliminate most of the remaining political controversy (involving the ward organizations) from the St. Louis school system.

issue. The other legislators wait for an "agreed bill" to be presented to them, and in the absence of local agreement, they say "No!"

Economic Interests

Missouri is often characterized as a conservative state. The principal evidence of conservatism cited is the relatively low level of taxes and services in the state. This evidence is often accompanied by charges that a rather generalized "they"—a combination of economic interests—run things for their own benefit and prevent the enactment of desirable programs. Conspiratorial theories of this kind are difficult to prove or disprove. However, our inquiry leads us to the conclusion that no pervasive conspiracy or alliance can be said to dominate the political process in Missouri and that, as is often the case, conspiratorial theories are of little use in explaining how policy is made.

Missouri may be a low tax, low service state, but it also has been relatively free of anti-labor legislation, agitation of rightist fringe groups, and other phenomena often associated with conservatism. There is no state minimum wage law, but neither is there a right to work law. Missouri legislators do not investigate "un-American activities." A state with a considerable Southern tradition, Missouri has nevertheless established an active Human Rights Commission and in 1961 passed an FEPC law. Rather than conservative, it might better be described as low-pressure. We have said that MSTA's activities are adapted to the low-pressure norms and expectations. So are the activities of the major economic interest groups in the state. Each group tends to seek a narrowly defined program calling for marginal adjustments in policy with as little fuss as possible.

Missouri presents no particularly unique combination of economic groups. Railroads and trucking companies, oil companies and highway contractors, Farm Bureau and Missouri Farmers Association, utilities, small loan companies, banks, insurance companies, and a host of other business and economic groups have stakes at issue in the state political arena. Similarly, a wide variety of labor unions participate vigorously in efforts to improve job security through state legislation. Two related generalizations apply to all these groups. None of them is large enough or, if large, sufficiently concerned to dominate the others. Secondly, none of these groups is actively interested in more than a few issues among all those under consideration at any given time.

When it considers matters of importance to these groups, the legislature may face a situation in which two rival economic interests are competing directly over a legislative proposal. Thus, oil interests battle contractors over gasoline tax increases, or railroads fight truckers over truck weight and height limitations. A second type of situation will find a particular economic group —for instance, dairy farmers—seeking legislative assistance and facing no particular opposition. Still a third pattern, and far rarer than the first two, would involve a broader alliance of groups in conflict with a rival alliance. Thus, when labor unions joined together in support of minimum wage legislation, they were opposed by a combination of farm and business groups. This kind of situation calls for expression of the traditional liberal versus conservative sentiments, and the political speeches as well as the final votes reveal the broad political convictions of the legislators and their constituencies.

But such issues are rare, and, being rare, do not govern the tone of the legislature. Neither the rhetoric nor the voting alignments on one issue will necessarily carry over to the next. Whatever alliances are formed are apt to be *ad hoc* rather than all-purpose. The broad-based economic groups—the Chamber of Commerce, the Associated Industries of Missouri, or the State Labor Council—find that their influence varies in some inverse proportion to the number of issues in which they interest themselves, so they tend to concentrate their attention on the bread and butter issues.

One must *never* assume that economic interest groups have

no significant influence on legislation. They do, and a large portion of the specific actions of the legislature may be viewed as responsive to *some* economic group. But the focus is on specific and incremental adjustments accompanied by a rationale which emphasizes job or investment protection against the impersonal forces of the larger world. No one seeks to depart from existing conditions in any dramatic, drastic, or rapid way, but rather to preserve things as they are, as far as possible. In this sense, labor groups are as conservative as business groups in the state, differing only in the specific objects of their conservative desire. Again, this emphasis reinforces the norms of the system, minimizes conflict, and encourages group spokesmen to employ the legislative tactics of quiet persuasion without ideological ferment.

An important consequence of this pattern for education policy is that MSTA rarely comes into direct conflict—or indeed contact—with the broad business, labor, or farm groups. Officially, MSTA regards all the big economic interest organizations as friends. "We get along fine with all of them. They all support better schools." But MSTA has so successfully defined the means to secure "better schools" in Missouri that there is little room left for argument from other groups. Indeed, MSTA has little need to call on its friends for overt demonstrations of support and prefers not to do so.

Finance is the one area of occasional conflict between MSTA and economic interests. MSTA supports all of the gubernatorial recommendations for increased taxes. These recommendations have included several to which labor unions take particular exception, notably, the sales tax and the cigarette tax. Union spokesmen outside and inside the legislature have expressed their objections to taxes which "bear heavily upon the workingmen" but as we shall see later, this does not affect many votes. MSTA leaders do not think this disagreement constitutes any basic antagonism and labor spokesmen agree. The same may be said of the opposition of some business groups to income tax withholding. The principal effect of such opposition is to reinforce MSTA's wariness, discussed earlier, of forming alliances with non-educational groups. Thus, on school issues, the major economic interests are, at most, of marginal importance to the outcome.

4

ARENAS OF CONFLICT

The early students of interest groups sometimes shocked their audiences when they suggested that groups might be observed pursuing their respective interests in all sorts of places. Not only legislative bodies but executive and administrative agencies and even the courts were arenas where groups contended for advantage. The selections in this part describe group activity in several different arenas of governmental decision. They are not written with a sense of alarmed discovery nor should they be read so. But they do remind us that interest groups, mainly organized groups in these selections, are ubiquitous in American political life.

Clement E. Vose wrote one of the first studies of organized group activity in the judicial arena, **Caucasians Only: The Supreme Court, the NAACP, and the Restrictive Covenant Cases.** In the selection here he continues this general line of inquiry, describing a number of less well-known groups, representing interests associated with local government, and seeking favorable court actions. Samuel P. Huntington examines the interest configurations of what has come to be called "the military-industrial complex." Joseph Palamountain describes the classic campaign of retail druggists to obtain fair trade laws from state legislatures. Harry M. Scoble examines the arena of electoral politics and the role played by organized labor in that arena.

Interest Groups, Judicial Review, and Local Government

CLEMENT E. VOSE

Past scholarship on judicial review of state and local government has been high on structure, power, and policy and low on process. The classic work of Dillon, McQuillin and McBain proved the power of courts in limiting municipal rule against state policy, and state action in many fields against federal constitutional limitations. Rhyne has shown, in an up-to-date treatise, that judge-made doctrines continue to govern state and local practice. The inferior position of these governmental units to both state and federal courts has long been illustrated in law school casebooks on municipal corporations and explained in political science texts on state and local government.

The importance of courts is well understood; the ways in which these passive instruments of government are stimulated to action is not. My attention to the details of litigation sponsored by organized interest groups flows from a central assumption that the important thing about appellate courts in the American system is that these courts govern by making policy. They may do this by deciding what is constitutional or unconstitutional and they may do it by the interpretation of statutes, administrative rules and regulations, the decisions of lower courts and so on. To say that courts are important in American

From the *Western Political Quarterly*, Vol. 19, No. 1 (March, 1966), pp. 85–100. Reprinted by permission of The University of Utah, copyright owners. Most footnotes omitted.

government is to speak the obvious. But emphasis on their importance because of their policy-making functions is not always the starting point in the textbook treatment of the judiciary. If it were, I believe there would be more attention to the ways cases are brought and to identify the true parties in such cases. Political scientists have not sufficiently moved off the dime of constitutional doctrine to describe the real gold of politics in the judicial process. This article looks at litigation conducted by action organizations and points to the importance of group agitation for judicial review of state and municipal public policy.

THE LEGITIMACY OF INTEREST GROUPS IN COURT CASES

The Supreme Court of the United States in 1963 vindicated the right of the most successful litigating organization of the day, the National Association for the Advancement of Colored People, to pursue its goals through the courts. In *NAACP* v. *Button,* the Court recognized the extent of group sponsorship of litigation and certified it against state legislation that aimed to severely limit cases brought by organizations. This was, of course, one way for a state government to protect its policies against judicial review. The failure of Virginia and other southern states to stop organizations from litigating, further legitimized judicial review and recognized the right of organizations to seek redresses in the judicial forum. This is what Mr. Justice Brennan said for the Supreme Court:

> . . . In the context of NAACP objectives, litigation is not a technique of resolving private differences; it is a means for achieving the lawful objectives of equality of treatment by all government, federal, state and local, for the members of the Negro community in this country. It is thus a form of political expression. Groups which find themselves unable to achieve their objectives through the ballot frequently turn to the courts. Just as it was true of the opponents of New Deal legislation during the 1930's, for ex-

ample, no less is it true of the Negro minority today. And under the conditions of modern government, litigation may well be the sole practicable avenue open to a minority to petition for redress of grievances.

• • •

The NAACP is not a conventional political party; but the litigation it assists, while serving to vindicate the legal rights of members of the American Negro community, at the same time and perhaps more importantly, makes possible the distinctive contribution of a minority group to the ideas and beliefs of our society. For such a group, association for litigation may be the most effective form of political association.

Academic categories of state and local government on the one hand and civil rights and civil liberties on the other have not kept organized interest groups from action. These are the propositions that link them together: (1) For some thirty years the Supreme Court has been nationalizing the constitutional rights of individuals. (2) In hundreds of decisions dealing with freedom of expression and religion, rights of defendants and rights of racial minorities against segregation and discrimination the Supreme Court has spelled out new constitutional doctrine. (3) The bulk of these cases have questioned state and municipal public policy with the result that many, many state statutes, municipal ordinances, and other forms of state action have been invalidated. (4) National organizations have participated in practically 100 per cent of these cases by providing financial or legal assistance, by appearing as *amicus curiae,* or by giving strategic advice.

The most active organizations include the following: the National Association for the Advancement of Colored People, the American Civil Liberties Union, the Commission on Law and Social Action of the American Jewish Congress, the American Committee for Protection of the Foreign Born, the Emergency Civil Liberties Committee, the Watchtower Bible and Tract Society (Jehovah's Witnesses), American Jewish Committee, Japanese American Citizens League, Congress of Racial Equality, and Protestants and Other Americans United for the Separation of Church and State. Attorneys employed by these and other organizations provide the expertise that continuous attention to a problem brings to practitioners. Their persuasive powers are applied to the courts in long series of cases which spread over many years. That this has, at least, sometimes been true may be seen by looking briefly at some of the most celebrated Supreme Court reviews of state and local government policy in civil rights and liberties.

The School Segregation cases of 1954 and 1955 were themselves the product of litigation sponsored by the NAACP Legal Defense and Education Fund. These five cases had been preceded by some fifty favorable Supreme Court decisions extending over the previous thirty years. Those decisions have been followed by a steady stream of litigation which has seen NAACP lawyers in an average of ten appearances a year in the Supreme Court. The Association has also participated in numerous cases in the lower federal courts. Certainly some 90 per cent of this vast litigation has put in question a policy adopted by Southern states and municipalities. Much of it has dealt with the segregation of school pupils but, of course, local school arrangements are public policy.

The Flag Salute cases of 1940 and 1943 as well as the Prayer cases of 1961 and 1963 dealt also with public school policy and resulted in the invalidation of local law by the Supreme Court. Manwaring has shown that the flag salute question had stood unanswered for years because no organization would challenge the practice in the courts. The Jehovah's Witnesses did so in the 1930's and after several tries gained review in the Supreme Court. They were finally successful in 1943 in having the obligatory flag salute for public school students invalidated.

Individuals who conscientiously opposed the recitation of

prayers in public school were parties to the recent cases on this question. This was necessary to establish standing as a party in the cases. But despite the national prominence of some successful parties in these cases—one thinks back to Mrs. Vashti McCollum as well as to Mrs. Pauline Murray, perhaps America's two most prominent lady atheists—organized interest groups have not been far behind the scenes. *Amicus curiae* briefs were filed in the most recent prayer cases by the American Humanist Association, the American Ethical Union, the Synagogue Council of America and the National Community Relations Advisory Council, and the American Jewish Committee and Anti-Defamation League of B'nai B'rith.

The extent of interest group activity in litigation is certainly not yet realized. Nor has the data so far collected been accommodated to a political theory of democracy. This article focuses on cases which define the limits of state and local governmental power and insists that group activity in the litigation is both widespread and legitimate. The large number of cases sponsored by organizations is a function of the power of courts to act. . . .

But courts are passive instruments of control and must be moved to decision by a party controverting government policy. The performance of this function has often been fulfilled by organized interest groups.

Interests opposed to each other in litigation are ordinarily not readily identifiable in the court reports. The parties are named and their counsel are listed but the parties are often there to give legal standing to the wider interests supporting a litigation. And the attorneys are representatives of those interests, often on a full-time basis. Little has been written on the function of interest groups in litigation. The current collection of examples will suggest something further about the variety of the phenomenon and show that group activity is not limited to celebrated cases on civil rights. Rather, litigation is a flow of pressure group activity that is old, common, and essential to the judicial review of the most controversial policies of municipal government.

PUBLIC SCHOOL CASES

Public education is important as a budget item and as a political issue in American communities. Many organizations have drawn the judiciary into the consideration of various aspects of local school affairs. Racial segregation was outlawed in cases initiated in this way and we are now well through the first decade of follow-up litigation to bring practice into conformity with constitutional doctrine. Court tests of school activities offensive to different religions have come up frequently in the past twenty years.

In 1933, well before this spate of cases on race and religion, an authority on the legal basis of school organization and administration wrote that "the relation of the school to civil society, on the one hand, and to the individual, on the other, is nowhere so well defined as in the great body of decisions rendered by the highest of our state and federal courts." Since then, outside control of education has advanced as activist judiciary has applied new tests to local practices. Of course, there is disagreement over whether these decisions are different from those in the first part of the century which Justice Holmes condemned because they prevented "the making of social experiments that an important part of the community desires, in the insulated chambers afforded by the several States." Edward S. Corwin believed that these issues are alike. After the decision in the McCollum case in 1948 outlawing released time practices in the public schools of Champaign, Illinois, Corwin said: "In my opinion the Court would act wisely to make it clear at the first opportunity that it does not aspire to become, as Justice Jackson puts it, 'a super board of education for every school district in the nation.'" Whatever one's view may be there can be no denying that court decisions are having important ramifications in the educational life of American communities.

INTEREST GROUPS IN ZONING CASES

The interest group approach follows the tradition of legal realism and emphasizes the political impulses behind litigation and the political results of judicial decisions rather than the arguments, reasoning and doctrines of law in cases. We are interested in the effect of judicial decisions on the distribution of power in communities. Take as an example the recent cases testing the authority of local zoning boards. In *Senior v. New Canaan Zoning Commission* the Connecticut Supreme Court of Errors, in 1959, held constitutional the upgrading of lots in a residential semi-rural zone from two to four acre minimums. The decision met with mixed reaction throughout Fairfield County. The Court noted in its opinion that "the town of New Canaan, as of the 1950 census, had the highest per capita income of any town, village, or city in the United States." It was not surprising to learn that the First Selectman of New Canaan described the ruling as beneficial. "It is good for the town to keep its prestige in a major suit of this kind," he said. There was general agreement that "the decision strengthened the power of zoning boards to decide the character of their communities." More recently *House and Home* has said that the U.S. Supreme Court's refusal to hear the arguments in the New Canaan Case "is seen as strengthening the power of zoning boards generally." Civic groups in other communities were encouraged to fight further for similar zoning for minimum lot area. It was also recognized that such zoning worked hardships on lower-income groups and believed by some that it prevented an orderly population growth. The effect of the Court decision upholding four-acre minimum lots was also said to be an increase in price of existing two-acre lots which were comparatively scarce. Quite certainly the courts which considered this case dealt with legal issues that touched not only the distribution of power within one community but in many similar suburban places and in central cities, as well. This was true for the Court of Common Pleas which, in the first instance, declared the zoning ordinance unconstitutional. It was also true for the Connecticut Supreme Court of Errors which reversed that decision and the United States Supreme Court which, on May 21, 1960, dismissed the appeal.

The pressures for and against acreage, or snob, zoning (called "Ivy League socialism" by Dean Jefferson Fordham of the University of Pennsylvania Law School) came to the surface in a case brought by a construction company against Easttown Township, a main-line suburb of Philadelphia. There a 1940 ordinance provided that a minimum lot area in an "A" residential district should be one acre, with a minimum frontage of 150 feet. The court test was begun when the applicant sought to build a dwelling on a site slightly less than a half-acre, with a frontage of 100 feet. The Easttown Township Board of Adjustment refused to grant a variance and this decision was supported by the Chester County Court of Common Pleas. The Supreme Court of Pennsylvania first reversed the lower court, by a vote of 6 to 1 on June 28, 1957, then granted a rehearing, vacated its order, and in a final order, on May 27, 1958, reversed itself by a 4 to 3 vote, and ruled the order of the Board of Adjustment to be valid. By the time the case reached reargument the defense of acreage zoning by Easttown Township and its Devon Citizens Association was supported by the *amici curiae* briefs of Lower Merion Township, Willistown Township, the Pennsylvania Local Government Conference, the Pennsylvania Planning Association, and George Wharton Pepper, Esquire, a well-known citizen of Easttown. The opposing position of the Bilbar Construction Company was supported in briefs *amici curiae* by the Home Builders Association of Philadelphia and the Home Life Insurance Company.

In stressing the organizations in a case there is danger of neglecting other important considerations. This is the problem of any interpretation built around a single approach. But the objective is understanding, not a complete explanation that would satisfy all social scientists and lawyers at once. Very important new doctrine may be found in the Easttown Township decision when the Pennsylvania Supreme Court ruled that the regulation need only have a substantial or reasonable relation to health, safety, morals, or the general welfare. This seemingly went against Dillon's rule in holding that the presumption of constitutionality of an ordinance is as strong as that attending an act of the legislature. With this and other decisions the importance of doctrine is assumed but the interest group environment in which these cases are decided is stressed.

Few major zoning disputes have been carried to the U.S. Supreme Court since the original case of *Euclid* v. *Ambler Realty Co.* was decided in 1926. The Village of Euclid had as counsel a young man named James Metzenbaum who has said: "It has been my understanding that the railroads, the industrial plants and the realtors (*then* afraid of zoning; now strong champions of zoning) paid the large fee to Mr. Newton D. Baker." There is little question but what zoning cases are rife with organized interests.

THE NATIONAL INSTITUTE OF MUNICIPAL LAW OFFICERS

In exploring the group nature of the litigation which gives rise to judicial decisions affecting municipal governments I shall first describe the side of government and, perhaps underplaying the role of the attorney for a municipality, tell of some organizations which stand behind him. Here is the defense of municipal power and the policies favored by the majority. Considering the values of local rule it is heartening to see that this defense is often well made. Then I shall identify groups which have lost out in municipal decisions and turn to the courts for relief. Considering that many of their cases are brought to protect citizen rights it is impressive that these groups bring zeal, skill, and money to litigation. Thus the place of courts in municipal power struggles will be reached indirectly[1]

Although the defense of actions by municipal corporations is formally in the hands of their chief legal officer, titled variously corporation counsel, law director or city, town, village, borough or county attorney, this work has been aided since 1935 by the National Institute of Municipal Law Officers. Known by its initials, NIMLO was an offshoot of the United States Conference of Mayors though always an independent organization. Its headquarters are in Washington where a full-time legal staff is maintained under Charles S. Rhyne, who has served as director since 1939. Its members are 1,200 American municipalities which rely on NIMLO as a collection center for their varied legal experience. A description by NIMLO shows it to be supported entirely by the annual membership fees paid by member cities. Interestingly, this tells that "information collected and on file in the Washington Office is never used by, nor made available to, any person other than an attorney for a NIMLO member so that there

[1]Bentley's proposition on the pressure of interests in the judiciary developed partly from his view of the Chicago traction company cases in which the Supreme Court limited the rights of the franchise street railways as against municipal control. *North Chicago City Railways Co.* v. *Blair,* 201 U.S. 399 (1906). He related the outcome in these cases to broad changes in public opinion over the previous decade more than to the conscious efforts of organized interests or to the labors of the attorneys. Arthur F. Bentley, *The Process of Government: A Study of Social Pressures* (Chicago: U. of Chicago Press, 1908), pp. 392–93. His conclusion was that Supreme Court justices are "a functioning part of this government, responsive to the group pressures within it, representative of all sorts of pressures, and using their representative judgment to bring these pressures to balance, not indeed in just the same way, but on just the same basis, that any other agency does, and that in this Chicago case they let a changing weight of group interests come very close to expression." *Ibid.,* p. 393.

is no possibility that this material will be employed against the cities which have collected it."

NIMLO represents a kind of perfect expression of a paradoxical development—the nationalization of municipal law. It aids the busy municipal attorney "who needs the strength flowing from joint support of many municipalities in instances where the protest of a single municipality would be ineffective." Or, put another way by NIMLO, "furnishes an effective agency through which municipal attorneys can take joint cooperative action on Federal legislation and on any other matter of nationwide consequence to municipalities on matters in Washington, D.C., with great effectiveness." NIMLO offers many services but two activities may be identified as directly shaping the legal position of municipalities: drafting model ordinances and defending them by briefs in the Supreme Court of the United States.

The very idea of model state constitutions and legislation, model city charters and ordinances has not been much explored. The phenomenon is very well known and accepted, for on its face it is easy to understand as necessary in a nation of fifty states and thousands of lesser governmental units. Yet the folklore of American government must yield a bit when it is realized that much modern local legislation has been drafted in Washington! At any rate, the *NIMLO Model Ordinance Service* is followed closely by most municipal law officers in advising local councils in the enactment of local legislation. The *Service* is in a loose-leaf binder to facilitate consistant revision and supplementation and "each model ordinance has tried and proven provisions with citations to the special studies or leading court decisions upon which it is based." And it may be truly said that "many of these model ordinances have already been adopted by hundreds of municipalities."

If a "test case" is one whose outcome will affect interests beyond those of the parties in the dispute then NIMLO's frequent interest in municipal ordinance litigation is to be expected.

In the bulk of instances cases involving model ordinances are settled at the state level and are prepared by the law officers of member municipalities. For example, in 1950 the NIMLO Model Sound Truck Ordinance, which had been adopted by the City of Allentown, Pennsylvania, was upheld by the Pennsylvania Superior Court. The case for sustaining the ordinance was made by the city solicitor of Allentown. The lower court's holding was affirmed by the State Supreme Court and an appeal from this dismissed by the United States Supreme Court. When cases involving member municipalities come before the Supreme Court, NIMLO takes action in two ways. The organization may provide assistance to the city law officer in charge of the case by making suggestions on the brief or on the approach to the oral argument. On occasion Charles S. Rhyne, Director of NIMLO, may join as a joint author of a brief for a municipality.

The second form of NIMLO support in court cases is by *amici curiae* briefs, an activity which seems to be flourishing nowadays. At least most of NIMLO's *amici* briefs have been in cases during the last three terms of the Supreme Court. There are nine cases which NIMLO has entered in this way. Of these, seven have supported city efforts to obtain lower gas and utility rates and two have involved municipal inspection practices.

NIMLO, as a kind of semi-governmental institution, acts with decorum and restraint in its work of ordinance design and defense. But, occasionally, an ally in extending and justifying municipal power may beseech the courts to act right by supporting a pet policy aim. A current example may be seen in criticisms of courts by supporters of urban renewal and slum clearance programs in American cities. In 1960 the *Cleveland Plain Dealer* addressed the courts editorially in this tone: "Frankly, we think the municipal judges who now try these cases have not given enough thought to the cancer which slums and rank overcrowding have created in this city. In our view, there consistently are too many postponements and too many suspended fines. . . . This wrist-slapping business must be stopped, for what's the use of hiring new inspectors and putting through a stricter housing code if the court doesn't follow up the good work?" This point of view was applied to courts in other cities in the spring of 1960 by the National Association of Housing and Redevelopment which criticized judicial leniency in Cincinnati, Dayton, and St. Louis. In those cities courts rejected evidence of violations obtained during inspections without search warrants. On June 20, 1960, a 4-to-4 tie vote in the United States Supreme Court let stand the arrest of a Dayton homeowner for refusing to admit a housing inspector without a warrant. The defense of the Dayton ordinance permitting such inspections was led by Charles Rhyne in cooperation with the city attorney and NIMLO filed an *amicus curiae* brief in support, also. However, the tie vote has no force or precedent, so this particular problem is not yet ended.

NIMLO protects local law in the courts as a matter of routine and as a primary obligation. There are other organizations, established to serve the interests of local government, which participate in law suits only occasionally. Thus, the United States Conference of Mayors has been involved in only one case since its founding in 1934. As an organization of mayors of approximately 300 cities with a population of 50,000 or more the Conference in 1957 filed a brief *amicus curiae* supporting a petition by Mayor Hartsfield of Atlanta requesting the Supreme Court of the United States to consider the constitutionality of the Georgia County Unit Primary. This brief contended that this system "represents a systematic discrimination against, and continuous debasement of, the political voice and position of municipalities and their citizens." And, "State Governments controlled by self-perpetuating rural minorities systematically discriminate against the interests of municipalities and their citizens." The Conference therefore entered its brief in order to place the Georgia County Unit Primary "in the larger context of urban underrepresentation," However, the Supreme Court denied review. It is fair to conclude that the United States Conference of Mayors ordinarily finds better expression of its goals than through litigation.

In contrast, the state leagues of municipalities act much more like NIMLO for, among many activities, they prepare codes of model ordinances appropriate in a single state and especially for smaller communities. These organizations also represent the interests of their member municipalities before state legislature, administrative agencies and courts. In a typical state, for instance, the League of Wisconsin Municipalities filed eight *amici curiae* briefs in state supreme court cases during the past decade. Ordinarily the preamble of such briefs explains that "the disposition of the matter before the court is of vital concern to all Wisconsin cities and villages." It is this judgment that the executive committee of the League applies in authorizing that a brief be submitted on behalf of its members. In Wisconsin the cities and villages which are members now number 492. State municipal leagues often decide whether to file briefs in cases partly on its view of the competence of the municipal corporation attorney for it continues to be a great irony of our judicial process that great principles affecting many interests not heard in a lawsuit may rise or fall in a quietly pursued litigation. The organizations that support the work of city law officers are understandable developments in this system of lawmaking.

Thus far I have assumed that municipal corporations have enough in common to join together in common defense when there are law suits questioning their powers, policies, and procedures. This view is supported by the program of the American Municipal Association, the national organization of the various state municipal leagues, which speaks of "the national municipal policy" which guides their activities. But while there are broad areas of agreement the differences in the size, location, financial condition and outlook among American communities are surely reflected in these organizations. Accordingly, the larger cities in a state are frequently at odds with the public position of their municipal league. And, no doubt, the American Municipal Association does not feel strongly about the need for reapportionment as does the United States Conference of Mayors. Certainly the litigation in which these groups are active reflects their different constituencies and outlooks.

Turning to the single municipality and its attorney one finds some well-established differences. Litigation for a large city is proportionately much greater than for a smaller place though rate of growth is a factor of importance. Tax and liability cases bulk large in this work while annexation and related issues shows up in the legal business of a growing place. While national and state organizations of government officials often contribute to the defense of municipal corporations in the courts, municipal law officers do not depend solely on this support. Political scientists should give attention to this office and the political factors which condition its conduct.

To the extent that local government policy is set by organized interests in a locality then the defense of that policy in the courts is also a defense of those interests. There are many instances where this private interest is given ample chance to speak officially in support of the policy. In *Dean Milk Co.* v. *Madison,* the city of Madison was represented throughout the litigation by the city attorney and an attorney for the Madison Milk Producers Association, as well. In *Zorach* v. *Clauson,* the city of New York was represented by its own counsel and by an *amicus* brief by a city-wide committee of Protestants, Catholics, and Jews which favored released time from the schools, for religious instruction. When the Borough of Rutherford, New Jersey, wished to defend distribution of Bibles in the public schools it accepted the support of the Gideons International as intervenor to defend the policy in the courts and carry the costs.

The frequent judicial defeat of states and municipalities a

generation ago was attributed by Justice Brandeis to inferior public counsel. He felt over and over again that attorneys representing private interests were abler men than those representing cities and states. It is hard to make a comparison today. No doubt the organizations of public officials, especially the National Institute of Municipal Law Officers, the state leagues of municipalities, and the National Association of Attorneys General, have provided vital skill in support of individual public law officers in crucial legal tests. Private supporters also volunteer legal aid to governments in court cases. Abler men, larger staffs and bigger budgets today enable cities to defend themselves in the courts to balance adversary proceedings which tend to be lopsided when superior private counsel is employed.

AMERICAN TRIAL LAWYERS ASSOCIATION—FORMERLY NATIONAL ASSOCIATION OF CLAIMANTS' COUNSEL OF AMERICA

Strong feelings of aggrieved parties, the devotion of able attorneys and associations of persons similarly situated go together in many of the best known actions against state and local government in recent years. In the city of New York, and elsewhere increasingly, a substantial part of the cost of operating the law department is due to the defense against "sidewalk injury cases." In 1959 the *NIMLO Municipal Law Review* reported that perhaps the most important problem of the municipal attorney is the question of tort liability. The report said: "This [condition] appears to be particularly true when consideration is given to the number of claims being presented, the large amounts now being awarded in damages, the often lack of funds with which to pay the same, the inability to secure adequate, if any, public liability insurance, and the removal by the courts and legislatures in various states of the municipalities' immunity from tort liability when acting in a governmental capacity." The assault on the doctrine of municipal immunity from tort liability has been led by the National Association of Claimants' Counsel of America. The 7,500 members of this nation-wide bar association, known as NACCA, are no doubt, the most zealous, hardest working best paid lawyers in the country. NACCA was founded in 1946. The National Association of Claimants' Counsel of America is made up of "attorneys specializing in the representation of injured persons." Through national and regional conferences, reports and the *NACCA Law Journal*, the organization has stimulated and applauded a sensational trend toward bigger and better damage suits. In 1965 the organization was renamed the American Trial Lawyers Association.

The opposing interests caught up by this trend were pointed up by the reaction of NACCA and NIMLO attorneys to the lifting of municipal immunity from tort liability by the Supreme Court of Florida in 1957 in the case of *Hargrove* v. *Town of Cocoa Beach*. This was an action by a widow against the municipality for damage for the alleged wrongful death of her husband who died of smoke suffocation in an unattended jail. (The court report says the "husband was incarcerated in the town jail while in a helpless condition because of excessive intoxication.") The trial judge dismissed the complaint on the theory that the town was immune to liability for this type of tort. On appeal, the Florida Supreme Court reversed and receded from its prior decisions holding a municipal corporation immune from liability for the torts of police officers. Positively, the court held "that when an individual suffers a direct, personal injury proximately caused by the negligence of a municipal employee while acting within the scope of his employment, the injured individual is entitled to redress for the wrong done." The court reasoned that the immunity doctrine was inappropriate in a modern, urban democracy where the city "is in substantial measure a large business institution." In departing from the rule of municipal immunity, the Florida Supreme Court explained that its conclusion had "not been hastily formulated" and added: "The matter was thoroughly briefed and argued by counsel for the parties. At the invitation of the Court, the Florida League of Municipalities filed briefs and through counsel ably presented the matter *amicus curiae*."

At the next annual convention of the National Institute of Municipal Law Officers, the city attorney of Pensacola reported that this opinion was most alarming and there was general concern that such judgments could "financially cripple any city or village at any time." The Pensacola city attorney's comments were uttered with some humor and, while it may be unfair to take them at face value, a quotation will reveal something of the spirit of one official faced with the prospects of damage suits in the future.

> . . . on leaving my home in Pensacola the other day I picked up a newspaper and read that in Miami a circuit court jury had returned a verdict in the sum of $23,000.00 because a man's arm was broken while he was being arrested. Of course, that's Miami. (Laughter.)
>
> . . . We look with a great deal of fear and trepidation to the decision in the *Hargrove* case in Florida particularly so in the Miami area where the verdicts are so fantastic. I hope that in the Northern part of Florida where the real Southerners of Florida live that they will be much more practical in their verdicts in the event that we have such a thoughtless officer on our police department as to break a man's arm when he is drunk. (Applause.)

In contrast, a note in the *NACCA Law Journal* praised the decision of the Supreme Court of Florida in the Hargrove case as "commendably repudiating the indefensible rule of municipal immunity from tort liability." Municipalities were described by the claimant's compensation attorneys as "one of the best loss-distributing units of society." The note said simply, but in emotion-charged words, that the immunity rule was "barefaced injustice." The NACCA position may be summed up as follows: "It is better that the losses due to the torts of city employees should fall upon the cities and for the latter to bear the cost of such casualties than upon the innocent victim of 'official' torts. Such losses should be regarded as the social cost of administering government, spread over the citizenry by the tax device, rather than have the cities partially subsidized by the coerced contributions of their victims." This view appears to be gaining popular and judicial acceptance. Without straining its implications too greatly one can see the obligations of local government and the tax burden growing through this judicial change of heart brought about, at least in part, by the zealousness of NACCA, henceforth to be known as the American Trial Lawyers Association.

COURT RULES AND INTEREST GROUP ACCESS

Among all litigants those who challenge municipal action perhaps have the easiest path. In conformity with "Dillon's rule," the powers possessed by municipalities are ordinarily interpreted in a restrictive way by the courts.[2] The troubles of municipal corporations are increased by the procedures of state courts which make them far easier marks than federal courts. Friendly suits are common. Advisory opinions are rendered in many states. The declaratory judgment is more fully developed. Class actions are permitted more readily. The rules for *amicus curiae* and

---

[2]"Dillon's Rule" was originally expressed as follows: "It is a general and undisputed proposition of law that a municipal corporation possesses and can exercise the following powers, and no others: First, those granted in express words; second, those necessarily or fairly implied in or incident to the powers expressly granted; third, those essential to the accomplishment of the declared objects and purposes of the corporation—not simply convenient, but indispensable. Any fair, reasonable, substantial doubt concerning the existence of power is resolved by the courts against the corporation, and the power is denied." [John F.] Dillon, *Commentaries in the Law of Municipal Corporation*, 5th ed. (Boston: Little, Brown, 1911, 5 vols.), I, 448.

intervenors are less stringent. Above all, the "taxpayer's suit" stands as a symbol of the many procedures by which state courts have been brought to exert such power over local government. This device led Sayre and Kaufman, in their study of New York City, to conclude that courts "offer nongovernmental groups in the city a chance to influence officials in the other branches indirectly when they cannot do so directly."

"Taxpayers' suits" satisfy the jurisdictional requirement that plaintiffs have standing to sue. Normally, this requirement means that the plaintiff must sustain specific personal injury before he is allowed to go to court. However, municipal action in virtually every state may be tested under this relaxation of the "standing" doctrine where a plaintiff's status as a taxpayer "has been held sufficient to allow damage to him which is shared equally with all members of the public to form a judicially cognizable issue." A taxpayer's suit has been defined as "a representative class action in equity, brought on behalf of all taxpayers against officials of the government unit challenged. In practice, the word "taxpayer" has been treated so loosely that a group of persons wishing to question governmental action in the courts need only find the money and a nominal plaintiff to do so. This is why "taxpayers' suits" have functionally become "citizens' suits."

A *Yale Law Journal* survey shows that the objectives sought by plaintiff-taxpayers have varied widely with the following in order of importance: (1) challenges to the use of the eminent domain power in connection with slum clearance, housing, highways, airports, and other public works projects; (2) attacks on the constitutionality of various methods of bond financing used by municipalities to circumvent limitations on indebtedness; (3) cases questioning the granting of franchises or licenses which represent public approval of privately owned but publicly used facilities; (4) efforts to withhold salary payments to civil servants who hold office in violation of statutory standards; (5) challenges to sales or donations of the public domain to private parties;

(6) cases to achieve civil liberties objectives such as the prevention of expenditures for illegal methods of law enforcement or expenditures which would violate the separation of church and state; (7) suits to reapportion election or judicial districts.

Taxpayers' suits were first allowed by American courts just prior to the Civil War but did not reach a great volume until the end of the nineteenth century. Then in the Populist and Progressive periods a number of devices of democratic intent were fashioned to cope with entrenched officials and vested interests. In this connection the taxpayer's suit should be linked with the initiative, referendum, and recall as a symbol of the era. In this century the taxpayer's suit has been one of the chief weapons in the arsenal of the good government movement. The editor of the Madison, Wisconsin, *Capital Times,* whose roots are deep in the LaFollette movement, in 1960 established a special fund of $10,000 to be used, as he said, "in the protection of the public domain which is being raided periodically by private interests at the expense of the public interest." He said that this fund would allow his newspaper "to start a taxpayer's suit where we believe that the state's lakes, rivers, streams, forests and parks are being taken over by private interests for private profit." Similarly, the Citizens Union of the City of New York, described as "probably the most widely known and influential organization among the city's multitude of nongovernmental groups," and with origins before 1900 in the good government reform movement, has begun numerous taxpayers' actions throughout its history. Its activity in the courts has also taken other forms and has varied with the character of the local government. During the administrations of Mayors John F. Hylan (1918–25) and James J. Walker (1926–32) the Citizens Union brought some nineteen lawsuits to restrain illegal expenditures of public funds and was successful in about twelve. The present counsel of the Citizens Union said recently that in the last few years he had "brought some half dozen suits to restrain various governmental actions which we believed to be illegal. In addition, the Citizens Union occasionally intervenes, by leave of the court, as *amicus curiae* or friend of the court, in suits brought by others." This use of taxpayers' suits by one newspaper and one civic organization is indicative of practices throughout the country.

The situation created by this easy access to the courts has been described by the *Yale Law Journal* in the following way:

> . . . Such litigation allows the courts, within the framework of tra-ditional notions of "standing," to add to the controls over public officials inherent in the elective process the judicial scrutiny of the statutory and constitutional validity of their acts. Taxpayers' suits also extend the uniquely American concept of judicial re-view to legislative action by allowing minorities ineffective at the ballot box to invalidate statutes or ordinances on constitutional grounds. . . . Taxpayers' suits thus create an army of potential private attorneys general acting on whatever private incentives may induce them to spend the time and money to bring a tax-payer's suit. . . . And since group financing of such litigation is not infrequent, taxpayers' suits also mobilize various voluntary associations seeking private, economic, or social objectives to fur-ther law enforcement and prevention of corruption in govern-ment.

The objections to the widespread use of taxpayers' suits are numerous. Even when unsuccessful the delay occasioned by such actions "may unduly obstruct the completion of public protests." These suits may harrass officials and immobilize local govern-ment thereby inhibiting progressive community action. But most important of all, "taxpayers' suits may push the concept of judi-cial review of legislative and executive action too far." The com-mon complaints about judicial review merit repeating:

> By calling upon the courts to sit in judgment of decisions taken by the political branches of government, when no one is suffi-ciently injured thereby to have standing as an individual, taxpayer litigation may undermine the independence and prestige of the

judiciary, impairing its ability to perform more traditional judicial functions. Since the courts are not designed, as are the political branches, to harmonize divergent views within the community and take action in accordance with the broadest possible concensus, such review may exceed their proper function. Moreover, placing the courts in the role of a "super legislature" may encourage irresponsibility and lack of creativity on the part of the political branches because they will be aware that decisions taken by them are always subject to judicial reversal.

This should suggest that the concept of judicial review, which is usually thought of merely in terms of Supreme Court review of acts of Congress and of state legislatures deserves consideration from the viewpoint of the government of communities, as well. The vast array of state and federal courts which may review the actions of community governments means that the scope of local power is always open to challenge by litigating interest groups.

Interservice Competition and the Political Roles of the Armed Services

SAMUEL P. HUNTINGTON

"Conventional wisdom" (to purloin a phrase from Galbraith) holds that interservice competion necessarily undermines economy, efficiency, and effective central control in the military establishment. The remedy is further unification, possibly even the merger of the services into a single uniform. The conventional wisdom also holds that political action by military groups necessarily threatens civilian control. The remedy is to "keep the military out of politics." The pattern of American military politics and interservice rivalry since World War II, however, suggests that the conventional wisdom may err in its analysis of their results and falter in its prescription of remedies.

I. THE ROOTS OF INTERSERVICE RIVALRY

Service political controversy between the world wars had two distinguishing characteristics. First, on most issues, a military service, supported, perhaps, by a few satellite groups, struggled against civilian isolationists, pacifists, and economizers. The Navy and the shipbuilding industry fought a lonely battle with the dominant forces in both political parties over naval disarmament. The Army lost its fight for universal service after World

From the *American Political Science Review*, Vol. LV, No. 1 (March, 1961), pp. 40–52. Reprinted by permission of the author and the American Political Science Association. Footnotes are omitted.

War I, and throughout the Twenties clashed with educational, labor, and religious groups over ROTC and with other groups over industrial mobilization preparation. In the annual budget encounters the issue usually was clearly drawn between service supporters who stressed preparedness and their opponents who decried the necessity and the legitimacy of substantial military expenditures. To the extent that the services were in politics, they were involved in conflicts with civilian groups. Behind each specific opponent of the moment was that broad and deeply ingrained anti-military sentiment which had characterized American society since the eighteenth century. By the end of the Coolidge administration this sentiment was so far in the ascendancy that the appropriations for the Army and the Navy together had been whittled to about $750 million in a total annual budget of just under $4 billion.

Second, each service waged its own political battles independently of the other. Throughout the 1920s and 1930s, the services cooperated in strategic planning through the Joint Board and in a few other enterprises. Strategic planning, however, involved no immediate claims upon scarce resources. It produced some disagreement but no real political conflict. The most significant intramilitary controversies involved the efforts of two semi-services, the Air Corps and, to a lesser extent, the Marine Corps, to achieve greater autonomy and *de jure* recognition as services. The two major services, however, seldom fought each other politically and virtually never helped each other. They were distinct departments. Separate legislation, handled by separate Military and Naval Affairs Committees in both houses, established and organized them, authorized their strengths and prescribed their systems of promotion and recruitment. Separate appropriations subcommittees provided their funds in separate supply bills. The political successes and failures of one service had little implication for the other: the National Defense Act of 1920 boded neither good nor ill for the Navy; the Vinson

Acts of the 1930s neither assumed nor precluded an increase in the Army. Each service struggled along in its own world with its peculiarities and preoccupations, its own friends and enemies.

In some respects this interwar pattern of relationships persisted into the postwar period. The traditional service-civilian conflict reappeared in the struggles between the Navy and the State Department over the Japanese mandates, the military and the scientists over the control of atomic energy, and the Army and a number of civilian groups over universal military training. These conflicts, however, were holdovers from a previous era. The primary locus of service political activity shifted drastically. World War II destroyed the separate political universes of the services. The development of new weapons and the emergence of a new role for the United States in world affairs meant a change in their old functions and activities. Service futures were now interdependent. The concerns which each service felt for the future tended to focus into a concern over the effect of the other services on that future. A unified defense organization meant competition over organizational position and strategic doctrine. A unified appropriations process meant competition for funds. The interservice battle over unification between 1944 and 1947 was not only a model of battles to come, but it also shaped the nature of those battles. Interservice rivalry was the child of unification. Both reflected the unity and complexity of modern war, and without the one, the other would never have come into existence.

The transition from civilian-service controversy to interservice controversy as the main focus of service political activity was graphically illustrated in the struggle over UMT between 1945 and 1948. The lines of battle were initially drawn between the Army and certain patriotic and veterans groups on the one hand, and various civilian educational, religious, pacifist, and farm groups on the other. The opposition, one War Department consultant declared, included "subversive groups and a large section of the public which does not think." The opponents replied with dire warnings of the dangers of militarization. Here was a conflict in the classic pattern of the 1920s and 1930s with all the familiar arguments, clichés, and symbolism. The resolution of the issue in 1948, however, reflected not so much the relative strength or persuasiveness of the two coalitions as it did the relative appeals of the Army and Air Force strategic doctrines. The issue was redefined from "UMT vs. no-UMT" to "UMT vs. a seventy-group Air Force." "The effect of the Fin-letter report and of the Brewster-Hinshaw Board," Forrestal noted in his diary for March 8, 1948, "has been to convince the country that by a substantial increase in appropriations for Air there would be no necessity for UMT . . ." Congress added $822 million to Air Force appropriations, and the UMT legislation died in committee. The conflict of the Army and its affiliated groups against an extensive coalition of civilian groups became a conflict of one service against another.

The rise of interservice rivalry had a direct impact on civil-military relations. Political conflict between civil and military institutions was sublimated and deflected into conflict among the services. Interservice controversy substituted for civil-military controversy. Two crucial foci of civil-military relations in modern states have been between the foreign office and the military, on the one hand, and between the military and the budgetary agencies, on the other. American civil-military relations in the postwar decade, however, were characterized by the relative lack of sharp conflict between a united military establishment and either the State Department or Budget Bureau. Service rivalry permitted the civilian agencies to pick and choose. When the State Department wanted to reinforce Europe in 1950, elements in the Air Force took a skeptical attitude, but the Army moved in to help develop and merchandise the policy. Conversely, when the Secretary of State later spoke of massive retaliation, the Army dissented, but the now-favored Air Force congratulated the diplomats on their military common sense. When the budget was reduced in Fiscal 1954, Vandenberg made his futile protests while the Army and Navy sat on the sidelines. When it was reduced in Fiscal 1955, the Air Force was pleased with the new emphasis, and the Army fought alone against the cuts. Civil-military relations before and after the Korean War would have been far different if the frustrations generated by the Johnson and Wilson budgets had not in part been dissipated in decrying other services and other strategic doctrines. Indeed, at no point after World War II were the President and his Budget Bureau confronted with a truly joint, integrated military program, publicly announced and supported by all military men as the indispensable minimum for national security. The *imprimatur* which the Joint Chiefs bestowed upon force-level recommendations was seldom more than *pro forma*. The "minimum" programs were service minimum programs for 70, 143, or 137 wings; for one *United States*, ten *Forrestals*, or a series of nuclear carriers; for twelve, twenty-four, or twenty-seven divisions. Each service chief tended to attack not the overall ceiling on the military budget but rather the allocation of the budget among the services. The oft-commented-upon failure of the American military to have a distinctive "military viewpoint" on national policy after World War II was not unrelated to the presence of distinctive service viewpoints.

In almost every modern state, the division of the military forces into two or more separate groups has been used to bolster civilian control. Totalitarian states create SS or MVD troops to check their regular forces. The Founding Fathers provided for both a militia and a regular army. After World War II, interservice rivalry played a similar role. "I want competition," Representative Vinson is quoted as declaring. Interservice rivalry not only strengthened civilian agencies but also furnished them with a whipping boy upon whom to blame deficiencies in the military establishment for which just possibly they could be held responsible.

Interservice controversy rendered unlikely any military rejection of the civilian world and its values, such as occurred in the late nineteenth century and between the two world wars. Civilian agencies were now more frequently arbiters than opponents, and each service was impelled to adjust its values and interests to those of influential civilians or to risk falling behind its rivals. Interservice conflict stimulated a politicization of the military which meant both a less military attitude in dealing with civilians and more sophisticated political techniques in dealing with other military groups. Implicitly, service activity directed at other services was more acceptable than service activity directed at civilians. The services themselves found it easier and more virtuous to tangle with each other than to challenge civilian groups and arouse the hallowed shibboleths of civilian control.

Despite these functions which it apparently served, interservice rivalry nevertheless was often denounced by civilians as the source of many evils in the Department of Defense. Interservice harmony, the elimination of duplication (rational organization), reduced costs, and greater unification were often seen as directly related; and the achievement of interservice harmony, it was argued, was a step toward the achievement of the others. If this were the case, however, it is indeed strange that political and military leaders so persistently refused to realize these values. Why wallow along with interservice bickering, duplication, needless expenditure, and administrative disunity, if they could all be eliminated or reduced together by taking a few simple steps? The relations among these goals were considerably more complex than they superficially appeared to be.

Interservice competition was not so much a cause of decentralization, duplication, and increased expenditures as it was the result of the desire to eliminate these supposed evils. More harmony among the services could be bought at the price of disunity, duplication, higher costs. It is generally conceded, for instance, that the less money there was in the military budget, the more intense and bitter was the competition of the services for it. Similarly, interservice competition in the postwar decade originated in unification, and efforts to increase unification usually tended to produce greater interservice competition. "If you try to put on the heat too much right now," Admiral Radford observed in 1958 with respect to the authority of the Secretary of Defense over the services, "they all take refuge in the law and you actually drive them apart." On the other hand, the less unification there was, the greater the freedom of the services to go their own way, the less they feared control by a central origin dominated by a hostile service, and the less the likelihood of serious interservice rivalry. In comparable fashion, duplicating ambitions were a cause of interservice rivalry; duplicating programs and functions a means of reducing that rivalry. Both the Army and the Air Force wanted to develop, produce, and operate intermediate range ballistic missiles. This conflict of ambitions was, in part, mediated by allowing both services to produce their respective missiles. In one sense, duplication was a result of interservice rivalry, but it was a result which tended to reduce its cause, and efforts to decrease duplication tended to increase interservice tensions.

Interservice harmony could thus be achieved at the sacrifice of reduced expenditures, rationalized organization, and greater unification. In addition, interservice peace would probably have certain costs in decreased civil-military harmony. Conversely, the achievement of these other values was only possible by accepting a considerable degree of interservice competition. One suspects that the real cause of the sustained depreciation of interservice competition was not its direct association with other evils in Defense Department management, but rather because it was a discomfort which had to be endured if these other evils were to be reduced. What people identified as the consequences of inter-service competition were in reality the alternatives to it. Inter-service competition became an ubiquitous, inherent, and permanent feature of the defense establishment because it would simply cost too much to eliminate it.

For the services, interservice competition was a justification for, as well as a cause of service political activities. Traditionally, and again immediately after World War II, service appeals to their officers to be public relations conscious stressed the close interrelation of political and military affairs and the general responsibility of military officers to enlighten the public on the needs of national security. Increasingly, however, the stress on the public relations responsibility of the officer assumed a service-oriented approach. Exhortations to political action were couched in terms of putting the service view across—informing the public of the indispensability of sea, air, or land power to national security. Competitive emulation thus provided the impetus for the multiplication of service political activities. "The Jupiter," as Wernher von Braun explained, "involves several hundred million dollars of the taxpayers' money. One hundred percent security would mean no information for the public, no money for the Army, no Jupiter. . . . The Army has got to play the same game as the Air Force and the Navy,"

Each service, with the notable exception of the Marine Corps, developed an image of itself as the "silent service," politically underprivileged, misunderstood by the public, incapable of competing equally in the public arena with its more articulate and dramatic rivals. Each service's feeling of inadequacy was undoubtedly real, and the ritualistic deploring of its inferiority furnished a perfect rationale for, and incentive to, political action. Contrary to what one might expect, however, the stronger a service was, the more it tended to deplore its inferiority. Perhaps the greater its power and the more extensive its activities, the more the service felt the need to justify them by stressing how weak it was. Conceivably, too, feelings of inadequacy derive more from the gap between a service's power and its aspirations than from its power relative to its rivals. Or, it may be that bemoaning the state of one's public relations is itself an inherent part of public relations activity and increases as the latter increases. In any event, by almost any standard, the Air Force was the strongest service politically during the postwar decade. It consistently out-scored its rivals, for instance, in public opinion polls, and after 1951 it regularly received the lion's share of the Defense Depart-ment budget. Yet the Air Force undoubtedly complained the most about its political weakness. The Air Force, one of its gen-erals declared, had "a special problem in public relations" be-cause most American did not understand the basic concepts of strategic air power and believed air power to be too expensive. "The Vice Chief of Staff," an Air Force journal reported in 1954, "is convinced that the Air Force has failed to keep the public properly informed." A distinguished lawyer and brigadier general in the Air Force Reserve compiled an imposing list of obstacles to the development of American air power:

> Air power is the victim of cultural lag. . . . The military commen-tators were brought up in the older services. . . . The Air Force lacks representation in the Office of the Secretary of Defense. . . . The Congressional relations of the Air Force are inferior to those of the other services. . . . The Air Force is really the silent serv-ice.. Its senior commanders do not write books and articles. . . . Those responsible for the development of national air power have not made use of the basic instrumentalities of information and enlightenment to get the public behind them.

The *Air University Quarterly Review* endorsed these conclusions and pointed out other deficiencies. Both the Army and the Navy had regular TV programs; the Air Force had none. Fewer movies were made about the Air Force than about the other services. The *Review* found just one area of Air Force superiority. "Only in the mass medium of the comics does the Air Force come out ahead, with 'Steve Canyon' and 'Terry and the Pirates' far outstripping any competition in that field of communication and public relations." The complaints of the other services differed only in quantity, not in quality, from those of the Air Force.

II. THE POLITICAL CASTELLATION OF THE SERVICES

Interservice competition tended to weaken the military as a whole but to strengthen the military services. Challenging the services, the rivalry also toughened them and forced them to develop the mechanisms and support necessary for survival in the pluralistic world of American politics. The expansion of their political activities tended to resemble a process of castellation. Building out from its inner keep, each service slowly constructed political, institutional, and legal defenses, after the fashion of an elaborate medieval castle with inner and outer walls, ramparts and barbicans, watch-towers and moats. The services, in short, entrenched themselves on the American political scene, as countless other interest groups, private and public, had done before them.

*Expansion of Public
and Congressional Relations*

Service emphasis upon reaching the public and Congress was concretely reflected in the elevation of these activities in the formal administrative hierarchy. During the 1920s and the 1930s, the Army and Navy public information sections occupied subordinate positions in the Intelligence branches of the services. Inevitably the outlook and values associated with the collection and interpretation of intelligence were not those which encouraged the collection and dissemination of news to mass media of communications. Congressional liaison responsibilities were dispersed among a number of bureaus in the Navy and assigned to the information offices in the Army and Air Force. By 1956, however, all three major services had similar organizational arrangements for public information and legislative liaison: two distinct offices at the highest level directly responsible to the service secretary.

The elevation of these offices was accompanied by an expansion and diversification of their activities. The Army Chief of Information, for instance, opened a branch office in Los Angeles in 1952 to improve relations between the Army and the movie industry, and another in 1956 in New York, designed, in the words of the Chief of Staff, to "assist in getting its story across to the public" through all the available news media. At the same time, the Chief of Staff pointed with pride to the award by the American Public Relations Association of three citations to Army organizations for outstanding public relations. Public relations was included in the Army Program System. Public information objectives were established quarterly, covering "those critical areas for which the Department of the Army particularly desires emphasis during the period." The parallel between the military services and the large industrial corporations was pointed out, and the military were urged to adopt the public relations philosophy of industry. General Ridgway's call in 1954 for the "creation of a public relations-conscious Army" had its counterparts in similar exhortations by the other services. Increased activities meant increased funds, and, reportedly, total military expenditures for legislative liaison doubled between 1953 and 1958.

"Backstop" Associations and the Articulation of Service Interests

A second aspect of the growth of service political activities in the post-war decade was the increased number, membership, and activities of service "backstop" organizations, private associations concerned with the support of the services and the articulation of their programs. The Navy League, oldest of the major associations, was formed by a group of civilians in 1902 to counter-bal-

ance the reaction against the Navy in the years after the Spanish-
American War. Prior to World War II, the League was an active
and devoted advocate of the Navy, but never a very large, affluent, or influential one. The unification controversy of 1945–1947,
however, gave the League a new role to play, not in fighting
anti-Navy midwesterners, but in fighting anti-Navy soldiers and
airmen. The Air Force Association was organized in 1946 and
the following year it took over the publication of the monthly
Air Force magazine, previously published by the Army Air Force.
In 1959, it had 55,000 members. The Association of the U.S.
Army was formed in 1950 by the merger of the Infantry and
Field Artillery Associations. In 1955 it assimilated the Anti-air-
craft Association, and by 1958 it had a membership of 50,000 and
almost a hundred chapters.

The development and vitality of the "backstop" associations
was particularly relevant to one major problem of service behavior in the postwar period: the definition and articulation of
service interests. Normally the leaders of a group are its natural
advocates and defenders. With the services, however, this is not
necessarily true. To be sure, the role of the service secretary differs little from that of the secretary in a civilian department. In
most civilian agencies, however, the definition, articulation, and
promotion of the agency's interests are also a function of the top
career leaders of the agency, those whose work-lives are continu-
ously-identified with it. The freedom of the military leaders to
perform this function, however, is restricted by their presumably
instrumental character. The Department of Agriculture, for example, has a responsibility for and to the farmers of the country
as well as a responsibility to the President and Congress. The
military, on the other hand, are responsible only to the higher
political authorities of government: their representative role is
minimal; this is the essence of "civilian control." Thus, the top
military leaders of a service—those who might be presumed to be
most active and influential in the defense of its interests—are

normally among those who must act with the greatest circumspection in this area. The "backstop" association, however, is uniquely able to perform this function. As a private group, it can openly criticize the Administration while service leaders limit themselves to oblique suggestions under the prodding of sympathetic congressmen. The Chief of Staff speaks for his service but also for the Administration and the Department of Defense. The service association speaks only for the service.

In addition, the association can engage in political tactics and methods which are denied to the service. The Regular Army, for example, in its struggles with the National Guard Association and the Reserve Officers Association, is, as one scholar has pointed out, handicapped "by its inability to throw charges— either reckless or responsible charges—into the headlines as its opponents frequently do." Service associations are under no such restraints, and the less directly they are associated with the service, the greater their freedom. On the other hand, they cannot become completely detached; if they are too distant from the service, they decrease their authority and responsibility and may misjudge the service's interests.

Preserving the balance poses problems with respect to membership. From the start the Navy League protected its freedom of action by barring from membership military men on active duty. The Air Force Association permitted active personnel to be members only in a non-voting, non-office-holding capacity. In contrast, the Army Association was originally composed largely of active officers. In 1956, however, it was reorganized, and the leadership was transferred to individuals not on active duty "so that the Association may exercise its right to express its own independent opinions." While they may in consequence have the freedom to do so, the service associations rarely, if ever, take stands opposed by the leaders of their service. The resolutions and programs adopted by the service associations at their annual conventions represent approximately what the leaders of the services would ask for if they were freed from Administration restraints. In 1959, for instance, the Administration advocated an Army of 870,000 men, the Chief of Staff one of 925,000 men, and the Army Association one of a million men.

Usually the service recognizes the unique position of the service association and the special relations which exist between them. At the same time, it also stresses the independence of the association. The Navy League, the Secretary of the Navy declared in 1958, is "the civilian arm of the service." Two months later, however, Admiral Burke told a Navy League audience that the Navy "has absolutely no control over your fine organization." Air Force sources have informally referred to the AFA as "our lobby," and in 1949, General H. H. Arnold even described the Association as "Air Force controlled." Yet its private character is also emphasized. The Secretary of the Army has declared that the relationship between the Department and the Association "although unofficial, must be close and cooperative." The "success of the Association," he said, "is a matter of vital interest to the Department of the Army."

Cultivation of the "Grass Roots"

The postwar period was also marked by increased service activities designed specifically to reach public opinion at the "grass roots." Service installations and activities, of course, were spread across the face of the land. A clear distinction existed, however, between the interest of a community in a particular installation and its interest in the service as a whole. The congressman from Charleston is an ardent supporter of the Navy—until the Navy proposes to cut its operations at the Charleston Navy Yard. Unlike many private associations and a fair number of governmental agencies, the services could not easily mobilize sentiment across the country in support of a national program. The problem which they faced was not dissimilar from that confronted by the large industrial corporations. Both the corporation and the service are national and highly centralized institutions. Political power in America, however, is to a large extent channeled through local organs. Individual political influence depends upon prolonged local residence and participation: the employees of the corporation and the service are continually on the move. On the one hand, the economic health of the local community may depend upon decisions by a General Staff in Washington or a board of directors in New York. On the other hand, the small community normally possesses direct access to state and local governing bodies, and frequently to Congress, in a way which is denied to the national organization.

Corporations have attempted to adjust to the decentralization of political power by supplementing their general public relations activities with other efforts specifically designed to reach local publics. The armed services have done likewise. Among them, the Army has been most active; more than the other services, it is apt to be concerned with issues where grass roots support is important. Shortly after World War II, for instance, when confronted with the need to stimulate recruiting and to arouse support for UMT, the Army sponsored the creation of Army Advisory Committees in numerous communities, each committee made up of leading local figures in business, religion, education, the press and radio, and civic organizations. "[I]nformation on our actual policies and actual plans," the Army's Chief of Information declared in 1947, "can be disseminated down through these advisory committees to all the various agencies that affect public opinion right out in the 'grass roots.' That is very important." Antedating the Committees, but subsequently closely associated with them, were the civilian aides to the Secretary of the Army. Their duties included advising the Secretary on matters relating to the public standing of the Army, investigating specific problems at his request, and cooperating with the local Army commanders in furthering their programs. The Navy's counterpart to the Army Advisory Committees was the Advisory Council on Naval Affairs, sponsored by the Navy League. The members of the Advisory Council were appointed by the commandants of the various naval districts and furnished the Navy with a means of reaching local opinion groups. In addition to these broadly purposed programs, all the services emphasized the importance of "community relations'" to the commanders of their posts and installations and urged them to carry on an active program of visits, support of local charities and projects, and sympathetic consideration of local interests.

The reserve structure was another means of reaching local public opinion. The reserve organization, and, to an even greater extent, the National Guard were influential with Congress simply because they were organized locally. As more than one congressman has noted, in contrast to the service "backstop" associations, the reserve organizations "have the votes." "Because the National Guard Association represents the fifty-one states and territories," as one National Guard leader put it, "and is able through its membership to bring considerable pressure to bear on Congress, it has consistently enjoyed a high respect from Congress." The strength of the Guard, he continued, lies both "in the state representation" and in "the potential vote represented by the 500,000 and their families." Army spokesmen and supporters frequently urged that efforts be made to utilize the reserves to put across the Army viewpoint. The very power of the reserve organizations, however, made them less susceptible to use by the service leadership and more likely to have interests different from those of the service. The Guard, for instance, was politically stronger than the Army reserve, but also more independent of the Regular Army.

Industrial Bulwarks

The high level of military spending required by the Cold War and the heavy concentration of that spending on complex weapons brought into existence a significant peacetime munitions industry for the first time in American history. In their search for support in civil society the services could hardly overlook their contractors. In mobilizing industry the Navy and Air Force started with two advantages over the Army. Both the Navy and the Air Force furnished a substantial portion of the total demand for the products of two distinct industries. The shipbuilding industry would always encourage a larger Navy, and the aircraft industry a substantial Air Force. The Army, in contrast, had no such concentrated source of industrial support. Secondly, the research, development, and, in some cases, the production of Army weapons was traditionally handled in government arsenals. The Navy made greater use of private industry, and the Air Force came into existence with little organized experience in research and development and hence depended very heavily upon the private aircraft companies. Army arsenals could generate support from the congressmen of their districts, but the aircraft companies could do this and also engage in all the public relations and propagandizing activities which their private status and funds permitted. "The aircraft industry," Senator Goldwater observed, "has probably done more to promote the Air Force than the Air Force has done itself."

Interservice rivalry stimulated industrial competition, and industrial competition, in turn, fanned the flames of interservice rivalry. In 1959, as the conflict between the Army Nike and the Air Force Bomarc came to a head, Boeing took newspaper and magazine ads to counter the "misinformation" spread about Bomarc, and Army officials urged Western Electric to increase its advertising on behalf of Nike. On the other hand, as General Gavin said, "what appears to be intense interservice rivalry . . . in most cases . . . is fundamentally industrial rivalry." Trade journals, Wernher von Braun declared, engage in "active instigation of interservice rivalry." They "often seem to feel that they owe it to their advertisers to go to bat for them" and to "publish quite frequently some rather vitriolic articles, taking a very one-sided stand in favor of one of the services." In nationwide advertisements, Chrysler proudly heralded the Army's successful Jupiter C space shot. Two weeks later Douglas retaliated with ads declaring that the Air Force Thor was "already in mass production." The Army Director of Special Weapons replied by referring caustically to a missile with "an apogee of four feet." The Air Force struck back by leaking information concerning its new solid-fuel Minute Man missile and at the same deprecating the expense of the Navy's solid-fuel Polaris missile. The Navy replied that Polaris was less vulnerable and much closer to operation than Minute Man. "Thus a publicity contest between two corporations," as William S. Fairfield observed, ". . . now involved the uniformed personnel of all three services."

The Thor-Jupiter controversy was perhaps a classic example of how interservice rivalry initially can open a choice to the top civilian leaders of the defense establishment and then, in effect, shut off that choice through competitive castellation of services. Thor and Jupiter were, as one general said, "about as alike as the Ford and the Chevrolet." The Secretary of Defense repeatedly asserted that only one or the other would be put into production. He delayed his decision, however, and in the end choice was impossible. "If the Defense Department suggested canceling the Air Force's Thor program," a former Pentagon official declared, "a Congressional delegation from California would be down our necks. And elimination of the Army Jupiter program would have half the Alabama delegation plus a couple of representatives from the Detroit area fighting us."

The shift from aircraft to missiles tended to broaden the ties of the aircraft industry with the services. The Navy, of course, had always been a significant purchaser of aircraft, and increasingly in the 1950s the Army also turned to the aircraft companies for its missiles. "The aircraft industry," one Air Force legislative liaison officer is quoted as saying in 1958, "just isn't likely to be as good a source for lobbying as it was two years ago." In the conflict between Jupiter (Chrysler) and Thor (Douglas), Douglas Aircraft was on the side of the Air Force. In the conflict between the Air Force Bomarc (Boeing) and the Army Nike (Douglas), however, Douglas was presumably on the side of the Army. As the major defense contractors in missiles and electronics increasingly held contracts with two or more services, the lines of industrial competition did not always coincide with and sometimes perhaps blurred those of interservice competition.

The Proliferation of Doctrine

After World War II, interservice competition contributed to increased service concern with, and output of, doctrine. Every bureaucratic agency, military and civilian, tends to develop a "bureau philosophy" or "ideology." The armed services differ from most civilian groups, however, in the extent to which the bureau philosophy becomes formal, self-conscious, and explicit. The philosophies of civilian agencies may be just as real as those of the military, but they are seldom codified into written statements of "doctrine." The importance of doctrine stems from the extent to which the military groups are perceived to be and perceive themselves to be simply the instruments of a higher national policy. The armed services explicitly rationalize their existence in terms of a higher national end, and each activity and unit is justified only by its contribution to the realization of the prescribed hierarchy of values and purposes. This instrumentalism is reflected in the emphasis, peculiar to the military, on the concept of "mission," and it manifests itself most concretely in the elaboration of doctrine.

Prior to the 1930s, doctrine was reasonably well developed in the Navy, somewhat less so in the Army. The rise of airpower, however, was a powerful stimulant to the military quest for ideology. Lacking secure organizational existence or general acceptance during the 1920s and 1930s, the supporters of airpower, like any new, crusading group, were tremendously concerned with the development of an intellectual rationale. The existence of the surface forces might be taken for granted; the need for an air force had to be demonstrated. Moreover, no longer was it possible for a service to elaborate a doctrine defining its importance to the nation and its relation to national policy without explicitly —and not just inferentially—defining the position of the other services also. Mahan had constructed a doctrine of seapower without specifically denigrating landpower. For the supporters of airpower, however, the attack on the surface forces was unavoidable. Once the Air Force was established, the intensity of its doctrinal concern perhaps moderated somewhat, but by this time the other services had felt compelled to reply in kind. Just as unification led to interservice political conflict, so it also stimulated interservice doctrinal conflict, and with the same power goals in view: jurisdiction, appropriations and influence.

The historical output of political theory, it has been suggested, correlates rather well with the presence of political crisis, turmoil, and conflict. So also, when vital controversies arise, military doctrine flourishes. After 1945, it proliferated in a variety of forms in manuals, speeches, journals, regulations, War College theses, and staff studies. The competitive spur to its formulation was concretely reflected in the creation of special staff units specifically designed to develop doctrine and arguments for use in the interservice debates, such as Navy's "Op-23," headed by Captain Arleigh Burke during the B-36 hearings, and the Army's Policy Coordinating Group, the head of which retired shortly after the interservice blow-up in the spring of 1956. Each service also attempted to formulate concise statements of doctrinal guidance for its members and persuasion for its potential supporters.

III. THE CHANGING CONTEXT OF INTERSERVICE COMPETITION

Interservice competition and the castellation of the services continued throughout the fifteen years after World War II. The content and the significance of the competition, however, changed markedly. In the immediate postwar period fundamental issues of service existence and strategy were at stake. After a major war, military policy is in a state of flux. The cake of custom, bureaucratic routine, and sustained habits of behavior—executive, congressional, and popular—are broken. Change is not only possible, but expected. In such periods, existing organizational units have the most to fear from major threats to their existence, and new organizational units have the best prospects for an easy birth or growth.

After World War II, each service and hoped-for service was anxious to carve out a role for itself suitable to its ambitions and self-conceptions before a postwar equilibrium was established and the patterns of organization and behavior jelled into enduring form.

• • •

The strategic debates of the late 1940s seemed equally momentous for the services. All agreed that the next war would be a total war. They did not agree how that war should be fought. In the Air Force image, the war consisted of an initially decisive—or airpower—stage in which victory would be irretrievably won or lost, and then a second mopping-up stage in which the other services might be of some use. The Army view (and essentially the Navy view, too) was that the initial air exchange would be indecisive until the surface forces had been built up to the point where they could move forward to seize bases and territories close to the enemy. After they had done their work, the air attack might play a somewhat more important role. But the final *coup de grace* would still be administered by ground forces moving in, defeating the enemy's land armies, and occupying enemy territory. Between these two concepts of a future war and the way it should be fought, no compromise seemed possible.

The debate, however, soon became obsolete. The war whose strategy the services were debating never occurred. Instead, the

Korean War and the development of thermonuclear weapons changed the framework of strategic thought. It became less and less likely that another war would be World War II plus nuclear weapons. The Air Forces no longer stressed the decisive aspect of airpower, but rather its deterrent quality. The experience of the other services in Korea was codified into a doctrine of limited war. Previously, the Air Force concept and the surface forces' concept of how to fight a general war had been completely incompatible. Deterrence and limited war, on the other hand, were complementary and competitive but not incompatible. Previously, any increase in the effectiveness of strategic airpower meant a decrease in the probable roles of the other services. Now, the more effective the massive deterrent became, the greater the probability of the smaller-scale disturbances with which the other services were primarily concerned. To be sure, the debates still continued over how much of the effort should be devoted to one purpose and how much to the other. All the services, however, accepted the necessity of devoting some resources to each. What had been conflicting images of a single-contingency future were replaced by general agreement on a multiple-contingency future, although the priorities and probabilities of the various contingencies remain in dispute.

In the middle 1950s, interservice debate was just as prevalent and intense as it had been previously. Strategic questions, however, had become less important and proprietary issues more important. The question was less what should be done than how it should be done and who should do it. Neither the fundamental existence of the services nor fundamental alternatives of national strategy were main issues, but rather marginal gains and losses of weapons and functions. Major strategic issues were still debated, but the debate was not so strictly along service lines. . . .

The relation of the services to fundamental issues of strategy in a sense tended to resemble the relation of the political parties to fundamental issues of national policy. The two parties have different centers of gravity with respect to policy, and yet each includes groups representing almost all viewpoints on the political spectrum. Similarly, while the outlook and doctrine of each service differs somewhat from that of the others, each service also has interests all across the strategic spectrum. At times, of course, there may be party votes on major issues of policy, and at times, also differences over strategy may coincide with differences between the services. Moreover, just as the parties exist independently of the issues of the moment, so also the existence of the service is independent of the strategy of the moment. The resolution of any particular set of issues, whether political or military, does not end the competition among the groups, whether parties or services. The competition continues, rising to peaks fixed by the calendar of biennial elections and annual budgets. Partisan debate and interservice debate are often carried on in clichés, slogans, and appeals, with little operational significance for governmental action. A member of a service is loyal to the service irrespective of its strategic function, just as a good organization Democrat or Republican is loyal to the party irrespective of its stand on policy. The existence of the services, moreover, like the existence of the parties, tends to obscure the issues of debate. The argument that the United States is well off to have non-ideological parties and that it would be unfortunate if the division between left and right coincided exactly with the division between Democrat and Republican may also hold true with respect to the services and strategy. Strategic issues are blurred by the overlay of service competition, and the proprietary issues at stake in the latter are inherently easier to compromise than basic issues of strategic principle.

The Cold War thus replaced the simple pattern of service-vs.-service rivalry by a complex matrix of rivalry between service and service, service and function, function and function. The multiplication of the lines of conflict also tended to minimize its intensity. In this, the evolution of military politics followed a classic American path. Overlapping memberships in interest groups moderate group conflicts. The conflict of interest groups within and across party lines moderates the party struggle. Party conflict across institutional boundaries moderates executive-legislative conflict. Similarly, in the military area, just as interservice rivalry moderated the potential conflict between military services and civilian agencies, the emergence of conflicting functional programs tends to moderate interservice rivalry.

• • •

Diversification of function also gave the services organizational flexibility and balance by freeing them from identification with and dependence upon any single strategic concept or functional mission. "The Army," its Secretary declared in 1957, "cannot—and indeed assiduously seeks not to—commit itself to any particular doctrine, strategy, or tactic." Non-commitment was the means of self-preservation. Shifts in emphasis in national policy from massive retaliation to limited war to continental defense would affect the relative standing of the services, but it was unlikely that they could threaten the existence of any service. The new role of the services was formally recognized in the Reorganization Act of 1958: the interservice and functional commands became clearly responsible for combat, the services for personnel, training, and logistics. By reducing the combat functions of the services, the act insured their continued existence.

If this tendency continued, eventually the services would end up as English regiments on a grand scale—administrative organizations rather than fighting organizations. Thus, at the very time when interservice competition was forcing the services to develop doctrinal justifications, the evolution of strategy was depriving them of their traditional source of doctrine. As a result, the doctrinal issues debated among the services often seemed to have but minor relevance outside the locus of interservice competition. Not infrequently they assumed a certain metaphysical quality, in arguments over whether landpower or airpower was the dominant force in modern war and whether guided missiles were aviation or artillery. Such issues had little practical consequence for policy, except—and it is a vital exception—so far as the future of the service was concerned.

The value of the services thus stemmed precisely from their incomplete commitment to any single doctrine. An organization such as SAC or the Continental Defense Command, which exists for only one strategic purpose, cannot be receptive to changes in its purpose or to the creation of new organizations embodying competing purposes. The functional commands of today are the vested interests of tomorrow. So long as the existence of no service, however, depends upon any single strategic purpose, no service has reason to oppose intransigently changes in strategic purposes. Organizational permanence is the partner of strategic flexibility. Thus the unified and specified commands may become the instruments of strategy, and yet the political castles of the services may also continue to stand, with their storied keeps of service loyalty and tradition, their inner and outer walls in the executive and Congress, their towers and barbicans in industry, their moats flowing with the currents of public opinion. Perhaps, at some point, a major political or military innovation may, like gunpowder, bring these political structures down in a heap of broken masonry. The experience of other established organizations in American politics, however, suggests a different fate; that the castles of the services, like many of their medieval counterparts, will remain in existence, battered but untaken, long after the decisive battles—both political and military—have shifted to other fields.

Retail Druggists
and the Fair Trade Laws

JOSEPH C. PALAMOUNTAIN

. . . [T]he crucial fact [about retail druggists] is a homogeneity and group cohesion so notably lacking among grocers. There are three major reasons for this. First, there is far less size variation among druggists. In 1939 the bulk of independent drug stores had volumes of between $10,000 and $50,000. Within this range lay 63.6 per cent of all druggists, accounting for 67.4 per cent of all sales, while only 34.5 per cent of all independent food stores, making 52.6 per cent of all independent food sales, fell within this range. 61.3 per cent of the independent food stores had a volume of less than $10,000, and 30.1 per cent of independent food sales were made by stores with sales of more than $50,000. It is possible to speak of *the* typical independent druggist with some accuracy, whereas it is necessary to speak of the typical marginal grocery store—a "Mama, Papa, and Rosy store"—the typical medium-sized full-service grocery store, and the typical large-volume self-service grocery. This means that most druggists are engaged in much the same *type, as* well as size, of operation. They share the same problems to much the same degree.

A second reason for greater group cohesion is that retail

Excerpted by permission of the publishers from *The Politics of Distribution*, pp. 92–105, 235–246. Cambridge, Mass.: Harvard University Press, Copyright, 1955 by The President and Fellows of Harvard College. Also reprinted by permission of the author.

pharmacy is a chosen occupation. Most druggists have undergone some training in preparation for a lifetime career. Entry tends to be limited to those who have some training and sufficient capital to carry a large stock. This again is in contrast to the grocery trade, which attracts a high proportion of the incompetent, the misfit, and the unemployed. And a mortality rate which is only from a half to a third of that for grocers enables greater stability and cohesion.

Finally, a third reason is that most druggists, being registered pharmacists, share an important bond and tend to regard themselves as professional men rather than as merchants. Thus to the ties of economic interest are added those of a profession —ties which usually cause those so united to share a feeling of exclusive superiority. Such a fusion of economic and professional bonds, as the American Medical Association demonstrates, can produce an unusually cohesive economic group with a strong sense of group purpose. It also tends to produce a conviction that their services should not be evaluated under solely economic criteria and that, accordingly, they should be protected from the rigors of the market.

This cohesion has characterized retail druggists for many years. The NARD [National Association of Retail Druggists], the politically most powerful of all retail associations, was organized in 1898. By 1906 it was powerful enough to enforce a "Tripartite Agreement" among drug manufacturers, wholesalers, and retailers. This agreement established uniform retail prices through manufacturers' sales contracts binding distributors to specified resale prices. Manufacturers were induced to sign contracts by a well organized program of blacklists, white lists, and boycotts by wholesalers and retailers. While this scheme was held to be a violation of the Sherman Act, and the NARD and the National Wholesale Druggists' Association (NWDA) were perpetually enjoined from continuing these practices, the scope and success of the Tri-partite Agreement do attest to the high level of organization achieved by both wholesalers and retailers, although the NARD was the principal force behind the agreement. And the NARD and other druggists' organizations were prominent in the political campaign for resale price maintenance legislation from 1914 on. Even in the absence of formal organization, group consciousness and joint action mark the druggists. In the late nineties druggists adopted a code word "pharmocist," which could be so marked on prescription copies that the original prescription price could be ascertained and matched when refilled by a second druggist. While the NARD may have been instrumental in the adoption of the code, it speedily dissociated itself from any responsibility for the practice. Yet in 1929, thirty years later, most druggists still honored code prices.

This cohesion has had important consequences throughout the trade. Price competition has usually been avoided without arousing consumer antagonism, for a customer is peculiarly helpless in his drug purchases: he is seldom capable of intelligent judgment about the prices and qualities of drugs and usually is equally ignorant about toiletries and related products. Indeed, a low price may be a competitive disadvantage if it is substantially below the price of similar products. In the absence of intertype competition there is a strong tendency toward price uniformity, price lines, and relatively high retail margins.

Here, too, the interrelations among horizontal, intertype, and vertical competition and conflict are complex. Retail emphasis on nonprice competition has combined with consumer apathy to cause manufacturers similiarly to stress nonprice competition. The unusual cohesion of retail groups has made the boycott a powerful weapon, and retailers' vertical strength has been enhanced by their influence over consumers. In his drug purchases the consumer often asks the druggist's advice, and that fact that the druggist is a white-coated professional man, a registered pharmacist, renders the customer susceptible to suggestion. Thus the retailer is often in the peculiarly strategic position of selecting which one of several competing articles will be bought. This power of selection makes boycotts most effective and causes manufacturers to compete for the support of retailers as well as of consumers. This competition is reflected in high retail margins and increases in normal margins through such devices as "free goods" and special allowances and discounts. Manufacturers may also provide demonstrators or pay commissions or "PM's" to drug clerks.

Some manufacturers may try to offset retailers' power by extensive advertising, using it not only as a weapon of horizontal competition but also as a tool in vertical relations. Others may accept retailers' power and try to harness it by such inducements as those just described. Sometimes the tribute paid to retailer power reaches major proportions, such as the payment of $25,000 to the NARD by the Pepsodent Company in order to be reinstated in the good graces of the retail druggists. Such special inducements, however, require a sizable staff of sales representatives and may tend to displace the wholesaler. But the general-line wholesaler is not easily displaced. . . . The stock requirements of a retailer make him dependent on his wholesaler for frequent delivery and usually for credit. Few other organizations can match the range of stock carried by a general-line wholesaler. Retailers who buy from voluntary group wholesalers, retailer cooperative warehouses, and cash-and-carry wholesalers, and even many chain drug stores, must patronize a general-line wholesaler for some purchases. He has the largest average volume of wholesalers in all trades, and his sales dwarf even those of the average manufacturer of drugs and toiletries. Furthermore, many wholesalers do much manufacturing themselves, producing a variety of products from their own formulae, from those of physicians who purchase from them, and from the American Pharmacopoeia. Finally, the fact that their numbers are so few enables them to organize cohesive and strong trade associations.

The power and strength of the general-line wholesaler has

produced a stable discount schedule and a fairly high wholesale margin. Despite his strategic position and his strength, however, he has been increasingly replaced by manufacturers' wholesale outlets. He can perform many services for the manufacturer, such as the anticipation of demand and the allocation of supply, but, carrying so many thousands of lines, he cannot sufficiently focus his attention to offer the many special concessions, allowances, services, and personal contacts which manufacturers desire in their competition for the favor of the retailer. A large manufacturer therefore may establish his own wholesale outlets in order to contact retailers and to tap their power. Despite the danger of incurring the wrath of the powerful wholesalers, many large manufacturers have undertaken the laborious and expensive chore of supplying directly about 58,000 drugstores rather than simply selling to 297 wholesalers who cover almost every retail outlet, thereby demonstrating the value they place on personal contact with retailers and their high evaluation of retailer power. In 1939, while general-line wholesalers were the largest single source of supply for all retailers, selling them 46 per cent of their supplies, retailers bought 19 per cent of their supplies from manufacturers' wholesale outlets, 15 per cent from specialty-line wholesalers, and 17 per cent directly from manufacturers.

Thus distribution by manufacturers is an important alternative marketing channel; it is in intertype competition with wholesalers. Unlike the channel opened by grocery chains, however, this medium is an extremely costly one, its operating expense in 1939 being about double that of general-line wholesalers. It has directly increased distributive costs and also has unnecessarily duplicated marketing facilities.

All the factors—horizontal, vertical, and intertype—thus far discussed have increased distributive margins. Indeed so powerful have retailers and wholesalers been that a retail margin of 33⅓ per cent—equivalent to a markup of 50 per cent on cost— and a wholesale margin of 16⅔ per cent have been traditional.

Although this retail margin has been reduced by competition on many fast-moving items, the full margin has long been a watchword among druggists and one of the major objectives of the NARD. Manufacturers have been forcefully acquainted with the desire of organized druggists for a 33⅓ per cent margin. Boycotts and the pushing or burying of products have vividly demonstrated the intensity of this desire and the great influence of druggists over consumers. Since consumers usually are not price conscious, manufacturers are often willing to grant such margins, especially since uniform margins may enable them to avoid price competition among themselves.

The simplest way for a manufacturer to guarantee a margin is to fix the retail, "resale," or "list" price of his item. Since he directly controls his price to wholesalers, he has now determined the combined wholesale and retail margins. The retail price is usually printed on the item's container, but this does not make it legally enforceable. The most effective method of enforcement is to sign contracts with distributors or to refuse to sell to price-cutting distributors. These actions have usually been held illegal, but the persistence with which manufacturers have nevertheless attempted to control resale prices is another tribute to the power of retail druggists. It also demonstrates the complex interrelations among the different planes of competition and conflict. Here retailers have used vertical power over manufacturers to induce them, in turn, to use *their* vertical power over retailers to control horizontal competition among retailers.

Attempts to maintain resale prices on drugs began in California as early as the 1870's. The primary pressure on manufacturers was at first that of wholesalers. After the creation of the NARD in 1898, the movement to force manufacturers to maintain resale prices became national in scope, and retailers became the primary force behind the movement. The initial program, as we have seen, ended with the outlawing of the Tri-partite Agreement in 1907. Meanwhile, the NARD had persuaded manufacturers to adopt resale price maintenance contracts together with a serial numbering of products to enable enforcement of the contracts—a program first developed by the Miles Medical Company in 1903 or 1904. At the NARD Convention in 1904 twelve of the largest drug manufacturers agreed to the plan. When this plan was declared illegal in 1911, druggists persuaded manufacturers to announce resale prices and then refuse to sell to wholesalers or retailers who did not observe these prices. In 1919 the Supreme Court appeared to sanction this method but later held refusals to sell illegal if they implied an agreement to suppress competition among retailers. Despite these decisions and vigorous enforcement by the FTC until the NRA, drug manufacturers still tried to enforce resale prices, and many successfully pursued refusal-to-sell policies.

Thus, once again, the vertical power of retailers, group organization and cohesion at both retail and wholesale levels, and consumer ignorance and inexperience have all combined to maintain relatively high margins. Indeed, despite the rise of some intertype competition, actual wholesale and retail margins in the late 1930's approximated the 16 per cent and 33⅓ per cent traditionally demanded. The same factors that produce high margins have also encouraged so much advertising and other sales expense that there is little correlation between manufacturing cost and retail price. It is notorious that many patent medicines selling for a dollar or more cost only a few cents. This is also true of many preparations which, although bearing brand names, are standard pharmaceutical formulae, and which can be made by a pharmacist for as little as one tenth of their *wholesale* price. . . .

• • •

. . . [O]ne of the strongest political drives will be that of retailers and wholesalers seeking to protect their margins. They can do this most easily by seeking legislative permission for them to compel manufacturers to guarantee margins. So strong are druggists that we may expect manufacturers to accept subordination to them [Fair Trade legislation was the device sought to bring about this result.]

THE FAIR-TRADE LAWS

The NARD's broad and forceful campaign for "fair-trade," or resale price maintenance, legislation—permitting the fixing of minimum wholesale and retail prices on trademarked goods—in the 1930's was extraordinarily successful. . . .

. . . Within an eight-year period, 1933–1940, the NARD secured the passage of resale price maintenance acts in 44 states —half again as many as passed chain taxes. In one year alone, 1937, 28 states passed such laws. That this was a centrally directed and carefully organized campaign is indicated by the fact that the acts of 16 states are closely modeled on the California statute, which had been passed at the insistence of the organized retail druggists of that state, and those of 20 states are direct or close copies of the NARD's "Model Act." These acts were such close copies and were pushed through so hastily that 16 states repeated California's wrongful use of the word "content" where "container" was intended, and 11 states actually copied a stenographic error in the California act which made an important section of the law unintelligible, substituting "in delivery" for "any dealer."

The NARD's success on the federal level was equally striking. It won passage of the Miller-Tydings Amendment to the almost sacred Sherman Act in 1937, despite the fact that every session of Congress since 1914 had seen that body reject resale price maintenance legislation and despite the opposition of a President who had just received overwhelming support in the 1936 elections.

Economic factors explain much of this legislative success. . . . There are many economic and other factors which make retail druggists more cohesive than perhaps any other retail merchants, enabling them to form a militant, well organized, highly disciplined trade association, capable of conducting effective political campaigns. Of probably equal importance is the trade's power structure. . . . The power structure within automobile distribution hindered dealers in mobilizing political power and narrowly confined the gains which could be won. The drug trade's power structure offers a sharp contrast. Because the retailer often performs the crucial function of selection—determining which brand a consumer will buy—manufacturers are dependent on his good will and hesitate to antagonize him. In addition, because of inelastic consumer demand for drugs and cosmetics, resale price maintenance, and its consequent raising of retail margins, does not lose manufacturers much volume. And, since the consumer had never made much use of his potential economic power and could be expected to be politically quiescent, druggists were relatively free to promote a program designed to increase retail margins.

Finally, it was unlikely that intertype competitors would muster strong political opposition to the druggists. The logical opponents, the chains, had come to accept nonprice competition and to mute their price appeal. The deepest price competition confronting druggists was that offered by pine-board stores and department stores. But the former's economic base was so marginal and personal—resting on their ability to secure distress merchandise, to get by with minimum product ranges, and to find low-rental quarters—that they could not generate or organize effective political power. Accordingly, the burden of mustering and expressing intertype political opposition to the NARD's program had to be borne by department stores, whose political strength was confined to cities.

Thus, the economic bases for a political victory of the independent retail druggists are readily apparent. Even a quick summary of the political campaign shows how much of its success is due to these economic bases. While other retailers—notably liquor dealers and booksellers—aided the druggists, this was the NARD's program, and it was the NARD which directed and organized the campaign and which exerted the preponderance of force in support of it. . . .

At work here was the same militant cohesion which had made the NARD one of the major forces behind the Robinson-Patman bill and which had enabled it, through an unusual amount of pressure, to obtain the most protective of all NRA retail codes. And retail druggists were considerably aided by their vertical allies. The wholesalers naturally allied themselves with the retailers. Maintenance of retail prices and margins would tend to protect wholesale margins. Indeed, there are some suggestions that drug wholesalers, especially McKesson & Robbins, played a major role in promoting and financing the campaign, but little concrete evidence is available. Manufacturers, too, were inclined to support resale price maintenance. A manufacturer whose product had been made a loss leader often found that, as a consequence, independents were reluctant to stock it and some consumers balked at paying its normal retail price. Retailers often were not content with purely voluntary support from manufacturers; they blacklisted or boycotted manufacturers who did not support their program, and maintained white lists of cooperating manufacturers. The experience of the Pepsodent Company is the best example of how a manufacturer could be "persuaded" to support the druggists. In 1935 Pepsodent withdrew from its California fair-trade contracts for fear of violating the Sherman Act. Druggists' associations quickly reacted by urging their members to boycott Pepsodent. Almost to a man the retailers responded. The executive secretary of the Northern California Retail Druggists' Association reported that

> . . . to my great delight and the great delight of our executive committee all the druggists in California refused to sell Pepsodent

toothpaste or Pepsodent products. They put them in the basement. Some were enthusiastic enough to throw them into the ash can.

The boycott was almost completely successful. For a while it was possible to buy Pepsodent products only in a few pineboards. News of the boycott was passed on to druggists in other states, and the Company's national sales fell appreciably. Here was a clear demonstration of the vertical power of druggists and of their surprising group solidarity. Pepsodent was a relatively powerful firm. Through extensive advertising it had won about as much consumer preference and hence had generated about as much vertical power as any manufacturer could. Yet it had been decisively defeated by the organized druggists. After a few months of drastically declining sales, Pepsodent capitulated, again signed price maintenance contracts, *and* donated a check of $25,000 to the NARD to be used in support of the campaign for fair-trade acts. Following this good-will offering, other manufacturers voluntarily contributed to the fund, and still others were requested to donate.

Their vertical power permitted druggists to present what appeared to be industry-wide support for price maintenance at Congressional hearings and probably at hearings before state legislative committees. At all Congressional hearings on the Miller-Tydings Amendment manufacturers as well as wholesalers joined retailers in supporting the legislation. Much of this support clearly was by command of the NARD. This political solidarity was possible because of the same factor which gave the retailers their economic power: the silence of the consumer—unorganized, inarticulate, and probably unaware. At these three hearings only one witness testified for the consumer, and she was a self-appointed representative. Spokesmen for the Farm Bureau Federation and the National Grange also opposed the bill in the interests of farmers as consumers, but their opposition was so perfunctory and ill-informed that the Congressional committees could have safely assumed that farmer-consumers were not much concerned.

That consumers are congenitally difficult to organize and arouse is a political truism. Yet the task is not hopeless. As we have seen, grocery chains finally mustered considerable consumer support in opposition to the Patman tax bill. This political support, however, had been based upon a prior economic support. Having successfully appealed to consumers with lower prices, the grocery chains were then able to generate some political support for a continuation of those prices. But drug chains had given up the effort to elicit consumer support for lower prices, accepting fatter margins in preference to promoting intertype competition. Where once they had vigorously opposed resale price maintenance legislation, they now supported it, seeking protection from pine-boards and department stores. "Today chains are working shoulder to shoulder with the independents in behalf of fair trade legislation," said the NARD. Consequently, if there were to be any consumers' tribunes to mobilize consumer support for a continuation of deep price cuts, they had to arise from the pine-boards or the department stores. But the former were too marginal and small to play an effective role, and sent not a single representative to the Congressional hearings. From among the ranks of the department stores, R. H. Macy, long a leading price-cutter, did try to assume this role. It fought federal and New York legislation vigorously and forcefully. But even in New York, where it elicited some consumer opposition, it could not prevent passage of a fair-trade act. In Washington it was almost alone in its opposition, commanding the support of only the department stores' trade association, the National Retail Dry Goods Association, and the Mail Order Association.

Thus the drug trade presented a united front, facing the opposition of only a few department stores. The economic bases, then, do explain much of the NARD's political success. Yet this is not a full explanation. Economic circumstances explain why virtually the whole drug trade supported fair trade; they do not explain how it was possible for the nation's 50,000 druggists, together with other drug interests, to gain such a sweeping political victory with so little support from other retailers. The absence of effective opposition from other groups is only a partial answer, for the Miller-Tydings Amendment was opposed by a strong President. And every previous session of Congress since 1914 had seen similar legislation fail, although many earlier bills were backed by broad group coalitions.

The political process was more than a simple reflection of underlying economic forces. The NARD's great success—the passage of 28 state acts and one federal statute in a single year—suggests extraordinary political skill and organization. The NARD was immodest, perhaps, but accurate in attributing victory to "a combination of brilliant leadership and direction, plus loyal and active support by the members." It has frequently taken pride in its "constant militance and vigilance" and has said that "legislative activity has been one of the major divisions of the Association's work since its beginning." Little wonder that its secretary should boast that "the NARD can do anything in reason that the retail druggists want it to do. . ." And the political skill of its leadership was matched by the cohesion and effectiveness of its organization. Its *Journal* was justified in exulting, after the passage of the Miller-Tydings Amendment, that "once again . . . ORGANIZATION WINS!" Its political skill and organizational cohesion were amply demonstrated throughout this decade. In addition to its sweeping fair-trade victory, the Association had been a major force behind the Robinson-Patman Act, had assisted in the passage of state chain taxes and unfair trade practices acts, and had induced at least 11 states and over 200 cities to confine the profitable sale of prophylactics to drug stores. This mastery of the political arts cannot be dismissed as a mere reflection of economic circumstances.

Not much material is readily available on the state campaigns conducted by the NARD, but apparently it took advantage of a relative lack of opposition to push through its legislation speedily and easily. This speed and ease are indicated by the number of bills passed in one year, by the fact that hasty legislatures enacted bills with stenographic errors, and by the fact that few legislatures even conducted hearings. The campaign was, however, centrally directed. "The outstanding work of the NARD has been of extreme importance in the enactment of these laws. The Association furnished state legislative committees with facts, figures, and a wealth of ammunition with which to fight these bills through legislatures." And druggists' pressure on state legislators paralleled the NARD's method of influencing Congress.

Under a "Captain Plan," first developed in California and then applied nationally, the NARD organized a contact committee in every Congressional district, headed by a "Captain," who was intimately acquainted with the district's Representative. By 1937 there were two thousand "Congressional contact men" in operation, and the number later rose to three thousand. Each of these men, in turn, was expected to form in his own local community a committee of ten other retailers "who will work and move as a unit when called upon by the NARD Washington Office." These committees exploited the especial malleability of candidates for office by approaching the nominees for House and Senate in the 1936 elections and asking for their pledges of support. With such a disciplined army in the field, the NARD's GHQ could conduct a most effective political campaign, attacking on broad fronts or concentrating fire on one point of resistance after another. They could bombard all Congressmen with demands for passage of the Miller-Tydings Amendment, producing "a flood of letters and telegrams coming from practically every community in the nation," or they could inundate members of a crucial committee. The *NARD Journal* for 1936 and 1937 reads like a file of battle orders. At one time one thousand communications were ordered sent to each member of a committee considering the bill; at another time each druggist was commanded to write a letter a week to his Representative and Senator; in the later stages of the bill's consideration "a constant barrage of letters and telegrams and letters" was ordered. Direct pressure was applied on the President and the FTC, and state governors were strongly urged to communicate their support of the bill to the President and the Commission. Determined and organized attempts were made to gain allies. Instructions were given on methods of securing consumer support and of lining up support from other retailers. Manufacturers were "persuaded" to support the bill and unsympathetic newspapers were attacked. In short, while the economic environment had minimized opposition and made victory possible, the achievement of that victory required positive political action and a mastery of the weapons of political warfare.

Equally responsible for its victory was the way in which the NARD had framed and presented the issues. Seeking to lessen criticism of its program as "price-fixing"—criticism which had defeated all earlier federal price maintenance bills—it combined an appeal to general antichain, antibigness sentiment with an appeal to equity. It argued that chains had grown primarily because of an unfair trade practice—loss leaders—and that only the prohibition of this practice would enable independents to survive.

> These unfair trade practices have . . . been peculiarly helpful to . . . large distributors. . . . Thus large concerns have become larger. . . . Monopoly now casts its insidious shadow over the land that was meant to symbolize free and open opportunity for all.

> We are up against the question of whether we want to protect small business enterprises against powerful aggregations of capital. . . . I am not out to destroy big business, but . . . it must be properly regulated . . . for not to regulate it so the small businessman can survive is to tend toward monopoly and no competition at all.

. . . [T]he small retail distributors are rapidly approaching the
time when they will be forced completely out of an independent
business existence. . . . Even if this situation were the outcome of
fair methods of competition . . . it would be deplorable. . . .
These small businesses have been and are the backbone of the
communities of this country. . . . If we ask ourselves, honestly,
whether we want this country to become a nation of clerks or to
remain a nation of opportunity for individual enterprise, there
can be only one answer consistent with American ideals.

The bill's supporters devoted most of their arguments to
attacks on loss leaders, which they assailed for injuring: a manufacturer, by cutting off some of his marketing channels or by
damaging the reputation of his products; a wholesaler, by disrupting "normal" trade channels; an independent retailer, by
cutting his sales; and a consumer, by deceiving him into the
belief that all products in a cut-rate store were priced on an
equally low level and by bankrupting the fully-stocked druggist
and so depriving the consumer of ready access to a full stock of
drugs. This was a persuasive argument. Loss leaders can be
defended as a method of advertising, but there are also sound
and, to the members of the Congressional committees, convincing
reasons for terming their use a deceptive, perhaps even preda-
tory, trade practice. But the argument against loss leaders was
only a smokescreen. Had it really been the NARD's goal to out-
law them, then the most direct method would have been state
acts prohibiting sales below cost. Indeed, 25 states had passed
such legislation by 1940. While these laws may be held unconstitutional unless cost is defined narrowly, they do effectively bar
loss leaders.

Fair-trade acts permit the manufacturer of a trademarked,
branded, or otherwise identified product, or his authorized agent
or distributor, to prescribe by contract the minimum prices at
which the product may be resold at wholesale and at retail. The
nonsigner clause of these laws makes the observance of the prices
set by a contract signed with any one distributor mandatory on

all other distributors within the state upon the serving of notice. Thus a manufacturer or his distributor can set minimum resale prices for his goods at all stages in their distribution. Although such contracts conflict with common-law doctrines of contract, in 1936 the Supreme Court sustained them as a valid method of protecting a manufacturer's good will, and upheld the constitutionality of the Illinois and California statutes.

[In recent years the political, legal, and economic circumstances affecting distribution have changed considerably. Discount houses are commonplace and resale price maintenance is only sporadic in actual operation. But the interplay of political and economic forces illustrated here remains highly pertinent, and the often complex links between the structure of economic interests and the substance of public policy still require careful scrutiny. Ed.]

Organized Labor in Electoral Politics: Some Questions for the Discipline

HARRY M. SCOBLE

ORGANIZED LABOR AS A SYSTEM OF ELECTORAL POWER

The CIO's Political Action Committee was created under and largely by Sidney Hillman in 1943 for the purpose of "nonparty, nonpartisan" politics. The American Federation of Labor hesitated just long enough, in its traditional reluctance to turn away from "business-unionism," to witness the failure of organized labor to defeat the Taft-Hartley Act in 1946; then it, too, took the path of electoral action, patterning its Labor's League for Political Education on the earlier PAC. (Since 1955 and the merger of the AFL and CIO, these political-action arms have slowly been merged into the joint Committee on Political Education.) These facts, which every politically oriented student of America ought to know, are repeated here to underscore the major point that the most fundamental postwar change in the structure and process of political parties has been the entrance of organized labor into electoral activity at the precinct level and on up.

But when one searches the literature of social science for a full description of what it is in fact that labor unions *do* in elections and for systematic analysis of such activity, one finds pri-

From the *Western Political Quarterly*, Vol. 16, No. 3 (September, 1963), pp. 666–686. Reprinted by permission of the University of Utah, copyright owners.

marily pronouncements and sentiments instead of facts and science. . . .

• • •

THE NATIONAL CONVENTIONS AND LEGISLATIVE RECRUITMENT

The available facts are pitifully few. Why should this be so? The area of national conventions and legislative recruitment provide illustrations. If one takes the date of the creation of the PAC as the proper starting point of the entrance of unions into elections, it is clear that nine national elections have now passed in which organized labor has participated; four of these were presidential elections. It seems not unreasonable to hypothesize that mass-membership interest groups will seek to seat their officers-members in the state delegations to the national nominating convention of that party with which the overwhelming majority of the interest group members identify. For example, Key noted that "around 200 unionists attended the Democratic National Convention as delegates or alternates in 1952; and anyone attending to his television set in 1960 could learn that there were 42 officers-members of the United Steel Workers alone among the total Pennsylvania delegation to the Democratic Convention. Furthermore, it is common knowledge among political scientists that the Brookings Institution has expended large sums of money and has produced several massive descriptions of national party conventions and of presidential elections; and in all that body of description, it is possible to learn that in 1948 labor union representatives constituted 2.1 per cent of the total Democratic delegations as against 0.2 per cent of the total Republican delegations while 1962 [sic 1956] data include information on the annual income, the education, and so on of the delegates (one may even discover the races of the ministers who prayed for those conventions)—but one cannot find information on the *occupations* or the *interest group memberships* of the delegations for 1952, or for 1956, or for 1960. This suggests that sheer description is not enough; the product amounts only to a dated edition of the *New York Times*. The conclusion is inescapable: if teams of political scientists are to describe complex political behavior such as a national convention or a presidential campaign, some organizing principles other than mere chronology must first be decided upon. It is my contention that group theory can provide organization and meaning where none now exist.

Candidate-recruitment presents another enigma. Labor's League for Political Education announced in 1949 that it would henceforth subsidize labor members of those state legislatures in which salaries were extremely low. The proposal was patterned on the long-standing practice of the British Labour party; its purpose was to increase the availability of labor union candidacies by organized compensation for social-structural processes noted at least as long ago as the time of Max Weber. Within the limits of the institutional and demographic gerrymander against the union vote in all state politics, the LLPE proposal might, *if carried out*, have had some measurable counterbalancing effect. But what political scientist in America even knows whether the policy was attempted, much less effective? One may, of course, suppose that the LLPE activists were somewhat naive in their public announcement: the reader easily imagine the editorial reaction to such a "radical" proposal in the pages of the *New York Times*, the *Wall Street Journal*, and almost every other newspaper in the land. It is not inconceivable that labor leaders might have decided that such policies are best carried out away from the glare of flashbulbs and klieg lights. But who in the political science profession is carrying out trend analyses to find out whether, regardless of labor propaganda, labor ideology is in fact being advanced by increasing union representation in state legislatures? It was like pulling teeth to find out that "laborers and craftsmen" constituted 5.5 per cent of all lower-house members and 2.5 per cent of all state Senate members in 1949; the combined percentage was 5.0, and such *possibly* union legislators were most *numerically* frequent in the legislatures of Rhode Island, Minnesota, Connecticut, and Pennsylvania, in descending order; on the other hand, in the most heavily industrialized states of Massachusetts, Michigan, New York, and New Jersey "representatives of labor were so few that in numerical terms they were of little significance, although in these states there were more labor leaders." That summarizes what is known.

LABOR AND THE PARTY APPARATUS

Suppose that one asks what is known concerning organized labor and the party apparatus, again with relation to the Democratic party. If it could be demonstrated that organized labor *is* sometimes the political party at city, county, and/or state levels, political scientists could finally turn away from the foolish distinction about nominations and begin to ask the more important questions: Under what conditions, with what tactics, and with what consequences do mass-membership interest groups become the party apparatus? The trend questions also then become appropriate.

To illustrate: in Rockford, Illinois, the CIO-PAC organized to elect precinct captains in order successfully to swing the election of the Democratic chairman for Winnebago County. Concerning *local* elections, the evidence—such as it is—is an odd mixture. In New Haven, Connecticut, the city itself is the fifth largest employer; most of its employees are now unionized and, along with other union members and union families, now constitute about 36 per cent of the electorate; these people have apparently voted as a bloc in at least one important election (1945)—but unionist activity has not become the apparatus for local nominations and elections, and the trade union leadership's activity and involvement is largely that of traditional lobbying "only on questions of the wages, security, and working conditions of city employees." A survey of the politics of education in Massachusetts also suggests that labor union leaders and members have not yet perceived local electoral activity as a means to their ends, relying instead on ineffectual traditional lobbying to promote the addition of pro-labor courses to the public school curriculum, to protest the politico-economic views of teachers, and to protest the use of NAM-supplied "educational materials" in the school system. In Madison and Kenosha, Wisconsin, on the other hand, evidence exists of direct and increasing union activity in local educational elections. The best available survey of New York City politics suggests the following: The Central Trades and Labor Council (AFL and representing about three-quarters of a million unionists) had initially de-emphasized its political purpose, but had "an almost unbroken history of endorsing the major candidates of the Democratic Party for city office" (with, however, an occasional split to a Republican candidate for Borough President and City Council in the last decade). Its electoral activity locally was directed primarily toward a broad concern for personnel and policy in the limited interests of the building trades, teamsters, and longshoremen's unions. Meanwhile the authors expected that the 1959 merger (with a million-and-a-half unionists) would lead to slow change in the direction of "greater and more unified influence" because of the CIO's greater concern for electoral action and also because of the 400,000 votes quadrennially mustered by the Liberal party (largely ILGWU).

The evidence that is available thus suggests that organized labor has not yet become the party apparatus of the community with regard to community or local politics; on the other hand, lacking "community political systems" analyses of Akron, Cicero, Gary, or Pittsburgh, it is wisest to suspend judgment on this point.

At least the study of organized labor with regard to nationally oriented party machinery has been a little more thorough and slightly more revealing. Recent studies of the successes of the

Democratic party in such widely separated states as Maine and Wisconsin provide brief generalized descriptions of union activity; at the lowest level of analysis, therefore, one may infer some effect. More directly descriptive of the relations between organized labor and the growth of successful party organization are recent studies of the Minnesota and Michigan Democratic parties. Mitau indicates the present importance of union-member identification with the Democrat-Farmer-Labor party in the former state while the studies of the Michigan Democrats by Calkins, by the Sarasohns, and by Eldersveld and his associates particularly highlight the role of unions in creating a party apparatus. In Michigan, for example, it is estimated that 821 of 1,000 members filing in 1948 for Wayne County precinct delegate were stimulated to action by their union-membership; shortly after that (the year of the first Williams victory) it was estimated that 64 per cent of all money donated to the Democratic State Central Committee and directly to statewide candidates came from United Auto Worker and other CIO-union funds. And, by the mid-1950's, evidence existed for concluding that CIO-PAC electoral action not only exceeded that of the regular Democratic organization in much of Wayne County but that "in fact, in a few of the Detroit Congressional Districts the regular organization has been largely supplanted by the CIO-PAC." More broadly, Heard has cited evidence indicating that in 1952, somewhere in the neighborhood of 1,000 unionists were active as full-time campaign workers in the closing weeks of the election in California, while in 1956 in the Detroit area 1,549 UAW temporary election workers were hired with dues money paid to local unions. Additional evidence of the integration of union structure and Democratic party structure comes from a study of precinct committeemen in Gary, Indiana; for the study by Rossi and Cutright indicates the importance of membership in and identification with the union, particularly the United Steel Workers, in leading into precinct political work. In the sample, 20 per cent of the white Democratic and 23 per cent of the Negro Democratic precinct committeemen gave union (or class-interest) responses as the "self-activating motive" for entering political work. Among Republican precinct workers the comparable percentages were zero. From such facts one may infer that since World War II union leaders and members alike have in large numbers come to the conclusion that political activism within—and public identification with—the Democratic party is an efficient means to personal and organization goals.

VOTE MOBILIZATION

Vote-mobilization is the third area of inquiry in this review of the scant factual material available about organized labor in electoral politics. Labor unions have carried out registration drives and get-out-the-vote drives in both primary and general elections and have done everything else that a political party does, including provision of free baby-sitting service on election day. At the level of description, facts abound; but at the level of analysis, knowledge remains fragmentary, shadowy, and highly unsystematic. For example, the New Jersey CIO-PAC carried on a self-appraisal of its early-registration drive; and at least one political scientist, having read this, stated that "convincing evidence is available to show that the CIO did a relatively better job in 1950 in registering its members than the general public"; while Heard more generally cites a Connecticut CIO Council report, "Voter Registration Survey—1954," to the effect that it revealed "startlingly low registration among union members, and the rewarding effects of attempts to raise it"—the sole references available in political science literature today that constitute anything close to evaluations of the effectiveness of such political action. This raises a series of interrelated questions: Have union political activists stopped attempting to appraise their activities since 1951? If not, have they "clamped a lid of secrecy" on such analysis?

Again if not, then have political scientists been remiss in not asking the right questions of the right people? A second comment must be made about the meager data: the correct baseline for the measurement of effect of any union political activity—registration or get-out-the-vote or directional-impact—is other unorganized workers and not "the general public." Thus when Jack Kroll wrote in 1951, estimating that roughly the first five years of labor voter-registration drives resulted in "about 55 to 60 per cent of labor union members" having been registered and that this constituted "only a slight edge on the general population," the political scientist ought to have been skeptical: organized labor has a vested interest in appearing efficient-but-not-too-efficient in American politics.

This is an exceedingly important point—what does activity mean?—and one on which, despite the repeated injunctions of Lasswell in favor of trend analysis and despite the welcome work of the Survey Research Center, it is apparently impossible to obtain relevant data for comparison over more than three successive elections in a time-series. For example, do union members vote (including register) more frequently than relevant others? Campbell and Cooper present data for 1948, 1952, and 1954 indicating that unionists voted 6.7 per cent more frequently than others—but the comparison is with the general population; but when union members are correctly compared only with non-union workers of comparable occupation, education, income, and status—for the two presidential elections on which data are available the unionists voted at an average of 16.0 per cent more. Both of these figures suggest that important differences in volume of political activity are associated with labor unions and that these differences between unionists and non-unionists (whether generally or specifically compared) *increased* between 1945 and 1955.

This brings us to the second point of inquiry. It is hardly esoteric social science knowledge that organized labor, at least since 1936, has consistently voted more Democratic than have other sectors of society. But all knowledge beyond this seems to be highly esoteric in the sense that it is extremely difficult to find intelligent appraisals of *how much* more Democratic and of trends. Illustratively, union families in Elmira, New York, whether of skilled workers or unskilled, were at least 24 per cent more Democratic than non-union families in both categories in the 1948 election; but that was an unusual election, as Dr. George Gallup and other commercial pollsters have revealed. Its uniqueness is evident in the 1948 "Iowa Poll" of the *Des Moines Register and Tribune,* which indicated that union members were 9 per cent more likely to report having had conversations concerning the election and were 18 per cent more "certain of vote" than the general Iowa sample *even with education controlled.* It is appropriate, therefore, to turn away from the "unique event" which plagues social science just as much as it does Dr. Gallup, although in somewhat different ways. Gallup data for the entire period 1936 through 1960 have recently been published indicating that "union families" voted an average of 6.7 per cent more Democratic than "all manual-worker families." An earlier Gallup analysis, covering only 1936 through 1948 *but* more directly comparing "non-union labor" with "union members,'" indicated that the latter were on the average of 12 per cent more Democratic than non-union labor. Furthermore, if in the depressing discontinuities of social science research it is permissible to consider four successive data points as constituting trend data, the spread between unionist and non-union has increased with the political activity of organized labor; for the 1936 and 1940 differences are the same (8 per cent) and only half the 1944 and 1948 differences. My belief that an *increasing* differential has occurred simultaneously with increasing electoral activity by unions is supported by the most recently published Survey Research Center data, in that a comparison of union members in 1956 with "a '*control*' group of non-members that matches the 'test' group of members on all important aspects of life situation save the fact of membership" indicated that the unionists were more than 20 per cent more Democratic than the control group, while union families were 17 per cent more Democratic than the matched control group.

These figures have been patiently reconstructed, and the bases of choice and comparison perhaps laboriously verbalized, in order to test the assumption of E. E. Schattschneider that the net electoral impact of organized labor is just under one million votes. My estimate is presented in Table 1. It suggests that the net gain of the Democratic party in presidential elections as a consequence of the existence of unions is perhaps as much as 2,800,000 votes; furthermore the *gross* impact of unionization may be estimated by alternatively hypothesizing what the Democratic vote would be if *all* 31,000,000 workers were unionized (over 16,000,000 votes) and what it would be if *none* of them were (just under 10,500,000 votes—) that is, the total variation for the relevant labor force could be as much as 5,848,700 votes at the present time and under projections of available data as to both turnout and Democratic-preference. And this is why my estimate is almost three times what Schattschneider's was: he assumed that the voting rate was "only about half of the membership" (i.e., for unionists); he assumed that there was *no* spread between unionists and non-unionists (the data available indicate it is about 16 per cent); and he lastly assumed a party-preference differential of only 10 per cent (whereas the conservative estimate used here is only 13 per cent, to compromise the differences between Survey Research Center and Gallup data).

Now, my point in all this is not to attack a single individual—Schattschneider's reputation was long ago established and at a deservedly high level—but rather to underline unmistakably how damningly difficult it is for *any* political scientist to obtain relevant and reliable data for comparative analysis,

TABLE 1. *Probable Net Democratic Vote Impact of Electoral Action of Organized Labor in Late 1950's and Early 1960's*

	Organized Labor	Unorganized Labor
Total numbers	15,000,000	16,000,000
Mean voting rate	75%	59%
Probable turnout	11,250,000	9,440,000
Mean Democratic per cent of the two-party vote	70%	56%
Probable Democratic vote	7,875,000	5,381,000
Probable Democratic vote with assumptions reversed:		
1. If organized labor behaved politically like unorganized labor	5,044,500	—
2. If unorganized labor behaved politically like organized labor	—	8,400,000
Democratic gain as consequence of unions	2,830,500	—
Republican avoidance of loss as consequence of lack of unionization	—	3,019,000

NOTE: This table is based on probable presidential vote; the 1960 Labor Force figures have been approximated; the turnout rates and the party-vote rates for union members have been averaged from Survey Research Center data . . . the differentials between union member and non-union member have been averaged between the SRC (higher) and the Gallup (lower) data.

because individually and collectively we have failed our profession. We have been anecdotalists and not empiricists; we have been individualistic librarianists and not field-oriented team- or group-researchers; and we have not as yet learned the inestimable quality and capacity for collective self-appraisals that appear regularly and usefully in sociology, psychology, and other social sciences. The only thing we have that I would not grant the other social sciences is a superior personal (and therefore modal-collective) political ideology, but in this we are not much different from members of labor unions; and, however superior the ideology for personal (and collective) action, it is not the basis upon which a social *science* can be founded.

MAGNITUDE AND METHOD OF FINANCIAL INVOLVEMENT

The analysis of voter-mobilization by labor unions in the preceding section leads to the conclusion that the *net* gain to Democratic presidential candidates during the 1950's was something under one-eleventh of the total popular vote necessary for election. But voter-mobilization is also the end-purpose of the flow of money into elections; therefore it is appropriate to examine in this section what is known concerning the extent, methods, and impact of labor money in politics.

To begin with, it is extremely difficult to obtain any reliable and comparable data that span more than two elections—as Alexander Heard, the author of the most exhaustive treatment of money in politics, has carefully noted. However, it is possible to examine a variety of alternative data presented by Heard in an attempt to establish the upper limit of the extent of spending in elections by labor unions. A first, and perhaps the best, measure is that of direct expenditure (for goods and services consumed during a campaign) by national-level campaign groups. For 1952, labor money constituted 15 per cent of all direct expenditures in behalf of Democrats, and in 1956 this proportion was 11 per cent. At a second and quite different level, Heard estimates that the *voluntary* political giving by some 17,000,000 unionists in 1956 constituted about $2,000,000 which in turn just about balanced the voluntary contributions in amounts of $500 or more recorded by 742 officials of the 225 largest business concerns in the nation. Approximately one union member in eight contributed voluntarily during this period, with the average contribution something less than $1.00 and with considerable variation: in highly political unions such as the UAW or the ILGWU, both the rate and the average amount of contribution were considerably higher (e.g., one in two members and an average of $2.57 in the latter union). But voluntary contribution is only part of the process, as Heard notes; for dues-money may flow into election campaigns through one or more of a wide variety of activities: donations (e.g., the ILGWU donated an average of $15,500 annually to the ADA in 1953–56); the maintenance of political departments, such as the "political shop-steward" program of the ILGWU; the creation of special "Citizenship Funds" (in the UAW, 5 per cent of the member's dues goes into such a fund maintained by the international and another 5 per cent into a local fund); the development of "education and information" programs, such as the IAM training classes on the relation between legislation and political activity; or undertaking communications and public service activities (e.g., the AFL-CIO sponsors Edward P. Morgan on ABC nationally, while the UAW sponsors the radio-television newscasts of Guy Nunn in the Detroit metropolitan area.) In addition, it should be obvious that electoral purposes may be served through union expenditures on: public relations and research; union legal departments; union-executive expense accounts; general administrative costs; and, of course, salaries. All of these account for some hard-to-measure but nonetheless real methods for organized investment in the electoral process by unions. In an effort to provide some estimate of the dollar magnitude of such investment, Heard has taken organized labor's numerical membership as a proportion of the potential electorate—roughly 17 per cent—and concludes that "labor money in politics from all sources pays *a much smaller share* of the nation's campaign-connected costs than union members constitute of the population of voting age." However, such an estimate may unintentionally conceal the significance of such labor money to the Democratic party. For example, one might arbitrarily take 10 per cent as labor's actual share of the roughly $165,000,000 in cash-and-kind costs for financing all the electoral activities entailed in a presidential election year; but that 10 per cent of the *total* would be highly significant in Democratic party finance for two reasons: very close to 100 per cent of all labor money goes to the Democratic side (see below) *and,* for the period under review, the two-party division of resources and expenditures was roughly 60–40 in favor of the Republicans; therefore the 10 per cent over-all share of labor actually would constitute close to 25 per cent of all Democratic funds. Whether the empirical basis for testing this tentative conclusion will ever be unearthed seems highly problematical; such a project would require even more time, money, and effort than were put forth in the heroic labors of the University of North Carolina (Heard) project. Meanwhile one may infer that the apparent autonomy, decentralization, and disarray of the organizational structure of unions provide national labor leaders with a convenient excuse for saying that they simply do not and cannot know all the facts; and one might equally suppose that some, perhaps many, Democratic (and Republican) candidates also prefer not to know too much about the entire process of money in elections.

When one turns from the *magnitude* of labor's financial involvement in elections to the *method* of its involvement, three additional aspects of Heard's analysis of labor money become relevant. Heard's available evidence on the geography of labor support in 1956 indicated that such support was concentrated within the ten states whose populations include two-thirds of all organized labor. His next analysis, focused on the partisan recipients of funds transferred by labor committees, showed the almost exclusive support of Democrats. In 1952, for example, $833,000 could be traced, and $5,450 had been transmitted to one senatorial and five House Republican candidates (an average of $908 each); the analysis for 1956 of $1,616,000 of national-level and of $430,000 of state-local-level labor committee transfers showed a total of $3,925 going to eight House Republican candidates (about $491 each). A final aspect of the method of labor's financial involvement as depicted by Heard is contained within the data of Table 2. The major point of interest in the table is the clear indication that labor union leaders desire to, and primarily do, deal directly with Demo-

TABLE 2. *Types of Recipients of Transfers of Labor Funds from National-Level and State-Local-Level Committees in 1952 and 1956ᵃ*

	Election Year, Type, and Number of Labor Committees Transferring Funds					
	1952 14 N-L		1956 17 N-L		1956 155 S-L	
Types of Recipients	*Amount*	*Per Cent*	*Amount*	*Per Cent*	*Amount*	*Per Cent*
At national level						
Labor and other non-party committees	$199,000	26	$297,000	25	$ 34,000	9
Democratic party committees	98,000		109,000		3,000	
At state-local level						
Labor committees	268,000	74	236,000	75	95,000	91
Democratic candidates on their committees						
– for the Senate	100,000		326,000		43,000	
– for the House	80,000		334,000		136,000	
Other (non-party) and miscellaneous	101,000		272,000		27,000	
Democratic party committees	67,000		42,000		24,000	
State-local candidates or their committees	—		—		68,000	

ᵃ Simplified and recomputed from data presented in [Alexander] Heard [*The Costs of Democracy* (Chapel Hill: University of North Carolina Press, 1960)], p. 185, Table 23.

cratic *candidates* (or their personal committees); they deliberately bypass the established Democratic party committees at both national and state-local levels. Heard also indicates the obverse of this, in that there is evidence that union leaders have frequently sought to prevent Democratic party solicitation within and among their local memberships. In the broader context of my analysis, these data on voter-mobilization are further indications of the tendency of interest groups to expend such potential resources as exist within the electoral process and to expend them at such a rate and with such efficiency that the group takes over *all* of the *relevant* functions of the political party.

This last broad generalization unfortunately creates more intellectual problems than it solves, for it begs three additional questions: How much in fact has organized labor committed its potential resources to electoral politics? How efficiently in fact has it exploited these committed resources? And what in fact have political scientists done by way of systematic analysis to answer these first two questions?

At several points in the preceding sections I have pointed out the lack of both data and analysis; consequently I recommended the following specific questions for focusing disciplined inquiry into the increasing electoral action of organized labor. Does a strongly held and economically based ideology—for business or for labor—lead to efficiency in electoral action? Does a left-oriented *labor* ideology incorporate, ignore, or conflict with the central cultural concept and value of "efficiency" in the first place? Furthermore, to what extent is organized labor activity confined to *general* elections? Are the electoral practices of organized labor similar in disbursement and endorsement to those of the party groups and of other non-party political groups? Does organized labor in its electoral action normally aid established incumbents, or do its major efforts go into support of non-incumbent challengers? Lastly, to what extent has political science analysis provided intelligible answers to these questions?

Before surveying the substantive material available for answering such questions, several explanatory comments are required. To begin with, as one committed to group theory I am acutely aware of gross inaccuracies in the monolithic assumption implied by speaking of "organized labor" or, conversely, "the business community." In my usage of "organized labor," therefore, let it be understood that I believe that sufficient evidence already exists to justify working upon the assumption that in political behavior a unimodal (rather than a bi- or multimodal) tendency exists and that political science can advance only by working out from this initial primitive—yet empirically based—assumption. After that, the necessary refinements can be made. Secondly, it should be clear from the particular phraseology of the questions posed in the last two paragraphs that I believe that the scheme of analysis framed by these questions is appropriate to the study of *all* interest groups that engage in electoral action. Finally, I am knowingly taking on the unpopular but necessary task of bringing to the threshold of consciousness the very perplexing question of just how much we political scientists really know.

What precisely have political scientists stated about the electoral impact of organized labor? One text notes that organized labor spoke of Election Day 1946 as "Black Tuesday" because only 73 of 318 House candidates and only 5 of 21 Senate candidates endorsed by labor won—but it is impossible to learn whether these were Democrats or Republicans, incumbents or non-incumbents, or how well labor did relative to, say, the Democratic party itself in that Republican year. One author has taken the analysis of 1946 somewhat further, however, in noting that California Republicans uniformly centered their campaign attack on CIO-supported Democratic congressional candidates; that this attack on "CIO-PAC package" candidates became a campaign theme for Republicans almost everywhere in the nation; and that CIO-PAC endorsement of some congressional candidates proved to be a "kiss of death" under certain circumstances. That is, in a number of constituencies the PAC leaders made only a public announcement of endorsement of the candidate and either did not think it important to, or in fact could not, commit labor to any other campaign acvitity; as a consequence, the labor endorsement in those constituencies provided an issue to opponents of the candidate and permitted them to activate their members and sympathizers with no offsetting gains for the labor-endorsee. As for 1948, which was critical in many ways, slightly more information and analysis are available. Hugh A. Bone pointed out that after the 1948 election the new Labor's League for Political Education (AFL) claimed 172 "friends" of labor elected and 106 "enemies" retired (i.e., now ex-incumbent). Interestingly the most sophisticated analysis of 1948 is to be found in Truman's book—published eleven years ago. Noting generally that the CIO-PAC had endorsed 215 House candidates in 1948 and that 144 of these were elected, the author breaks down the 144 victories in several ways: first, 64 were of incumbents, 74 involved defeating incumbents, while the remaining 6 were in non-incumbency situations; next 57 of the labor-endorsed incumbents re-elected had voted against the Taft-Hartley Act of 1947 while all 74 of the incumbents defeated had voted for it; and finally, a partial analysis of such factors as the two-party division of the popular vote at the last election and the partisan control of the constituencies leads to the conclusion that "the changes in 1948 were of major importance. Presumably the CIO-PAC efforts had something to do with them."

Despite the fact that a tentative scheme for analysis has been in existence for at least a decade, neither textbook writers nor the researchers they cite have done anything further on this subject. To be sure, one can find conclusions that, for example, in 1950 "the labor-endorsed candidates took a fearful drubbing," or that "in California, following the 1958 elections, labor's power emerged as a great part of the substance behind the Democratic Party's victory." What one finds is unrelieved anecdotalism, and not very good anecdotes at that. This may be partly a result of the combined tendency of politicians (including labor politicians), news media, and the political scientist audience alike to personify the issue of labor's electoral activity in one key race at a time, *viz.*,Taft and Ohio in 1950 or Goldwater and Arizona in 1958. And there is some evidence that labor, especially in its allocation of funds, may be inefficient in such races. For example, organized labor *reported* expenditures of $180,880, Senator Taft *reported* expenditures of $243,740, and probably more than $2,000,000 was spent in that one 1950 contest. As for 1958, the close reader of the *New York Times* found that "Rumor has it that the national COPE organization has been pouring money—as much as $400,000—and political workers into Arizona to defeat Senator Goldwater. . . ." COPE officials and Arizona labor leaders immediately denied this, of course, indicating that labor's financial involvement would be about the same as the $33,000 expended in Arizona in 1956; but when the battle had ended, labor's reported contributions to McFarland (Goldwater's opponent) interestingly totaled only $3,500. Meanwhile, Goldwater's re-election effectively obscured the fact that two other COPE-endorsed Arizona candidates had been elected with impressive vote-margins. The focus upon one great personalized contest at a time may also result from the facts that organized labor, even the AFL-CIO, has no centralized endorsement machinery and that it is therefore difficult, though hardly impossible, as indicated below, to learn what the state, district, and local political units of labor are doing; and as a general rule in this country, that which it is difficult to learn normally goes unreported and necessarily unanalyzed.

But at least one political scientist has provided interesting

clues concerning the behavior of organized labor in endorsements. In a tentative survey of CIO-PAC activity in the Detroit
area, Nicholas Masters has generalized that "the PAC attempts
to endorse the candidate who most nearly meets the claim of
the group and who commands the greatest prestige, but it will
endorse the mediocre or weak candidate if he is opposed by a
candidate who is closely identified with business groups." Thus
there is evidence of the push and pull of ideological stereotypes
in electoral behavior. Furthermore, Masters has noted that the
Democratic partisanship of the candidate is the primary criterion
for PAC endorsement in Wayne County, with liberal position
coming next in importance; and—

> The term "liberal" does not puzzle PAC leaders as it does acade-
> micians. A candidate may prove his liberalism by allowing the
> PAC to evaluate his stand on ten or twelve key and current issues
> with which the CIO is concerned. *The usual method for evalua-
> tion of a candidate, however, is to tabulate his recorded votes on
> such issues. Thus the incumbent has the inside track for endorse-
> ment.* . . .

This in turn is evidence—if tentative and subject to further
testing—that the influence of organized labor, even in a labor-
dominated area, may be inoperative or ineffectual until *after*
the candidate has established himself; it may also mean that
organized labor operates as a conservative force in the limited
sense of freezing out challengers and preventing intraparty conflict; at the minimum Masters' evidence suggests that repeated
endorsements of incumbents is the major factor in explaining
the high rate of success of the CIO-PAC in the 1946–55 period.

More information is available concerning the national level
of politics and especially concerning the 1960 election. For
example, that election is the first in which data both on the
Senate campaign committees and on labor endorsements and
disbursements are readily available to the political analyst. Using
such data, then, Table 3 compares the Democratic Senate

Campaign Committee and the AFL-CIO. Labor made only approximately half as many major-support decisions (defined as allocations of $5,000 or more) as did the DSCC in 1960; sight inspection of this figure also shows that the order or preference varied considerably between the two groups; and a rank-order correlation coefficient (Kendall's *tau*) of the candidates appearing commonly in both the DSCC and the AFL-CIO lists was only + .143—quite close to full independence—for the particular election.

TABLE 3. *Rank-Order Comparisons of Major-Support Decisions (of $5,000 or More) Made by the DSCC and by the AFL-CIO Respectively in 1960 Senate Elections*

DSCC			AFL-CIO		
Rank	Name	State	Rank	Name	State
1	Frear (Delaware)		1	Kefauver (Tennessee)	
2	Anderson (New Mexico)		2	Humphrey (Minnesota)	
3	Bartlett (Alaska)		3	Douglas (Illinois)	
4	Humphrey (Minnestoa)		4	McNamara (Michigan)	
5	Whitaker (Wyoming)		5	Neuberger (Oregon)	
6	Neuberger (Oregon)		9	O'Connor (Massachusetts)	
7	Pell (Rhode Island)		7	Pell (Rhode Island)	
8	Metcalf (Montana)		8	Knous (Colorado)	
9	McLaughlin (Idaho)		9	Metcalf (Montana)	
10	McNamara (Michigan)				
11	Burdick (North Dakota)				
12.5	Knous (Colorado)				
12.5	Kerr (Oklahoma)				
14	Randolph (West Virginia)				
15.5	Long (Missouri)				
15.5	McGovern (South Dakota)				
17	Douglas (Illinois)				

SOURCE: *Congressional Quarterly Almanac,* 17 (1961).

We may also compare the disbursement practices of the AFL-CIO with those of the political party Senate campaign committees (in Table 4). These data for 1960 show several

TABLE 4. *Major-Support Decisions (of $5,000 or More) of Senate-Oriented Party and Labor Political Groups in 1960 Elections—Analyzed by Incumbency and Non-Incumbency Situations*

Political Group	All Major Support		Incumbent Support		Non-Incumbent Support	
	Mean Amount	No. of Races	Mean Amount	No. of Races	Mean Amount	No. of Races
DSCC	$ 9,880	17	$10,876	10	$ 8,457	7
AFL-CIO	14,511	9	20,980	5	6,425	4
RNCC	8,327	22	8,119	10	8,500	12

SOURCE: *Congressional Quarterly Almanac*, 17 (1961).

interesting behavioral differences. First, as many political scientists have long suspected, the DSCC in 1960—at least—operated to the distinct advantage of incumbent members of The Club—by a mean difference in excess of $2,400. The Republican National Campaign Committee, secondly, contested the greatest number of races at the level of major-support and, also presumably reflecting the mathematical decline of Republicans in the Senate since 1952, the party allocation policy actually worked to the slight advantage of their non-incumbent candidates. In between these two, the AFL-CIO concentrated its activity—disbursing a much higher mean contribution to a much reduced total number of candidates. Furthermore, for an established electoral interest group such as organized labor, 1960 must be regarded as a year of consolidationist effort. That is, the AFL-CIO devoted its major efforts to helping re-elect five preferred incumbents, disbursing to them almost three times the mean amount contributed to non-incumbent Democratic candidates.

The question of electoral efficiency (and power) can be dealt with least satisfactorily here. At best, until comparable data for a sequence of elections become available, I can only illustrate the types of assumptions that seem immediately relevant to this question. The crudest measure of efficiency, of course, is whether the endorsed-supported candidates or the electoral interest group in fact win their elections. By one form of this measure—examining the proportion of all disbursements (not just major-support allocations) according to the final division of the two-party total vote in the constituency—Table 5 indicates that the AFL-CIO was more efficient than either party campaign committee, for it allocated 81 per cent of all 1960 disbursements to winning candidates whereas its closer competitor (the DSCC) could claim only 61 per cent here. But the data previously given, regarding incumbencies, suggest that this very primitive assumption on which Table 5 is based is appropriate only where one has a very limited number of cases with which to deal. When the number of cases has increased significantly, the analyst would do well to invoke a second assumption here, already implied by the construction of Table 5, that devoting group efforts to "close" contests is more efficient—in terms of the psychology of indebtedness—than either winning too easily (presumably by backing only incumbents) or losing too badly. As the number of cases becomes truly adequate, a third and more important assumption is necessary: that it is more efficient to help a non-incumbent challenger defeat an incumbent than it is merely to aid an already-incumbent candidate win re-election. Furthermore, in this context, efficiency is a function of *net* impact on the distribution of legislative seats (i.e., victories minus losses) rather than of *gross* (victorious) behavior alone. But such more sophisticated and, it is believed, realistic analysis clearly requires detailed information on individual constituencies not now available in any numbers.

TABLE 5. *Relative Efficiency of Senate-Oriented Party and Labor Groups in 1960 Elections—Measured in Terms of Proportion of Disbursements to "Close" and "Not Close" Races*

Senate Races: Division of Two-Party Total Vote	Party & Labor Political Groups		
	DSCC	AFL-CIO	RNCC
"Not close"—more than 55 per cent	39	52	23
"Close"—50+ through 54 per cent	22	29	27
"Close"—46 through 50 per cent	23	8	25
"Not close"—less than 46 per cent	16	11	25
Total	101[a]	100	100

[a] Errors due to rounding.
SOURCE: *Congressional Quarterly Almanac,* 17 (1961).

To conclude this section, then, one must presently fall back upon fragmentary and discontinuous *aggregate* data such as have been brought together in Table 4. This table provides a framework for summary analysis of four aspects of the electoral activity of organized labor. A first cluster is indicated in

Table 6: for example, the magnitude of organized labor's electoral involvement in House races has significantly diminished in the past fifteen years; and I infer from this that labor strategists have acquired experience in limiting labor money to the lesser number of constituencies in which it can make a difference. (When the post-1960 Census redistricting is completed, probably by the 1964 election, the number of House seats that labor can hope to contest should increase.) As for the Senate, analysis of the geography of endorsements indicates that labor now participates in virtually the full 100 per cent of contested general elections, reflecting the greater advantage of statewide constituencies for labor's electoral resources. And, lastly, labor's electoral efficiency—measured solely by percentage of victories—has closely paralleled the ebb and flow of Democratic party fortunes in the past fifteen years.

TABLE 6. *Type, Number, and Frequency of Victory of Organized Labor Endorsements in Selected Congressional General Elections*

Year	House of Representatives			Senate		
	Con-tests	Vic-tories	Per Cent	Con-tests	Vic-tories	Per Cent
1946 (CIO-PAC)	318	73	23	21	5	24
1948 (CIO-PAC)	215	144	67	—	—	—
1954 (CIO-PAC)	256	126	49	26	16	61
(AFL-LLPE)	—	154	—	30	18	60
1956 (AFL-CIO)	288	159	55	29	12	41
1958 (AFL-CIO)	199	—	—	34	24	71
1950 (AFL-CIO)	193	106	55	21	12	57

NOTE: This table has been pieced together from the sources previously cited in this section plus *Congressional Quarterly Almanac*, 15 (1959), and 17 (1961).

A related aspect, not revealed by Table VI, is the fact that labor money is almost wholly concentrated within the Demo-

cratic party, probably more so recently than Heard's earlier figures indicated. For example, of 199 money-endorsements for
House seats in 1958, only 6 were of Republican candidates. In
1958 senatorial races, only 2 of 34 candidates supported by labor
were Republicans; one of these (Knight of California) received
less than one-twenty-fourth the sum contributed to his Democratic opponent, while the other (North Dakota's Langer) was
noted as a domestic Democrat. In 1960's Senate races, 3 of 21
labor-endorsed candidates were Republicans; 2 of these received
relatively token contributions of $500 each (incumbent Cooper
of Kentucky and successful challenger Boggs of Maryland)
while in the third contest, in New Jersey, incumbent Case received $2,500 to the $1,000 given to his Democratic opponent.

The influence of incumbency may be treated as a third
aspect of analysis, in that endorsements of incumbents seem to
account for a greater proportion of labor victories in the House
than in the Senate. The data are not extensive, but they indicate
the following: 10 of the 24 Senate victories in 1958 and 7 of
the 12 in 1960 involved support of a successful incumbent,
while in the case of the House, 95 of the 106 victories claimed
in 1960 were of re-elected incumbents.

A final point may be gleaned from the available data,
namely the fact that labor-money activity is *not* confined, as the
limited data that Heard had available seemed to indicate, to
those seventeen states in which three-quarters of all unionists
reside. In 1960, for example, a full half of labor's major financial efforts for the Senate fell outside those seventeen states;
despite the artificialities of federalism, money is a highly mobile
political resource, and the recent extension of this activity by
both business and labor would seem both a cause and a reflection of the nationalization of electoral politics in America.

Between the Depression and the end of World War II,
business unionism essentially achieved its three major goals of
union recognition, shorter hours and higher wages, and control

of the job market. The Employment Act of 1946 should be
viewed as symbolic of the transition from business unionism to
political unionism—in the sense that unions have been able to
survive as a social movement in America by the development
of a logical succession of goals. Since 1946, labor's goals have
been employment, security, and peace. But business unionism
could not directly contribute to the achievement of such goals.
Each of these new goals was significantly affected by what the
national government would or would not do. Therefore business
unionism has now been replaced by a political unionism based
upon the realistic and realizable premise that political action is
necessary to control the government that in such a major way
conditions achievement of the newer and broader goals of
organized labor.

From the sketchy evidence available, political unionism—
consciously undertaken within the framework of the existing
national two-party system—has meant that organized labor acts
as a party-within-a-party. But the descriptions available *are*
fragmentary and discontinuous. Lacking adequate descriptive
bases, we are necessarily precluded from experimentation with
logical methods for evaluating the efficiency of power-oriented
action. Lacking both description and evaluation, there can be
no political *theory* as distinct from political philosophy. Therefore, at numerous points in this article I have referred to the
sins of omission of political scientists. But guilt is not ours alone,
for no one else has yet attempted systematic appraisal of organized labor's role in American politics. For example, respected
research organizations—such as the National Bureau of Economic Research, Incorporated—have neither conducted nor sponsored research on organized labor in electoral politics. The social
scientists who control client-oriented educational institutions—
such as the University of Wisconsin's School for Workers—have
apparently lacked inclination, resources, and/or ability for research into labor's political activities and power. The modern

myriad of corporate-financed "educational" foundations—such
as the American Enterprise Association or the Foundation for
Economic Education—publish only unreliable polemics on this
subject. And organized labor itself understandably is no more
anxious scientifically and publicly to appraise its efficiency and
power than any other group in the political arena. In this sense—
but in this only—the future is bright: it now remains to be seen
which of the sectarian fields of social science will contribute to
understanding of a major political phenomenon.

5

LOBBYING AND LOBBYISTS

The usual beginning point of an interest in interest groups, whether by journalists, academic observers, or citizens, has been lobbying. What might be called the traditional indignant view tended to regard lobbying as so pervasive that its pressure on hapless or at least spineless government officials accounted for most of what governments did. More recently, perhaps since World War I, the indignant view has moderated somewhat, regarding only some of what government does to be the result of pressure groups activity. Whatever may once have been the case, most observers now agree that (1) lobbying in Washington, and in many states and cities too, seldom involves overt corruption and probably accounts for less of the policy result than we imagine, and (2) relations between lobbyists and governmental decision-makers are more complex and varied than we once believed.

Oliver Garceau and Corinne Silverman illustrate one case of this richly complex pattern by examining the Associated Industries of Vermont at work in a legislative session. Lester W. Milbrath reports the results of interviews with more than one hundred Washington lobbyists concerning what they do and what they believe to be effective.

A Pressure Group and the Pressured: A Case Report

OLIVER GARCEAU AND CORINNE SILVERMAN

The organized interest group does not make the laws of the land. It must devise means for gaining access to and influencing those who are constitutionally empowered to make, administer, or otherwise define the law. This study deals with the efforts of one organized group, the Associated Industries of Vermont, to secure its objectives in the 1951 session of the Vermont legislature. The study is correlatively concerned with the legislator's view of the AIV activities and, more broadly, of the legislative process.

I. THE PRESSURE GROUP

The Associated Industries of Vermont is a "peak" association; an organized business group which acts as spokesman for many diverse business interests in the state. The membership, which ranges from small manufacturers to the National Life Insurance Company, totaled some 450 concerns in 1951, the year in which the events to be described took place. Membership is by indi-

From the *American Political Science Review*, Vol. XLVIII, No. 3 (September, 1954), pp. 672–91. Reprinted by permission of the authors and the American Political Science Association.

The research, of which this article is one report, was assisted by grants to Bennington College from the Carnegie Corporation of New York and the Rockefeller Foundation.

viduals, firms, and a few trade associations. Included were almost all the textile, the granite and marble, and the machine-tool companies in the state—representing three of the state's important industries. A rough estimate of the total payroll of the member concerns was about half of the total payroll of the state. A few retailing and other non-manufacturing members had recently been added.

This study does not attempt to deal with all the events of the 1951 session, nor even with the myriad ways in which business opinion in Vermont gained or failed to gain acceptance on a range of issues. It is concerned primarily with the overall strategy of the staff of the Associated Industries to gain access to the legislature, and with the specific tactics used by the AIV.

Access to the Vermont legislature is always difficult for the Associated Industries. No matter what the nature of the issues, the AIV is certain to face a legislature more sympathetic to the Farm Bureau than to a business group. Since each township in the state, irrespective of population, is entitled to one representative in the 246-member lower house, the natural preoccupations of the state with agricultural problems are further magnified in the legislature. Although 30.5% of the population live in towns of 5,000 or more, only 5.3% of the members of the lower house represent towns of that size. More than half of the AIV's membership in 1951 were located in towns of more than 5,000 population, which means, of course, that access to legislators through AIV-member-constituents was singularly limited.[1]

Despite these characteristics of the state and the legislature which continually handicap the Associated Industries in attempts to gain access to the legislators, AIV appeared to be in a strong

---

[1]As far as the party division in the legislature is concerned, it should be sufficient to say that the Democrats counted among their members 21 representatives (8.5%) and one senator. On all matters, including that of organization of the House and Senate, a Democrat in the Vermont legislature is indistinguishable by his voting behavior from a Republican.

position when the 1951 session opened. Although it could not appeal to the mass of legislators, the formal leadership of both houses was decidedly receptive to consideration of the AIV point of view. In fact, the formal leaders of the houses were themselves key figures in the formation of the AIV point of view. The Lieutenant-Governor and President of the Senate, Joseph Johnson, was at that time on the Executive Committee of the AIV. He had been a vice-president of the Association, a member of the 1949 AIV Legislative Committee, and had been under consideration for the presidency of the Association until his election as Lieutenant-Governor. In private life he had been vice-president of a large machine-tool company. The Speaker of the House, Wallace M. Fay, was a director and a member of the Executive Committee of AIV. He, too, had been a member of the 1949 AIV Legislative Committee. Fay was vice-president of the Vermont Marble Company. The President Pro Tem of the Senate, and chairman of the Senate Rules Committee, Merrill Harris, who was president of one insurance company and a director of another, was also at that time a director of the AIV.

The chairmen of the standing committees in the legislature are not designated by virtue of seniority. They are appointed by the Speaker or by the President of the Senate. The AIV was directly influential in the appointments of chairmen and members of the committees considered of probable concern to the business group. The chairman of the House Commerce and Labor Committee, Walter Malmquist, president of a wood products company, had been a member of the 1949 AIV Legislative Committee together with Fay and Johnson. The chairman of the House Social Security Committee, while not a member of the Association, was appointed on the recommendation of Theodore Kane, the Executive Vice-President and manager of the AIV. The two other AIV members of the legislature were appointed chairman of the Senate Finance Committee and chairman of the Senate Commerce and Labor Committee, respectively. However, these two, although members of the AIV, were not as active as Fay, Johnson, Harris, and Malmquist, all of whom had held or were holding positions of responsibility in the formal organization of the group.

The AIV also had reason to suppose that the newly elected governor, Lee Emerson, would have a readier ear for its opinions than had Governor Ernest Gibson. Although both governors were, inevitably, Republicans, this meant less than the fact that Gibson was associated with one faction of the Republican party in the state, and Emerson was allied with the opposing faction.

The development of the factional split in the Republican party is a major part of the story of the progress of the 1951 session, and is tied in some measure to an understanding of the role of the Proctor family in Vermont politics. This role reaches back to 1878 when Redfield Proctor started on an active political career, serving as governor in 1878, as Secretary of War under Benjamin Harrison, and in 1902 as United States Senator. During this period, the Vermont Marble Company, owned by the Proctor family, became the largest single company in the state. The Proctor family continued throughout the years to take an active interest in the politics of the state; and although the process of gaining office is certainly not a simple one, the history of the Proctors would seem to substantiate the folk tale that as soon as a Proctor reached the proper age he was elected governor of the state. Between 1878, when Redfield Proctor was elected governor, and 1944, when Mortimer Proctor became governor, three other members of the Proctor family served in that position. The Proctors were not and are not today political "bosses" of the state. Although the family might almost be viewed as a fixed pole in Vermont politics, it is fixed not in terms of ideology but in terms of repeatedly occupying an influential position in the political power structure of the state.

Until the middle 1930's, knowledgeable informants agree, there was no serious or lasting cleavage in the Republican party of an ideological nature. But in 1934 appeared the first glimmer of a split which could be viewed as other than over personalities. In that election the Farm Bureau moved toward a formal endorsement of candidates in the primaries, and successfully backed Charles Smith for the governorship. In 1936 George Aiken was elected governor, again with the support of the Farm Bureau, which also supported his successful campaign for re-election in 1938. In these campaigns, the Farm Bureau in effect opposed Proctor candidates. During the war years Vermont politics quieted down, and Mortimer Proctor was elected in 1944, fully expecting re-election in 1946 for the traditional two terms of office. But in 1946 Ernest Gibson returned from the war and upset the proprieties by defeating Proctor in the primary and gaining the governorship, with the public endorsement of the Farm Bureau.

Gibson's election provoked a split in the Republican party of a type and meaning which remain somewhat enigmatic. Part of his opposition was made up of those who were irritated at the violation of the second term tradition, which would have given Mortimer Proctor a second term in office. To some observers, the split is a "liberal-conservative" one, with Gibson as a "New Deal kind of Republican" opposing the "Old Guard." Yet his program and policies in his two terms of office centered around major points which it would be hard to view as the foundations for a deep ideological cleavage. Gibson opposed the construction of a dam on the Connecticut River on the grounds that it would flood good farm land. This endeared him to the Farm Bureau and solidified the Aiken-Farm Bureau-Gibson combination. It also evoked murmurs of discontent from the private utility companies. The utilities were further incensed when in 1949 Gibson proposed to establish a Vermont Power Authority to negotiate for and distribute electric power produced by the St. Lawrence Seaway developments, if and when such developments occurred. The Farm Bureau backed Gibson fervently on this proposal which was, however, defeated. For Senator Aiken this was one facet of his participation in the struggle for federal endorsement of the Seaway. In Vermont, Gibson's proposal brought cries of "socialism" and established him as something of a radical. Other programs included a Department of Health to administer mobile health units, and a State Police system to augment the local sheriffs. He pressed for additional construction of state institutions, projects which had been ignored during the war years. He created a Development Commission to encourage industrial expansion in the state, to attract new business to the area, and thus to stem the steady outflow of Vermont's younger generation. These policies were viewed by many as radical and involving a wanton expenditure of money. They were acclaimed by others as "progressive" and as sensible investments in the state's health. When, in 1949, Gibson resigned from the governorship to accept a Truman appointment to the federal court, many felt that the accusations of radicalism were vindicated.

The 1950 campaign was a complicated affair, with candidates for the Republican primaries announcing first for one office and then another in a whirl of indecision. When the merry-go-round slowed down there were three candidates for the Republican nomination for governor. One of them, Peter Bove, was generally regarded as "a Gibson man," but without as broad a backing as Gibson himself had had. The second, J. Harold Stacey, although he had been Gibson's Speaker of the House in the 1949 session, was considered to be nobody's man and a middle-of-the-roader, whatever that might mean in the low temperature politics of the state. Lee Emerson, the third and successful candidate, had been Lieutenant-Governor in Mortimer Proctor's term as governor, although this did not necessarily mean that he was "Proctor's man." The Proctors, in fact, did not appear to take much interest in the 1950 campaign until the last two or three weeks, when, it is often reported, they decided upon Emerson as the least of three evils and it became generally known that he had their backing.

The Associated Industries scrupulously refrained from taking any part in the 1950 campaign. Although the AIV had no direct connection with Governor Emerson, the links were there, and the campaign situation did nothing to weaken the possibility of cooperative relationships between governor, legislative officers, and the business group. At the very least, it was clear that the new governor could expect little support from former Gibson associates. As the new administration began and the legislature convened, the AIV made the explicit assumption that the official climate of opinion in the state government would be more congenial than in recent years and its own problems of effective access much simpler and more direct.

II. THE 1951 LEGISLATIVE SESSION[2]

The AIV did not concern itself actively with the full range of issues in the 1951 session. Rather, the staff focussed a major portion of its energy on one bill, the proposal of the labor groups to include certain occupational diseases under the Workman's Compensation Act. Theodore Kane, Executive Vice-President of the AIV (and for all practical purposes "the staff"), told the Association's members that this was "the most important legislation affecting industry to come before the 1951 session."

The development of this issue in the 1951 session is a not unrepresentative example of a process of inter-group negotiation characteristic of state legislatures when dealing with issues of something less than first-rank drama and political potential. The nature of such negotiations among interests is often assumed

[2]Much of the material presented in this section is based on reports of participant observers who were employed in the offices of the Associated Industries and the Vermont Farm Bureau during the 1951 legislative session.

to be characteristically one of mutual hostility. Rather than assuming the legislature to be subject to a barrage of independent and divergent pressures, it may be closer to reality to conceive of a pattern, shifting through time, of alliances of interests which engage in negotiations and compromise outside the legislature. The rather picturesque comment of one member of the Vermont House is suggestive. Commenting on the AIV-labor negotiations on the occupational disease bill, he said that there were too many bills to keep track of in the session, and "if it is satisfactory to them you figure you're not cutting anybody's gut." The example of the occupational disease bill is also a cogent illustration of the role such group negotiations play in broadening access to the legislature for one group or another. The labor groups in Vermont had, with the exception of three or four friendly legislators, little or no opportunity for gaining access *except* through the AIV.

The occupational disease bill story begins in 1947 when the granite workers, concerned about silicosis, sought to have it covered under Workman's Compensation. Procedure followed the pattern prescribed for most legislative proposals of even ordinarily controversial nature: a temporary committee was set up which recommended further study by a five-man commission. The commission was established and reported to the 1949 session, presenting a majority report and a minority report. The AIV, although it preferred the majority report if forced to make a choice, offered still a third course; and the labor groups, although they preferred the minority report if forced to make a choice, came up with a fourth proposal. All four of these proposals reached the floor. The Vermont House normally consists of more than 50% "first-termers" who are unaccustomed for the most part to legislative routine and are traditionally prone to vote "no" on everything when confronted by confusion of amendments, substitutions, and other sophisticated parliamentary practices. Acting in true form, the 1949 House defeated the majority bill, the minority bill, and labor's proposed substitutions, and passed the AIV's suggestion, which was to authorize the establishment of a Division of Industrial Hygiene in the Department of Health whose function it would be to recommend better methods for preventing occupational diseases.

For the time being, this was doing nothing about workman's compensation. However, the granite industry and the AIV, and most especially Mr. Kane, were well aware of the fact that the labor groups would make another try in the 1951 session. Despite the conservative drift of opinion in state and nation, and the exceptional access to the legislature enjoyed by AIV in 1951, it was never concluded by Mr. Kane that business interests could call the tune, even with relation to labor. This, be it noted, was not because labor was strong, but because business interests remained essentially weak. Farm leaders were characteristically Bull Moose progressive on business issues, disliked bankers for the record, distrusted big business and Wall Street to notable political advantage. Vermont legislative policy had, on a number of issues, been liberal to an exceptional degree, considering the conduct of some of the neighboring states and the very limited per capita wealth of the state. Business endorsement of a policy was considered, in the AIV office, a surety of defeat. This gloomy assessment may well have been an exaggerated projection of the 1930's, but it significantly conditioned the course of the negotiations. Since it was judged doubtful that an occupational disease law could be postponed indefinitely, the better strategy seemed to be for industry itself to take the initiative, present its own bill, and start any negotiations in an offensive rather than defensive position. Although it is not possible to place responsibility for this decision, it is more likely that it was Kane's rather than that of the Barre Granite Association, many of whose members were opposed to the passage of any bill.[3]

In December, just prior to the opening of the 1951 session,

[3]The Barre Granite Association included among its members almost all of the 117 granite companies in the state, and had joined the AIV as an association, paying a lump sum annually as dues.

a meeting of minds was achieved between the leading members of the Granite Association and Kane, and a bill was drawn up. This bill resembled in its essence the majority bill of 1949, although the form was greatly simplified, especially by the omission of the innumerable "except as hereinafter otherwise provided" clauses to which the minority report had strenuously objected. The bill was taken to the Governor by the AIV and all seemed to be well. Two days later word came from Emerson that there were objections to the proposed bill. Kane would have to reach agreement with labor or there would be trouble in the legislature, trouble in the form of opposition on the floor by one or another of the handful of legislators friendly to labor. Such objections threatened a repetition of the events of the 1949 session, where the confusion of disagreement on the floor led almost inevitably to legislative disapproval.

The course followed by Kane to secure agreement was to set in motion a series of sessions with the CIO, or as some legislators termed it, "a horse trade." The AIV had planned to introduce in this session three bills aimed at tightening the qualifications for workers claiming benefits under the Unemployment Compensation Law. It is not impossible that these bills were planned as bargaining items, although intrinsically they were compatible with AIV aims. Labor in turn hoped for an increase in the maximum duration of unemployment benefits from 20 to 26 weeks, and for an increase in the maximum weekly payments from $25 to $30.

Kane and the CIO representative went into a determined huddle over who would give up what in return for what. Labor's concern was to get an occupational disease bill on the books in some form or other. The AIV, on the other hand, felt that its legislative position was stronger in this session than it had been for some years and that it might be in sessions to come, and therefore wanted to get an occupational disease law in a form acceptable to business. Labor knew that the most it could hope for in a future legislature would be an increase in the number of "friendly" legislators from the three or four in the 1951 session to a possible five or six. Unless the AIV felt that labor was "cooperative," labor demands might be ignored. It was only through the maintenance of reasonably amicable relations with the Association that labor interests could look for success in the legislature. Labor finally agreed to the occupational disease bill in the form in which the AIV had drawn it, and agreed also to withdraw all its proposals for increasing unemployment benefits and extending the duration of payments. The AIV in turn agreed that it would withhold in this session the bills tightening qualifications for unemployment compensation.

These negotiations were carried on completely outside the legislative halls with only two legislative participants. One, Walter Malmquist, was the AIV-picked chairman of the House Commerce and Labor Committee. However, his role was not that of active negotiator but that of liaison between the AIV and the legislature, a role which he played throughout the session on all AIV issues. He kept Speaker Fay and some of the more important legislators informed on this and all other situations in which the AIV was concerned. The other legislator present was the representative from Barre Town, Ralph Smith, who was recognized as the principal legislative spokesman for labor. One or two other legislators were involved in some portions of the bargaining process, and although they did not know the details of all that had happened, they knew that, since agreement had been reached, the bill should be approved. The vast majority of the legislators, however, knew only that both Malmquist and Smith rose on the day of debate and announced that both industry and labor thought the bill should pass. They sat down, the vote was taken, and an occupational disease bill passed the House. The Senate, also noting that Malmquist and Smith urged the bill, granted its approval and the bill became law.

The passing of this bill was not accomplished by any visible lobbying. No attempt was made by either of the interested parties, industry or labor, to "buttonhole" members of the legislature and persuade them of the righteousness of the cause. There was no pleading before legislative committees. Rather, the differences of opinion within industry were first resolved and then agreement on the nature of the bill was reached between the representatives of organized industry and labor. Agreement to pass the bill came as a result of swapping and cancelling out objectives announced for the 1951 session. Bargaining was readily achieved by virtue of a long-standing "open-door" policy which existed between Kane and John Mitchell, the representatives of the AIV and CIO, respectively. Success for each of them depended upon maintaining an attitude of willingness to bargain with the other, although this dependence was more keenly felt by the CIO then by the AIV. The bulk of the legislators were more than willing to accept the bill without feeling a need to know what had happened behind the scenes, or if anything had happened. Their attention was caught by the more dramatic bills which had not been so resolved and which thus resulted in a clash of interests on the floor.

These more dramatic clashes, which in 1951 centered about the problem of the Governor's budget and tax policy, illustrate the limitations of the above methods. One factor important to the success of the occupational disease negotiations was that the bargaining and the legislative action came relatively early in the session. The bill was passed by the House in the last days of March and by the Senate in the first week of April. Up to that point the social and political organization of the legislature had been comparatively unstructured, and factional lines had not yet become sharply defined. Less than a week after passage of the occupational disease law, the entire character of the legislature changed and "the honeymoon was over." If the occupational disease bill had come up any later than it did, Administration support might have proved a liability and the issue might well have become entangled in the struggle which characterized the remainder of the session.

Governor Emerson, in his inaugural address and budget message, proclaimed an era of economy. No state department was to receive funds for additional personnel or new projects; wherever possible duplication was to be eliminated and consolidation of agencies effected. Above all, no new taxes were to be levied, except for a half-cent increase in the gas tax, which in Vermont is earmarked for highway development. This program in itself, while perhaps not entirely realistic in an inflationary period, would not have alarmed most members of the state legislature. What did arouse comment, and eventually deep acrimony, was the detail of this program. For the departments and agencies singled out by Emerson as those in which the greatest cuts could be made performed services inaugurated by his predecessor, Ernest Gibson. The Vermont Development Commission was to be virtually eliminated, and the new State Police was to be merged with the Motor Vehicle Department. Savings from these two reorganizations were budgeted as sufficient to avert tax increases. The Governor warned that if his program were not carried out, the burden of balancing the budget would rest upon the members of the legislature.

These two issues were seized upon by those in the legislature who had been Gibson supporters, and by much newspaper opinion, as purely "political" maneuvers, designed only to "undo all Gibson had done." By the time the two bills reached the House in early April they had become regarded as Emerson's "test of strength." In the event, they demonstrated that the Governor could not effectively "control" his legislature, for the House voted $100,000 to the Development Commission instead of the Governor's proposed $20,000, and defeated the proposed State Police-Motor Vehicle Department merger. The Senate restored another $100,000 to the Development Commission, or all but $40,000 of the Commission's original budget request of $240,000.

It was not to the advantage of the AIV to become embroiled in either of these issues. Factions in Vermont do not have the stability of established parties in other situations. Today's opponents may well be tomorrow's political compatriots. The Association managed to stay clear of the merger issue almost entirely. However, the Development Commission battle was more difficult to avoid. When a public hearing was scheduled on the proposed cut, Kane received word from the President of AIV to appear at the hearing and support the Governor's proposal. However, there were pressures in the opposite direction. Among the more determined opponents of the proposed cut were the local chambers of commerce, and the resort and hotel interests. Many of the latter were recent additions to membership. Kane could not afford to alienate one part of his membership in order to satisfy another. Furthermore, perhaps the most determined opponent of the proposal was the Vermont Farm Bureau. Since the Farm Bureau was unquestionably the most powerful organized group in the state, it was never to the advantage of the AIV to appear in direct, certainly not in open, opposition to it, if such a position could be avoided. The day of the hearing found Kane with important matters to attend to elsewhere.

Although the AIV managed to remain nominally neutral in these two issues, the Governor's defeat affected the AIV in the consequent problem of taxation. When both of the Governor's major proposals for economizing were defeated, and when the legislature also passed a bill raising the salaries of state employees, it was clear the budget would not be balanced unless new taxes were levied. As he had promised, Emerson had no tax proposal to offer. The legislators were in this difficulty despite his warnings, and the legislators would have to get out of trouble by themselves.

This interpretation of the role of the executive resulted in something close to chaos in the legislature. No one in the legislative branch considered himself responsible for working out an overall tax program. As one senator pointed out, "it's not very smart politically to introduce tax bills. That's supposed to be the job of the Administration, and everybody was glad to leave it to them." However, a small group of leaders of the Governor's faction attempted to solve the problem by introducing a series of small taxes which became known as the "patchwork taxes." Rather than raise the state income tax, a policy which Emerson had disapproved in his budget message, and rather than leap to the politically unpopular sales tax, this group proposed increases in the taxes on beer, on soft drinks, and on amusements. None of these proposed taxes had the official blessing of the Governor. Contradictory reports about his preferences flowed freely in the legislative corridors. Since the patchwork taxes were being proposed by legislators regarded as "Emerson men," there was some feeling that Emerson was backing the patchwork program; and in fact Emerson was meeting regularly with this group of legislators to discuss the possible methods of passing these taxes. The patchwork program was speedily defeated.

Kane did not find it appropriate to take the initiative on new taxes. The membership of a business group is not likely to be tolerant of the staff's proposing a more active tax program than those emanating from the executive and legislative branches. Furthermore, over the objections of a number of his members, Kane had actively supported a withholding tax earlier in the session. This was not a "new tax," but a new method of collecting taxes. Since it was to be retroactive, it was to result in an immediate "windfall" of several hundred thousand dollars of revenue. Kane, and the Governor as well, had harbored some hopes that this windfall would lessen the pressure for any further taxes. Having gone beyond his membership in this, Kane was unwilling to approve, in the name of the AIV, any further tax proposals.

Finally, though none of the industries presently in the AIV would have been hit by the patchwork taxes, Kane was trying to broaden the base of membership in the Association to include, among others, business at which the taxes were directed. Kane was not prepared to alienate these potential members.

It was now the middle of May. The 1951 legislature had already broken all records for length of session, and a solution to the tax problem was not yet in sight. A sales tax proposal was thrown into the hopper, but did not receive the approval of even 15% of the House. It was generally recognized that a tax of this sort required more preparation than a day or two spent copying a bill currently proposed in New Hampshire.

The legislature finally turned from the confusion to a 15% surtax on the state personal and corporate income tax, a solution proposed and introduced in the House by a legislator readily identified as "a Gibson man." This was the only tax on which the Governor had explicitly taken a stand, stating clearly in his budget message that "I do not favor any change in the existing income tax law at this time." It was the tax which the AIV would logically have wanted to defeat. But the AIV was by this time in a changed position. The Association had, at the outset, enjoyed access to the legislature through the formal leadership of the House and Senate. By the end of the session, the formal leadership did not coincide with the actual leadership. The Governor by his policy throughout the session, and by withdrawing himself from leadership on the whole question of taxes, had precipitated the latent cleavage in the legislature. Two sets of informal leaders had emerged.

It could be argued, no doubt, that the Governor and the AIV had not been wholly realistic in assuming that Emerson's program would be adopted in full and that therefore no tax program would be necessary. It might have been wise to have considered early in January what program would be preferred in the event that some new taxes became necessary. When the major decision of tax policy had to be faced, AIV had neither a policy known and acceptable to its members, nor access to the leadership which had developed in the legislature.

III. THE PRESSURED

After this summary of the 1951 legislative session from the perspective of the Associated Industries, it is appropriate to report how the events of the session looked to some of the members of the legislature. The questions to be explored are how these legislators themselves perceived the legislative process; what they thought was their own role in the process; and what place they attributed to organized group interests and activities. More specifically, what issues stood out for these legislators as "important," and for what reasons? What did they think was the role of organized interest groups in shaping the decisions on these or other issues? How much activity and what kind of group activity were, in fact, visible to the legislators?[4]

The legislators, who were interviewed from two to four

[4]The sample of legislators who were interviewed is not statistically representative of the membership of the 1951 session of the Vermont legislature. Forty members of the 246 representatives were interviewed, and 16 of the 30 senators. Half of the members of the House sample were selected by the participant observers in the Associated Industries and the Farm Bureau as either accessible to the interest groups under study, influential in the legislature, or both accessible and influential. The remaining half of the House sample was selected on a random basis. It was originally planned to interview the entire membership of the Senate, but interviews were completed with only slightly more than half of the senators.

Despite the fact that the entire sample was not chosen on a random basis, the sample as it was drawn is representative in certain characteristics considered relevant. The geographic distribution of the members and the party division in the legislature are quite accurately reflected in the sample, as is the distribution by previous legislative experience. The 40 members of the House under-represent slightly the proportion of representatives from the smaller towns, and the proportion of farmer-representatives, and over-represent slightly the proportion of lawyer-representatives.

months after the close of the 1951 session, did not tell a uniform story of what had happened during the five-month session. They chose for themselves several different kinds of signposts as guides through the confusion and stress of the session. They had different ways of structuring the experience, different perspectives on the elements of the legislative process.

Among the members of the lower house there appeared to be four different ways of describing the session. One group of House members were distinguished by their reluctance to impose any intellectual scheme or interpretation on the events of the session. All of the many episodes of the session were remembered, often with some difficulty, as so many separate items. There was a striking tendency among these representatives to refer questions about specific issues to the report of the committee which had handled the bill, although this is not to say that they remembered very clearly which committee had indeed handled which of the bills under discussion. Unable to see relationships in the handling of different issues, or relationships among informal groups of legislators, these representatives, making a virtue of necessity, seemed to cut down the confusion by taking the "safest" course. They argued that the standing committee members ought to have the "right decision" on each bill, and that the committee reports ought to be followed by the legislature. These legislators had not evolved broad standards for judging the issues as matters of social policy. They did not see the legislature as a forum for rival parties, factions, or interests. They did not identify leaders in the legislative process. Their interpretation of events was in terms of a traditional democratic morality. As representatives they were under obligation to their own consciences to do the right thing. The standing committee was to define, from its hearings and special competence, what was right. As observers of the interaction patterns in the 1951 session, they were "non-generalizers," and will be so termed below.

A second group of members of the lower house was sensitive primarily to the factional cleavage among the Republican legislators. Although these representatives could identify some of the more specific issues on which the cleavage had been apparent, they tended to discuss the cleavage as a conflict between rivals seeking advancement and power in state politics. For them a great many of the events of the session had turned on which group of factional leaders were the more effective or persuasive. These representatives will be referred to as the "faction-oriented."

A third group of the legislators added a further dimension to the process. They were aware of the factional clashes. They saw also a relation between the Governor's program and the emergence of factional alignment. Among this group, the Emerson supporters felt that his original message of economy in state programs, to avoid tax increases, had been sound. Although they had doubts of varying degrees about the specific proposals which were to effectuate this program, they cast their lot with the overall aim. Those who developed into "the opposition" had in some cases been Gibson supporters in previous years, and in other cases had been uncommitted. But they agreed that the reorganization and decimation proposals were unacceptable, whatever the merit of economy in general. For these legislators, the session was a struggle between factions emerging out of the Governor's program. They were essentially "program oriented" in their answers to questions covering the range of legislative activity.

A fourth group of representatives, "policy-oriented," saw the relation between broad program and faction. But their concern was with their own role as active leaders promoting particular policies or seeking to take care of policy in what might be called an issue area. Three were focussed on the interests of labor, and a fourth dealt with education. To these legislators the story of the session was the story of their own activity with relation to these policy matters and their own negotiations with interest groups and legislative factions. To a degree they sought for themselves a limited and special role as factional leaders; but their purpose and their interpretation of events were in terms of particular policies.[5]

IV. LEGISLATIVE VIEWS OF ISSUES AND GROUPS

The research used a focussed interview. At the outset the legislator was asked what he considered the most important problem of the session. It was mainly from the responses to this question that the varying perspectives emerged.

With one exception, all the "policy" and "program-oriented" legislators selected as the most important problem of the session the question of the Governor's program and budget, which led them immediately into a discussion of the policy of economy, the State Police merger and the Vermont Development Commission questions, the various tax programs, and the split in the Republican party.

Most of the "faction-oriented" selected the merger, the Vermont Development Commission cut, or one of the tax proposals. The biggest difference between this group and the "policy-" and

[5]These perspectives and the analyses to follow must of necessity be impressionistic and based on rough quantification. The sample is too small to allow more rigorous validation. The number of representatives who fall into each group should be kept in mind.

Group	Number of Representatives
"Policy-Oriented"	4
"Program-Oriented"	12
"Faction-Oriented"	13
"Non-generalizers"	11
Total	40

The Senate sample is too small to analyze separately. All quantifications are based on the representatives. The findings reported on the representatives appear as tendencies in the Senate. The two samples have not been combined, since the two populations differ in intrinsic characteristics.

"program-oriented" groups was the failure of the "faction-oriented" to see the interconnections between any of these issues and the entire range of issues which had made up "the problem" for the first two groups of legislators.

As for the fourth group, the "non-generalizers," almost every representative in this group picked a different issue as "the most important problem in the session." A few chose one or another of the tax proposals, but the range of issues selected was widely scattered. Every issue appearing in the interview with a member of this group was treated by him as a discrete issue with no apparent sense of interconnections.[6]

The most striking fact which emerged from the interviews as a whole was the extremely low level of recognition of interest group activity. Although every representative interviewed knew

[6]After the legislator had completed his discourse on "the most important problems," specific issues were introduced unless volunteered by respondent. Since the interest group activity on these issues was available from the participant observers, one purpose of the legislative survey was to complement this story with a picture of how the process appeared to the legislator. Accordingly, it was planned to include discussion of the questions on which the AIV had been most active and interested: the occupational disease and unemployment compensation bills which had been involved in the business-labor negotiations. Each interview was also intended to include a discussion of the Governor's budget, the proposed State Police merger, the proposed cut in the Vermont Development Commission appropriations, the "patchwork" taxes, and the sales-income tax alternatives.

In addition, the interviews were planned to include discussion of two matters on which the Vermont Farm Bureau had been active: a proposal to permit the sale of colored oleomargarine; and two proposals relating to the St. Lawrence Seaway, one memorializing Congress to approve the Seaway, and another establishing an agency in Vermont which would be authorized to negotiate for power resulting from any St. Lawrence development.

The interviews did not follow a prescribed sequence, nor were they confined to these topics. They did not always achieve complete coverage, either because respondent lacked information or interest in the proposed items, or because the interview developed respondent's concepts of party, faction, interest group, executive roles, and issues by other means.

of the Vermont Farm Bureau, more than a third had never heard of the Associated Industries of Vermont, and only a few more had any notion that the labor interests in Vermont were organized. One third of the representatives had never heard of Arthur Packard, for a generation the president and lobbyist for the Farm Bureau, and about two thirds of them were unable to identify the lobbyists for either the AIV or the CIO. Even fewer were able to recall more than one issue in which these groups had been interested.

TABLE 1. *Per Cent of Representatives Interviewed Who Were Able to Identify Organized Groups, Their Lobbyists, and Issues in Which the Organized Groups Were Interested*
(N = 40)

Question	Per Cent Able to Recognize		
	Farm Bureau	AIV	CIO/AFL[a]
Group itself	100.0%	62.5%	77.5%
Lobbyist	70.0	40.0	37.5
More than one issue	60.0	30.0	30.0

[a] Although John Mitchell, the labor lobbyist identified here as the most active during the session, represents officially the CIO, he was considered to have been representing both the CIO and the AFL. The granite quarry workers belong to the CIO and the stone cutters belong to the AFL.

These differentials in the ability of the representatives to recognize organized groups, their lobbyists, and issues in which the groups were interested are closely linked to the different ways the various legislators structured the session. The representatives who made the more complex analysis of the legislative process, the "policy-" and the "program oriented," saw more group activity than did the "faction-oriented." The "non-generalizers" had the lowest level of recall and recognition of organized group activity. Their concept of the legislative process did not require it of them. Or was it that, lacking recognition of

TABLE 2. *Representatives in Each Category of Perspective on the Session Who Were Able to Identify Organized Interest Groups*

Legislative Perspective	Number	Per Cent Able to Recognize Organized Interest Group		
		Farm Bureau	AIV	CIO/AFL
"Policy-Oriented"	4	100.0%	100.0%	100.0%
"Program-Oriented"	12	100.0	100.0	100.0
"Faction-Oriented"	13	100.0	56.2	76.9
"Non-Generalizers"	11	100.0	45.4	45.4
Totals	40	100.0	62.5	77.5

TABLE 3. *Representatives in Each Category of Perspective on the Session Who Were Able to Identify the Lobbyists for Each Group*

Legislative Perspective	Number	Per Cent Able to Recognize Lobbyist of the Group		
		Farm Bureau	AIV	CIO/AFL
"Policy-Oriented"	4	100.0%	100.0%	100.0%
"Program-Oriented"	12	75.0	75.0	41.7
"Faction-Oriented"	13	84.6	23.0	23.1
"Non-Generalizers"	11	36.4	00.0	27.3
Totals	40	70.0	40.0	37.5

TABLE 4. *Representatives in Each Category of Perspective on the Session Who Were Able to Recall More Than One Issue in Which a Group Had Been Interested or Active*

Legislative Perspective	Number	Per Cent Able to Recognize More than One Issue in Which Each Group Had Been Active		
		Farm Bureau	AIV	CIO/AFL
"Policy-Oriented"	4	75.0%	100.0%	100.0%
"Program-Oriented"	12	83.3	58.3	33.3
"Faction-Oriented"	13	61.5	7.7	23.2
"Non-Generalizers"	11	18.4	9.9	18.4
Totals	40	60.0	30.0	30.0

interest groups, their concept of process had to build without such elements? The data allow the question to be raised, but do not answer it.

The level of recognition or recall of group activity involved in this analysis is not exacting. It is based on the ability of the legislator to recognize or recall the existence of the organized farm, business, and labor interests; to recognize or recall the name of any of the lobbyists for these groups; and to link either the organized group or its lobbyist to issues which had arisen in the 1951 session. There was far less recognition of inter-group bargaining, techniques of lobbying, and patterns of individual interaction. Only two of the representatives interviewed were fully aware of the inter-group negotiations which had taken place on the occupational disease bill. Two or three others knew that some negotiations had taken place, but did not know that concessions had been made by the two sides. They referred questions about such details to Representatives Ralph Smith or Walter Malmquist, who, it will be recalled, were the two representatives actually involved in the whole range of negotiations. Another two or three representatives knew that business and labor—and they only presumed that it had been Kane and Mitchell—had somehow managed to agree on the occupational disease bill, but had no idea of what the agreement had involved or that it had taken the form of a *quid pro quo*. The remaining representatives could recall the occupational disease bill only dimly, and associated it vaguely with labor, but for the most part did not recall that the AIV or "business" had been concerned with it, and had no knowledge of "business-labor" conferences, negotiations, or compromises.

This less than a dozen representatives who had been aware to varying degree of the protracted and, to the AIV and labor, highly important negotiations, were almost without exception the only ones who were able to discuss in any detail the nature of the membership of the Associated Industries, and it was not clear to all of them how the diversity of membership had influenced

Kane's ability to act in the development of the tax program. The other representatives were hardly aware of the existence of the AIV and had no conception of the nature of its membership. All those with the "policy-oriented" perspective and half of those with the "program-oriented" perspective knew that the AIV had a high degree of interest in the various tax alternatives which were being proposed, and they had been watching to see whether the group would, in fact, take a position on tax changes. None of the other representatives (who constitute 75% of the sample of the lower house) had any notion that the AIV was interested in the tax proposals.

The dimensions of a legislator's awareness of group activity do not appear to be related to respondent's affiliation with one faction or another. Faction was also unrelated to the representative's conception of the process in the legislative session. As noted above, however, there was a relationship between the way the legislator structured the events of the session and his ability to report the activity of organized groups. Furthermore, it was

TABLE 5. *Relationship Between Perspective on Legislative Session and Socio-Economic Variables*

| | | Per Cent of Legislators Within Each Category | | |
Legislative Perspective	*Number*	*From Towns with Pop. of More than 2,500*	*With Previous Leg. Experience*	*With College Education*
"Policy-Oriented"	4	100.0%	75.0%	100.0%
"Program-Oriented"	12	50.0	66.7	58.3
"Faction-Oriented"	13	15.4	53.8	30.8
"Non-Generalizers"	11	0.0	27.2	9.1

not unexpected that the more complex patterns were seen by respondents of longer legislative service, more education, less geographic isolation, and more urban background.

Widely different attitudes and value judgments emerged from the interviews as to the role of interest groups in the decision-making process. A number of the legislators, mostly "policy-oriented" or "program-oriented," recognized the importance of inter-group negotiations in softening the edges of conflict among interests, be they organized or unorganized. Some legislators cited instances when they themselves had urged such negotiations. Others had sought to establish that such inter-group conferences had taken place and that the results were acceptable to the participants. One legislator, for example, discussed the occupational disease bill by saying:

> . . . that was one thing John Mitchell was very interested in. I saw him around and asked him about it, and he told me to vote for it. I asked him if he was satisfied with it, and he said "no," he wasn't, but "go talk to Ted Kane—he isn't satisfied with it either. Or talk to (Ralph) Smith—he isn't satisfied either. None of us are satisfied, but it gets a bill on the books." So it was a compromise bill, and I voted for it.

Then there were the legislators, also among the "policy-" and "program-oriented," who pointed out that unilateral pressure was not ordinarily effective in changing opinions:

> Lobbyists are effective only when opinion is not already made up, or when there is a propensity in that direction anyway. I can't think of one instance when an actual switch was brought about by lobbying.

A few others, not so facile with abstractions, confirmed this opinion. One legislator, a farmer himself, told of an attempt made by the Farm Bureau to persuade him to vote against the State Police merger when he himself had been in favor of it:

> This was the bill I was most pressured on. The Farm Bureau tried to change my vote. Each county has a Farm Bureau branch, and each branch has a legislative committee of about five people, not themselves legislators. They discuss the issues they think are going to come up and pass resolutions. During the session the local committees meet and talk about the bills. The ____ County

committee had decided that they were against the merger. After the second reading when they found out that I had voted for the merger they came to me and asked me to change my vote on the third reading. I said I didn't think I would, and I didn't. There was nothing they could do about it.

In another instance a farmer-legislator had been subjected to vigorous argument by the retail grocers, who were working for repeal of laws against the sale of colored oleomargarine: "I guess it will get passed eventually," he said sadly. "More and more seem to be for it; but I couldn't come home and look one of my cows in the eye if I voted for it."

Some of these legislators were anxious to point out that a discussion of interest groups cannot be confined to what is ordinarily termed "lobbying." Said one legislator:

> You can't talk about "Farm Bureau" activity on this bill. Farm support or opposition is not always organized. It's the same with any group. For example when this bill came up, or when any bill comes up, the members of the Agriculture Committee sit around for a while in their committee room and discuss the effects of the bill on them as farmers. Sure, they're all farmers and probably all Farm Bureau members. But is this an organized group? Not really. At least not organized in such a way that you can point to direct Farm Bureau influence.

Another legislator talking about the influence of one of the lobbyists who had at one point in his career held state office, had this to say:

> It's not so much a question of cornering this one or that in lobbies, . . . had a room on the second floor of the hotel and so did a number of influential legislators. He'd go out about 10 P.M. and get together with a few of them. He's an old guy, very lively and highly respected. They'd pat the man on the back and invite him in. Then he'd say, "you know, about this bill and that. I think this and that." And he'd be listened to. It's much more this kind of thing than actually speaking in hearings, although he did that too.

These were the legislators, too, who considered various organized groups and their lobbyists to be sources of information not only on the actual content of bills, but on attitudes about the bills. A few first-term members reported that they had consulted with the politically experienced lobbyists to get their opinions on techniques of legislative strategy.

In sharp contrast to those who viewed the interest groups as the instruments for softening conflict, defining alternatives, and conveying information, were the legislators who expressed highly negative opinions about the role of interest groups in the legislative process. Some of these fell into the category of "faction-oriented," but most of them were the "non-generalizers." "Lobbying is immoral, indecent, and unnecessary," was a fairly representative statement among this group. "There were lots of lobbyists around, but they knew it wouldn't do any good to talk to me, and I left them alone too," said another. Running through most of such interviews was a concept of an undefined "they." For the most part, unable to fit into their framework of process the activities of organized groups, these legislators could say only that "they killed it," or "they got it passed," but could not identify who "they" actually were, or how "they" had managed to kill or pass the bill.

V. LEADERSHIP IN THE LEGISLATURE

At the close of the interview each legislator was asked to nominate the members of the legislature whom it would be most valuable for the research team to visit and question. A noticeable pattern was a pronounced regional division of the state. Legislators from the southern part tended to suggest only other legislators from the south, and northern legislators tended to feel that only other legislators from the north were "worth talking to."[7]

[7]This division was a real surprise. Preliminary talks with knowledgeable people had described the political organization of the Republican party as dividing between east and west, with an alternation in office for the two sides of the mountains.

In addition, a simple count of the number of times any legislator was recommended revealed an informal structure in the legislature. Certain legislators were recommended many times more frequently than others, and their nomination was independent of respondent's factional preference or geographic residence. Without exception, those nominees appearing in the sample interviewed were "policy-oriented" or "program-oriented" in their own interpretation of the session. Parenthetically and understandably, the "non-generalizers" made the fewest nominations, and made them with the greatest reluctance.

These nominated legislative leaders, who commanded an important position in the informal structure of the legislature, appeared to have played a significant part in interpreting and reporting events for the others. They seem to have defined for the others both the nature of reality and the alternative means for bringing such reality into better adjustment with the legislator's personal preferences. They did not influence to any noticeable degree the final choice among these alternatives for the other legislators, as evidenced by the roll-call votes on crucial issues, and by the factional allegiances of respondent and nominee.[8]

[8]Though the data available from the interviews do not bring it into clear focus, there is a further variable related to the informal leadership structure of the legislature. To some members, service in the legislature is a strictly amateur undertaking, pursued for many motives, it is true: out of a sense of civic duty; as an enormously entertaining pastime to relieve the rigor of a northern winter; a varied social occasion; a chance to make business contacts or advance personal status in the home community. To others, it is part of their professional vocation. The professionals may go no further than the legislature, and may not expect to. Or they may be moving rapidly through a series of public offices. They may be freshmen or have many years of experience. In any case, the professional member must bring to his role a different perspective of the process and a different stance in his own activities than does the amateur. Further research is needed to develop the relationships between these roles and the materials analyzed in this case study.

VI. REVIEWING THE RECORD

The 1951 session afforded the Associated Industries of Vermont some interesting surprises. On the policy issue defined in advance for action, the strategy of inter-group negotiation worked admirably. The advantage of access gained from the 1950 election was put to immediate use. The substance of the bill was satisfactory to the business members. The timing was right in the legislature. The relations with other groups remained cooperative and available for further issues. The tactical moves were made out of the public eye. The requisite appearance of harmony was sustained; there were no complicated reservations, no outcries of frustration, to precipitate a negative vote.

But the case study suggests forcefully that the business group had interests at stake on many fronts, and was far from free to have its own way. Sure of access to the executive and to both houses of the legislature, convinced that the climate of opinion in the election had been sympathetic to its needs and aspirations, careful to avoid the limelight, aware that the label of business was a handicap to a policy proposal, active to form alliances with labor on social insurance and with agriculture on federal control of inflation, the AIV nonetheless ran into heavy weather. Representatives of business had worked closely with the new governor in preparing the budget message. Economy and no new taxes were the keynotes of the executive program. But an absolute freezing of appropriations was not realistic in a year of inflation. The proposed reorganization of agencies became a symbol of factional rivalry. The informal leadership emerging during the session left the AIV with notably diminished access. The timing on the major issue of the new taxes turned out to be all wrong. The AIV had not anticipated the problem, and lacked a policy and a strategic plan. The rotten-borough, rural-dominated legislature, with short tenure, afforded little opportunity for AIV to develop a case for business views of fiscal policy. A final irony of the 1951 episode was the 1952 election, in which Governor Emerson, seeking re-election, was widely criticized for the overwhelming surplus in the state treasury, product of these increased personal and corporate income taxes under the stimulus of the Truman boom.

The widely varying conceptions of the legislative process that turned up in the legislative interviews after the session explained much about the cautious approach used by AIV. Kane did not try to be invisible, and there is little to be said for stereotypes of invisible governments and pressure group politics. But, to a political scientist, it is reasonably astonishing to discover how few of the legislators could name the interest groups correctly or associate group executive with group or issue. The amateur legislature, meeting biennially, for nominal compensation, is a remarkably relaxed forum of political behavior. The issues are viewed as postponable. The temperature is kept moderate by this basic technique of resolving conflict. In this case the interest group had to play the game of politics with a legislature that was essentially unorganized until the game was better than half over.

Lobbyists Approach Government

LESTER W. MILBRATH

In discussing the methods lobbyists use to communicate with governmental decision-makers, it might be wise to emphasize that lobbyists must not only send communications, they must also design them so that they will be favorably received. The only *effective communications* are those which penetrate the perceptual screen of the receiver. . . .

There are several barriers to effective communication that lobbyists must overcome. Each governmental decision-maker has a set of predispositions which derive from a variety of sources: heredity, environment, conditioned learning, current role constraints, physiological needs, etc. These personal predispositions are enduring rather than transitory and provide long term guidance for behavior. An individual's predisposition complex can be called his personality. The important thing about predispositions for our analysis is that they not only guide behavior but also provide a perceptual screen allowing some stimuli to pass through while arresting or shutting out others. It is well know that different people viewing the same event may perceive it quite differently. Anyone reading congressional hearings, for example, must conclude that most members of Congress hear what they want to hear from witnesses. The most significant barrier to effective com-

From *The Washington Lobbyists,* Chicago: Rand, McNally & Company, 1963, pp. 209–254. Reprinted by permission of the publisher. Footnotes omitted.

munication facing the lobbyist, then, is the perceptual screen of his intended receiver.

There are other barriers as well. Officials suffer from a serious overload of communications. It is physically impossible for any governmental official to attend to all the communications directed to him. Officials use their personal perceptual screen to protect themselves from some of this overload. They also have devised some institutional means, such as staff assistants and data coding, to help them sort, condense, and comprehend as much of the incoming information as possible. In the scramble for limited attention, the lobbyist must plan carefully and seize a rare moment of receptivity to drive home a communication.

Another condition to be met is that the lobbyist must make his communication credible. In some ways the credibility barrier is similar to the perceptual screen—except that the perceptual screen is unconscious, whereas decisions about credibility are usually conscious. Government officials receive many messages containing conflicting or contradictory information; they soon learn that they must evaluate all messages. One guide to credibility is the extent to which arguments are backed up by facts and research data.

A clear and straightforward presentation also suggests credibility to a receiver. However, clear presentations backed up by data are proven incorrect from time to time; therefore, government officials look to the source of the data for an additional guide. The sender's reputation for integrity and trustworthiness is often decisive in determining the credibility of communications. This point was reiterated again and again both by congressional and lobbyist respondents. Competitive organizations comb each other's communications for mistakes or misrepresentations, which they use to the disadvantage of the original sender. One lobbyist said that once he had found over fifty mistakes in a report made by an opponent, exposition of these mistakes destroyed the credibility of the writer of the report. A quotation from a lobbyist respondent emphasizes the necessity for credibility:

> A reputable lobbyist must be very careful whom he represents. He may lose a great deal of prestige if he represents cases or clients that may come into conflict. It is extremely important that a congressman think of a lobbyist as a kind of doctor that he can depend on. Unless a congressman has real confidence in a lobbyist, that lobbyist simply does not have much influence. The greatest compliment one can get is for a member of Congress to say, "whatever that fellow tells you, you can depend on it."

Officials emphasize that information must be reliable not only because they need it for their own decisions, but also because they use this information in communications with other officials and with the public. An official who has committed himself using information supplied by a lobbyist which is later proved incorrect will be seriously embarrassed and will cut off further access for that lobbyist. Practically, the interdependence of lobbyist and governmental decision-maker requires that their relationship be built on trust and integrity.

To surmount these barriers lobbyists use both direct and indirect methods to communicate with governmental decision-makers. Some direct methods are personal presentations of viewpoints and research findings, and testimony at hearings. Some indirect methods are approaches through constituents and friends, letter and telegram campaigns, public relations campaigns, and the publicizing of voting records; these will be discussed in the next chapter. Both kinds of communications contain arguments and supporting facts; they differ only in the distinction between the lobbyist's speaking directly to the decision-maker or through an intermediary.

. . . Respondents were initially asked an open-ended question: "What approach do you generally follow to try to get a member of Congress or other public official to agree with your point of view?" About 80 per cent of the respondents said they prefer direct methods. . . .

Why the general preference for direct methods? Assuming equal receptivity, direct communications are simpler, less dangerous, and less expensive. Using indirect methods, there is some danger that an intermediary will garble the message, and it is certainly more trouble to work through someone else. As pointed out previously, receptivity for a direct message cannot be assured, and when direct methods fail, lobbyists turn to indirect communications. However, lobbyists can turn to constituents to convey the message only if the membership is substantial and willing to act on signal from Washington. Moreover, lobby organizations must have large staffs to be able to convey messages through intermediaries. As a consequence, it is likely that only lobbyists for large-membership or rich organizations can effectively utilize indirect methods. Even in these cases, lobbyists sometimes emphasize and prefer direct methods and utilize indirect methods to supplement and amplify the direct messages. . . .

• • •

PERSONAL PRESENTATION OF VIEWPOINTS

Lobbyists normally present their views personally by paying visits to governmental decision-makers and delivering their messages in face-to-face conversation. They sometimes deliver messages over the phone or via written letter or memo. Many messages are received first by staff assistants who may or may not pass them on to the official. A puristic definition would require transmission through staff assistants to be considered indirect communication. For our purposes, however, we shall make no distinction between messages transmitted through staff and those received personally by the decision-maker. Staff members are usually very close to their superiors and know in advance how the officials would deal with messages if they received them personally. It is highly realistic to consider staff members as integral parts of the official decisional units.

As groups have set up lobbying operations over the years, they seem to have operated on the following assumptions: a direct personal visit by an envoy is more effective than a written communication in gaining access; a message delivered in person can be more fully elaborated; a personal message is more likely to reach a decision-maker when he is in a receptive frame of mind.

A group with a personal envoy is thought to have a competitive advantage over a group without an envoy; consequently, an ever-increasing number of groups have sent such envoys. Now, however, the number and variety of lobbyists competing for the limited personal attention of decision-makers is so great that the Washington atmosphere is filled with noise. Having a personal envoy no longer assures a hearing. Lobbying resources have increasingly been diverted from direct communication to communication through intermediaries who are presumed to have better access. . . . [L]obbyists spend relatively little time in direct conversations with officials. Members of Congress with some years of experience, and other observers as well, have noted the shift from direct to indirect methods of communication.

Despite this shift to indirect communication, lobbyists still believe that their most effective tactic is the personal presentation of their case to the official. In response to the open-ended question about their preferred method, sixty-five respondents say they prefer and generally use personal presentations. . . .

• • •

When lobbyists make personal presentations, they do not aim their messages indiscriminately. For each problem there is a key man or group of men to whom others will look for guidance; it is especially these men whom the lobbyists try to persuade. In Congress, the members of the committee handling a given bill are the special targets of lobbyists concerned with that bill. The chairman of the committee is usually the key decision-maker and therefore draws the heaviest flow of lobby communications. If the committee has a particularly able and respected staff member (whom the members of the committee look to for guidance), he often becomes the target for heavy lobby communications. In the executive branch, lobby messages generally are directed to the top decision-maker or the particular staff assistants on whom he leans most heavily for advice. Lobbyists, then, must locate the key people—those who are so well respected that their decisions are likely to be influential to many others. Failure to locate such key persons may result in the sending of many superfluous messages, and if the key persons cannot be persuaded, there is a high likelihood that the decision will go adversely.

Some lobbyists direct their messages to persons who are undecided on a given question. When lobbyists have scarce resources, this is most economical. Some find it wise also to communicate briefly with decision-makers favorable to their point of view to encourage them to vote according to expectation. Most lobbyists do not bother to communicate with those they know are opposed; this is both painful and thought to be a waste of time. A few lobbyists, however, deliberately call on the opposition; a well-executed visit may reduce animosity even if it changes no votes.

Usually a single lobbyist calls on a single decision-maker, but this is not universally true. Some lobbyists prefer to call as a delegation; this is more likely if several groups are collaborating. Another tactic is a conference attended by several lobbyists and several decision-makers through which the group process is used to try to convince the decision-makers. Conferences are also useful in finding compromise solutions when persistent differences make that necessary. They are, however, rather cumbersome and difficult to manage; they may even have results contrary to the wishes of the organizer. Since decision-makers have tight and varied schedules, finding a convenient time for all concerned is nearly impossible unless the participants place very high priority on the meeting. Conferences, then, can be used only on very important questions.

Some lobbyists spoke of a necessity for securing a champion for their cause in Congress. This is important for relatively minor bills, since issues of major public importance tend to attract their own champions. A champion is needed to introduce the bill, call for hearings, see that the bill is voted on in committee, see that it is called off the calendar and voted on by the house. These are tasks that only a member (usually a key member) can perform; therefore, if a lobbyist fails to enlist a champion, he has little chance for success with a bill. A bill that has no member or members pushing for it (there are hundreds of them each session) will be by-passed, languish, and die.

At each legislative stage, key people must be convinced to allow the bill to pass to the next stage. Bills must be passed by subcommittees, full committees, often by the Rules Committee in the House, and the full house in each house of Congress. If the versions of the two houses differ (they usually do), the bill must go to conference committee and then back for approval to each house before being submitted to the President for approval. At each stage, there are different key people. The lobbyist must time his messages to reach the appropriate key people at the right time. A message that comes too soon may be wasted and may foreclose entree for later messages. Timing is one of the main reasons that knowledge of the legislative and political process is so important for lobbying. One lobbyist respondent explained the problem rather well:

> It is important to direct the legislative effort at the level where a bill is . . . When a subcommittee is considering a bill, it's useless to turn one's energies to the full committee, and it is too early to alert the membership of the association to contact the

entire House. A great deal of effort is wasted and it even tends to dry up possible sources of support if one pushes the wrong action at the wrong stage and before the thing is ready to be voted on. In order to avoid this, we withhold all bids for support until the proper time. Occasionally we get caught short and have to send out five thousand telegrams in a hurry to get the support rolling in, but this cost is worth it to avoid wasting our efforts before the time is ripe.

Another reason that timing is important is that entree must be saved for a time when lobbyists have something very important to discuss. Lobbyists who do not go to decision-makers until they definitely need to not only do the decision-makers a favor but help their own cases. One respondent uses infrequent visits to dramatize the urgency of his coming when he does have a problem to discuss. Smart lobbyists do not dissipate good will on any but the most important matters. This, then, is another reason why lobbyists spend so little time talking to members of Congress.

Appointments with senators are more difficult to obtain than appointments with representatives, but there is no automatic entree even with the latter. Successful lobbyists are resourceful and imaginative in discovering techniques for gaining entrance to see officials. Methods must be varied with the target and some require considerable time and energy for execution. Friends and constituents are regularly used to get appointments. The following quotation illustrates the mood and approach of many lobbyists:

I'm in the business of communicating with these people, and if they don't have an open mind, I don't get to first base. I understand perfectly well that members of Congress are busy people, and I have a great deal of sympathy for that problem, but I can't be stopped by that. If a member tells me that he is too busy to see me, I find someone who is not insulated from the member, and I ask him to contact the member. I ask him to get my point of view over to the member, or I ask him to make an appointment so that I can get it across.

The comments of both lobbyists and congressional respondents on the kind of lobbying approach they consider effective are so similar that they shape into a set of norms. Not all actors fully perceive all of the norms, but the more effective lobbyists follow them rather closely. Decision-makers are in a position to enforce these norms because they can cut off access to those who do not conform. Even if they grant an audience, they sometimes fail to listen or they may vote against the transgressing lobbyist. So many compete for a decision-maker's attention that he can readily justify setting down conditions for giving his attention and applying sanctions to those who fail to comply.

ELEMENTS OF A SUCCESSFUL PRESENTATION

The series of dos and don'ts that follow are collated and condensed from extensive comments by both lobbyists and congressional targets of lobbying. Some of the points may seem rather obvious, but they were stressed very strongly by many respondents, and supposedly they are violated from time to time.

1. Be Pleasant and Non-Offensive

• • •

Pleasantness is probably the most important factor in obtaining and maintaining access to decision-makers. Harried officials naturally defend themselves against lobbyists, and it is up to the lobbyists to overcome that barrier. One clever respondent uses the tactic of asking members of Congress to tell him their troubles. The troubles elicited generally relate to the lobbyist's own area and help to drain off some latent resentment against the organization he represents. This deliberate "tripping of their mechanism" serves as a novel introduction and helps to bring the conversation around to the subject of the visit in a smooth and unobtrusive way.

2. Convince the Official That It Is Important for Him to Listen

Some officials appear to listen to whomever is talking to them, but in many cases audiences with lobbyists are *pro forma* occurrences which have little impact. Lobbyists must convince the official that he has something at stake. Since elected officials are nearly always concerned with constituent interests, a demonstration of constituent interest is one of the best ways to insure attention. Whenever possible, lobbyists try to show members how certain behavior will help them in their districts. To do this, lobbyists must be aware of political pressures and have a realistic knowledge of the legislative process. . . .

• • •

3. Be Well Prepared and Well Informed

This is by far the most important aspect of a successful presentation. Respondents in Congress and lobbyists mention it repeatedly. Some respondents use the phrase "having a good case," which to them means essentially the same thing. Capable lobbyists are well informed not only in their own fields but on a broad range of other issues as well. They know the appropriate phrases and words to use; they know when and with whom to communicate. They know not only when and how to act but also where to get the inside information they need to do their jobs.

• • •

Officials require lobbyists to be knowledgeable because they need information and want something in return for the time and attention they give. Some lobbyists try to meet this need by operating service offices to assist officials on any problem for which assistance is requested. They give reliable expert information on short notice; thus they must have a highly capable staff. An office which establishes a reputation for reliable information and assistance on a variety of subjects is in a peculiarly strong position to affect governmental decisions. . . .

• • •

4. Be Personally Convinced

The legal profession has a tradition that the guilty as well as the innocent have a right to advocacy; accompanying this is the notion that an advocate need not believe in the truth of his case. It is the responsibility of the adversary to expose falsity; full exposure and truth are supposed to derive from the clash of the adversaries. There is a natural temptation to transfer such ideas to lobbying and conclude that lobbyists personally need not believe in what they are advocating. In lobbying, however, the advocate who is not personally convinced is less successful in pleading a case. The advocate in the court room does not personally have to withstand cross-examination; in lobbying he does. Officials opposed to a lobbyist's pleas may deliberately expose his insincerity (questioning the witness in a congressional hearing where penalties for perjury apply, for example). The lobbyist who is interested only in his fee has a difficult time justifying himself and his argument. In the competition for attention, the sincere voice is more easily heard.

• • •

5. Be Succinct, Well Organized, and Direct

Time is a precious commodity in Washington. The challenge to the lobbyist is to communicate the greatest amount of relevant information in the shortest possible time. Presentations should not only be short but simple, well organized, and direct. Simplification should not take the form of talking down to the official, but the message should be carefully drawn so that it is easy to grasp. The lobbyist who violates this norm challenges his listener to devise ways to dismiss him; he stands to lose the official's attention for not only this but also future presentations. . . .

• • •

6. Use the Soft Sell

Some lobbyists make the mistake of pushing their case too hard. They ask for the whole pie and accept nothing less than everything they have asked for. This is foolhardy in the atmosphere of compromise that inevitably prevails in legislative decision-making:

> If you insist on it being all or nothing, you usually get nothing. We look for a language in a bill which will help us to get all we can out of a situation. We try to write the bill so that it pleases as many people as possible and yet gives us as much as we feel we can get.

The sensitive lobbyist pleads but does not demand. He does not pressure the official to commit himself to a definite line of action. Above all, he does not threaten—that would only create antagonisms which would destroy his case and cut off access. Present-day lobbyists are more inclined to use the "soft sell" than lobbyists of bygone days. Several old-timers in Congress reported this:

> There now seems to be a lot more emphasis on working through the people back home and not so much emphasis on personal contact. I probably don't see a lobbyist a week here. The present-day lobbyists are cuter, too. They don't come around and try to pressure you, they just drop in and present their case. You get the impression they are afraid you won't understand their case.

• • •

7. Leave a Short Written
Summary of the Case

Most officials prefer to have something in writing to relieve them of the necessity of taking notes and to insure correctness of information and interpretation. They often file this for consultation when the official makes his decision or talks with others about the issue. Some lobbyists send this written summary in advance of the oral presentation; then when the official or his staff man talks to the lobbyist, he can ask questions in areas or topics that need clarification or amplification. Written statements from lobbyists are used by officials in speeches to other officials (on the floor of the House or Senate, for example) or to the public. Sometimes campaigning officials contact lobby organizations for arguments justifying stands they have taken. . . .

• • •

PRESENTATION OF RESEARCH RESULTS

Most lobbyists consider research results to be integral components of their presentations. . . . Lobbyists for organizations with a specialized subject matter emphasize research more than others. And lobbyists for small organizations emphasize research more than those from large organizations. Large organizations are less inclined to be specialized, and they generally have greater political resources to throw into the battle.

Lobbyists in most roles rank research second or third among the fourteen tactics. Legislative staff persons are notable exceptions, however; they rate research high but rate other tactics such as collaboration, constituent contact, hearings, and letters, higher. This exception is not clearly explicated by the data, but the data do suggest some hypotheses. Since legislative staff persons generally work more closely with Congress than other lobbyists, they may reflect feedback from Congress. Research has become honorific in modern American society; members of Congress are bombarded with research results. In many cases, the findings are not in agreement; they may, in fact, point to diametrically opposite conclusions. Recipients of conflicting research results are forced to the realization that the quality of research depends very much on the quality of the researcher and his methods. Most of these people know that statistics can be found to support almost any view. Consequently, every research report must be carefully evaluated in terms of the method, the reputation of the researcher, and the strength of the impact of the findings. In certain instances, facts may be dramatic, irrefutable, and point to an obvious conclusion—as such they have tremendous power. When they are not, however (as is the usual case), they must be evaluated personally by each decision-maker; such judgements sometimes develop into bitter disputes over method and reputation. Congressional respondents also appear to reflect an ambiguous attitude toward research; very few give it a top rating, but most rate it highly.

Some persons, of course, have little or no respect for research of any kind. They believe that science (especially social science) can never be sufficiently precise to be informative and prefer to depend on their own limited observations and experiences as a basis for deciding what they will believe and disbelieve. The presentation of research results to such an official has little or no effect. Most officials, however, are pleased to have information and ideas supported by research. Some lobbyists confine their presentations almost totally to research findings; they leave persuasion to the constituents of the official. Few lobbyist roles are so narrow, however.

TESTIMONY AT HEARINGS

Hearings are a formal communication procedure provided by congressional committees and some independent regulatory commissions. They are available to nearly anyone wanting to present his point of view. Not only do congressional committees feel compelled to hold hearings on every major bill, but all lobby groups concerned feel compelled to testify. Committees fear criticism from groups and individuals if all are not allowed to be heard at open hearings. Similarly, lobby groups fear criticism from officials—especially committee members and committee staff—and from their own members if they do not take the opportunity to testify. . . .

•   •   •

Testifying at hearings (going on the record) is often seen as a defensive action that dare not be neglected. Hearings, requiring only a single presentation which then becomes available to all concerned, appear to be an efficient means of communication. Yet both lobbyists and congressional respondents rate hearings considerably below personal presentation of viewpoints and equal to contact by constituent and public relations campaigns. Congressional respondents also rate friend contact and campaign work equally high. That rating of hearings does not significantly correlate with preference for direct communication or with rating of personal presentation of viewpoints.

There are several reasons for the imperfection of hearings as a communication device. Although messages are transmitted both orally in the hearing room and later in writing via hearing reports, there is no guarantee that the intended receivers are listening. Hearings are often held with only one member of Congress present. Even if members are present, they may not be listening. They are frequently called out of hearings to attend to something more urgent. Most members have somewhat fixed opinions about the topics on which hearings are held; thus their predispositions are likely to screen out non-congenial messages. If a member serves on a committee for several years (a common practice), he will probably have attended several hearings on the same subject. He is certain to become bored listening to the same people repeatedly saying more or less the same things.

• • •

A message on the hearing record is available in print to officials (and to the public) at no cost to the lobby group. But again, there is the problem of the overload of messages. It is simply impossible for officials to read transcripts of all hearings relevant to the decisions they must make. Most volumes of hearings are unduly long and difficult to sift through. Committees try to circumvent this by asking their staffs to present résumés of the hearings as they meet in executive session. In this process, however, the lobbyist's most important point is sometimes dropped out altogether. The function of preparing summaries makes committee staffs as much a target of lobbying as the members themselves.

• • •

It is important that, although the lobbyist dare not pass up an opportunity to testify, he also cannot count on hearings to get his message across to officials. He must use other methods as well. Some lobbyists do not expect to change the minds of any officials by testifying at hearings, but they think that hearings are useful in "strengthening the backbones" of persons who might be wavering. They also provide questions, information, and arguments that can be used by the committee members in floor debate. One lobbyist reported that he uses every opportunity to testify not because he hopes to change anyone's mind, but rather because his performance on the witness stand might fix an impression of him as a person in the minds of his listeners. This impression is useful in gaining access and rapport when he later contacts the official for a personal conference.

Gaining attention at a hearing may partly make up for sparse attendance by members; reporters are generally assigned to cover hearings, and one of the Washington newspapers occasionally picks up a bit of a lobbyist's testimony. In fact, lobbyists sometimes play to the mass media rather than to the committee members at hearings. Some, perhaps many, members read the newspapers more carefully than they read hearings. Seeing an issue or a lobbyist's testimony spotlighted in a newspaper may raise that point higher on the member's agenda of attention.

• • •

COLLABORATION BETWEEN
GOVERNMENT OFFICIALS AND LOBBYISTS

Communications and influence attempts flow in both directions between officials and lobbyists. . . .

• • •

Officials often initiate communications with lobby groups to gather basic intelligence about their environment. They need to know where various groups—especially those which are powerful politically—stand on issues. Usually these stands are so public and visible that the official need not inquire; sometimes, however, he must make a special investigation. A member of Congress planning to introduce a bill for example, sometimes checks with groups likely to be affected to see what they think about it. Intelligence gathering is basically defensive; it is only good sense to be well informed before exposing oneself.

Occasionally officials initiate communications with lobbyists to promote a bill or policy. Certain kinds of bills require considerable external pressure on members of Congress, and interested officials may set up a super-lobby group (usually called a "citizens committee") to stimulate and organize the support of lobby groups. Nearly all congressional respondents report that they collaborate with lobbyists in this fashion from time to time.

As one vigorous old warrior in the House expressed it: "Yes I do. I think every member who is worth a damn does that kind of thing." A similar comment came from a senator:

> I would not hesitate to spur on a pressure group in an activity directed to my colleagues. I might contact some farm groups or some business groups and say to them, "You know, you have been very silent on this tax proposal; I wonder why you haven't spoken up on it."

Sometimes members collaborate with sympathetic lobby groups in staging hearings. They review the testimony of witnesses in advance so that the witnesses can prepare answers. They also plan the order of witnesses to maximize the impact on the public of the desired viewpoint. Such collaboration promotes a policy and stores up good will on behalf of officials with lobbyists. A smoothly staged hearing impresses the officers and members of the pressure group. Conversely, an embarrassing hearing may lead a testifying officer to conclude that the lobbyist staff is inadequate.

• • •

Other favors are available to officials for building good will with lobby groups. Officials "leak" advance information to interested lobbyists—usually not improperly, for the lobbyist would hear about it in due time. The speed with which the lobbyist is informed constitutes the favor. Lobbyists who were former staff members on the Hill often receive their "leaks" from congressional staff persons. Officers and executives of lobby groups, who generally operate on a somewhat higher level, usually learn advance information from members of Congress themselves.

Members also assist lobby groups and lobbyists to get publicity. A favorite device is to praise a group's stand or activity on the floor of the House or Senate. Members also insert speeches or statements in the *Congressional Record*. The relevant material can then be reproduced at low cost exactly as it appears. Some enthusiastic members distribute the material postage free under their own franks. Even if publicity does not directly allude to the lobby group, a public endorsement of the group's policy stand is considered a favor. These gestures not only promote the policy of the group, they may also enhance the standing of its leadership with the group's membership.

Members of congress contact lobbyists for such services as speech-writing, preparing reports, answering correspondence, writing legislative bills, entertaining out-of-town visitors, and so forth. Some lobbying offices are, in effect, adjuncts to certain members' offices. This is seldom pushed too far because members generally keep close control of things going out over their name, but greatly overworked congressional offices welcome the free services of lobby groups in time of need. Lobbyists, for their part, are delighted to provide these services; they know no better way to affect policy than to be in on its creation. These relationships develop only when there is very close agreement on policy between the member and the lobby group; therefore, the relationship is not invidious or an abdication of functions by the member. Each participant does what he would do in any case; their cooperation merely increases their efficiency.

• • •

COMMUNICATION THROUGH INTERMEDIARIES

Several intermediary routes are used by lobbyists to supplement direct communications. . . .

• • •

Most lobby groups use both means of transmission of messages; it is difficult, then, to attribute success or failure to either method. This accounts in part for the inability of respondents definitively to evaluate the methods. The high competition of lobbyists trying to deliver direct messages to officials encourages lobbyists to seek alternative transmission routes which have better access. . . .

• • •

Here is a comment from a lobbyist:

> I'm convinced that the grass-roots support is the important thing rather than my contacts. I know this from my experience on the Hill where I have been on the receiving end. I can go up and explain the technical end of the thing, but it's the grass roots that lets the member of Congress know who is behind it. I would give 75 per cent to the grass roots.

The competition for the attention of officials has taken a new turn, however. Decision-makers, especially members of Congress, are deluged with messages from constituents. To be sure, some of these messages come spontaneously and with genuine conviction, but officials know that many others have been inspired by lobbyists and pressure groups. The net effect is that no single type of message or source can be assured attention. The competitive clamor of lobbying carries its own control. The legislator drowned in a Babel of voices is probably more free to consult wise counsel or his own conscience than one who receives only a few messages. Members must, of course, heed genuine ground swells of public opinion, which they have always done, but ordinary messages tend to cancel one another out.

Lobbyists react to this situation in several ways. Some are shifting back to direct communication. This is especially true of lobbyists for groups with specialized or technical policy concerns or with little power at the polls. Indirect communication methods are generally more time-consuming and costly. Lobbyists make tactical decisions when they allocate their resources. Smaller and poorer organizations concentrate primarily on direct methods;

larger and richer organizations utilize both indirect and direct methods. Direct methods are not likely to be neglected even if indirect methods are used. . . .

•   •   •

APPROACHES THROUGH CONSTITUENTS AND FRIENDS

From time to time lobbyists fail to get appointments with officials or a favorable reception for their messages. If it is important, they must find another means of gaining acceptance of the message. A favorite tactic is having the message conveyed by someone to whom the official is more sensitive, such as a constituent or a friend; if constituent and friend are combined in the same person, so much the better. At times messages are conveyed in writing; sometimes the intermediary pays a personal visit or calls the official on the phone.

. . . [L]obbyists clearly prefer constituents as intermediaries; while congressional respondents rate friend contact just a little higher than constituent contact. Lobbyists were asked to rate the tactics according to the way they use them in their work; whereas congressional respondents were asked to rate tactics in terms of their effect on themselves. From the perspective of the recipient of lobbying, contact by a friend is just as impressive as a contact by a constituent. Lobbyists, however, have discovered it is much easier to find constituents who will contact an official than to find a friend who will do so. Officials have only a limited circle of intimate friends. Also, constituents are generally less reluctant than friends to use the power of their relationship to influence the official. An official is less likely to resent being importuned by a constituent than by a friend.

Constituents are not always available as intermediaries either. . . . [R]espondents vary greatly in their evaluation of constituent contact. Representatives of groups with large memberships rate this tactic higher than representatives of small membership groups. Representatives of farm groups, big labor organizations, and church and humanitarian groups rate this tactic quite highly. Some farm and labor groups bring their members to Washington by the busload ("bus trippers" they are called), give them some hasty training in lobbying techniques, and send them out to call personally on governmental decision-makers. Each man focuses most heavily on his own representative and senators.

Constituent contact is also rated highly by persons who have observed closely the way officials react to constituents. Lobbyists who have had experience on the Hill or who are on a legislative relations staff rate constituent contact higher than other lobbyists. Some respondents even go so far as to use constituent contact exclusively. One lobbyist who has a rather weak case to sell says he never attempts to promote his proposal on its merits. The only point he brings up in personal visits to officials is the power of the constituents; he then stimulates constituent contact in an effort to drive his point home.

Most lobbyists use constituent contact rather carefully. They use it more for gaining access than for "making the pitch" to officials. It is common practice for the constituent and the lobbyist to call jointly on an official. The constituent has the entree and can answer questions about his personal situation; the lobbyist usually presents the main argument with the broader picture. Constituents who call on officials alone must be carefully chosen for their knowledge in depth and their ability to communicate. They are usually thoroughly briefed. Officials are themselves usually well informed, and they are not likely to be impressed by a poorly informed constituent. Some members of Congress report that they like to have constituents call on them even if they hold opposing views; this gives the member an opportunity to try to talk the constituents out of their positions.

Some members feel that pressure groups overstep the bounds of propriety in utilizing constituent contacts from time to time.

One member reported an instance in which lobbyists for a certain group called on him but failed to convince him of their case. Their proposal was voted down in committee. The lobbyists next hired an attorney from the member's home town to present the case once more. The member considered the maneuver deceptive, was angered, and stiffened his opposition.

Personal friends of officials are utilized similarly—except that the difficulties are even greater. All officials have a few friends whom they respect so highly that they will always listen to them. Such close associations can only be built up gradually on the basis of reciprocal obligations, mutual respect, and non-exploitation. The relationship carries its own control, for few friends would endanger a relationship by exploiting it. One senator said, "A friend that contacts me should be doing it to help me, not someone else. If he is being used by someone else and I discover it, he is no longer a friend."

• • •

LETTER AND TELEGRAM CAMPAIGNS

One of the surest ways to influence an elected official is to convince him that a given proposal has strong or overwhelming support among his constituents. Deluging the official with letters and telegrams is frequently presumed to convince him of this fact. In fact, most letter and telegram campaigns have little impact on the decision of officials. To be effective, a campaign must be very large and weighted to one side of the issue or it must appear to be spontaneous. A campaign which is both large and genuine in appearance is most potent.

The official cannot ignore a big campaign because of the sheer political weight which it represents. Some respondents characterized it as a "hurricane warning." Often, officials simply batten down for the storm and wait for it to pass. Members of

Congress philosophically wait for the public to move from one wave of sentiment to another. While the interviewing for this study was being conducted, Congress was flooded with letters in favor of an "economy drive"; legislation which might have been adversely affected by the drive was simply postponed until it could be considered in a more favorable climate.

Letter campaigns have an irritation value, since the over-worked staffs of members must respond to the letters. Sometimes the mere threat of such a campaign accomplishes the lobbyist's purpose. Another result of a big campaign is that it actually stimulates closer scrutiny of the proposed legislation.

•   •   •

Lobbyists know that members of Congress try to distinguish between pressure mail and letters that are written spontaneously from a genuine concern in the minds of the constituents. It then becomes a game in which the lobbyists try to launch a campaign which does not look like one, and the members try to spot a campaign and discount it. Smart lobbyists do not prepare mimeographed messages for members to sign and mail to members of Congress; neither do they supply suggested wording for messages. It may even be dangerous to supply points or topics to be mentioned in the letters. Lobby groups find the best tactic is to try to teach their members how to write messages to officials and trust them to make relevant points. . . . Some groups print pamphlets showing how to write spontaneous letters, or hold short courses on stimulating spontaneous grass-roots sentiment.

The difficulty with this game, from the lobbyist's point of view, is that it depends too much on untrained, unskilled persons. Often members are tipped off because some constituent has been sloppy. One member told of a local club that, not wishing to waste postage, put all their letters in a hosiery box and mailed them to the member. Sometimes a constituent sends the bulletin giving instructions for letter-writing to the congressman. Members spot campaigns from similarities in envelopes, stationery, stamps, postmarks, even the special characteristics of certain typewriters. Occasionally an overzealous constituent sends messages on behalf of his friends without consulting them. Such a tactic is generally uncovered when the letter or telegram is answered and the unconsulted constituent communicates his surprise to his representative. Because of these kinds of difficulties, letter and telegram campaigns are less frequently used now than in the recent past.

Another reason members of Congress discount letter and telegram campaigns, even the spontaneous ones, is that they realize that only a small portion of the population will take the trouble to write. If a congressman should get thirty thousand letters on an issue, this would be considered a great number; yet it would account for no more than 10 per cent of his constituency. The persons who do write may well feel more strongly on an issue than those who are silent, but the views of the writers should not, for that reason alone, be given preference. Writers tend to be drawn from the upper socio-economic strata of the population; persons who perceive themselves as poorly educated or of lower status are hesitant to approach officials, even by letter. Persons of lower status are less likely to be alerted to impending legislation that affects their interests; this does not mean their interests ought not to be protected.

• • •

As was noted earlier, members of Congress deluged with letters to take a stand they do not want to take may ask an opposition group to produce an equal or greater number of letters on the other side so that they will be left free to vote their convictions. Members differ in their reaction to mail; some readily conform to the pressure; some react strongly against it; others react mildly or not at all. Some members like the attention of letter or telegram campaigns; these are known as members who "court mail." Some need to lead their constituents, and respond to a mail campaign with a communication of their own setting forth their reasons for taking their own position. They sometimes also use the mass media to educate their constituents.

• • •

Even if an organization has the membership to stage mass letter or telegram campaigns, several other factors are considered when the group is deciding on use of this tactic. Certain subject matters of technical or narrow interest are not adaptable to broad pressure tactics. Also, the campaign may backfire if it is poorly executed. Most important, it is difficult for any organization to stimulate its membership to send messages to officials; they can call on the membership only a limited number of times (perhaps three per session). Therefore, letter campaigns must be saved for the most important issues. One lobbyist for a mass organization says he does not expect letters to accomplish much toward influencing the decisions of officials, but he thinks they are useful in stimulating the political interest of the membership. Any member of his organization who writes a letter is likely to watch the performance of his congressional representative more closely; if the official does not perform to expectations, the letter-writer is more likely to retaliate at the polls.

These summary comments might be made about letter and telegram campaigns. Officials appreciate thoughtful well-reasoned letters: "One thoughtful letter is worth five hundred uniform ones." Therefore, letters generally are superior to telegrams. Campaigns are discounted when officials know that someone is turning a crank. Even tremendous campaigns may well not accomplish their purposes. One committee staff member reported that eighteen sacks of mail piled up in the committee office during one campaign, but the legislation still did not pass. It is almost impossible to disguise a letter campaign so that officials will not detect it as such. Lobbyists vary considerably in their rating of letter campaigns. The organizations that use them think of letters from the grass roots as a reinforcing tactic to back up other methods of communication.

PUBLIC RELATIONS CAMPAIGNS

Public relations campaigns are much more indirect than letter campaigns; therefore they are less efficient and most costly. On the other hand, they are not so likely to be detected as a pressure tactic. One supposition behind such campaigns is that if enough people can be convinced to favor a given viewpoint, this viewpoint and the power behind it will be communicated in various ways to government officials. Another supposition is that such [a] campaign will have long-range effects on the voting behavior of the public and thus will find policy expression through the selection of governmental decision-makers. Successful public relations campaigns set the stage or create the climate within which governmental decisions are made. Any given climate will facilitate certain decisions and exclude others. The climate created by a successful "PR" campaign also sets the limits for the transmission and acceptance of messages. A message that might have been ignored in one climate may be favorably received in another.

A PR campaign can be partially effective even if the people send only a few communications to officials. Officials are more likely than voters to perceive public relations campaigns. If they begin to think that the views of the public are indeed being affected, they may begin to adjust their behavior even before they hear from the constituents.

Lobbyists report that the effects of PR campaigns are so diffuse and delayed that they are difficult to evaluate. . . . [A]nother reason that PR campaigns are rated so unevenly by lobbyists is that these campaigns must be very large and expensive to be successful. Therefore only a few organizations can afford to use them. Organizations that cannot afford PR campaigns naturally rate it very low. . . .

The PR campaign of the margarine manufacturers to abolish the federal tax on margarine and the campaigns of the American Medical Association to defeat Presidents Truman's and Kennedy's health insurance programs are notable postwar examples of successful public relations campaigns. Each cost several million dollars. Less ambitious campaigns have effects so diffuse that the public may not be visibly moved. If officials do not perceive that the public is actually manipulated, they are less likely to respond.

· · ·

Although PR campaigns are so expensive that only certain organizations can use them, some of the costs are passed on to the public or consumers. Advertising expenses, even for institutional advertising which is often semi-political, can be deducted from corporation income tax as a business expense; therefore, PR campaigns are partially publicly supported. PR campaign costs are also passed on to consumers as higher prices for products and service. Indirectly, this is true of all lobbying expenses; consumers ultimately pay for all lobbying.

Public relations campaigns that are big enough and clever enough to establish a climate of opinion are very effective for influencing governmental decisions. Such campaigns are not widely used, however, because they are so costly. They may also stimulate counter-campaigns by opponents, the two campaigns cancelling each other. Moreover, the public is not passively pushed hither and yon by PR campaigns. A public discussion, once begun, carries its own momentum. People have their own ideas on public policy which they communicate with one another. The total political climate resulting from this multitude of interactions may have much wider ramifications and results quite different from those anticipated by the planners of the PR campaign.

PUBLICIZING VOTING RECORDS

Roll-call votes in both houses of Congress are part of the public record available to anyone who is interested. A few lobby organizations give roll-call votes wide publicity, so that many more voters know the voting records of officials than would otherwise be the case. Curiously, the wide publicizing of a public record is rejected and resented by most lobbyists. . . . [P]ublicizing voting records is a powerful and dangerous political tactic open only to groups with considerable power at the polls. . . .

The tactic is dangerous because most members of Congress perceive it as punitive and sometimes unjust; they may retaliate against the organization or lobbyist who uses it. Members quite accurately feel that pressure is being applied to force their vote in a certain direction. Many also object because they think that the particular combinations of votes published by some organizations present unfair pictures of their voting records. . . .

• • •

In an effort to set the record straight, some members have publicized a voting record compiled by themselves which they feel is more fair than that circulated by the lobby group.

Publicizing voting records has been pursued most diligently by labor and other large membership groups. Most labor lobbyists are convinced of the wisdom of the tactic:

> I think it's important. Of course we make people mad at us at times. Bill ___ is sore as hell at me now because we published his records. But I think we are going to make up—I kind of like Bill and I think he kind of likes me. I really don't get particularly bothered if they do explode. We find this especially valuable in

the case of a congressman who comes from a very close district. He's got to have labor votes in order to win, so he will certainly come around. The reason I am so convinced that they are helpful is that I get many calls from members saying, "Couldn't you keep that vote off the record?" and "Do you have to have this vote on the record." I reply that the record is purely objective and we've got to report whatever they do.

• • •

The vulnerability of a member to pressure arising from publicizing his voting record depends on his strength in his constituency. A man who is fairly certain of re-election is not very concerned if his record is published. If his re-election is doubtful, he is not in a position strong enough to protest vigorously to a politically powerful organization which has published his record. He can, however, end all the future access for which a group with little power at the polls publishes his record; that is why such organizations do not use the tactic.

• • •

The Impact of Lobbying on Government Decisions

LESTER W. MILBRATH

Perhaps the most difficult question about lobbying is that of the extent of its influence or impact on governmental decisions. No one has a definitive answer to that question. Yet an understanding of the influence of lobbying is essential to a full perspective on the topic. This study was not designed to measure the impact of lobbying and can offer only partial answers. Still, quite a number of observable facts contribute some enlightenment. Some have been alluded to previously. In this chapter, all findings relevant to the impact of lobbying will be reviewed to provide as broad a perspective as possible.

Inquiring about the influence of lobbying is not the same as inquiring about the influence of pressure groups. Admittedly, the factors are highly related, but they are not identical. Some lobbying is carried out on behalf of individuals or corporations as well as groups. On the other hand, some of the influence of pressure groups is not exerted through lobbying (using a special envoy at the seat of government) or lobbyists. It will not be necessary to maintain a clear distinction between lobbying and pressure groups, but the reader should be aware that the primary purpose of this chapter is to evaluate the influence of lobbying, not that of pressure groups.

From *The Washington Lobbyists*, Chicago: Rand McNally & Company, 1963, pp. 328–354. Reprinted by permission of the publisher. Footnotes omitted.

• • •

Congressional respondents were asked the following question:

> Whenever a person must decide how he will vote on an issue or a bill, he must take several factors into account, such as: the wishes of his constituents, the views of interest groups, the recommendations of his colleagues and friends, and his personal feelings. Which of these kinds of factors are uppermost in your mind as you arrive at your decisions?

Members have complicated and varied answers reflecting different backgrounds and different situations. Before discussing each factor more fully, some quotations from members will point up the complexity of the interrelationships:

> That is the sixty-four-dollar question to ask a member of Congress. I think it varies. If it is a question which affects the national security, why I invariably vote the way the best information for me indicates I should vote regardless of the constituents.

• • •

> I take them all into account, but I almost always vote the way I personally decide. I don't make this decision naïvely, by the way. My own view is that it is good politics to take a personal position, and that is the way representative government should function. However, it is not as simple and clear-cut as that. Many times you may see an issue very clearly at the beginning of a session, and you know how you are going to stand on that issue, but by the time you get to the end of the session, it may become confused because there are so many compromises and changes. You wonder if the problem is being evaded and how you should really stand on it. . . . I would say by and large I have a view of my own before I am approached by an interest group. The lobbyist may bring me the first information on a "cat and dog bill"; those are bills without much consequence for the public. I don't remember a time when a position I had was changed by a contact. I do recall making at least one recognizable mistake each year I have been in Congress. The only one that ever upset me was one time when I voted on both sides of an issue; I voted for the bill

and then voted to sustain the President's veto. I tried to explain it to the people in the next campaign and discovered it had no effect on my election; since then I haven't been too worried about making a mistake once in a while.

• • •

You haven't listed the most important one—that is, the merits of the legislation. There is an interaction in the mind of the legislator which considers all those factors. The attitude of every member is influenced by his over-all background and the nature of his constituency. Members are either born economizers or born spenders, and this is influenced by the nature of his constituency. Most members are more or less predisposed toward an issue before they get to it. We take a pretty common sense approach to the views of interest groups: Are they selfish or unselfish? How does opinion run in one's district? Is there undue advocacy or undue advantage? How the views are presented is a lesser factor but still a factor.

• • •

Your first claim is to your district or you won't be here next time. Second comes the desires of the President; I am his leader in the House, and I wouldn't desert the President or the aims of the administration unless there were a mighty weighty reason. I am a member of the team, and this is uppermost in my mind on most questions. I don't take the views of interest groups too seriously. Actually, I don't get too much pressure; I have a very good district in that respect. Maybe it is because I have been here thirty years; they know what to expect. Either they have confidence that I will do the right thing, or they figure it is hopeless—either way I don't get a lot of letters.

• • •

The number one factor is that you make sure it doesn't adversely affect the people you represent. If it doesn't hurt your people or you feel it might be good for them, you also try to weigh the public or the national interest and try to decide what the legislation will do over a long pull. If you decide it is a good bill and it is lasting, why this is a very persuasive factor in one's decision.

What your colleagues think about an issue or a bill doesn't enter into your decision. All of these people have their own problems, and just because one guy is in favor of a bill doesn't mean you should be. He may have different problems with his constituency. What shall it profiteth a man if he vote to save the country and lose his own seat? . . . I do discuss certain problems with other members; these are men I have come to know and trust over the years.

It can be seen from the quotations that the wishes of a member's constituents are an omnipresent factor, and, in a broad sense, they are decisive. The desires of constituents might be conceived of as boundaries beyond which a member dare not step without suffering dire consequences. These boundaries might be very wide on certain questions and very narrow on others. If a constituency is vitally interested in a question—for example that of segregation (for a southern district)—the boundaries are very tight, and the representative can take only one action if he hopes to be re-elected. The folkways of the Congress recognize these restrictions, and a member who breaks with the leadership to please his constituency on such a tight matter will be forgiven. If a constituency is not so vitally interested, the boundaries are broader, and on some questions there are no boundaries at all. Lobbying has greater opportunities for influence when the constituency is not very interested and the decision-maker has greater decision latitude. If the constituents are interested and aware, their desires are undoubtedly the most important factor. A congressman put it this way:

Well, of course the views of the constituents are always uppermost in the politician's mind. We jokingly make a distinction between a politician and a statesman, but we are all politicians, too. As statesmen, we are delegated to represent not only the views of our constituents but also their best interests. If we could count on the people being properly informed, well then, their views would be all that is necessary, but unfortunately that cannot always be counted on. When you come up here they expect you to study and advise them, and I try to do so. I lead them a little bit, but in the end, their views tend to be uppermost.

A clerk for a congressional committee said:

> If I had to select one as the most important day-in-and-day-out, I would say it is the appraisal of the member of what his constituents think. He may not know what his constituents think; he has no really good measure; but it is what he thinks they think that is important. Even if he believes his constituency is not too interested in a bill, he may try to parlay his vote on that bill into an advantage for him in his constituency on some other kind of issue. Ninety-nine per cent of the money spent on lobbying falls short because it ignores that fact. . . . To the extent lobbying can influence public opinion, it has some impact because voter reaction is the most important thing in Congress.

Most lobbyists also recognize the predominating influence of voter desires:

> Most of what happens in the legislative area is at least 80 per cent determined on the day of election; in addition, much of the legislative activity throughout a session of Congress is actually a setting of the stage for the next election. It is impossible for a lobbyist "to make a silk purse out of a sow's ear." . . . You do not change a member of Congress by buying him or browbeating him or otherwise attempting to change him.

The smart lobbyist tries to demonstrate to a member that following a particular course of action will help him in his constituency. The member usually listens attentively to such information, but he also learns that he must view claims of constituency support with some skepticism. Reliable information about constituent desires is difficult to obtain. The leaders of large membership organizations generally claim that they speak for all their members, but this is a claim they can hardly substantiate.

> You can't be a public official without having considerable knowledge in your own right, and you learn to discount what these groups say. I come from a farm district, and it makes a difference if the Farm Bureau is for or against a piece of legislation. But I

have learned that the top people in these organizations often have views that are different from their members down below who are my constituents; therefore, I discount what they say a little.

Following constituent desires too closely can be harmful in certain cases. Constituents generally do not and cannot follow the development of information and arguments on an issue. The complexion of the issue may change, and the available alternatives may shift to such an extent that constituent desires provide little or no guidance. Many members also take the traditional Burkean perspective that constituents really elect a man's judgment and that it is proper to vote according to their own judgment even if it goes against the desires of the constituents. Members report that they feel compelled on occasion to vote against their constituents, especially if they believe it is for the good of the country:

> It so happens that practically all of my votes are the way that the prevailing opinion is in my district. This is probably because my own philosophy of government is the same as that of the people in my district. However, there are times when we differ, and in such cases I vote the way my best judgment indicates. In the long run, this is in the interests of the people, and they do have an opportunity to express approval or disapproval at the next election. The Lend-Lease and defense acts early in World War II were opposed by 75 per cent of the people in my district; yet I voted for every one of them and in so doing I was performing my representative function.

· · ·

> There are two types of issues. When it doesn't involve a profound decision or doesn't strongly affect the government or there will be no great disparity in cost, I give the weight to what the people feel strongly about. There are other kinds of decisions that are weighty and will affect the security or solvency of the country. On those kind your own convictions are dominant. The people are very understanding even if you go against their wishes. If you

frankly tell them that it wasn't wise for the country, they are not going to turn against you. You can try to educate them, but generally you can't make them change their mind. They may still be against you, but they will realize there are two sides to the question, and they will not turn against you.

If the boundaries set by the constituents on an issue have left some decision latitude to the member, the next most important factor is likely to be his personal convictions about the issue. Most members have a long-established political philosophy which guides their decisions. Through their political philosophy they "know" what is good and bad for the country and the people. Furthermore, a man who has served in public office for some time has had to take a stand on most issues in the past. A prior stand tends to freeze his current position. A change from a past position can easily be interpreted as a tacit admission that the prior position was incorrect or possibly that undue influence was used.

On broader legislation which affects the lives and future of the people, I vote according to my philosophy of government. Some people in government stress the money values and some stress the human values. Without disregarding money values, my emphasis is on the human values.

. . .

When lobbyists work on broad national policy, their effect is very minor. Lobbyists are effective when they are urging what you are for and not effective when they are urging what you are not for. I have watched people come and go on the Hill here for fourteen years, and I have seldom seen a change in a fellow's basic philosophy even though he has been subject to all sorts of pressures.

. . .

Everyone has a political philosophy and is seldom talked out of it. If they have been re-elected, they feel it has paid off in getting them re-elected. Lobbying might have some effect on insignificant facets of legislation, but it doesn't have much effect on the philosophy of a senator. The longer a senator has been here, the more he is convinced the people back home like his philosophy and the less susceptible he is to lobbying. . . . You can pretty well judge in advance how a senator will vote on something because he has been voting that way for years. You really can't get them out of their rut, and the pressure groups tend to freeze them this way; they feel they must hold these people within the traces. If a senator kicks over the traces, the pressure groups generate indignation all over the country.

It is important to keep in mind that simple "yeas" or "nays" are not the only alternatives open to a member when an issue is up for decision. A wide range of actions is possible—from campaigning on the issue, to mere voting, to abstaining. . . . Most lobbying effort, then, is aimed not at conversion but at activating the favorable member or at least at ensuring that he remains committed and votes "correctly."

Every public official is interested in making a "good record." A "good record" is instrumental in maintaining and enhancing his position. It brings increased influence, which is important to all public officials. Further, when an official pursues policies that fulfill his political philosophy, he thinks that he is making a "good record"; this is important in satisfying his ego needs (his conception of himself). But no public official can make a "good record" by himself. He must have the cooperation of other officials. To obtain this cooperation, he must be prepared to bargain and must learn to play as a "member of the team." Former Speaker Rayburn is reputed to have said, "The way to get along is to go along."

The organization of a majority to get a bill passed requires some minimum amount of discipline and compromise. Once the "team" position on a given piece of legislation has emerged, the pressures for the members of the team to "go along" become rather intense. Failure to "go along'" lower one's standing within the team and lessens one's chances for advancement in the system; it may even result in negative sanctions such as withdrawal of campaign support or loss of preferred committee assignments, although Congress is generally reluctant to apply such severe sanctions. The major penalty for not playing as a member of the team is loss of reputation or standing, which provide influence or power. Certain members can be characterized as very powerful; their power generally derives from the respect they have gained from their fellow members as they have played by the rules on the team over the years. A non-team player never gains that respect and influence.

When a member's political party holds the Presidency, his team grows to include the presidential office and even the executive departments. His leader becomes the Presidnt, and much of the policy initiative flows from that quarter. Presidential and departmental recommendations become important influences on his voting decisions. These recommendations are backed by superior information and research as well as all of the influences associated with the team effort.

Officials cannot avoid making decisions though they generally must make them on the basis of somewhat imperfect information. To fill the gap, they usually welcome or actively seek out information. The need for facts provides lobbyists with their best opportunity to influence decisions. But even here, lobbyists must compete with many other sources of information and advice. Information and recommendations of colleagues are very important in this process. Officials are inclined to accept information and advice from a colleague if they respect his integrity and wisdom and believe that he has superior knowledge. The complexity of modern legislation and the norms of the institution encourage members to develop knowledge in depth in only a few legislative subjects. In subjects about which they are not so well informed, members lean heavily on committee recommendations or on the advice of a member of the relevant committee.

Informal circles of friends with similar political philosophies spring up in Congress. Information on forthcoming developments is exchanged within them. Respect for one another's specialties within such a circle can be so great that the recommendation of the specialist in a certain policy area can determine the votes of the entire friendship circle. One lobbyist said that at the time when he was a member of Congress he belonged to a circle of friends with similar political philosophies. Each member of the group served on a different committee, and they met weekly at lunch to report to one another on developments in their respective committees. Asked if he accepted the recommendations of his colleagues without further investigation, the respondent rocked back in his chair, thought for a full minute, and then said quite decisively, "Yes, by God, I did."

Staff assistants to decision-makers also exercise an important influence on the information and advice accepted by officials. Staffs not only process incoming information, they also take the initiative in digging out information. Staff persons are appointed by their superiors and are supposed to be alter egos for them, but since staff members are individuals, they may have some political convictions which intrude into the performance of their tasks. It is impossible to say with any precision how much decision-makers lean on their staffs; some are probably much more dependent than others. Dependence on staff recommendations probably increases if decisions involve technical or specialized questions and as decision-makers become more rushed.

Since officials have several alternative sources for information and advice, it is difficult to measure how effective lobbyist messages are. . . . [O]fficials do attend to lobbying information; they welcome it even if they do not feel very dependent on it. A rough indication of the value decision-makers place upon messages from lobbyists also can be derived from answers to the question of how often decision-makers come to lobbyists for information and advice.

Table 1 shows how often lobbyists have been solicited for their views and the kind of views sought. Twenty-four per cent report that they have never been solicited; 44 per cent say it has happened no more than ten times a year; 18 per cent say it occurred eleven to twenty-five times a year; and 14 per cent say it has been continual. Most lobbyists report that communications initiated by decision-makers are confined to requests for information to which the lobby organization has unique access or to views on issues on which the organization has strong and established opinions. A prime aim of most lobbyists is to develop confidential relationships with decision-makers which will provide regular opportunities to exert influence. These data suggest that no more than 10 per cent of the lobbyists achieve this with even one official; only 9 per cent are consulted frequently on a wide range of policy issues. There is no evidence in this table that lobbying messages are widely sought after by decision-makers.

The representatives of large organizations with considerable power at the polls, such as labor and farm groups, report being solicited for their views more often than other lobbyists. This again reflects the power of the constituents; the stand of an organization with power at the polls may be important information when an official is making a decision. Organizational executives and officers who are the spokesmen for their organizations are solicited more often for their views than lobbyists in other roles. Lawyers in private practice are seldom solicited. Lobbyists who have previously had confidential relationships with decision-makers tend to carry part of that confidence over to their new role; former office-holders, those with Hill experience, and those who are very active in groups, tend to be solicited more frequently. Political activity also seems to be rewarded by increased solicitation of one's views; political contributors, especially political fund-raisers, are solicited more than those who do not so participate.

TABLE 1. *Decision-Makers' Solicitation of Policy Views from Lobbyists*

	Frequency of Solicitation						
Type of Views Solicited	*Never*	*2 Times a Year or Less*	*3–10 Times a Year*	*11–25 Times a Year*	*On-going Activity*	*No Response*	*Total*
None	24						24
Inquiry confined to organizational views or information		13	25	15	8		61
Wide range of issues		2	2	3	3		10
Confidential conversations					3		3
No response		1	1			14	16
Total	24	16	28	18	14	14	114

These data do not precisely indicate the extent to which lobbyists are heard. However, where lobby groups have useful information, it is heeded; and when their stand has important political implications, it is heeded. But we must also say that many lobby messages fall on deaf ears. Decision-makers occasionally seek information and advice from lobbyists, but very few of these interchanges are on a confidential and wide-ranging basis. Very few lobbyists report, and none of the congressional respondents report, having such confidential relationships.

Looking back now on the factors that decision-makers consider as they make their decisions, we can more clearly evaluate the range of lobbying influence by inquiring into the probability that lobbying or lobbyists can affect these factors. Lobbyists and lobby groups have a very limited ability to control the selection of officials or to affect the likelihood that an official can keep or enhance his position. . . . [L]obbyists and lobby groups are reluctant to become involved in partisan politics. They also find it difficult and very expensive to try to manipulate public opinion; many of them have great difficulty manipulating even the opinion of their own membership. This is not the same as saying that groups have little influence on politics; they obviously do have considerable influence; however, the influence of groups is derived from the fact that members of groups are citizens and the political system is designed to respond to the influence of their votes.

In similar vein, lobbyists and the leaders of lobby groups cannot, by themselves, make an official look good or bad. They have little to say about whether an official makes a "good record" or not. They can, of course, offer support to or oppose an official, and that may have some little impact on his public image; but they do not have votes on bills that they can use to bargain with officials in the way officials bargain for one another's votes. They are not members of the team and do not have team norms and sanctions to use to control the behavior of officials. They have little or no success in changing the political philosophies of officials. Even their impact from supplying information and suggested policy alternatives to officials is diluted by the many alternative sources officials have for information and ideas.

The kinds of rewards and punishments that lobbyists are in the best position to offer have relatively low priority for the officials. It has been shown that entertainment and parties are not even considered a reward by most officials. Favors and bribes are not highly valued and are considered very dangerous by both officials and lobbyists. Lobbyists do have a kind of nuisance impact. They can make life somewhat unpleasant for officials who do not go along with them: It is embarrassing to vote against someone who is watching; it is difficult to vote against a group that has sent six thousand letters; it is hard not to listen to someone who is very persistent; it is hard to stand up to scorn by the public media. On small matters these nuisance factors may have considerable impact; they may even be decisive; but on matters of large public import such factors are rarely, if ever, of any great importance.

It has been suggested that the impact of lobbying on governmental decisions varies with the nature of the issue. On broad political issues commanding considerable public attention, the major determinant is the desire of the public. Lobbyists can do very little to affect the outcome, though they may influence the details of the bill or the specific language of small sections. If the legislation is specialized and affects only a small segment of the population, lobbyists are more likely to play a larger role. A member of the Ways and Means Committee of the House told a story about representatives of two large whiskey distilleries who came before the committee to argue about when the tax on whiskey should become due and payable. Each was seeking a competitive advantage over the other. There was no governmental or public interest to be served or disserved. The issue received no attention in the press. The committee listened quietly to the pleas from both sides and then made its decision (handed down its judgment). Lobbying may have been important on this bill, but was the bill really important?

> It is the demands of the people that start the country on a certain broad road policy-wise. Lobbyists may affect the language of the bills and legislation that come out in conformity with this broad policy, but they have little influence on the general outcome. They may not have any influence about the choice of the road to drive on, but they do have something to say about the way we drive on the road once we are on it.

· · ·

> I think lobbying plays a role in shaping the final content of a piece of legislation. We went out and slugged for an amendment to the highway act and got it tacked on. We couldn't affect the outcome of the bill very much, but in this technical way lobbying plays its role.

· · ·

> I think over the long haul that lobbying hasn't too much influence. I think they do have some impact on the details, and considerable impact on specialized legislation.

· · ·

> The lobbyists are really interested in the details, and this is where they have their effect. On over-all policy, however—the 1954 tax code for example—I don't think they are particularly effective. I suppose on broad policy if you get enough lobby organizations heading in the same direction, it has some effect. But once a coalition is built up on one side, it stimulates an opposing coalition on the other side, and Congress is caught in the middle.

Some observers argue that lobbyists have their greatest power when the issue is closely contested and switching a few votes here or there may turn the tide. It is rather superficial, however, to give lobbyists credit for the outcome if they have switched a few votes in a close contest. It ignores all the factors that originally made the contest close, the influences that created the firm stands of the persons lined up on both sides of the issue. In legislative votes, the factors that determine one vote are as important as those that determine any other vote. If two hundred House members, acting on their political beliefs, were to line up on each side of a bill and the tide were turned by a dozen votes that were influenced by lobbying, would it be correct to say that the votes of four hundred persons acting on political conviction were outweighed by the dozen acting on pleadings from lobbyists?

THE BALANCE OF POWER IN LOBBYING

An important factor attenuating the impact of lobbying on governmental decision is the fact that nearly every vigorous push in one direction stimulates an opponent or coalition of opponents to push in the opposite direction. This natural self-balancing factor comes into play so often that it almost amounts to a law. The great numbers of lobbyists in Washington may actually be a blessing instead of a threat to the governmental system. When groups push on both sides of an issue, officials can more freely exercise their judgment than when the groups push on only one side.

The theory that countervailing power will cancel out some of the one-sided strength and evil effects of lobbying is an old one in Washington and is criticized vigorously by some persons. One criticism is that certain interests, such as consumers, have no one to represent them and that, therefore, any pressure against the welfare of these weakly organized interests is not resisted adequately. Although there is some truth to that criticism, the point is often overstressed. From time to time, consumer representatives are placed on boards and other decision-making bodies. More important, consumers, and any other poorly organized group, have a voice through constituent pressures and the vote.

In addition, it is common for one of the organized interests to have an interest coinciding with unorganized interests. For example, in the struggle over the tariff, the direct interest of the consumer is in free trade; the goods he purchases will be cheaper. Every time tariff decisions must be made, some organized interests lobby vigorously in favor of free trade.

A more telling criticism of the theory of countervailing power is that there is some danger that such an overwhelming coalition of groups may be organized on one side of an issue that the beneficial effect of competition may be outweighed by the irresistible force of combination. This criticism can be over-emphasized, too. If an overwhelming combination of powerful groups were on one side of an issue, the public would probably also favor that side of the issue. In such a case, the outcome would be completely in accord with our beliefs about how the political process should work. If the public were not behind the coalition of groups, the decision-makers would have sufficient public support to decide without being irresistibly influenced by the coalition.

When thinking about the theory of countervailing power, it is important not to think of decision-makers as inanimate objects which are manipulated by group pressures. Officials have beliefs and values of their own which are important guides to their decisions. The group or coalition with the greatest numbers, or the most money, or the loudest noise will not necessarily prevail, especially if their prevailing is not in the public or national interest. As we saw above, the pressures of groups are but one of the factors considered by decision-makers—and by no means the most important one.

Another false notion in thinking about the impact of lobbying is the condemnation of all pressure as bad. It is a fact that life, especially organized community life, does not exist without pressure of one kind or another. Pressure is effective when it is backed by sanctions. The sanction with the greatest impact on the public official is the decision of the voters to support him or not. Every vote is a unit of pressure on a representative. Every communication from a constituent to his representative is a pressure. Our political system was designed to register those pressures, and we consider it proper when public officials respond to them.

All other forms of pressure derive meaning only as they are converted into voter pressure. If a lobby group can use money and other resources to convince the body politic that a certain policy should be followed, that conviction will be registered in pressure at the polls, and it will be proper for the system to respond to that pressure. We would not, in fact, want public officials who were insensitive to pressures at the polls. The only feasible and legitimate way to counteract political pressures is to form opposing groups and to try to convince the public that the original pressure group is wrong. If a group can sway the body politic, that is exactly what our system responds to and should reward.

ESTIMATIONS OF LOBBYING SUCCESS

Lobbyist respondents were asked to make several subjective evaluations of their success and of the contribution of lobbying to the policy-making process. In addition, they were to name the most successful lobby organization in town. Some consensus in this selection was expected. Lobbyists do not agree on the most successful lobby group in Washington; no organization received more than eight or ten choices. One reason for this is that judgments of success are very subjective. Different lobbyists use different standards. Some evaluate the percentage of bills passed that a group supported. This fails to come to grips with the question, however; one does not know whether the same bills would have passed if the lobby group had done nothing. Others use a broader criterion of long-range progress toward a distant goal. The subjective component of this kind of appraisal is readily apparent. Still others use a negative criterion of a group's ability to prevent potential damage to its interests.

Another reason for the lack of agreement on the most successful lobby group was that lobbyists naturally tend to choose a recent opponent as the strongest or most successful group. Psychologically, one enjoys believing that one's opponents are strong. Like anyone else, lobbyists need to believe they are succeeding. The feedback from their activities, however, is very ambiguous and difficult to interpret. They naturally interpret their progress as favorably as possible; this helps to maintain their self-respect. Believing that one's opponent is very strong, a lobbyist who wins a point scores a striking success in his own mind. Even if he should be defeated, his deflation is minimized because one could not really expect much more when opposing such a strong adversary. About 15 per cent of the lobbyists choose a major opponent as the strongest group in town. There are also psychological rewards for believing that one's own organization is the strongest in town; about 14 per cent of the lobbyists believe that.

Despite the subjective difficulties in estimating group success, lobbyists tend to pick large membership organizations—like farm groups, veteran groups, and labor organizations (especially the railway labor unions)—as the most successful. About one-third of the lobbyists choose a large membership organization as the most successful. This is consistent with the contention that power at the polls is the greatest power in lobbying. The American Medical Association and the oil and gas lobbies are the specialized groups most often listed as quite powerful. The reputation of the AMA stands out quite sharply and stems largely from their successful public relations campaigns to label proposed national health insurance plans as "socialized medicine." Another source of the AMA's strength is their firm policy that the organization shall take public stands only on medical matters.

On the whole, lobbyists rate the success of their own organizations rather highly. None calls his own organization a failure, and only six report that they do poorly. About one-fourth think they have moderately good results, and about one-half say their results are good; only one-sixteenth think they are resoundingly successful. Respondents tend to estimate that the odds against great success are rather high. They made such statements as, "Considering the odds against us, I think we did rather well." Estimations of success vary with the kinds of goals the group sets for itself; usually these goals are broad and long-range— more than simply a successful outcome on particular bills. Naturally it is easier to obtain specific limited objectives than to realize broad long-range goals.

These varying goal standards for measuring organization success produced interesting results in the data. Most observers would agree that organizations with great power at the polls generally have lobbying power superior to those with little power at the polls. High-poll power organizations, however, tend to set broad, long-range goals which are difficult to attain. Thus, representatives of organizations with high power at the polls are no more inclined to claim high success for their organization than representatives of organizations with less power at the polls. Rather significantly, few lobbyists claim outstanding success. If the total lobby setting results in a balancing of groups, we should find, as we do, that groups claim moderate success against strong odds. If a substantial percentage claims resounding success, it would signal that a balancing process might not be functioning.

It is a truism that it is easier to stop a bill at some one hurdle in a legislative passage than it is to get it over all the hurdles (eight or ten in a two-house legislature) and signed into law. From this observation it is often suggested that "defensive organizations" (those trying to maintain the status quo) will generally be more successful in lobbying than "offensive organizations" (those trying to change the status quo). The organizations represented by respondents in this study were categorized according to whether the policy of the group was primarily designed to preserve the status quo in society or to change the status quo. The results show no relationship between these categories and respondents' appraisal of the organization's success. This suggests that the generalization that defensive organizations find more success than offensive ones must be examined more rigorously. The lack of correlation between defensive-offensive postures and appraisal of organization success probably results from several factors. Group success depends on many factors in addition to defensive and offensive posture; it is also appraised by varying goal standards. In addition, the legislative process is not so neatly arranged that defensive organizations will nearly always attempt to defeat bills while offensive organizations will nearly always attempt to pass them. Both types of organizations attempt to pass some bills and to defeat others. This results mainly from the fact that numbers of bills are introduced on all sides of questions in each Congress.

One lobbyist for a deprived minority group attributes much of his organization's considerable success to the fact that there is basic and clearly recognizable justice in his pleas. He believes that decision-makers recognize this fundamental justice and that this prevails as they make their decisions. Yet, careful examination of the data does not show that organizations trying to correct a basic injustice have any more success at lobbying than other kinds of organizations. The success of this respondent's lobby group probably stemmed more from the fact that the rationale for the original injustice had disappeared and that no organization is pushing on the other side. In many other cases of injustice, the organization, or organizations, benefitting from the injustice is still active on the other side.

Lobbyists' estimations of their personal success are highly correlated with estimations of their organization's success . . . Most lobbyists report moderate or good results from their personal efforts; only two report poor results; and only three report resounding success. Most lobbyists take a rather long-range view of their efforts. One reports, "I have only been on this job for five years, and that's not long enough to find out how successful I will be." Lobbying success is very much dependent on tenure, since acceptability of messages from lobbyists by officials can be gained only if the lobbyist builds a reputation for reliability. Most lobbyists hold their job for some time and plan to make a career in lobbying. Feeling successful goes along with liking the work and planning to make a career of it. The lobbyist's feeling of personal success shows no relationship to the poll-power of his organization. This finding was not unexpected; lobbyists for weak organizations take that fact into account as they appraise their personal success, and lobbyists for strong organizations realize that organizational success is due to many other factors in addition to their personal efforts. It also seems to be generally true that every lobbyist aspires to more than he achieves; he must then decide what he might reasonably expect to achieve.

EVALUATIONS OF ALL POLICY INFLUENCES

In attempting to make an over-all evaluation of lobbying impact on governmental decisions, it is important to place lobbying within the setting of all the factors influencing public policy. The final question of the interview with respondent was:

> We all know that lobbying is just one factor in making public policy. The President, Congress, executive agencies, political parties, opinion leaders, and voters also participate in policy-making. How would you appraise the relative influence of these various forces as they operate in making policy?

More than half of the respondents pick the President or the executive branch as the most important factor in making policy; even lobbyists with experience on the Hill and congressional respondents tend to give first rank importance to the executive branch. About 20 per cent of the lobbyists give the voters first rank importance. (These people tend to give unqualified approval to lobbying.) Many congressional respondents also rate voters first. Approximately 10 per cent of lobbyists give first rank importance to Congress. Congress is most often named second (about 35 per cent) and is followed closely by the executive branch (30 per cent). Opinion leaders and political parties are named relatively few times.

Most important for our purposes, only one lobbyist gives first rank importance to lobbying, and only five rate it second. Congressional respondents also accord very slight importance to lobbying in making public policy; about half of them, in fact, place lobbying at the bottom of the list. It is rather striking that both the practitioners and the recipients of lobbying think that lobbying is of so little importance in making public policy. One lobbyist struggling with this question said:

> I don't know where in the world I would fit the lobbyists as a group. Some of them have been up here for years battling for lost causes. On the whole, and speaking of all lobbyists in general, I think they are a lot less effective than most people believe.

The tendency of the public to overestimate the impact of lobbying on public policy is curiously seductive. If one assumes that lobbying is bad and ought to have little or no influence on policy and then discovers that lobbying does have some influence, it is easy to leap to the conclusion that lobbying is powerful and exercises inappropriate influence. If, on the other hand, one assumes that lobbying is legitimate and then evaluates all the other influences on public policy, he concludes that lobbying has relatively little impact on policy when compared with the other factors. Persons who believe human nature is essentially evil seem to be able to find sinister influences everywhere; finding a few sinister influences in lobbying, they are overeager to condemn all lobbyists.

The strong influence of the President and the executive branch on public policy is attested to by some very knowledgeable leaders in Congress:

> You would almost have to put the President number one. He has such a tremendous command of the sources of information, this automatically gives him an advantage. Next I suppose you would put the sources of information such as press, mass communications, political commentators, and other opinion leaders. The public opinion they create is reflected from the districts back into Congress. Congress has some leadership in policy but it is more difficult to pinpoint than the leadership of the President.

> • • •

> Policy is made largely by the executive and the legislative party leaders; these two most important factors are somewhat influenced by the other factors. Lobbyists have very little to say on legislation so far as I can see. . . . I have known lots of party chairmen and the party on the national scene is not very effective. I never saw a chairman who would swear he had any effect on policy whatsoever. Any attempts to influence policy would be instantly resented either by leaders in the executive branch or leaders of the legislative party in Congress.

> • • •

> There is just no way of getting around it, the President is the dominant force in policy-making. The President is one man, and when he speaks he has the attention of the world. He can mold public opinion, and he also tends to have the confidence of all the people. There is no one member of Congress who has that much respect. If it should become a popularity contest, the President will always win out. All policy is made from a view of what the public demands; political figures orient to it. I doubt if the lobbyist has much to say except when he gets down to specific language of particular sections of bills; he is not very effective on broad policy.

The lobbyist-son of a former President said:

> The President is certainly the most influential—this is without any question. Second I would put the head of an executive department who is putting up a real fight and is backed by the President. The most important single element is the President's backing up of a fighting cabinet officer.

THE DANGERS OF LOBBYING

The weight of the evidence that this study brings to bear suggests that there is relatively little influence or power in lobbying per se. There are many forces in addition to lobbying which influence public policy; in most cases these other forces clearly outweigh the impact of lobbying. Voters set the broad trends of public policy which all the other influences on policy must follow. It is for this reason that so many forces battle to manipulate public opinion. Public opinion is a factor which sets the boundaries for the policy struggle. On certain questions the boundaries are closely restricted, and the policy decisions of officials must closely follow public demands. On other questions, the boundaries may be broader, leaving wider discretion to decision-makers and more possibility for lobbyists to influence their decisions. Questions of large public attention and import are chiefly determined by considerations of political success and winning the next election. The chief executive, through his political leadership, has ability to mold public opinion, and his command of the resources and imagination of the executive bureaucracy, has the greatest single impact on the shape of public policy. Questions of small technical nature, which attract little public attention, are more subject to lobbying influence. The growth of one lobby group or coalition generally stimulates the development of an opposing group. Most careful observers of governmental decision-making have concluded that the over-all impact of lobbying is relatively minor.

• • •

Index